Native Americans and the Law

*Contemporary and Historical Perspectives on
American Indian Rights, Freedoms, and Sovereignty*

Series Editor

John R. Wunder
University of Nebraska-Lincoln

GARLAND PUBLISHING, INC.
New York & London
1996

Contents of the Series

The Indian Bill of Rights, 1968

Edited with introductions by

John R. Wunder
University of Nebraska-Lincoln

GARLAND PUBLISHING, INC.
New York & London
1996

Library of Congress Cataloging-in-Publication Data

The Indian Bill of Rights, 1968 / edited with introductions by John R.
 Wunder.
   p.   cm. — (Native Americans and the law ; 3)
   Includes bibliographical references.
   ISBN 0-8153-2487-1 (alk. paper)
   1. Indians of North America—Civil rights.   I. Wunder, John R.
 II. Series.
 KF8210.C5I53   1996
 342.73'0872—dc20   96-29375
 [347.302872]   CIP

Printed on acid-free, 250-year-life paper
Manufactured in the United States of America

Contents

Series Introduction

N. Scott Momaday, in his masterful *The Way to Rainy Mountain*, tells a story of a Kiowa family—a father, mother, and son. During one evening, while the father was resting inside their tipi, the mother was preparing a meal over the fire. She gave a piece of meat to her young son. He went outside to eat it, but soon came back in and asked for another piece. This happened three more times in succession, and when he came back once again he brought several enemies into the tipi. They told the Kiowa parents there were many other enemies nearby who also wanted food, but if they were fed now they would help the family against those other enemies and not harm them.

The father did not think this story was quite right, but he pretended to believe it. As his wife put a large amount of fatty meat on the fire to cook, he went outside the tipi and proceeded to hide the enemies' horses. He did not see any other enemies. Once the father was a short distance away, he sang in the voice of a bird. The mother knew now it was time to act, so she set fire to the fat and threw it all around upon those who were sitting nearby. While the enemies screamed, she grabbed up her little boy in her arms, ran outside the tipi, and without hesitating sprinted upstream to be reunited with her husband. As the Kiowa family escaped, they turned and saw the fire destroying all of their belongings and heard the cries of their enemies.[1] They thought of their terrifying duress they had so suddenly experienced, of their disastrous and sacrificial loss of their home, and of their forced removal. They also remembered their resistance and their survival.

*   *   *   *   *

Within this story are some of the characteristics that help to describe the legal relationship of Native Americans to law in the United States. Such traits include duress, disaster, removal, resistance, sacrifice, and survival. Each of these, among others, can be applied to a legal understanding of the past, present, and future. The relationship of American Indians to law, in particular to federal law, is one highlighted by ambiguity, confusion, and all too frequently imbalance. There are many colonial manifestations as well. No other group in the United States has been the subject of more litigation than Native Americans. Throughout the nineteenth and continuing into the twentieth century, these legal relationships have not been resolved and likely never will be. So litigious are the issues that the famous John Marshall decision, *Worcester v. Georgia* (1832), remains one of the most cited court decisions in United States legal history.[2] The fat, we might say, is constantly in the fire.

As Sidney Herring has pointed out in his recent book, *Crow Dog's Case*, there are two basic legal traditions at play in modern considerations of Native Americans and law. There are the constitutional and common law structures of the state and federal governments. But Indian tribes also have their own laws and customs that have evolved through time and have been practiced by succeeding generations. Although these traditions have been modified and attacked, most significantly in the twentieth century, they continue to be practiced. These legal traditions are very rich, reflecting the diversity of Native peoples in North America. Thus, federal Indian law is a conflict of laws exercised in theory, but seldom is Indian law analyzed in legal determinations outside of tribal courts. The history of Native Americans and law is the history of this curious duality inherent in two competing legal systems.[3]

These legal relationships are dynamic and frequently changing, as this six-volume collection of articles will show. For the first time, more than 70 scholarly essays concerning the legal history of Native Americans and law are offered. They represent a wide variety of expertise, including writings from Native leadership, practicing lawyers, legal scholars, anthropologists, and historians—a vast interdisciplinary wealth of authors who normally would not be bound together.

This anthology is divided into two sections. How the United States attempts, generally unsuccessfully, to make Native Americans fit within a federal legal framework is the primary theme of these essays. The first four volumes offer a historical survey of the development of Indian legal relationships within their communities and from without. Volume 1 covers the evolution of legal cultures among Native peoples from pre-1776 through an era of colonialism to 1903. Volume 2 next considers the first sixty years of the twentieth century built around the theme of constitutionalism. Here there is an emphasis on the intersection of the U.S. government and tribal law when so many legal changes were made. Of particular significance is Volume 3, the first collection of essays published on the Indian Bill of Rights, legislation passed by Congress and signed by President Lyndon Johnson that encompassed six sections of the Civil Rights Act of 1968. The last of the historical survey volumes, Volume 4, considers recent legal issues, from 1968 to the present. Included among those discussed are fishing and hunting rights, water law, zoning, the Indian Child Welfare Act of 1978, taxation, gaming, and repatriation.

The last two volumes of this series each stand on their own, representing important themes in Native American law. Volume 5 considers cultural and religious freedoms that have evolved from important legal confrontations between Native American societies and the United States government and from those legal decisions reached. Volume 6 offers assessments of the various legal nuances and meanings of sovereignty for Indian tribes. These two volumes also present the historical underpinnings of the exercise of cultural and religious freedoms and sovereignty rights entailed in today's legal arena.

*   *   *   *   *

The preparation of this collection involved the work of many people. I am most grateful for the scholarly expertise of Mark Ellis of the University of Nebraska-Lincoln, Department of History, and his help in this endeavor. In addition, the staff of the Center for Great Plains Studies at the University of Nebraska, notably Gretchen Walker and Linda Ratcliffe, were instrumental in the timely preparation of materials. While editing these six volumes, I held the position as Bicentennial Fulbright Chair in North American Studies at the Renvall Institute of the University of Helsinki, Finland, and there the assistance of its director, Eino Lyytinen, the Institute staff, and my Finnish students in American legal history and Native American history classes were indispensible. Thanks also go to Carole Puccino, Leo Balk, and the Garland staff for their careful and steadfast work on this intricate project.

NOTES

1. N. Scott Momaday, *The Way to Rainy Mountain* (Albuquerque: University of New Mexico Press, 1969), p. 44.
2. See John R. Wunder, *"Retained by The People": A History of American Indians and the Bill of Rights* (New York: Oxford University Press, 1994), 219, n. 25.
3. See Sidney L. Herring, *Crow Dog's Case: American Indian Sovereignty, Tribal Law, and United States Law in the Nineteenth Century* (New York: Cambridge University Press, 1994).

Volume Introduction

The year 1968 was a time of political assassinations, urban riots, and anti-war protests. It was also the year a new civil rights act was passed that would have significant implications for Native Americans. The Civil Rights Act of 1968[1] was conceived as a response to the murder of Martin Luther King Jr. and the plight of black urban Americans, but in the heat of the moment Senator Sam Ervin of North Carolina succeeded in attaching an Indian Bill of Rights to this statute, which became law with the touch of President Lyndon Johnson's pen.

The new law represented a major legal change for American Indians. No longer were Native Americans who lived on reservations immune from some Bill of Rights protections. This was very important, for previously they were not covered. But the nature of this new coverage, the way in which individual Indians could achieve their rights, and the extent to which these new provisions could be used to dismantle tribal government powers, proved controversial.

Under the new law, some, not all, of the Bill of Rights were extended to American Indians. Those rights not extended included rights to bear arms or to be immune from quartering soldiers, rights to jury trials, rights to free counsel in judicial proceedings, the Ninth and Tenth Amendments, the establishment clause of the First Amendment, and the right to "life" under the Fifth and Fourteenth Amendments. Why these exceptions were made is difficult to explain. Some were made based upon rational objections, such as the problem of the establishment clause for the Pueblo peoples of New Mexico. But others defy categorization. In addition, the redress for infringement of the rights provided in the statute was through habeas corpus actions only.

Almost immediately challenges were made to this important change in Indian legal relationships. The first involved the Navajos and their right to banish from their reservation an unpopular non-Indian director of the Navajo legal services, Dinebelina Nahillna Be Agiditahe, Inc. or DNA. The federal appellate court in *Dodge v. Nakai* (1969)[2] held that Theodore Mitchell, the attorney receiving banishment, had not received proper due process and had had his freedom of speech infringed. This decision went beyond mere habeas corpus requirements and allowed a significant opening for suits against tribal governments. Court actions were then filed challenging voting rights, representative governments on reservations, and discrimination by tribal governments. That door was eventually slammed shut nearly ten years later by the U.S. Supreme

Court in its important decision, *Santa Clara Pueblo v. Martinez* (1978)[3] Here the Court upheld Santa Clara Pueblo patrilineal tribal membership requirements and returned to a strict interpretation of the Indian Bill of Rights in terms of forms of redress.

The essays that follow represent the first collection ever published on the Indian Bill of Rights. The first essay, written by the editor, provides a survey of the historical background to the Civil Rights Act of 1968, a summary of the act's contents, and the legal implications for Native Americans. It is followed by two specific legal summaries, one positive in its assessments by Donald L. Burnett Jr. and another, somewhat critical, by Arthur Lazarus Jr.

Understanding the rights guaranteed by the Indian Bill of Rights is the subject of the next essay by G. Kenneth Reiblich. He catalogues how the Indian Bill of Rights applies and its potential usages. Next comes the first of two articles by attorney Alvin J. Ziontz. He explains in his essay, "In Defense of Tribal Sovereignty: An Analysis of Judicial Error in Construction of the Indian Civil Rights Act," how the federal courts misconstrued the nature and meaning of the Indian Bill of Rights. He anticipates correctly how *Dodge v. Nakai* and other federal district and appellate court interpretations erred. There was simply no standing to sue based upon the law, and by allowing such standing, tribal governmental stability was seriously threatened.

One of the important changes brought by the Indian Bill of Rights concerned the application of the "equal protection of the laws" concept to Native Americans. Ralph W. Johnson and E. Susan Crystal explain this complicated concept and how it applies to American Indian rights. Their essay is followed by a perceptive summary of the controversies raised over political rights and equal protection concepts by Dennis R. Holmes. The exercise of voting rights, who could vote, apportionment, and other issues associated with government and politics were decided by courts interpreting the Indian Bill of Rights.

The last two essays concern the landmark case of *Santa Clara Pueblo v. Martinez*. First, Andra Pearldaughter explains the problems with this decision with reference to Indian women and their desire to achieve sexual equality. The *Santa Clara Pueblo* decision struck down the attempt of Julia Martinez, a Santa Clara Pueblo in good standing, to give her children, raised at the pueblo and in Pueblo culture, membership in her tribe. Alvin J. Ziontz concludes this volume by explaining how the Supreme Court, through the *Santa Clara Pueblo* opinion written by Justice Thurgood Marshall, attempted to weigh the damage being done to the authority of tribal governments and the ability of Indians to make decisions about basic aspects of their own culture against the rights of individual Native Americans and the role of the federal judiciary to intervene.

Sherman Alexie, in his recent novel, *Reservation Blues*, offers some observations about Native American life that has significant bearing upon the short history of the Indian Bill of Rights. Alexie relates how two Pacific Northwest Indians have a free ranging conversation about Christianity and a general faith in life as they travel from Seattle back to the Spokane Reservation. Thomas Builds-the-Fire initiates the conversation, "You have to have faith." His girlfriend Chess Warm Water answers, "But what about Hitler and Ted Bundy? How do you explain George Bush and George Custer? If God were good, why would he create Rush Limbaugh?" "Really," ponders Chess. "How do you explain all of that? How do you explain all of the murdered

Indians?" The van rolled on. Chess thought some more. "How do you explain Gandhi and Mother Theresa?" Chess asked. "How do you explain Crazy Horse and Martin Luther King? There's good and bad in the world. We all get to make the choice. That's one of the mysteries of faith."[4] Certainly, there are good and bad in history and law, and the Indian Bill of Rights, now nearly thirty years old, contains both characteristics in significant quantities. We are just beginning to understand its historical and legal ramifications.

NOTES

1. *U.S. Statutes at Large* 82 (April 11, 1968): 73–92.
2. *Dodge v. Nakai*, 298 F.Supp 26 (1969). This federal appellate court decision is known as *Dodge II*. An earlier decision made in a federal district court is found at *Dodge v. Nakai*, 298 F.Supp 17 (1968), known as *Dodge I*.
3. *Santa Clara Pueblo v. Martinez*, 436 US 49 (1978).
4. Sherman Alexie, *Reservation Blues* (New York: Atlantic Monthly Press, 1995): 166–76.

FURTHER READING

Vine Deloria Jr. and Clifford M. Lytle, *American Indians, American Justice* (Austin: University of Texas Press, 1983).

David H. Getches and Charles F. Wilkinson, *Federal Indian Law: Cases and Materials*, 2nd edition (St. Paul, Minn.: West Publishing Co., 1986).

Gary D. Kennedy, "Tribal Elections: An Appraisal After the Indian Civil Rights Act," *American Indian Law Review* 3, no. 2 (1975): 497–508.

James R. Kerr, "Constitutional Rights, Tribal Justice, and the American Indian," *Journal of Public Laws* 18 (1969): 311–38.

Mary L. Muehlen, "An Interpretation of the Due Process Clause of the Indian Bill of Rights," *North Dakota Law Review* 51 (Fall, 1974): 191–204.

Frank Pommersheim, "Tribal Courts: Constitutional Decision Making and an Opportunity for Transformation," in John R. Wunder, ed., *Law and the Great Plains: Essays on the Legal History of the Heartland* (Westport, Conn.: Greenwood Press, 1996): 151–82.

Joseph de Raismes, "The Indian Civil Rights Act of 1968 and the Pursuit of Responsible Tribal Self-Government," *South Dakota Law Review* 20 (Winter, 1975): 59–106.

The Indian Bill of Rights, 1968

The Indian Bill of Rights

The social and political upheaval in the United States peaked in 1968. The year began with a presidential announcement of the drafting of over 300,000 men for the Vietnam War, including many Native Americans. The war itself was not going well; the Viet Cong besieged the United States Marine base at Khe Sanh throughout February. One month later, Lyndon Johnson announced to a stunned nation that he would not run for another term as president. Earlier he had fared poorly in the New Hampshire presidential primary against Senator Eugene McCarthy of Minnesota, a critic of the Vietnam War. The violence abroad came home with the assassination of Martin Luther King, Jr., on April 4 and the resulting urban riots. One week later, Congress responded with the passage of another civil rights act, this one aimed at preventing discrimination in the sale and rental of housing.

Students all over the country tried to take over their colleges, and they marched in the streets demanding an end to the war and to discrimination. Before he was assassinated, Martin Luther King, Jr., had planned the Poor People's March in Washington, D.C., to dramatize the extensive poverty in the country, and in May the Poor People's Campaign, led by the Reverend Ralph Abernathy and composed of many poor people, mostly African Americans, converged on Washington and camped near the Washington Monument. On June 5, Robert Kennedy, senator from New York and former attorney general, won the important California Democratic primary, edging out Eugene McCarthy, but that evening he was fatally shot after making a victory speech.

During the late summer, the main political parties held their conventions. In early August, the Republican party nominated Richard Nixon, Eisenhower's vice president and the 1960 presidential nominee, as its standard bearer. During the last week in August, the Democrats gathered in Chicago to choose their candidate. After Johnson's withdrawal, his vice president, Hubert Humphrey, declared his candidacy, and their supporters controlled the Chicago convention, nominating Humphrey on the first ballot. Although Humphrey prevailed at the convention, he and his supporter, Chicago mayor Richard J. Daley, could not prevent bloodshed and mayhem on the city's streets. Hundreds of disappointed anti–Vietnam War protesters were attacked by Chicago police, and the bedlam came into the hall during a famous speech to the delegates by Senator Abraham Ribicoff of Connecticut. In October, the vicious third-party candidacy of segregationist George Wallace of Alabama emerged, but on election day Richard Nixon eked out a narrow presidential victory. By the end of 1968, the nation was trying to come to terms with its horrors, including the deaths of 30,000 Americans in Southeast Asia, by celebrating the success of *Apollo 8* in its orbiting of the moon. It had truly been a year to remember.

Native Americans also remember 1968, and those memories are both complex and vivid. The 1968 Congress, federal and state judiciaries, President Johnson, candidate Nixon, and the Civil Rights Act of 1968 were important to Indians as well. Moreover, also occurring in 1968 was the surprise creation and passage into law of the Indian Bill of Rights, a statute that significantly changed the legal relationships of Native Americans. Issues not yet resolved—from the Indian Claims Commission and termination to relocation and the applications of Public Law 280—were also addressed in 1968. In the end, a new federal policy—that of Indian self-determination—founded on old ideas, was introduced, encompassing a different kind of hope for a sustained legal parity.

Mandate and Morass:
Setting a New Agenda from Old Legalisms,
1968

American history is not filled with numerous periods of upheaval. Although social change has occurred in the United States, there have not been the kinds of violent movements in the society as there have been in others, such as in Russia, China, the Middle East, or Ireland. So when things fell apart in the United States in 1968, the American people and scholars looked for reasons to explain this unusual time.

The year 1968 has been and will continue to be the subject of numerous histories and films. It is featured in texts as a time of troubles when the fabric of American society began to unravel. But within this societal dysfunction was an era of reform. The anti–Vietnam War movement acted as an umbrella over numerous calls for social change, including women's rights and civil rights. Native Americans were also involved in the rhetoric and action of reform, but they did not speak loudly or with unanimity. Moreover, the larger national movement did not address the legal disparities of Native Americans. Indian issues were not issues of the civil rights movements. Instead, women, African Americans, and Latinos came to the fore with their agendas for social change.

Thus for Native Americans, 1968 was an ambivalent time. It was not so much the violence, the war, and the assassinations that made Indians cautious; some remember vividly the Sand Creek Massacre, the numerous wars with the United States Army, and the political murders of Crazy Horse and Sitting Bull. Here in 1968 was a movement in history during which the racial dimension to American society was carefully scrutinized, and Indians were being left out. Then, much to everyone's surprise, an Indian Bill of Rights was born.

Legal Highlights for Native Americans in 1968

Shortly before he was murdered in 1877, Crazy Horse of the Oglalas reportedly observed the following about American power and the defeat of his people by the United States government: "We preferred our own way of living. . . . All we wanted was peace and to be left alone."[1] Nearly a century later, these words might easily be applied to the extension of American law over Indians. In 1968, Congress and other political and legal institutions were not about to leave Native Americans alone.

During 1968, the federal and state governments were especially active in assessing Indian law. The first four months saw Congress pass nine pieces of Indian legislation, the first eight concerning specific tribes and a variety of funding and land issues. The ninth piece of Indian legislation was a last-minute amendment to the Civil Rights Act of 1968. This was the Indian Bill of Rights, a pet project of Senator Sam Ervin of North Carolina. Since 1961, Ervin had held hearings on the legal rights of

Native Americans, and he had become convinced that Indians should have the same individual rights as those guaranteed to all other Americans by the Bill of Rights.

Assessing his motivation is not easy. Clearly, Ervin listened to Helen Scheirbeck, a Lumbee from Ervin's home state who was his aide on the Subcommittee on Constitutional Rights. Ervin admired the acculturation of the nonreservation Lumbees and saw them as models for other Indians. But Ervin was also a segregationist who wanted to delay or stop the extension of civil rights to African Americans. By trumpeting the lack of individual Indian rights, Ervin might have thought that he could build a coalition with western senators to prevent general civil rights legislation from passing.[2]

To be fair, however, we must add that Ervin felt strongly that all Americans deserved the protection of the Bill of Rights. He later stated that "even though the Indians are the first Americans, the national policy relating to them has been shamefully different from that relating to other minorities."[3] The problem was that most Indians believed they were different and wanted to stay that way. Ervin and other senators were quite surprised to learn that the Bill of Rights in 1968 did not apply to Indians living on reservations. Such a notion was "alien to popular concepts of American jurisprudence."[4]

Presidential leadership sought to define Indian programs and legal relationships during 1968. In March, President Johnson, seeking to distance himself and his administration from the Kennedy and Eisenhower years, sent a message to Congress declaring that Indian policy should be guided by a doctrine of self-determination, not termination.[5] Johnson then issued an executive order establishing the Council on Indian Opportunity, whose primary mission was to coordinate federal programs and create a full partnership between Indians and the federal government.[6] During the presidential campaign, Richard Nixon echoed these sentiments. He opposed termination, favored self-determination, and supported the Council on Indian Opportunity.[7]

Like the other branches of government, the judiciary—including the Supreme Court, other federal courts, and the state courts—was also active on Indian issues. The effect of termination on the overall sovereign rights of the Menominees was decided.[8] Clarifications regarding the extent of rulings by the Indian Claims Commission were made.[9] Public Law 280, the power to tax on reservations, and extradition rights were the subject of litigation.[10] Limitations on hunting and fishing treaty rights were beginning to be heard by federal courts, as Indians, particularly in the Pacific Northwest, sought to test state regulations restricting long-standing hunting and fishing practices.[11] By the end of 1968, even the new Indian Bill of Rights was the subject of a dispute over its interpretation.[12] This was a busy time.

Lingering Legal Entanglements

Fresh from another renewal of its existence, the Indian Claims Commission continued to review allegations by Native Americans about the abridgment of treaty rights and human rights. The commission's procedures still hamstrung the process. In an effort to move ahead more quickly on the huge backlog, starting in 1968 the commission allowed one commissioner, rather than three, to hear a case. In addition, pretrial activities were tightened, and experts were required for the first time to submit written reports before a trial.[13] Despite these improvements, the commission's decisions and those appealed to the Court of Claims provoked controversy.

The Peoria Tribe in Oklahoma made a treaty with the United States in 1854, in which the Peorias ceded tribal lands to the United States on the condition that the federal government would sell them at a public auction with the proceeds invested in bonds, whose interest would be annually paid to the tribe. The United States violated the treaty. It sold the lands to private individuals, not at a public auction, and it did not invest the proceeds. When the Indian Claims Commission was established, the Peorias made their claim. At a hearing, the ICC held that the Peorias were entitled to only the difference between what the lands would have sold for at a public auction in 1854 and the funds actually received from the private sales. This amounted to $172,726. The Peorias appealed to the Court of Claims, which affirmed the ICC's decision, and the Peorias then appealed to the Supreme Court.

The federal government argued before the Supreme Court that it was established law for Indian claims that the United States was not liable for interest on claims against it. In *Peoria Tribe of Indians of Oklahoma et al. v. United States* (1968), the Supreme Court, however, refused to accept this argument, instead finding that there were specific treaty obligations to invest the funds and pay an annual income to the Peorias. In a brief unanimous opinion by Justice Potter Stewart, the Court remanded the cases back to the ICC to determine the amount of damages to be awarded to the Peorias. The ICC and the Court of Claims were thus curtly reversed.[14]

The Justice Department seemed intent on tightening any potential loopholes in ICC proceedings. Two small tribes in Arizona, the Gila River Pimas and the Maricopas, attempted to sue the United States for inadequate educational, health, and administrative services provided to them through the years based on the jurisdiction in the Indian Claims Commission Act requiring "fair and honorable dealings" by the federal government in its relationships with Indians. Here the Justice Department vociferously argued that the United States had no specific responsibility for providing incompetent services. The ICC ruled that no compensation could be paid because there was no specific standard of care for providing these federal services. The commission ignored the Supreme Court holdings in *Sweatt v. Painter* (1950) and *Brown v. Board of Education* (1954). African Americans were entitled to equal educational opportunities, but Indians were not. The Gila River Pima–Maricopa community appealed this decision to the Court of Claims, which supported the ICC.[15] The commission clearly did not want to open the door for tribes to claim that they had historically experienced damages as a result of incompetent teachers and doctors being sent to the reservations.

The ICC also heard the case of the Northern Paiute Nation, which claimed that their lands in Nevada, Idaho, Oregon, and California had been taken from them by the United States without proper compensation. The commission agreed with the Paiutes' claims and assessed more than $15.7 million in damages. What made the claims so valuable was the finding that the Comstock Lode in Nevada was located on the Paiutes' homelands.

The federal government appealed the decision to the Court of Claims, and the Paiutes filed a counterclaim. The court reached its holding in April 1968, dismissing both claims and reprimanding the Justice Department for trying to argue that the Treaty of Guadalupe Hidalgo extinguished all Indian claims to subsurface minerals. The court went into great detail regarding Spanish mineral law and showed where the government was deliberately misleading in its presentation of the evidence. On the other side, the Court of Claims had little patience for the Paiute attorneys, who tried to assess the same evaluation standards applied to the Comstock Lode for all the silver mines in the region. This made little sense to the court and smacked of lawyerly greed. Thus Indian mineral rights were not eliminated, nor were irrational evaluations for worthless mines allowed as compensation.[16]

In 1968, the Indian Claims Commission continued to process claims and make rulings on narrow grounds. Its findings appeared to be modestly favorable to Native Americans when compared with the aggressive challenges made by the federal government's lawyers. Still the Supreme Court, such as in the *Peoria* decision, had to watch the commission carefully to ensure some semblance of fairness.

By 1968, nobody seemed to like termination, but no one wanted to end it, either. Presidents declared it a dead policy. Congress even tried to grapple with it. At the instigation of Senator George McGovern of South Dakota, Congress went on record as guaranteeing "moral and legal obligations" to Native Americans through federal policy.[17] Some representatives and senators thought this to be an overriding of House Concurrent Resolution 108, and some Indian leaders remained hopeful. Said Earl Old Person, chairman of the Blackfeet, about the word "termination": "You have caused us to jump every time we hear this word." Old Person stressed the development of Indian reservations rather than termination. He wanted the government to stop talking about termination and instead anchor its policy on economic investment and Indian self-help. Not directly ending the termination policy was "like trying to cook a meal in your tipi when someone is standing outside trying to burn your tipi down."[18]

The Supreme Court, however, was the only American legal institution to curtail the legal meaning of termination. As soon as the Menominee termination order was implemented in 1961, the state of Wisconsin began the process of trying to regulate the Menominee lands and people. In 1962, Wisconsin decided that the Menominees were subject to all state hunting and fishing regulations. For Menominees this meant the loss of many of their remaining means of survival as well as their treaty rights. The Menominee Termination Act of 1954, argued the state of Wisconsin, ended all fishing and hunting rights guaranteed in the Wolf River Treaty of 1854, which had been signed a full century earlier by the United States and the Menominee Nation.

For Justice William O. Douglas and a majority of the Supreme Court, this was sheer folly. In *Menominee Tribe of Indians v. United States* (1968), Douglas found that termination did not mean the abrogation of existing treaty rights.[19] To end treaty rights required specific language in law to do so, and the Menominee Termination Act did not specifically override the Wolf River Treaty of 1854. Moreover, Douglas tied the termination acts to Public Law 280. In a rather novel legal twist, the Court ruled that the language in Public Law 280 ("Nothing in this section . . . shall deprive any Indian or any Indian tribe, band, or community of any right, privilege, or immunity afforded under Federal treaty, agreement, or statute with respect to hunting, trapping, or fishing or the control, licensing, or regulation thereof") did not allow any state or federal official to reduce the treaty rights.[20] In fact, by specifically guaranteeing hunting and fishing rights and by not specifically ending the Menominees' nineteenth-century treaty with the United States, Public Law 280 doubly protected the Menominees.

For the time being, the Menominees' treaty rights were sacrosanct. The Supreme Court narrowly defined termination as the loss of federal support services, not the legal abolition of a tribe and its membership. If the state of Wisconsin wanted to abolish the Menominees' hunting and fishing rights, it would have to persuade Congress and President Nixon, an opponent of termination, to pass a new termination act specifically ending the Wolf River Treaty. The effect of the *Menominee* decision did not, however, undue the damage done by termination. The Menominees' tribal government was moribund. Of all the terminated tribes, only the Klamaths had been able to sustain any continuing tribal political manifestations.[21] *Menominee Tribe of Indians v. United States* simply put a stop to further denials of Indian rights.

The ironic coupling of termination with Public Law 280 brought to full circle the Indians' animosity regarding the direct loss to the states of their sovereignty over their reservations. They renewed their arguments that they had never been consulted about Public Law 280. For the most ardent foes of Indian sovereignty, such an undemocratic process was hard to rationalize. In addition, those states that assumed jurisdiction over Indian reservations were finding it to be an expensive process that they were not willing to fund fully, if at all. Thus a movement toward retrocession, the return of criminal and civil law functions to the federal government and tribal governments from state governments, began.

Retrocession was not debated during consideration of Public Law 280, nor was it placed in the legislation. As a legal concept, it awaited congressional approval. But some states did not even wait. Montana passed a statute in 1966 recognizing tribal consent to withdraw jurisdiction, and Nebraska tried unsuccessfully to implement retrocession on all the reservations in the state, with or without Indian consent.[22] With so many constituencies in agreement, the abolition of Public Law 280 when considering an extension of the Bill of Rights to reservations was easily available for the taking.

The Legal Origins of the Indian Bill of Rights

In 1968, the estimated number of Native Americans in the United States as counted by the BIA was approximately 760,000. Seventy percent, or approximately 530,000, lived near or on reservations. More than 85 percent of all Indians lived in eight states: Alaska, Arizona, Montana, New Mexico, North Dakota, Oklahoma, South Dakota, and Washington. The populations were concentrated even more, with 65 percent of all Native Americans residing in just four states: Alaska, Arizona, New Mexico, and Oklahoma.[23]

When Indians lived off the reservation, they were subject to the civil and criminal jurisdiction of the state in which they lived unless they were charged with one of fourteen crimes listed in the amended Major Crimes Act of 1885: murder, manslaughter, kidnapping, rape, carnal knowledge of any female not one's wife who was not yet sixteen, assault with intent to commit rape, incest, assault with intent to commit murder, assault with a dangerous weapon, assault resulting in serious bodily injury, arson, burglary, robbery, and larceny in Indian country.[24] If they committed any of these crimes on a reservation, they came under federal jurisdiction. In both state and federal courts, the Bill of Rights was a part of normal criminal and civil procedure, although many state courts were lax in their treatment of Native Americans.

Courts on Indian reservations assumed extensive powers. They had misdemeanor and some felony criminal jurisdiction when Indians were defendants and fairly wide civil jurisdiction with exclusively Native American parties and concurrent civil jurisdiction with the states when the parties were both Indian and non-Indian. Three kinds of courts existed on Indian reservations in 1968: fifty-three tribal courts, twelve Courts of Indian Offenses, and nineteen traditional courts.

The federal government recognized 435 tribes and bands in 1968, and 247 of these formally organized tribes had constitutions. Of those, 117 tribes included bill of rights provisions in their tribal constitutions, although these provisions were incomplete. Some of these tribes also had tribal courts. Although many of the tribal courts operated under a tribal constitution with bill of rights provisions, it did not matter because the

Supreme Court, beginning with *Talton v. Mayes* (1896), ruled that the federal Bill of Rights did not apply to Native American governments or courts.[25] Moreover, most of the courts on reservations did not offer rights to counsel, rights to remain silent, rights to a trial by jury, or rights of appeal to litigants. Rarely were records kept of judicial proceedings. Few judges were trained; in 1968, only five of the sixty-eight judges in tribal courts and Courts of Indian Offenses were lawyers. Clearly, Indians on reservations who were parties to disputes did not have available to them Bill of Rights protections, due process of law, or equal protection of the laws.

Beginning in 1961, two special committees, one federal and the other private, focused on Indians and the Bill of Rights. The Special Task Force on Indian Affairs recommended to the Department of the Interior that tribes protect civil liberties by passing and enforcing new ordinances. The Commission on the Rights, Liberties, and Responsibilities of the American Indian, financed by the Fund for the Republic, urged that Indian tribal governments be placed under the federal Bill of Rights because not to do so put in jeopardy "the very assumptions on which our free society was established."[26] The terminationists and acculturationists concluded that if they could not abolish the IRA governments, the least they could do was to have Indian institutions placed fully within constitutional constraints. The stage was set for Senator Sam Ervin of North Carolina to begin conducting hearings before his Subcommittee on Constitutional Rights into the Bill of Rights and Native Americans.

Ervin's subcommittee collected information for seven years. It sought testimony from Native Americans and interested parties. It heard stories of the abrogation of religious freedoms and personal liberty by some tribal governments. Shoddy court practices by all three kinds of Indian courts were documented. The causes of injustices on reservations were traced mainly to the judges' lack of legal training and experience, minimal resources, and the failure of the states covered by Public Law 280 to enforce laws on reservations. Field hearings by the committee recorded almost 1,100 pages of testimony.[27]

Most of those testifying explained that deprivation of rights for Indians was principally the result of improper federal and state actions. Indians were treated as slaves in local South Dakota jails; the police in Pocatello, Idaho, and Gallup, New Mexico, let Shoshonis and Navajos die in jail rather than call a doctor. The Courts of Indian Offenses cooperated with police to kidnap Indians on reservations and take them

11

off the reservations in order to facilitate arrests. Rights to counsel were denied in state courts; not-guilty pleas were not allowed; and states included in Public Law 280, such as California, refused to allot sufficient funds for law enforcement on reservations.[28]

At the same time that the Ervin subcommittee was documenting the condition of justice on reservations, other developments concerning Indians and the Bill of Rights were taking place in state and federal courts. Before 1968, most courts adhered to the *Talton v. Mayes* decision and the Doctrine of Sovereign Immunity.[29] Tribal governments claimed that they could not be sued unless they gave permission, and they were not giving permission. Indeed, all Indian Claims commission proceedings since 1949 were predicated on this very concept. The tribal courts took the Doctrine of Sovereign Immunity seriously, but the state courts were anxious to intervene.

The full erosion of the *Talton* Doctrine came in the *Colliflower v. Garland* (1965) dispute. Madeline Colliflower, a Gros Ventre living on the Fort Belknap Reservation in Montana, was jailed after she refused to remove her cattle from tribal lands. She filed a writ of habeas corpus, and the Ninth Circuit Court of Appeals ruled that tribal courts function as federal agencies and, as such, must uphold basic concepts inherent in the Rill of Rights, such as allowing the right to counsel, the right to confront witnesses, and the right of appeal.[30] Madeline Colliflower was ordered freed from the reservation jail. *Colliflower v. Garland* was a major departure from the *Talton* rule, but as Attorney General Robert Kennedy observed in 1968 when he testified before the House Subcommittee on Indian Affairs, the *Colliflower* holding "virtually stands alone in upholding the competence of a federal court to inquire into the legality of an order of an Indian court."[31]

Although the Indian Bill of Rights adopted the legal pronouncements of the *Colliflower* decision, two other cases that resulted in holdings favorable to tribal governments probably had a greater impact on Senator Ervin and his subcommittee staff. Both disputes involved First Amendment rights. In 1953, the federal district court of New Mexico heard a dispute between the Jemez Pueblo government and six Jemez Pueblo Indians, members of several Protestant denominations who claimed that they were being religiously persecuted. The court ruled that it had no jurisdiction to hear *Toledo v. Pueblo de Jemez* (1954) because the First Amendment, as well as the Fifth and Fourteenth Amendments, did not apply to tribal governments.[32] At the same time as the Jemez

Pueblo dispute, the Navajo Tribal Council restricted religious freedoms by prohibiting the use of peyote on the Navajo Reservation. Navajos participating in Native American Church services were arrested, charged, and convicted of violating the Navajo ordinance. The Tenth Circuit Court of Appeals refused to recognize the Bill of Rights as protecting Indian religious freedom.[33]

Thus the historical and legal setting was ripe for Senator Ervin to introduce his version of an Indian Bill of Rights. Most Native Americans continued to reside on reservations or at least maintain some connection with reservation life, and Ervin's subcommittee discovered a mixed bag of Indian courts and councils. Pressures were building in the federal and state legal establishments to clarify the Indian relationship to the Bill of Rights. It seemed that only through federal legislation might this legal ambiguity be resolved, although at least one circuit court was willing to cross the lines drawn in *Talton v. Mayes*. This situation was further exacerbated by the First Amendment cases decided by the federal courts in favor of tribal institutions. Restrictions on basic religious freedoms, particularly when they might have an impact on mainstream Christian denominations, simply would not be tolerated by most Americans, regardless of the reason. As was the situation before the successful passage of the Dawes Severalty Act by Congress, assimilationists and civil rights advocates surprisingly found new ground for agreement, this time in 1968 over a new federal statute—a Bill of Rights for Native Americans.

The Indian Bill of Rights

The civil rights movement of the 1960s was powerful, successfully advocating social changes that altered the fundamental nature of American society. The challenge for Indians was to define the movement in ways that complemented their circumstances. They had to find a method to persuade Congress to abolish termination, to end relocation, and to outline Indian rights without compromising their sovereignty.[34] To shape the movement meant that Native Americans had to grasp the initiative in Congress, but few vehicles or congressional advocates were available to them. Before Indians could interpret the civil rights cause for themselves and for Congress, Senator Ervin introduced his Indian Bill of Rights.

Ervin's Subcommittee on Constitutional Rights first submitted nine bills for the Senate's consideration. Five of the proposals were aimed at correcting specific abuses in the tribal court system. Three bills offered practical protection to those who claimed that their constitutional rights had been infringed: criminal appeals from tribal courts went to federal courts for a completely new trial; a specific model code was to be created for the Courts of Indian Offenses; and the United States attorney general was charged with investigating complaints from Indians about the deprivation of their constitutional rights. All eight of the proposed new laws built on the bulwark of the Ervin subcommittee's investigations.

The ninth bill stated that "any Indian tribe in exercising its powers of local self-government shall be subject to the same limitations and restraints as those which are imposed on the Government of the United States by the United States Constitution."[35] This in essence imposed the entire Constitution on tribal councils and courts. In particular, the Bill of Rights and provisions in the Fourteenth and Fifteenth Amendments were to be extended to tribal legal institutions.

There were objections to this proposal. Many Indians thought that it posed as serious a threat to their existence as termination and relocation had. Even the Department of the Interior believed that the Ervin bill went too far. Some tribes, particularly the Pueblos, were theocracies, and they feared that the proposal would destroy their way of life. Others were concerned about the definition of tribal membership and whether it could stand up to constitutional scrutiny. Tribal resources would be severely taxed to implement the kind of judicial system mandated by the Bill of Rights, and the criminal justice system used in state and federal courts placed greater value on confrontation and punishment than did the Indian system which sought accommodation and protection of the tribe.[36]

Senator Ervin took these objections seriously and rewrote the bills. What emerged was the Indian Bill of Rights (IBR), which encompasses six sections—Titles II through VII—of the Civil Rights Act of 1968.[37] Title II was borrowed directly from the Bill of Rights and the Fourteenth Amendment. First, Indian tribes, the powers of self-government, and Indian courts are defined, and then Title II states: "No Indian tribe in exercising powers of self-government shall— . . ."[38] This is quite similar to the prohibitions of federal action in the First Amendment and state action in the Fourteenth Amendment.

Ten subsections of Title II specifically prohibit a number of Indian tribal actions against individuals. The first prohibits tribes from preventing the free exercise of religion, abridging freedom of speech or of the press, and forbidding the right to assemble or petition for a redress of grievances. These are traditionally termed First Amendment rights. The second subsection prevents tribal governments from conducting unreasonable searches and seizures or issuing warrants without probable cause. This is a Fourth Amendment right. The third subsection prohibits a person from being subjected to double jeopardy; the fourth prevents a person from being a "witness against himself"; and the fifth prevents private property from being taken for a public use without just compensation. These are Fifth Amendment rights. The sixth subsection guarantees a defendant the right to a speedy and public trial, the right to know specifically about any criminal charges, the right to be confronted by hostile witnesses, the right to subpoena witnesses, and the right to counsel at one's own expense. These are found in the Sixth Amendment, with the exception of requiring private payment for counsel. Another Sixth Amendment right is found in the tenth subsection, in which tribal governments are prevented from denying any person accused of an offense punishable by imprisonment the right to a trial by a jury of no fewer than six persons, a direct consideration of the situation in *Talton v. Mayes*. The seventh subsection prohibits excessive bail or fines, cruel and unusual punishments, and convictions for any crime for which the penalty is greater than six months in jail or a fine of $500 or both. These rights are similar to those in the Eighth Amendment. Thus Subsections 1 through 7 and 10 cover portions of the First, Fourth, Fifth, Sixth, and Eighth Amendments.

Two subsections go beyond the Bill of Rights. Subsection 8 prohibits the denial to any person of the equal protection of the laws or the deprivation of liberty or property without due process of law. These individual rights are found in the Fifth and Fourteenth Amendments. The ninth subsection does not allow tribal councils to pass bills of attainder or *ex post facto* laws. This is similar to portions of Article I, Section 9, as applied to Congress and Section 10 as applied to state legislatures.

What, then, is missing from the Indian Bill of Rights? In a sort of nineteenth-century carryover, individual Indians were accorded neither the Second Amendment right to keep and bear arms nor the Third Amendment right to be immune from the quartering of soldiers on one's property in time of peace. The Seventh Amendment, which allows the right to a jury trial in civil suits exceeding $20, was not extended to

Indian courts, principally because of the cost to tribal governments and Indian litigants.

The Ninth Amendment, the general clause retaining for the people those rights not covered in the Constitution, and the Tenth Amendment, reserving for the states or the people those powers not delegated to the federal government or prohibited to the states, were not added. Also left out was the Fifteenth Amendment, prohibiting discrimination in the right to vote based on race. The last omission was intentional, as many tribes believed that the inclusion of the Fifteenth Amendment might make it difficult for them to determine their own membership qualifications based on descent or blood quantum.

In addition to the omission of the Second, Third, Seventh, Ninth, Tenth, and Fifteenth Amendments from the Indian Bill of Rights, portions of other amendments were excluded. Noteworthy was the establishment clause of the First Amendment. The Ervin bill deleted the establishment clause after hearing extensive testimony from the theocratic Pueblo tribes of New Mexico, which argued that the establishment clause would destroy their tribal culture. The grand jury provision of the Fifth Amendment, requiring an indictment to be held to answer for a capital crime, was deleted, and the Sixth Amendment right to counsel at the expense of the government was not included. Here the Senate reasoned that tribal governments simply did not have adequate resources to retain counsel for indigent litigants, and most tribal courts did not use lawyers but instead provided tribal members for advice as needed.

The Fifth and Fourteenth Amendments were altered in the Indian Bill of Rights. The Fifth Amendment states that the federal government cannot deprive a person of "life, liberty, or property, without due process of law." Similarly, the Fourteenth Amendment stipulates that states cannot deny a person "life, liberty, or property, without due process of law; nor deny to any person within its jurisdiction the equal protection of the laws." Subsection 8 of the IBR provides that no Indian tribe can "deny to any person within its jurisdiction the equal protection of its laws or deprive any person of liberty or property without due process of law." The *life* provision of the Fifth and Fourteenth Amendments was deleted in the Indian Bill of Rights, and it is these provisions in the IBR guaranteeing due process and equal protection of the laws that have proved so contentious and litigious.

The last section of Title II also proved controversial. Initially, Ervin provided for appeals from Indian courts to federal courts to result in a trial de novo. This was challenged by many who believed that this would destroy the Indian court system. Thus in the final version, challenges to Indian government and court malfeasance were channeled through the privilege of filing a writ of habeas corpus. The only way that a person dissatisfied with his or her treatment could have that action reviewed was if the person was incarcerated. This was a narrow means of review. No language was provided in the IBR stipulating that other forms of appeal were not prohibited; they simply were not mentioned. However, if congressional intent can be measured, there is evidence that Congress preferred restricted appellate grounds.

Title II is the heart and soul of the Indian Bill of Rights. Its three sections—the definitions, the ten incorporations of selected portions of the federal Bill of Rights and other constitutional provisions, and the appellate provision using habeas corpus—constitute the only means by which individual Indians on reservations are accorded traditional Bill of Rights protections. Because Indians were not considered to be covered directly by the Constitution, the only possible vehicle available to those who wished to extend Bill of Rights concepts to Indian tribes was through congressional legislation.

Other sections of the Civil Rights Act devoted to Indian law were also path breaking. Title III directs the Secretary of the Interior to draw up a model code of justice for Congress's approval that applies to Courts of Indian Offenses. Title IV revised Public Law 280 by preventing a state from assuming criminal or civil jurisdiction over reservations without the consent of the Indian tribe or tribes in residence and by allowing any state to retrocede criminal or civil jurisdiction or both to the tribes, although no Indian consent is required. It is important to note that Public Law 280 was amended and not repealed. Title V revised the Major Crimes Act, adding assault resulting in serious bodily injury to the burgeoning list.

In the course of the Ervin committee hearings, senators discovered that the Department of the Interior had been obfuscating the ability of tribes to hire legal counsel and to know their constitutional rights and obligations. Consequently, Title VI stipulates that the Department of the Interior has ninety days to consider an Indian tribe's application for approval of a lawyer. If the agency does not make a determination, then the request is considered granted. In Title VII, the Secretary of the Interior is required to update the document "Indian Affairs, Laws and Treaties," to republish the treatise *Handbook of Federal Indian Law,* and to compile all official Interior Department opinions, published and unpublished. All these materials are to be made available to all recognized Indian tribes, bands, and groups.

The Indian Bill of Rights was indeed a significant and historic milestone for Native Americans. Its provisions changed the fundamental way in which tribes looked at themselves and their people under law. Even the partial application of the federal Bill of Rights to reservations altered forever some traditional practices. Moreover, acculturated Indians were not satisfied with a narrow interpretation of the IBR, but pressed for further expansion of this document.

Reactions to the Indian Bill of Rights

Reactions by non-Indians to the new Indian Bill of Rights were generally quite favorable. Most were surprised only to learn that Native Americans on reservations did not have access to the federal Bill of Rights, and they did not comprehend the implications of the new legislation.

The Indians' reactions were mixed. Some leaders favored the IBR. Wendall Chino, tribal chair of the Mescalero Apaches, believed that the act was an important step and hoped that the next Congress would abolish termination with a law and then adopt a major development program for the tribes. To Chino, the Indian Bill of Rights was something for all Indians to build on. The Association of American Indian Affairs also expressed its support.[39] Robert Burnette, leader of the Rosebud Sioux and former director of the National Congress of American Indians, strongly suppported the act:

> The Indian people do not have any rights. None of us are able to enter a United States district court and settle our grievances against our own elected leadership. We spent nine years fighting for the Indian Civil Rights Act. I do not think there is hardly an Indian leader today who realizes that Public Law 280 disappeared because of this act.[40]

Burnette and others mistakenly believed that Public Law 280 had been repealed.[41] One Indian present at its creation remained supportive. Helen Scheirbeck, director of the United Indians of America, believed that violations of religious freedom, the need for tribes to have their lawyers approved, and restrictions on Public Law 280 required this corrective legislation.[42]

There also was opposition. Most Native Americans were apathetic, and some were even hostile to the Indian Bill of Rights. Leslie Chapman of the Laguna Pueblo criticized the act as treating all Indians alike. She singled out Pueblo courts and Pueblo legal traditions as contrary to the IBR provisions:

> Even within the Anglo system, you can see the Constitution and due process do not necessarily yield justice. If you are concerned with how people feel and what is the effective way, what is functional in terms of the people on the reservation, the recognition of the differences is going to have to be made.[43]

The chair of the All Indian Pueblo Council, Domingo Montoya, asked for a revision of the Indian Bill of Rights to exempt all the Pueblos of New Mexico. Montoya expressed fear that the Pueblo political and legal systems would not stand up to constitutional mandates such as equal protection of the laws and "one man, one vote" reapportionment requirements.[44] Perhaps the most realistic reaction was expressed by Gerald Wilkinson, executive director of the National Indian Youth Council. To him, "every Indian is opposed to the Indian Civil Rights Act . . . until he has been screwed by his tribal council."[45]

Most of those opposing the Indian Bill of Rights felt that the act was contrary to the newly stated Indian policy of Presidents Johnson and Nixon. Opponents saw the IBR as incompatible with Indian self-determination. How, they questioned, can Indian tribes under the Indian Bill of Rights make decisions based on cultural considerations if these determinations violate Western European legal traditions? They believed that much more damage than good would result.[46] Proponents cited previous abuses and insisted that the protection afforded by the Indian Bill of Rights was justified. They also discounted the possible erosion of tribal sovereignty and treaty rights and instead saw the Indian Bill of Rights as strengthening tribal legal institutions.[47] With the first test case of the Indian Bill of Rights, this argument was demolished.

Dodge v. Nakai *(1968)*

The same week after the Indian Bill of Rights became law, the Navajo Nation was in turmoil. On April 16, 1968, the Navajo Tribal Council met to consider the operation of Dinebeiina Nahiilna Be Agiditahe, Inc.

(DNA), a nonprofit legal services corporation financed by the federal government's Office of Economic Opportunity. Earlier, the tribal chairman, Raymond Nakai, had asked the Office of Navajo Economic Opportunity (ONEO), the contracting agency with DNA, to consider rescinding its contract because Theodore Mitchell's conduct was embarrassing Nakai. Mitchell, a non-Indian, was the director of DNA. The executive director of ONEO, Peter McDonald, a political rival of Nakai and future Navajo tribal chairman, refused Nakai's request.

Frustrated, Nakai took his concerns to the council, which responded by holding two days of hearings on Mitchell and his policy of intervening in issues before Navajo agencies. Of particular concern was Mitchell's actions on behalf of several Navajos in a dispute over the operation of the Chinle school system on the reservation. The council decided not to ask that Mitchell be temporarily relieved of his duties.

Not all council members were satisfied. Annie Wauneka, a member of the council and of the Navajo Tribal Council Advisory Committee, sought out Mitchell the next day and told him that she believed he was detrimental to the Navajo people and should leave the reservation. In the next week, conditions deteriorated to the point that the Advisory Committee passed a resolution demanding Mitchell's dismissal. On July 3, Tribal Chairman Nakai told Mitchell that he had fourteen days to remain as director of DNA or the Advisory committee would take further action. Nothing happened.

On August 5, the Navajo Tribal Council Advisory Committee held a meeting in the council chambers. At the meeting were representatives of the Department of the Interior to discuss the implications of the new Indian Bill of Rights Act. Also present were DNA officials, including Theodore Mitchell. Annie Wauneka asked whether the act prevented the Navajo Nation from evicting persons from the Navajo Reservation. Durard Barnes, Acting Associate Solicitor on Indian Affairs from the Department of the Interior, asked Wauneka whether she had anyone specific in mind. She interrupted and stated that she did not, but at this point extremely loud, derisive, and insulting laughter erupted from several in the audience, the most noticeable coming from Mitchell. The next day, the meeting continued. At this meeting, Wauneka got up from her chair and confronted Mitchell. She demanded to know whether he intended to laugh at the Navajo Council again. After Mitchell said something to her, Wauneka slapped him several times and told him to leave the chambers. Mitchell left.

The next day, August 7, the Advisory committee passed a resolution requiring the immediate removal of Mitchell from the Navajo Reservation. He could then return on August 8 for a hearing about his permanent banishment. Navajo police were dispatched to remove Mitchell; he was taken from the reservation; and on August 8, there was a hearing at which Mitchell was allowed to make a statement before the Advisory committee. The committee then formally declared by a vote of 12 to 3 that Mitchell was banished from the Navajo Reservation.[48]

Two important issues surrounded the banishment order. First, Mitchell's conduct during the Advisory Committee's meeting was more than reprehensible. According to Navajo culture and tradition, disruptive, antisocial conduct is essentially a crime against the tribe. To some, including council member Annie Wauneka, such an action is tantamount to a serious felony. Second, even though Mitchell's action involved illegal personal activity on his part, *banishment* is essentially a civil action, not a criminal finding. Because it is a civil action and the restitution for any wrongful action does not require imprisonment or fines, tribal judicial institutions have jurisdiction. Banishment allows for the restoration of tribal harmony. Antisocial conduct on a reservation by an Indian or a non-Indian can be considered by tribal courts or, as in this case, a quasi-legislative/judicial tribal council advisory committee.

Mitchell brought suit in federal court to reverse his banishment. As a plaintiff, Mitchell joined eight Navajos from the board of directors of DNA and a class of indigent Navajos who used the services of DNA. One of the Navajos representing the class was John Dodge, a relative of one of Raymond Nakai's political opponents. Mitchell sued Nakai, chairman of the Navajo Tribal Council; V. Allen Adams, superintendent of the Navajo police; and Graham Holmes, area director of the Navajo Reservation for the BIA.

The district court in Arizona agreed to hear arguments regarding whether it had jurisdiction as a result of the new Indian Bill of Rights. Mitchell peppered the court with possible ways in which the federal courts could assume jurisdiction. Most were rejected, although the court did accept two of the arguments he raised. First, the district court ruled that the Navajo Tribal Council Advisory Committee's action was subject to treaty interpretation and so allowed for federal jurisdiction. Although that was sufficient, the court went further. It ruled that when Congress passed the Indian Bill of Rights, it intended to "make substantial changes in the manner in which Indian tribes could exercise their quasi-sovereign powers." This, to the court, opened the door to federal juris-diction. The legislative intent behind the IBR was so broad that the fact that Mitchell did not exhaust the Navajo court system before he came to the federal court was unnecessary. Moreover, the lack of a writ of habeas corpus was not even fully discussed.[49]

The court also dealt with the *Colliflower* precedent. The Navajos' case presented a different situation. The Navajos never approved the New Deal governments, so their government was based on treaties. Consequently, the federal court in *Dodge v. Nakai* could not declare the Navajo Advisory Committee as an extension of a federal agency in order for jurisdiction to be attached.

After agreeing to hear the case, the court eventually issued its opinion in March 1969. It found that under the Indian Bill of Rights, the actions of the Navajo Nation violated Theodore Mitchell's rights by not accord-ing him due process of law (Title II, Section 202[8]) and freedom of speech (Title II, Section 202[1]). The Advisory Committee also violated the Indian Bill of Rights by passing what the court determined to be a bill of attainder (Title II, Section 202[9]). The court held that the banishment provision of the Navajo treaty with the United States in 1868 required fundamental aspects of due process and that any action of the tribe activating such "a severe remedial device" must be in full compliance with its own Navajo tribal code.[50]

Dodge v. Nakai was a massive hemorrhage in the tribal sovereignty of the Navajos and that of all Native American nations. Treaty rights were attacked. Narrow jurisdictional limits placed in the Indian Bill of Rights were expanded significantly. Restrictions placed on banishment as a remedy for tribal governments made it almost impossible to obtain. Due process of law would be applied to tribal courts as if it were a federal rather than a tribal legal concept. Even Senator Sam Ervin had not anticipated such a sweeping interpretation of his Indian Bill of Rights.[51]

■   ■   ■

"Will Capture had told his daughter a lot about old Eagle Capture, how much he had admired his father and wanted to please him," writes Janet Campbell Hale. Hale, a Coeur d'Alene, explains in her novel *The Jail-ing of Cecelia Capture* that Cecelia Capture, Will's daughter, is in jail remembering a childhood event that she now understands. At the time, it did not make sense why her father threw away all of his law books. Eagle Capture

> was the one who had brought the white man's system of justice to the tribe. He believed that the key to survival was legal representation. If the Indian people had had adequate legal representation, there would have been no Little Bighorn or Wounded Knee. It wouldn't have been possible for the white-eyes to steal land and murder Indians. Legal representation was the key.[52]

Cecelia, who had shared her father's hopes, now shared her father's doubts.

This year, 1968, was indeed important to the relationship of Native Americans to the Bill of Rights. It began with the foment associated with an unpopular war and a nation attempting to come to grips with the fundamental legal and moral inconsistencies in its race relations. The assassination of America's foremost civil rights leader punctuated the nation's agony, and the political system could not contain the confusion. Another assassination brought memories of a slain president from the death of his brother. One president gave up; a new one was chosen. Indians had some cause to worry. Richard Nixon's previous federal experience was as vice president for Dwight Eisenhower, the primary advocate of termination and relocation policies in the 1950s.

For Indians in 1968, a renewed threat to tribal sovereignty appeared in the form of the Indian Bill of Rights. It was not enough for the Indian Claims Commission to continue slowly down its terminationist path or for the federal courts to make war on tribal governments. The protection afforded tribal courts and tribal councils from *Talton v. Mayes* was eliminated by Congress. Moreover, with the *Dodge v. Nakai* decision, it appeared that tribal ways of life were about to come to an end. The very nature of Indianness was at stake.

With these serious and threatening legal signs for Indians and the tempo of the times, it is not surprising that 1968 also ushered in a new way of thinking for some Native Americans. Red Power came of age. Young Native Americans, many living in the cities, the victims of relocation, proclaimed their own social movement. Northern Plains Indians in Minneapolis started a new organization, the American Indian Movement, known as AIM. Its founders, notably Dennis Banks (Chippewa), Russell Means (Sioux), Hank Adams (Assiniboine), Clyde Warrior (Ponca), and Clyde Bellecourt (Chippewa), fashioned rhetoric that appealed to the young. The activists in AIM developed a militant program that targeted corrupt tribal governments, the BIA, the FBI, the state courts and police, and irrational federal policies.

After 1968, what might the 1970s and 1980s bring? Self-determination and economic development were federal policies debated front and center. Richard Nixon offered some surprising new initiatives, and Native Americans embarked on a perilous journey with their new Bill of Rights.

AN HISTORICAL ANALYSIS OF THE 1968 'INDIAN CIVIL RIGHTS' ACT

Donald L. Burnett, Jr.*

Introduction

In the Indian Civil Rights Act,[1] enacted as a rider to the Civil Rights Act of 1968,[2] Congress faced a number of the problems involved in the relationship between the various Indian tribes and the federal constitutional system. In order to properly understand its provisions, however, the Act must be seen in historical perspective — in terms of the development of the place of the Indian in the American legal system and of the legislation itself. Because the debate in 1968 over the Civil Rights Act centered on the sections intended primarily to benefit other minorities, so have most of the commentaries written on it since then, and the necessary historical analyses of the Indian provisions have not been undertaken.

Judicial sensitivity is especially important in the area of Indian civil rights. The United States Commission on Civil Rights recently noted: "In enforcing the act, the courts will have the serious responsibility of drawing a balance between respect for individual rights and respect for Indian custom and tradition. Many important questions . . . will not be answered until the courts have settled them."[3] In deciding cases involving these provisions, some courts have not engaged in the sort of historical discussion and analysis that should be essential.[4] An underlying thesis of this article is that a sense of history will engender greater judicial sensitivity for the need to preserve effective tribal institutions. A better understanding of the relevant history should aid judicial analysis and guide the courts and the agencies implementing the legislation.

---

*Clerk to Henry F. McQuade, Supreme Court of Idaho; Member of the Idaho Bar; B.A., 1968, Harvard University; J.D., 1971, University of Chicago.

1 25 U.S.C. §§ 1301-03, 1311-12, 1321-26, 1331, 1341 (1970).

2 82 Stat. 73 (codified in scattered sections of 18, 25, 42 U.S.C.).

3 United States Commission on Civil Rights, American Indian Civil Rights Handbook 11 (1972).

4 See, e.g., United States v. Brown, 334 F. Supp. 536 (D. Neb. 1971).

This article, first briefly outlines the history of the issue of Indian tribal sovereignty and the ways in which federal law in this area has developed. It next traces the legislative process, especially the part played by Senator Sam Ervin of North Carolina, which resulted in the Indian civil rights provisions. This analysis focuses on Senator Ervin's apparent objectives, the interests of the affected parties, the areas of conflict and accommodation, and the process of enactment. It then examines the ways in which various courts have interpreted the Act and how the tribes have been affected by it.

I. TRIBAL SOVEREIGNTY FROM 1786

A. *The Early Years: Seminal Concepts*

The federal government's Indian affairs policy originated in times when it regarded the tribes as enemy nations. In 1786, Congress delegated responsibility for Indian affairs to the War Department.[5] The Bureau of Indian Affairs (BIA) was created in 1824, and President Jackson appointed a Commissioner of Indian Affairs within the War Department in 1832.[6] The responsibility for administration in the field rested with the local agent, often a cavalry officer, who was given broad powers "to manage and superintend the intercourse with the Indians" and "to carry into effect such regulations as may be prescribed by the President."[7] The President, in turn, was "authorized to prescribe such rules and regulations as he may think fit."[8]

The states took little part in the management of Indian affairs, for the Removal Act of 1830[9] transferred many eastern tribes to the plains west of the Mississippi River where no states yet existed. Moreover, in *Worcester v. Georgia*,[10] the Supreme Court held that native tribes were not subject to the jurisdiction of the states in which they were located. Chief Justice Marshall described the

---

5 H. DRIVER, INDIANS OF NORTH AMERICA 485 (2d ed. rev. 1969).
6 *Id.* at 482.
7 Act of June 30, 1834, ch. 162, § 7, 4 Stat. 736-37.
8 *Id.* at § 17, 4 Stat. 738.
9 Act of May 28, 1830, ch. 148, 4 Stat. 411-12.
10 31 U.S. (6 Pet.) 515 (1832).

Cherokee tribe as "a distinct community, occupying its own territory with boundaries accurately described in which the laws of Georgia can have no force."[11] In an earlier decision holding that the Cherokees were not a foreign nation within the meaning of the Constitution for the purpose of determining the Supreme Court's original jurisdiction, Chief Justice Marshall had described the tribe as a "domestic dependent nation" and had likened each Indian's relationship to the federal government to that of a "ward to his guardian."[12] These analogies reflected the traditional view that Indian tribes remained sovereign bodies empowered to regulate their own affairs, limited only by acts of Congress.[13] By virtue of the federal government's conquest, Congress was viewed as enjoying plenary authority over Indian affairs.[14] The treaties enacted under congressional authority often reserved to the Indians the right to retain their traditional institutions and to continue such essential activities as hunting and fishing.[15] Their implications were commonly broad, "[giving] the Indians every warrant to believe that they could retain their lands, their governments, and their way of life as long as they wished."[16]

Thus, the place of Indians and Indian tribes in the American system was uncertain. Indians were commonly regarded as federal wards; yet tribal organizations were acknowledged as "distinct communities" of a sovereign nature.

B.   *The Era of Conquest: The Rule of the BIA*

Following the Bureau's transfer from the War Department to the Department of the Interior in 1849,[17] BIA policy continued to

---

11 *Id.* at 560.

12 Cherokee Nation v. Georgia, 30 U.S. (5 Pet.) 1 (1831).

13 *See* Note, *The Indian Bill of Rights and the Constitutional Status of Tribal Governments*, 82 HARV. L. REV. 1343, 1347 (1969).

14 *See* Crosse, *Criminal and Civil Jurisdiction in Indian Country*, 4 ARIZ. L. REV. 57 (1962).

15 *See* 2 C. KAPPLER, LAWS AND TREATIES, S. DOC. No. 452, 57th Cong., 1st Sess. (1903).

16 W. BROPHY & S. ABERLE, THE INDIAN: AMERICA'S UNFINISHED BUSINESS 25 (1966) [hereinafter cited as BROPHY]. This volume expands FUND FOR THE REPUBLIC, REPORT OF THE COMMISSION ON THE RIGHTS, LIBERTIES AND RESPONSIBILITIES OF THE AMERICAN INDIAN (W. Brophy & S. Aberle eds. 1961).

17 DRIVER, *supra* note 5, at 482.

reflect these conflicting views. The field agents still exercised the broad statutory power previously noted, but they also created indigenous police forces and courts or retained them where they already existed. Of course, this policy was not simply a concession to the sovereign powers of the tribes. The Indian police, directed by the local agent, served not only to enforce law and order, but also to set examples of acculturation to the native communities and to undermine the authority of recalcitrant chieftains and councils.[18] In the 1890's the Indian police were instrumental in suppressing the Ghost Dance movement among the Sioux, the last great organized resistance to the inexorable white dominance.[19]

The law enforced by these indigenous police detachments was a mixture of tribal custom and rudimentary codes drafted by the BIA in the early 1880's. In part, these codes were intended to supplant native customs, but they were also required because the trauma of conquest had weakened traditional social controls.[20] The "successful" experiment with Indian police encouraged the BIA to establish Indian courts with native judges. Courts of Indian offenses were established by the Secretary of the Interior in 1883, and that year's Annual Report of the Commissioner of Indian Affairs set forth rules, approved by the Secretary, governing the operation of the new courts.[21] In practice, these courts operated very informally.[22]

By the mid-1880's a structure for Indian affairs management had emerged. Alert to the uncertain legal status of the tribes and the unclear extent of their sovereign powers, the BIA adopted a middle course. Certain trappings of tribal sovereignty (in the form of Indian police and courts) were encouraged, but matters of pol-

---

18 W. HAGAN, INDIAN POLICE AND JUDGES 69-79 (1966).

19 *Id.* at 103. For an examination of what underlay the Ghost Dance movement, see P. FARB, MAN'S RISE TO CIVILIZATION AS SHOWN BY THE NORTH AMERICAN INDIANS FROM PRIMEVAL TIMES TO THE COMING OF THE INDUSTRIAL STATE 280-84 (1968).

20 HAGAN, *supra* note 18, at 9.

21 SUBCOMM. ON CONSTITUTIONAL RIGHTS OF SENATE COMM. ON THE JUDICIARY, SUMMARY REPORT OF HEARINGS AND INVESTIGATIONS ON CONSTITUTIONAL RIGHTS OF THE AMERICAN INDIAN, 99th Cong., 2d Sess., 14 (Comm. Print 1964) [hereinafter cited as SUMMARY REPORT OF HEARINGS].

22 The extent to which the native judges served the will of local BIA agents varied with circumstances and personalities; but a report of the Board of Indian Commissioners in 1892 charged that agent influence remained unduly strong, partly because appeals from court decisions could be taken to BIA administrators. HAGAN, *supra* note 18, at 110.

icy, such as the drafting of codes, remained exclusively in the hands of the Bureau.

C.   *The Settlement Era: The Indians and the Law*

As white America pursued its "Manifest Destiny," Indian country ceased to be remote. Law and order on the reservations gravely concerned burgeoning numbers of settlers, and the increase in crimes committed by whites on reservations troubled the Indians as well. The new courts of Indian offenses exercised jurisdiction in civil and criminal cases in which both parties were Indian and also occasionally in cases involving whites on the reservations. But the creation of states as sovereign entities and a reluctance by the settlers to entrust serious criminal cases to Indian tribunals resulted in a substantial limitation of Indian court criminal jurisdiction.

State jurisdiction over crimes committed by whites on the reservations was extended in *United States v. McBratney*[23] in which the Supreme Court held that the United States Circuit Court for Colorado did not have exclusive jurisdiction over the murder of one white man by another on the Ute Reservation in Colorado. The Court said that the United States did not have exclusive jurisdiction over a reservation unless Congress had expressly exempted it from state jurisdiction when it had admitted the state to the Union. No such exemption had been made with respect to the Ute Reservation,[24] and, as a result, Colorado had "acquired criminal jurisdiction over its own citizens and other white persons throughout the whole of its territory . . . including the Ute Reservation. . . ."[25]

As the Supreme Court extended state criminal jurisdiction over whites on the reservations, Congress limited Indian court authority over Indians committing crimes against other Indians on the reser-

---

23 104 U.S. 621 (1881).

24 The Court sought support from United States v. Ward, 28 Fed. Cas. 397 (No. 16,639) (C.C.D. Kan. 1863) and The Kansas Indians, 72 U.S. (5 Wall.) 737 (1866). But these cases held merely that where express provisions *did* exist, Indian lands were exempt from state jurisdiction. They did not hold that express provision was an absolute prerequisite. Nevertheless, pressure to extend state jurisdiction, founded partly in fear of reservations becoming "no man's lands," was so great that *McBratney* became a landmark precedent.

25 United States v. McBratney 104 U.S. 621, 624 (1881).

vations. In the celebrated *Crow Dog* case,[26] the Oglala court had convicted the defendant of murder and ordered him to make restitution in the form of services and property to the victim's family. This form of penalty was fully consistent with traditional tribal practices, but outraged whites demanded a more severe punishment. The defendant was tried again and convicted in a Dakota Territory district court sitting as a United States circuit court. The Supreme Court held that the district court did not have jurisdiction over a crime committed in Indian country by one member of a tribe upon another of the same tribe.[27] In response, Congress eliminated tribal jurisdiction over cases involving serious crimes.

The Seven Major Crimes Act[28] gave territorial courts jurisdiction over enumerated major offenses committed by Indians within a territory, whether or not on a reservation and gave federal courts jurisdiction over such offenses when committed by Indians on a reservation within a state. The validity of the Act was established in *United States v. Kagama*,[29] in which the Supreme Court upheld the exercise of federal jurisdiction over the murder of an Indian by two other Indians on the Hoopa Valley Reservation in California. The Court recalled Congress' plenary power and reiterated Marshall's wardship concept: "These Indian tribes are the wards of the nation. They are communities dependent on the United States. Dependent largely for their daily food. Dependent for their political rights."[30]

At the same time, state courts and lower federal courts began to extend the logic of the Seven Major Crimes Act to give the states

---

26 *Ex Parte* Crow Dog, 109 U.S. 556 (1883).

27 *Id.* at 562.

28 Indian Appropriations Act of 1885, 23 Stat. 385 (1885) [informally and hereinafter referred to as Seven Major Crimes Act], *as amended* 18 U.S.C. § 1153 (1970). In the original Act of 1885, federal courts and law enforcement agencies were granted jurisdiction over cases of murder, manslaughter, rape, assault with intent to kill, arson, burglary, and larceny committed by one Indian upon another on the reservation. Incest, assault with a dangerous weapon, and embezzlement were added later. Pub. L. No. 89-707, § 1, 80 Stat. 1100, and Pub. L. No. 90-284, § 501, 82 Stat. 80, *amending* 23 Stat. 385 (1885). The Act did not abrogate existing treaties. 18 U.S.C. § 1153 (1970) (as amended). The Cherokee, expressly granted jurisdiction over all crimes committed on their reservation by 1785 treaty (7 Stat. 18), were unaffected.

29 118 U.S. 375 (1886).

30 *Id.* at 383-84.

criminal jurisdiction over Indians off the reservation.[31] The resulting diminution of the jurisdiction of tribal courts to include only less serious offenses committed by Indians while on the reservation led an Oregon district court to declare that the Indian courts were merely "educational and disciplinary instrumentalities, by which the government of the United States is endeavoring to improve and elevate the condition of these dependent tribes to whom it sustains the relation of guardian."[32]

In 1896, however, the Supreme Court clearly reaffirmed its adherence to the principle of tribal sovereignty. *Talton v. Mayes*[33] presented the question whether a Cherokee practice of using a five-man jury to institute criminal proceedings violated the grand jury requirement of the fifth amendment. In a landmark opinion, the Court held that the requirement was applicable only to the federal government,[34] saying that because the sovereign powers of Cherokee governing bodies had existed prior to the white man's arrival, the Indian courts were not federal agencies subject to the fifth amendment.[35] This reaffirmation of tribal sovereignty carried into the present century as tribal governments were acknowledged to enjoy immunity to suit without prior consent. In *Turner v. United States*,[36] the Supreme Court indicated this view as dictum, and in 1940, it held flatly that "Indian Nations are exempt from suit without Congressional authorization."[37]

---

31 *In re* Wolf, 27 F. 606 (W.D. Ark. 1886) (conspiracy of Indians to obtain money from tribe under false pretenses); Pablo v. People, 23 Colo. 134, 46 P. 636 (1896) (murder of Indian by Indian); Hunt v. State, 4 Kan. 60 (1866) (murder of Indian by Indian); State v. Williams, 13 Wash. 335, 43 P. 15 (1895) (murder of Indian by Indian).

32 United States v. Clapox, 35 F. 575, 577 (D. Ore. 1888).

33 163 U.S. 376 (1896).

34 In this respect, *Talton* paralleled Hurtado v. California, 110 U.S. 516 (1884), in which the Supreme Court had held that states were not required by the due process clause of the fourteenth amendment to prosecute only after indictment by a grand jury.

35 Recently, one distinguished commentator has suggested that *Talton* means only that a tribal government will not be required to grant a *remedial* right under the Constitution, the question of *fundamental* rights being left open. Lazarus, *Title II of the 1968 Civil Rights Act: An Indian Bill of Rights*, 45 No. DAK. L. REV. 337, 341 (1969).

36 248 U.S. 354 (1919).

37 United States v. United States Fidelity Co., 309 U.S. 506, 512 (1940). The Court also held the tribes immune to counterclaim except as authorized by statute.

D. *1920 to 1940: Nations in a Nation*

After World War I, Congress passed the Indian Citizenship Act, which provided that "all noncitizen Indians born within the territorial limits of the United States [are] declared to be citizens of the United States."[38] Most states extended the franchise with this new citizenship although several states did not.[39]

Following this grant of citizenship, the Secretary of the Interior hired the Brookings Institute to survey Indian tribes and to recommend further steps to bring the Indians more completely into the American mainstream. In 1928, the Institute issued the Meriam Report,[40] which revealed grim economic, educational, and health conditions on the reservations and stressed the impossibility of integrating the Indians directly into white society.[41] The Report was highly critical[42] of the Indian General Allotment Act of 1887,[43] which was an earlier attempt to achieve rapid assimilation. That Act had distributed Indian land to individual natives in 40, 80, or 100 acre allotments. Through white exploitation of native ignorance of the formalities of land titles, Indian land holdings decreased from 138 million acres in 1887 to 48 million acres in 1934.[44]

Drawing heavily on the Meriam Report and work begun during the Hoover administration,[45] New Deal appointees to the Department of the Interior were instrumental in drafting and guiding through Congress the Indian Reorganization Act of 1934,[46] a major reform measure. It cancelled the general allotment policy and radically changed BIA procedures regarding economic development and community self-government. The most important self-government provision was section 16, which authorized the tribes to adopt

---

38 8 U.S.C. § 3(c) *amended* 8 U.S.C. § 1401(a)(2) (1970). A number of Indians, such as those who had previously enlisted in the armed forces or who had accepted land allotments were already citizens by previous legislation. Rice, *The Position of the American Indian in the Law of the United States*, 16 J. COMP. LEG. & INT'L L. 78, 86 (3d Ser. 1934).

39 *E.g.*, Porter v. Hall, 34 Ariz. 308, 271 P. 411 (1928) (holding Indians ineligible to vote under a state statute denying the franchise to "persons under guardianship").

40 L. MERIAM, THE PROBLEM OF INDIAN ADMINISTRATION (1928).

41 *Id.* at 86-90.

42 *E.g., id.* at 7.

43 Act of Feb. 8, 1887, ch. 119, 24 stat. 388.

44 BROPHY, *supra* note 16, at 20.

45 *Id.* at 181.

46 25 U.S.C. §§ 461-79 (1970).

their own constitutions and by-laws, to be ratified by a majority of the members and by the Secretary of the Interior. An elected tribal council was authorized to pass ordinances consistent with the tribal constitution.[47] The Act authorized the establishment of tribal courts, to be manned by judges elected by the tribes or appointed by the councils and to be guided by rules drafted by the tribes themselves, subject to the Secretary's approval. Wherever a tribal court was established, it superseded the court of Indian offenses if one existed.[48] Finally, the Secretary was authorized to draft a model code as a guide to the tribes and as an operative code for those tribes who did not draft their own.[49] Although the original version of the Act provided for a court of Indian affairs with appellate jurisdiction, this provision was removed before passage, leaving unchanged the old system of appeals to BIA administrators and ultimately to the Secretary.[50]

The motivation behind the Indian Reorganization Act was to encourage the establishment of Indian governing bodies to exercise the sovereign powers which the Supreme Court in *Talton* had said belonged to the tribes. This view was expressed by Felix Cohen, one of the drafters of the Act: "These powers are subject to qualification by treaties and by express legislation by Congress, but, save as thus expressly qualified, full powers of internal sovereignty are vested in the Indian tribes and their duly constituted organs of government."[51] This notion of "internal sovereignty"[52] was to become the watchword of the courts in ensuing decades.

Because many tribes, however, were ill-prepared for self-government, the BIA often simply imposed its own code and created the tribe's constitution, by-laws, council, and court.[53] "While the trappings of autonomy had been created the substance was lacking.

---

47 The Act provided no express authority for the Secretary to review council-passed ordinances, but it became customary for him to do so through his local superintendent. *See* 25 C.F.R. § 11.1(e); *see also* SUMMARY REPORT OF HEARINGS, *supra* note 21, at 3.

48 25 C.F.R. § 11.1(b) (1969).

49 25 C.F.R. § 11 (1969).

50 H.R. REP. No. 1804, 73d Cong., 2d Sess. 6 (1934).

51 U.S. SOLICITOR FOR DEPT. OF INTERIOR, FEDERAL INDIAN LAW 143 (1940).

52 "Internal sovereignty" was contrasted with "external sovereignty" — the tribes' powers vis-a-vis non-Indians. The tribes enjoyed full sovereign independence from outside forces except for the federal government.

53 Oliver, *The Legal Status of American Indian Tribes*, 38 ORE. L. REV. 193 (1959).

No major transfers of governmental functions from the Bureau of Indian Affairs to the tribes took place."[54]

In fact, the 1934 Act strengthened the role of the BIA in tribal affairs, and the Secretary's review powers ensured that the BIA would still have considerable influence even among those tribes capable of creating their own governing bodies. While the Bureau role at first seems inconsistent with the principle of tribal sovereignty which the Act was apparently designed to implement, BIA involvement conformed with the Meriam Report which had acknowledged that true Indian self-government was a long-term objective at best, and that Indians should prepare for the eventual control of their own affairs through the gradual extension of tribal power.[55]

E. *World War II to 1955: Termination and Assimilation*

Nearly 25,000 Indians served in the American armed forces during World War II, and almost twice that number worked in industry.[56] As had been the case following World War I, new efforts were made after World War II to bring the Indians into the mainstream of American society. It appeared, however, that while white America was making room for the native American, it also threatened to destroy his Indian identity.

> The cultural conquest of the recalcitrant red man, by cajoling and by assimilation was at hand. He was measured for the melting pot. It was with this hope in mind that the Hoover Commission on postwar governmental reorganization, which had been appointed by President Truman, recommended "complete integration" .... Evidently it was thought that if the Indian could fight and work like everyone else then he must be like everyone else.[57]

Advance warnings of an attempt to remove the confining but protective fabric woven into the 1934 Act appeared as early as 1943, when the Senate Indian Affairs Subcommittee called for liquidation of the BIA and termination of its services.[58] In 1947,

---

54 Schifter, *Trends in Federal Indian Administration*, 15 S.D. L. Rev. 1, 4 (1970).

55 Meriam, *supra* note 40, at 86-90.

56 Driver, *supra* note 5, at 495.

57 S. Steiner, The New Indians 23 (1968).

58 S. Rep. No. 310, 78th Cong., 1st Sess. 17 (1943).

the Commissioner of Indian Affairs presented a plan to the sub-committee for termination of federal services to some more "advanced" tribes.[59] The Hoover Commission, in 1948, coupled its plea for integration with a proposal to terminate federal services to tribes and to transfer these functions to the states.[60] The next year, measures were introduced in Congress to abolish the BIA[61] and to amend the Constitution to eliminate the power of Congress over Indian affairs.[62]

In 1948, Congress authorized New York to assume criminal juris-diction over all Indians residing within its borders,[63] and a year later it extended coverage to include all civil disputes.[64] Because the Indians in New York were relatively assimilated and voiced no objection to the legislation, these actions created little controversy. The movement for further extension of state jurisdiction over Indian reservations throughout the country was slowed tempo-rarily in 1948 when a bill to that effect failed in the Senate after passing the House.[65]

However, the move to transfer tribes from BIA guardianship to state jurisdiction gained momentum as the Bureau brought dis-credit on the system created in 1934. In 1950, Dillon Myer, former director of the World War II Japanese-American Relocation Pro-gram, was named Commissioner of Indian Affairs. In order to implement the BIA's plan to relocate Indians into the cities, Myer used the Bureau to control or to dispose of reservation lands and individual property.[66] The BIA also allegedly meddled in tribal politics, froze tribal funds to quiet dissent on the reservations, interfered with the tribes' efforts to obtain legal counsel, and re-

---

59 STEINER, *supra* note 57, at 23.

60 Report of the Committee on Indian Affairs to the Commission on Organiza-tion of the Executive Branch of the Government (Oct. 1948), cited in BROPHY, *supra* note 16, at 36. The idea of turning Indian problems over to the states was an old one. In 1882 the Commissioner had recommended that when the Dakota and New Mexico territories became states they be given jurisdiction over reservations, but four years later the Supreme Court warned: "They [the Indians] owe no allegiance to the States and receive from them no protection. Because of the local ill feeling, the people of the States where they are found are often their deadliest enemies." United States v. Kagama, 118 U.S. 375, 383 (1886).

61 S. 2726, 81st Cong., 1st Sess. (1949).

62 95 CONG. REC. 9745 (1949).

63 25 U.S.C. § 232 (1970).

64 25 U.S.C. § 233 (1970).

65 H.R. 4725, 89th Cong., 2d Sess. (1948).

66 *See generally* STEINER, *supra* note 57, at 179.

fused to build permanent community facilities on reservations (such as a hospital in Papago country) because it would encourage the natives to remain on their land rather than to relocate.[67]

The BIA's abuse of its power to prepare Indians for self-sufficiency moved Congress to attempt "to get out of the Indian business."[68] After bills to set tribes "free" under state jurisdiction nearly passed the Eighty-second Congress, the Eighty-third Congress adopted House Concurrent Resolution 108, stating in part:

> [I]t is the policy of Congress, as rapidly as possible, to make the Indians within the territorial limits of the United States subject to the same laws and entitled to the same privileges and responsibilities as are applicable to other citizens of the United States, to end their status as wards of the United States, and to grant them all of the rights and prerogatives pertaining to American citizenship . . . .[69]

Bills to transfer jurisdiction over Indians to California, Minnesota, Nebraska, Nevada, Oregon, and Wisconsin were introduced.[70] Of these, H.R. 1063 was enacted and became known as Public Law 280.[71] Although originally drafted to affect only Indians in California, in its final form it covered Indians in Minnesota, Nebraska, Oregon, and Wisconsin. Sections 6 and 7 permitted states whose constitutions contained disclaimers of jurisdiction over Indian affairs to amend their constitutions to exercise such jurisdiction. In making this open-ended transfer of authority Congress did not even require that the Indians be consulted before a state assumed jurisdiction over them. President Eisenhower signed the bill reluctantly, terming the legislation an "unchristianlike approach" to Indian problems, and noting further:

---

67 Cohen, *The Erosion of Indian Rights, 1950-1953*, 62 YALE L.J. 348, 352-59 (1953).

68 *Hearings on H.R. Con. Res. 108 Before the Subcomm. on Indian Affairs of the House Comm. on Interior and Insular Affairs*, 83d Cong., 1st Sess., ser. 7, at 28 (1953) (remarks of Representative Saylor of Pennsylvania), *quoted in* Oliver, *The Legal Status of American Indian Tribes*, 38 ORE. L. REV. 193, 238 n. 247 (1959).

69 H.R. Con. Res. 108, 83d Cong., 1st Sess., 99 CONG. REC. 9968 (1953).

70 These states had no disclaimers of jurisdiction over Indians written into their constitutions, and their tribes had been previously "consulted" about the transfer, although no claim was made that their consent had been obtained. H.R. REP. No. 848, 83d Cong., 1st Sess. 7-8 (1953).

71 Act of August 15, 1953, 67 Stat. 588, *as amended* 18 U.S.C. § 1162 (1970) and 28 U.S.C. § 1360 (1970).

> The failure to include in these provisions a requirement of full consultation in order to ascertain the wishes and desires of the Indians and of final Federal approval, was unfortunate. I recommended, therefore, that at the earliest possible time in the next session of the Congress, the act be amended to require such consultation with the tribes . . . .[72]

The administration, however, did not submit a bill to implement the President's recommendation. While several members of Congress responded in the Second Session of the Eightythird Congress and continued to introduce modifying legislation during the remainder of the decade,[73] none was successful.

In 1954, Congress proceeded with legislation to terminate federal services to selected tribes, as contemplated by House Concurrent Resolution 108.[74] Several bills proposed to terminate tribes throughout the west and midwest. The most significant legislation to emerge was the termination of the Menominee,[75] Klamath,[76]

---

72 *Hearings on S. 961-968 and S.J. Res. 40 Before Subcomm. on Constitutional Rights of the Senate Comm. on the Judiciary*, 89th Cong., 1st Sess. 243 (1965) (testimony of Eagle Seelatsee, Chairman, Yakima Tribal Council) [hereinafter cited as *1965 Hearings*].

73 S. 2625 and S. 2838 were introduced by Senators Murray and Goldwater, and H.R. 7193 by Representative Metcalf, in the next session; all of these bills died in committee. Similar bills were introduced in later years by these members of Congress, joined by Representatives Rhodes, Senner, and Olsen, and Senators Burdick and Mansfield. One bill was successfully shepherded through the Senate by Senator O'Mahoney of Wyoming, despite resistance of Senator Watkins of Utah, Chairman of the Indian Affairs Subcommittee, and despite an adverse report from the Interior Department. 102 CONG. REC. 399 (1956). However, the bill failed to clear the House Interior and Insular Affairs Committee. *Id.* at 661.

74 House Concurrent Resolution 108 states in part: ". . . [A]t the earliest possible time, all of the Indian tribes and the individual members thereof located within the States of California, Florida, New York, and Texas, and all of the following named Indian tribes and individual members thereof, should be freed from Federal supervision and control and from all disabilities and limitations specially applicable to Indians: The Flathead Tribe of Montana, the Klamath Tribe of Oregon, the Menominee Tribe of Wisconsin, the Potowatamie Tribe of Kansas and Nebraska, and those members of the Chippewa Tribe who are on the Turtle Mountain Reservation, North Dakota. It is further declared to be the sense of the Congress that upon the release of such tribes and individual members thereof from such disabilities and limitations, all offices of the Bureau of Indian Affairs in the States of California, Florida, New York, and Texas and all other offices of the Bureau of Indian Affairs whose primary purpose was to serve any Indian tribe or individual Indian freed from Federal supervision should be abolished." H.R. Con. Res. 108, 83d Cong., 1st Sess., 99 CONG. REC. 9968 (1953).

75 25 U.S.C. § 891 *et seq.* (1970).

76 25 U.S.C. § 564 *et seq.* (1970).

and various western Oregon[77] tribes. The Klamaths promptly lost most of their timberlands and farmlands, which a Portland bank acting as trustee sold to the government and to private users following what appeared to be little consultation with the tribe. The tribe then began to disintegrate as a political and social organization.[78] The termination of the Menominee also caused the disintegration of the tribal structure, in addition to the near insolvency of several large tribal enterprises and the depletion of its treasury reserves before an adjustment to the new situation could be made.[79]

The termination policy sent a shock through Indian country which continues to this day.[80] The termination controversy also split the Department of the Interior and the BIA.[81] To calm the storm around him, Secretary Seaton announced in a radio broadcast that henceforth no tribe would be terminated unless it fully understood the program and clearly consented to it.[82] An old lesson had been re-learned: "The Indian tolerates his present impotent and unjust status in his relations with the Federal Government because he sees the Bureau of Indian Affairs as the lesser of two evils. . . . [T]he Bureau and only the Bureau stands between the Indian and extinction as a racial cultural entity."[83] The federal burden was again accepted as part of white society's debt to the Indian:

> As to special Indian rights, since being an Indian is hereditary, the rights at first glance seem anomalous in a democracy; when we study them, however, the anomaly fades. They are part of a quid pro quo promised solemnly by us in treaties, agreements and laws, and upheld over and again by our courts, in exchange for the whole area of the United States and for the ending of rightful independence.[84]

---

77 25 U.S.C. § 691 *et seq.* (1970).

78 BROPHY, *supra* note 16, at 199.

79 *Id.* at 201-03.

80 "Fear of termination pervades Indian thinking. It colors the Indian's appraisal of every proposal, suggestion and criticism." E. CAHN, OUR BROTHER'S KEEPER: THE INDIAN IN WHITE AMERICA 16 (1969).

81 BROPHY, *supra* note 16, at 182.

82 105 CONG. REC. 3105 (1959).

83 CAHN, *supra* note 80, at 14.

84 LaFarge, *Termination of Federal Supervision: Disintegration and the American Indians,* 311 ANNALS 41-42 (1957).

F.   *The Recent Years: The Indians and the Courts*

In *Tee-Hit-Ton Indians v. United States*,[85] the Supreme Court held that certain tribal property rights established by occupancy "since time immemorial" could be cancelled by Congress at its discretion and without compensation. This much-criticized decision[86] has been seen to undercut the principle of the Indian's sovereign control of tribal lands and to run counter to the spirit of a decision in 1941 upholding the notion of sovereign control and requiring compensation for cancellation of that control.[87] In *Tee-Hit-Ton* the Court declared: "Our conclusion . . . leaves with Congress, where it belongs, the policy of Indian gratuities for the termination of Indian occupancy of government-owned land rather than making compensation for its value a rigid constitutional principle."[88] As termination fever cooled, the significance of *Tee-Hit-Ton* diminished. A number of subsequent decisions by the Court of Claims recognized the tribes' sovereign control of their lands and resources and ordered compensation on statutory, not constitutional, grounds.[89]

Lacking clear direction, lower federal courts rendered divergent, uncertain opinions on issues of tribal sovereignty. The Eighth Circuit, for example, took the traditional position in *Iron Crow v. Oglala Sioux Tribe*,[90] upholding the enforcement of a tribal court's sentence for adultery. The Tenth Circuit was guided by similar principles in *Martinez v. Southern Ute Tribe*[91] as it declined to review a decision by a tribal council which allegedly denied an Indian the benefits of tribal membership. In *Oglala Sioux Tribe v. Barta*,[92] however, a district court agreed to hear a tax collection action brought by the tribe against a non-member who was leasing tribal land. Normally such a matter would be

---

85 348 U.S. 272 (1954).

86 *E.g., The Supreme Court: 1954 Term*, 69 Harv. L. Rev. 119, 150 (1955).

87 United States v. Santa Fe & Pacific R.R., 314 U.S. 339 (1941).

88 348 U.S. at 290-91 (1954).

89 *See, e.g.,* United States v. Seminole Indians, 180 Ct. Cl. 315 (1967); Whitefoot v. United States, 155 Ct. Cl. 127 (1961); and Tlingit and Haida Indians v. United States, 147 Ct. Cl. 315 (1959).

90 231 F.2d 89 (8th Cir. 1956).

91 249 F.2d 915 (10th Cir. 1957), *cert. denied,* 356 U.S. 960 (1958).

92 146 F. Supp. 917 (D.S.D. 1956).

under tribal court jurisdiction. The court suggested that the 1934 Act had changed the tribe from a sovereign entity to a federal agency: "Thus the rights derived from original sovereignty have been directly channeled into a Federal statutory scheme and all tribal powers are exercised under Federal law."[93] When the lessee appealed, the Eighth Circuit upheld the tribe's right to exact a discriminatory tax on non-Indians on the reservation, despite the due process protections of the fifth amendment or the equal protection clause of the fourteenth.[94] It also held that the lower court had not acted improperly in hearing the cases.[95] Thus, the appeals court implied that federal jurisdiction rested on the tribe's operation under federal law but that provisions of the federal Constitution remained inapplicable.

A less puzzling retreat from the tribal sovereignty principle appeared when the plaintiff in *Martinez*,[96] who had failed in federal court, sought a remedy in Colorado courts. The Colorado Supreme Court,[97] noting that the plaintiff's remedy had been denied in tribal and federal courts, reasoned that to deprive her of any remedy whatever would deny her equal protection of the laws and agreed to hear the case. The court maintained that incorporation under the 1934 Act constituted an expression of consent by the tribe to be sued in state court, because as a corporation, the tribe had recourse to state courts for protection of its rights, and it should, therefore, be required to answer the claims of others in state courts as well.

Notwithstanding the Colorado Supreme Court's decision, the movement away from tribal sovereignty during the years following 1954 slowed as two widely publicized decisions in Navaho country again reaffirmed the principle of tribal sovereignty by denying constitutional guarantees of individual rights to Indians in disputes with their tribal governments. In 1959, members of the Native American Church brought a first amendment attack in federal court on a Navaho ordinance which prohibited them from using or possessing peyote, a mild hallucinogen, as a substitute for the usual

---

93 *Id.* at 918.

94 259 F.2d 553, 556-57 (8th Cir. 1958), *cert. denied*, 358 U.S. 932 (1958).

95 *Id.* at 555-57.

96 Martinez v. Southern Ute Tribe, 249 F.2d 915 (10th Cir. 1957), *cert. denied*, 356 U.S. 960 (1958).

97 Martinez v. Southern Ute Tribe, 150 Colo. 504, 374 P. 2d 691 (1962).

Christian sacraments. In an earlier first amendment action, charging infringement of religious freedom of Protestants in a Catholic pueblo, a federal district court had dismissed for lack of jurisdiction;[98] but in *Native American Church v. Navaho Tribal Council*,[99] the Tenth Circuit did not refuse jurisdiction, even though the Navaho tribe had not organized under the 1934 Act. Rather, the court held that, with respect to freedom of religion, the Constitution did not apply to the Navaho tribe. The first and fourteenth amendments were interpreted as restrictions on the state and federal but not on tribal governments. The argument that the tribe was actually a federal agency was dismissed.

In the same year, the Supreme Court clarified limitations of state jurisdiction over civil disputes on the reservation in cases where the state had not assumed full jurisdiction under Public Law 280. In *Williams v. Lee*[100] the Court held that a state court could not compel payment by Indians for goods purchased on credit at a non-Indian's store on the reservation. The Court noted that the Navaho court system could exercise broad criminal and civil jurisdiction over suits by outsiders against tribesmen. It issued a sweeping endorsement of tribal sovereignty, suggesting the following guideline for allocating disputes between state and tribal courts: "Essentially, absent governing Acts of Congress, the question has always been whether the state action infringed on the right of reservation Indians to make their own laws and be ruled by them."[101]

Students of Indian problems, deeply affected by the failure of instant assimilation, entered the 1960's with a renewed awareness of the need to retain sovereign power in tribal institutions. This theme was struck in an independent report,[102] in the report of a Department of the Interior Task Force created by the newly ap-

---

98 Toledo v. Pueblo de Jemez, 119 F. Supp. 429 (D.N.M. 1954).

99 272 F.2d 131 (10th Cir. 1959).

100 358 U.S. 217 (1959).

101 *Id.* at 220. *But cf.* Organized Village of Kake v. Egan, 369 U.S. 60, 75 (1962) (dictum). The restriction of non-Indians to tribal courts or courts of Indian offenses for certain civil remedies, by *Williams* and subsequent decisions such as United States *ex rel.* Rollingson v. Blackfeet Tribal Court, 244 F. Supp. 474 (D. Mont. 1966), is said to have caused concern among white businessmen on the reservations. Often viewed by the Indians as exploiters, they feared they could not expect impartial treatment from a native tribunal.

102 FUND FOR THE REPUBLIC, REPORT OF THE COMMISSION ON THE RIGHTS, LIBERTIES AND RESPONSIBILITIES OF THE AMERICAN INDIAN (W. Brophy & S. Aberle eds. 1961).

pointed Secretary of the Interior, Stewart Udall,[103] and in the Declaration of Indian Purpose issued from a native American convocation at the University of Chicago in 1961.[104] Unresolved was the fundamental problem of how tribal institutions should relate to the constitutional system of the surrounding society.

II. THE ERVIN INDIAN INQUIRY AND PROPOSED LEGISLATION

A. *Senator Ervin and the Indians*

When Congress passed the Removal Act of 1830,[105] Andrew Jackson deployed troops throughout the southeastern United States to force the Indians westward. One hundred thousand Indians were resettled, and thousands more died along the "Trail of Tears" to Oklahoma. However, some tribes, including the Choctaw, the Seminole, and a band of the Cherokee, resisted. After $50 million and 1500 men had been lost pursuing the Seminole in the Everglades for two decades, further efforts to enforce the Removal Act against southern tribes were abandoned.[106]

Unlike the Seminole who remained isolated in the Everglades and the Choctaw who regrouped in sparsely settled areas of Mississippi, the surviving Cherokee continued to live in close contact with southern white society. Acquisition of a small reservation in North Carolina over which federal jurisdiction was concluded in 1868[107] established the Cherokee people as permanent residents of that state.

The co-existence between the white man and the Indian in the South, nurtured perhaps by a sense of common defeat at the hands of armies sent from Washington, has resulted in what one observer has termed the "romantic" southern affection for the Indian and his heritage.[108] Among the southerners who have publicly proclaimed this feeling for the Indian is Senator Sam Ervin of North

---

103 TASK FORCE ON INDIAN AFFAIRS, A PROGRAM FOR INDIAN CITIZENS (1961).

104 American Indian Chicago Conference, Declaration of Indian Purpose (June 13-20, 1961).

105 Act of May 28, 1830, ch. 148, 4 Stat. 411-12.

106 DRIVER, *supra* note 5, at 486.

107 *Id.* at 499.

108 Letter from Arthur Lazarus, Jr., counsel to the Association on American Indian Affairs, to the author, March 3, 1970, on file at office of Harvard Legislative Research Bureau.

Carolina.[109] His professed interest in Indian affairs may also be reinforced by a large naitve-American constituency in his home state.[110] It has surely been augmented by his repeatedly demonstrated concern for the protection of constitutional rights.

When the *Williams*[111] and *Native American Church*[112] decisions reaffirmed that systems of tribal government were largely unregulated by the Constitution, Helen Scheirbeck, a Lumbee serving with Senator Ervin's Subcommittee on Constitutional Rights, initiated a preliminary inquiry to determine whether such immunity from constitutional restraint had resulted in actual deprivations of constitutional rights by the Indian tribes. As the investigation progressed, it broadened into one of Indian rights in general, as the Subcommittee staff received numerous complaints about violations of constitutional guarantees not only by tribal authorities but also by federal, state, and local officials. However, Senator Ervin appeared to find the conflict between the Constitution and tribal sovereignty more intellectually stimulating than the broader issue of white relations with the Indians.[113] Furthermore, Senator Ervin, who had opposed previous civil rights measures, was careful at this time to separate the fledgling Indian project from the volatile issues of race relations concerning other minority groups.

In order to maintain his stand on Negro civil rights while investigating those of the Indian, Senator Ervin and his staff deftly distinguished red from black. Indians came to be known as "the minority group most in need of having their rights protected by the national government."[114] Senator Ervin was later to claim, "[e]ven though the Indians are the first Americans, the national policy relating to them has been shamefully different from that relating to other minorities."[115] The Indian project in fact later

109 110 Cong. Rec. 22081 (1964).

110 With 40,000 Indians in 1960, North Carolina trailed only Arizona, New Mexico, Oklahoma, and California in Indian population. Steiner, *supra* note 57, at 324. 1970 figures reveal approximately 45,739 Indians in the state. United States Bureau of the Census General Characteristics of the Population.

111 See text at note 100, *supra*.

112 See text at note 99, *supra*.

113 *See, e.g.*, 107 Cong. Rec. 17121-22 (1961).

114 Letter from Lawrence M. Baskir, Chief Counsel and Staff Director, Subcommittee on Constitutional Rights of the Senate Comm. on the Judiciary, to the author, March 5, 1970, on file at office of the Harvard Legislative Research Bureau.

115 114 Cong. Rec. 393 (1968).

provided Senator Ervin with occasional opportunities to embarrass his northern liberal colleagues, who were allegedly less interested in the first Americans than in the politically powerful black community.

Senator Ervin could politically afford to support Indian rights largely because of the extensive assimilation of North Carolina Indians into southern life. The Cherokee and Lumbee settlements had been fully integrated into the state's governmental structure as counties and municipalities.[116] It has been said that they represent a small, unaggressive, poorly differentiated minority in the state.[117] This integration has been facilitated, especially in the case of the Cherokee, by the early evolution of legal institutions modeled after those of their white neighbors. Their codes, courts, sheriffs, and police forces, for example, have long been in existence.[118]

While this fact freed Senator Ervin to investigate Indian rights without political difficulty at home, it limited his perspective. During the hearings, he revealed his inclination to try to duplicate the North Carolina assimilation experience on a national level. He demonstrated this predilection by focusing on how the systems of tribal justice outside North Carolina failed to conform to the country's constitutional scheme. As Senator Ervin launched the investigation, he cited the preliminary inquiries of his own staff, the Fund for the Republic Report, and the Department of the Interior Task Force Report, as factors in his decision to proceed.[119] Each had advanced the conventional thesis that deviations from constitutional government in the United States were improper in themselves and required eventual correction.[120]

---

116 *Hearings on Constitutional Rights of American Indians Before the Subcomm. on Constitutional Rights of the Senate Comm. on the Judiciary*, 87th Cong., 1st Sess., pt. 1, at 4 (1961) [hereinafter cited as *1961 Hearings — Part 1*].

117 In a 1970 school desegregation dispute, the BIA declared that the Lumbees lacked a tribal culture and did not constitute a tribe. Franklin, *Indians Resist Integration Plan in Triracial County in Carolina*, N.Y. Times, Sept. 13, 1970, § 1, at 78, col. 4.

118. HAGAN, *supra* note 18, at 19-21.

119 107 CONG. REC. 17121 (1961).

120 This language from the Fund for the Republic Report, is expanded in BROPHY, *supra* note 16, at 44: "No government should possess the authority to infringe fundamental civil liberties . . . . For any tribe to be able to override any of them violates the very assumptions on which our democratic society was established."

B. *The Subcommittee Field Hearings*

For the Subcommittee's first official hearing on Indian rights, Senator Ervin turned to non-Indian authorities.[121] An assistant secretary of the Department of the Interior, various BIA administrators, and interested members of Congress were heard first. Then the hearings moved west to Colorado, New Mexico, Arizona, North and South Dakota, and California before returning to Washington where further sessions were held in 1963 and 1965. Native testimony mixed self-interest and tribal loyalty, bitterness about white mistreatment and cautious acceptance of Anglo-American precepts. From this mixture emerged a broad picture of constitutional neglect which Senator Ervin was determined to remedy. The focus fell first on the tribal system.

1. Constitutional Guarantees and the Tribal System

Tribal politics is politics in a closed circle; it is intense and deeply personal.[122] Traditionally, tribal government has been fully participatory, controlled mainly by the prospect of shame before the group. One commentator described nineteenth century tribal systems:

> Law in the sense of formal written codes, of course, they did not have, but there were clearly defined customary codes of behavior enforced by public opinion and religious sanctions . . . . For most Indians the prospect of scornful glances and derisive laughter from the circle around the campfire was the chief instrument of social control.[123]

In this century, group pressure remains central, but individuality is not stifled; rather, the security of tribal identity has encouraged differentiation without fear of being ostracized and isolated. Thus, the "[c]ommunality of tribalism does not diminish the Indian's individuality. On the contrary it protects him socially and thus frees him individually. . . . The more secure his tribe is, the more secure the Indian feels — and the more independent and

---

121 *1961 Hearings — Part 1, supra* note 116.

122 Note, *The Indian: The Forgotten American,* 81 HARV. L. REV. 1818, 1830 (1968).

123 HAGAN, *supra* note 18, at 11.

self-confident he is."[124] Because the individual's sense of well-being is based in part on the security of the tribe, an Indian will frequently react more strongly to an attack on tribal institutions than to an attack on his own individual rights or powers.[125] This tribal orientation has been reinforced by the fact that all of the rights which the United States reserved to Indians by treaty pertained to the tribes as group entities rather than to individuals and in light of the conflict with white society over control of group-owned reservation resources.[126]

The traditional lack in most tribes of established social classes further cements tribal ties since there are fewer sources of localized power and sub-group disaffection. Tribes of the plains, prairies, and the East (such as the Cheyenne, the Creek, and the Iroquois) had well-defined systems of rank, but these were primarily based on achievement and only secondarily on heredity.[127] Certain tribes of the Northwest which maintained slave systems and the Pueblo communities of the Southwest were exceptions to this general rule. The Pueblo communities have been termed theocratic, because seats on the governing council were filled by the leaders of the many religious societies.[128] The social adhesive in the tribal systems appears to have been the collective manner in which decisions were made — community consent was required before the council would act. The emphasis was on group harmony: "In council meetings, it was considered bad form to become self-assertive and vociferous, and those who did almost never gained the assent of the council to their proposals."[129] There is some evidence that the aura of harmony was protected in the past by a policy of expurgation, as deviants were occasionally expelled or put to death.[130] Thus, no decisions were made without group consent, but the group was constantly adjusted to render consent possible.

The scope of tribal governments is generally similar to that of

---

124 STEINER, *supra* note 57, at 140.

125 *1961 Hearings — Part 1*, *supra* note 116, at 223 (statement of Arthur Lazarus, Jr.).

126 *Id.* at 187.

127 DRIVER, *supra* note 5, at 298, 341.

128 *Id.* at 297.

129 *Id.* at 338-39.

130 *Id.* at 297.

state or municipal governments in non-Indian communities.[131] These bodies make, enforce, and interpret laws affecting the general welfare, including the control on the reservation of criminal behavior not within federal jurisdiction by the Seven Major Crimes Act. Testimony in Washington revealed that of 247 organized tribes, 117 (most of them organized under the 1934 Act) operated under constitutions protecting individual civil rights, while 130 did not.[132] What rights provisions there were in these constitutions, however, were often incomplete.[133] In addition, 188 other tribes or bands were not organized under any tribal constitution.[134] In tribal courts, the absence of guaranteed rights was illustrated in four critical areas of due process — right to counsel, right to remain silent, right to trial by jury, and right to appeal.

The testimony at the hearings made it clear that few, if any, tribal courts allowed professional attorneys to appear before them. Courts of Indian offenses had been prevented by federal regulation from hearing professional counsel until the Secretary of the Interior revoked the regulation on May 16, 1961.[135] Generally, representation by another member of the tribe was permitted, but an assistant secretary of the Interior informed the Subcommittee that he knew of only one Indian lawyer practicing with his tribe.[136] Consequently, a de facto prohibition of professionals prevailed, in keeping with the informal nature of low-budget courts, managed by a single judge, without aid of a prosecutor.[137]

Many courts failed to advise defendants of their right to remain silent. In Phoenix, a BIA area director indicated that he knew of no tribe with protection against self-incrimination written into its constitution. In practice, however, courts for tribes which were capable of devoting substantial resources to evidence-gathering

---

131 BROPHY, *supra* note 16, at 24.

132 *1961 Hearings — Part 1, supra* note 116, at 121.

133 *Hearings on Constitutional Rights of the American Indian Before the Subcomm. on Constitutional Rights of the Senate Comm. on the Judiciary*, 88th Cong., 1st Sess., pt. 4, at 823 (1963) [hereinafter cited as *1963 Hearings*].

134 *1961 Hearings — Part 1, supra* note 116, at 166.

135 26 Fed. Reg. 4360 (1961).

136 *1961 Hearings — Part 1, supra* note 116, at 23.

137 The Criminal Justice Act of 1964, 18 U.S.C. § 3006A later provided legal assistance for Indians charged with violations of the Seven Major Crimes Act, and tried in U.S. district courts, but the 1964 Act did not extend to violators of tribal regulations brought before tribal courts.

usually protected the right to silence.[138] Smaller tribes, with less adequate enforcement facilities and personnel, did not offer this protection. Asked if he believed silence would prejudice a defendant's case, a Pima-Maricopa judge replied, "It certainly would."[139]

Most tribes provided for jury trial in some form, following the pattern established by regulations governing the old courts of Indian offenses. Even in those cases, however, the right to jury trial was often partially abridged. Typically, the jury consisted of six persons. They received compensation of only 50 cents per day, making it very difficult to assemble a jury. Accordingly, defense challenges were limited to three members of the jury panel. To prevent hung juries and new trials, verdicts could be decided by majority vote.[140] In some areas, moreover, the right to jury trial was lacking entirely. The Southern Utes of Colorado, for example, had no provision in their code for jury trials.[141] At Fort Totten-Devil's Lake, a BIA-appointed judge, pressured by the tribal council and police to maintain a high conviction rate,[142] simply refused all pleas of not guilty.[143] Similarly, a Standing Rock Sioux judge occasionally circumvented jury trials by incarcerating defendants even if they had not pleaded or been found guilty.[144]

Appellate procedures were similarly attenuated. Among many tribes, such as the Navaho, the court of appeals was comprised of all the trial judges sitting together as a panel.[145] Tribes with only a single judge devised more ingenious procedures; for example, the Shoshone-Bannock system provided trial by jury on appeal,[146] while the Pima-Maricopa tribal council appointed two laymen

---

138 *1963 Hearings, supra* note 133, at 862.

139 *Hearings on Constitutional Rights of the American Indian Before the Sub-comm. on Constitutional Rights of the Senate Comm. on the Judiciary*, 87th Cong., 1st Sess., pt. 2, at 366 (1961) [hereinafter cited as *1961 Hearings — Part 2*].

140 25 C.F.R. § 11.7(d) (1971).

141 *1961 Hearings — Part 2, supra* note 139, at 436.

142 A BIA practice of receiving efficiency reports on judges from law enforcement personnel made such pressure inevitable. *1961 Hearings — Part 1, supra* note 116, at 88 (statement of Senator Quentin Burdick).

143 *Hearings on Constitutional Rights of the American Indian Before the Sub-comm. on Constitutional Rights of the Senate Comm. on the Judiciary*, 87th Cong., 2d Sess., pt. 3, at 769 (1962) [hereinafter cited as *1962 Hearings*].

144 *Id.* at 734.

145 *1963 Hearings, supra* note 133, at 862.

146 *Id.* at 826.

when the need arose to serve with the tribal judge on a three-member appeals panel.[147]

The principal reason for the denial or abridgement of these rights was apparently the paucity of resources which most tribes could allocate to law enforcement. Prohibition of trained lawyers made possible the continued functioning of the tribal court system with untrained judges and without prosecutors. Compulsory testimony of defendants eased the costly burden of police investigation. Eliminating the jury or shifting it to the appeals level relieved pressure on court budgets. Redundancy of judges at the trial and appeals levels and ad hoc appointment of laymen for appealed cases produced similar savings. Despite strivings toward professionalism and the acceptance in principle by many tribal courts of due process requirements,[148] budgetary restrictions made infringement of these rights unavoidable. Average family incomes of $1,500,[149] land held in trust by the BIA, and meager royalties received for white development of reservation resources[150] provided inadequate bases for tribal revenue. The approximately 6000-member Pima-Maricopa tribe allotted only $4,500 annually to cover all court and police operations.[151] Even larger more affluent tribes, such as the Warm Springs Confederation, which spent $50,000 annually on judicial and law enforcement activities, regarded the financial burden of putting trained personnel in tribal courts as "impossible." The Confederation's general counsel observed that without financial assistance, "imposition upon the tribal courts of all the requirements of due process as we non-Indians know them, would mean the end of our tribal courts."[152]

Infringement of constitutional rights by tribal councils, in contrast to that by the tribal courts, appeared to manifest more than

---

147 *1961 Hearings — Part 2, supra* note 139, at 366.

148 Representative E. Y. Berry later informed Congress that the tribal judges had formed their own professional society, whose purpose was "to upgrade the Tribal court system through professional advancement and continuing education." 115 CONG. REC. 938 (1969).

149 Current estimates of Indian family income are generally in the area of $1500. CAHN, *supra* note 80, at viii; Collier, *The Red Man's Burden*, RAMPARTS, Feb., 1970, at 30.

150 CAHN, *supra* note 80, at 82-92.

151 *1961 Hearings — Part 2, supra* note 139, at 367-68.

152 *1963 Hearings, supra* note 133, at 872.

simply budgetary distress. One issue which drew Subcommittee attention to the abuse of council power was freedom of religion. The refusal of the Tenth Circuit to void the Navaho ordinance prohibiting the use of peyote in *Native American Church*[153] clearly illustrated the power of tribal councils. Outlawing the use of peyote was tantamount to outlawing the Native American Church. In the hearings, members of the Church complained to the Subcommittee that they were also victims of police harassment and of employment discrimination, even at the hands of the BIA, as a result of religious affiliation.[154]

Other witnesses also charged that some tribal councils violated individuals' constitutional rights. An attorney for the Rosebud Sioux claimed that many South Dakota tribal councils had with BIA approval enacted unconstitutional ordinances prohibiting private drunkenness.[155]

2.   Constitutional Guarantees and the BIA

As the discussion of the authority of tribal councils has indicated, the BIA frequently shared culpability with tribal councils for failure to observe the requirements of due process. Because the Bureau was decentralized, with little upward accountability, there was considerable potential for the abuse of authority at the local agency level.[156] One Shoshone-Bannock attorney charged the BIA with neglect of reservation law enforcement. He claimed that although the tribe was authorized to have two chief judges and three associate judges, the BIA had without cause refused to provide more than one; and that one was considered arbitrary and prejudiced. The BIA refused to remove her from office, even when petitioned by the tribal council to do so.[157] When pressed by Subcommittee counsel in the initial hearings, Interior's Assistant Solicitor for the Division of Indian Affairs testified that he knew of no systematic study undertaken by the Department to ascertain if the code contained unconstitutional provisions.[158]

The director of the BIA's law enforcement branch further ad-

---

153 See text at note 99, *supra.*
154 *1961 Hearings — Part 2, supra* note 139, at 467-78.
155 *1962 Hearings, supra* note 143, at 608.
156 CAHN, *supra* note 80, at 147-55. Reforms in 1970, especially elimination of area offices, may help to alleviate this problem.
157 *1963 Hearings, supra* note 133, at 817.
158 *1961 Hearings — Part 1, supra* note 116, at 112.

mitted that the Bureau had never attempted to supply Indian courts with adequate law libraries and had failed even to request funds for this purpose.[159] The executive director of the National Congress of American Indians subsequently charged that the Bureau's neglect also extended to inadequate facilities, personnel, and training; the BIA simply had refused to request greater appropriations for these purposes.[160]

The Subcommittee received testimony alleging that in numerous instances attorney contracts requiring BIA approval had been delayed for such extended periods as to deprive the Indians of legal counsel. The Shoshone-Bannock reported a delay of eight months,[161] and the Quechan (Yuma) testified that a delay of 13 months had caused its prospective attorney to withdraw without ever serving.[162] The Navaho reported in later hearings that the entire staff of the tribe's chief counsel had resigned because of Bureau delay of contract approval.[163]

The Bureau's refusal to act on requests for code review, pleas for adequate resources for law enforcement, and submissions of attorney contracts contrasted sharply with its conscientious screening of tribal council legislation for adherence to BIA policy. Yet the Subcommittee failed to find statutory authority for this sort of activity.[164] Subcommittee counsel noted that there was no provision for further review by the courts of such BIA decisions; appeals were confined to the Interior bureaucracy.[165]

The thrust of the testimony was that the BIA was less interested in the adequacy of law enforcement on the reservations and in the constitutional rights of the people for whom it was responsible than in maintaining control over tribal courts and councils and over the affairs of individuals. The attitude was neatly expressed, said the Shoshone-Bannock attorney, in a remark attributed to a BIA employee at Fort Hall: "We didn't have any trouble with the Indians until they found out they had constitutional rights."[166]

---

159 *Id.* at 152.
160 *Id.* at 190, 202.
161 *1963 Hearings, supra* note 133, at 824.
162 *1961 Hearings — Part 2, supra* note 139, at 410.
163 *1965 Hearings, supra* note 72, at 300.
164 Summary Report of Hearings, *supra* note 21, at 3.
165 *1961 Hearings — Part 2, supra* note 139, at 317.
166 *1963 Hearings, supra* note 133, at 819.

3. Constitutional Guarantees and State and Local Authorities

Subcommittee counsel indicated that a principal reason for investigating Indian rights was the large number of complaints about civil liberties violations by federal, state, and local agencies.[167] The hearings, however, produced only scattered complaints about federal officials outside the BIA.[168] Rather, if the volume of complaints is any guide to the seriousness of a problem, the greatest threat to the civil liberties of Indians was presented by the enforcement of state criminal laws by local authorities in communities relatively near Indian reservations.[169] For example, the Shoshone-Bannock and Rosebud Sioux asserted that police from surrounding communities entered the reservations, where they lacked jurisdiction, to make arrests.[170] Moreover, the Cheyenne River Sioux claimed that Indians were frequently arrested for crimes for which whites would not have been prosecuted.[171]

Testimony also revealed occasional mistreatment of Indians while in custody. The South Dakota Indian Commission charged that Indian prisoners in some city jails were compelled to perform manual labor not demanded of non-Indian prisoners.[172] The Shoshone-Bannock testified that a tribesman intoxicated on cleaning fluid was jailed by Pocatello authorities who allegedly were aware that he required hospitalization. The Indian died within

---

167 *1962 Hearings, supra* note 143, at 769.

168 A tribal judge for the Hualapai claimed that the United States attorney repeatedly refused to prosecute major criminal cases that were placed under federal jurisdiction by the Seven Major Crimes Act. *1961 Hearings — Part 2, supra* note 139, at 383-4. The Crow tribe of Montana charged federal game wardens with failing to enforce hunting and fishing regulations against non-Indians on Indian reservations. Moreover, the tribe claimed, one federal official had used his airplane to drive elk herds off the Crow Reservation into Wyoming, where white hunters waited. *1963 Hearings, supra* note 125, at 887.

169 *1961 Hearings — Part 1, supra* note 116, at 224 (testimony of Arthur Lazarus, Jr.)

170 *1963 Hearings, supra* note 133, at 827; *1962 Hearings, supra* note 143, at 639.

171 *1965 Hearings, supra* note 72, at 331.

172 *1962 Hearings, supra* note 143, at 588. The deliberate nature of this discriminatory treatment was illustrated in the testimony of the Chairman of the Crow Creek Sioux who quoted a police commissioner in a small South Dakota town: "Well, I think the boys are going to have to get some more Indians in jail, because we need a lot of snow moved over there on the north side of town." *1963 Hearings, supra* note 133, at 898.

hours.[173] The Navaho charged police in Gallup, New Mexico, with "frequent" murder of Indians, citing as a typical case the black-jack bludgeoning of a tribesman jailed for drunkenness. He died in his cell the next day without having received medical treatment.[174] Spokesmen for the Crow tribe alleged that police in Billings and Hardin, Montana, customarily released intoxicated Indians at the city limits, dropping them there even in sub-zero weather.[175]

During these hearings, non-Indian courts were linked with non-Indian police as villains.[176] The Shoshone-Bannock charged that Indian defendants confronted a presumption of guilt in courts off the reservation.[177] The Hualapai claimed that these courts cooperated with police who had made unauthorized arrests on reservations by attempting to sentence the defendants even though the courts knew they lacked jurisdiction.[178] Representatives of several tribes, as well as an assistant attorney general of South Dakota, testified that these courts sentenced Indians to penitentiary terms for "escape" when the local police negligently or intentionally allowed the prisoners to "walk away" before completing jail terms served for misdemeanors.[179] One such court was accused of ordering the release of Indian prisoners from jail and causing them to be transported to another state, where they were turned over to a farmer and forced to harvest crops.[180]

Attorneys also related to the Subcommittee deprivations of due

173 *Id.* at 820-21.

174 *Id.* at 860-61.

175 *Id.* at 882-83.

176 Witnesses also claimed that their rights off the reservations were being violated by local and state officials other than those involved in law enforcement. Numerous instances were reported of Indians who lived off the reservation and were legal residents of the states involved being denied care at state hospitals. *E.g., 1961 Hearings — Part 2, supra* note 139, at 650. Senator Burdick of North Dakota testified that reservation Indians were denied use of state correctional schools and that they could not be accepted in state mental institutions because they were not considered residents of the states. *1961 Hearings — Part 1, supra* note 108, at 88. Indians residing off the reservations in South Dakota were said to be issued periodic certificates of non-residency, rendering them ineligible for state welfare benefits. *1961 Hearings — Part 2, supra* note 139, at 603.

177 *1963 Hearings, supra* note 133, at 828.

178 *1961 Hearings — Part 2, supra* note 139, at 373-75.

179 *E.g., 1962 Hearings, supra* note 143, at 631, 699.

180 *1963 Hearings, supra* note 133, at 860.

process in arraignment. Right to counsel allegedly was denied or was not explained to defendants.[181] Instances of local judges disallowing pleas of not guilty were recounted.[182] One attorney claimed that in a number of cases when he surprised the prosecutor by appearing for Indian defendants, the charges were dropped. In many other cases, he asserted, the presence of a lawyer resulted in lesser sentences; in general, unrepresented Indian defendants received heavier penalties than their white counterparts.[183]

Testimony received in California revealed another form of discriminatory treatment. California was charged with failing to devote adequate resources to law enforcement on its reservations after jurisdiction over them had been extended following passage of Public Law 280. The Quechan (Yuma) testified that after California had obtained jurisdiction over its reservation, the tribe was "left stranded." Its own law enforcement system was dissolved, but the California county officials claimed that because the reservation remained federal land, the county had no jurisdiction. The tribe was, therefore, required to re-hire and to pay its own law enforcement personnel.[184] Joined by the Rincon, Pala, and Puma representatives, the Soboba Band of Mission Indians reported problems of inadequate police protection of their lands and claimed that the local sheriff occasionally failed to respond to calls for assistance.[185]

Frequently, the failure of state officials to provide law enforcement services on reservations where they were empowered to do so resulted in legal "no man's lands."[186] Such a situation had been created on the Soboba reservation. The Navaho reported a similar

---

181 *1962 Hearings, supra* note 143, at 598.
182 *1961 Hearings — Part 2, supra* note 139, at 375.
183 *1962 Hearings, supra* note 143, at 634-35.
184 *1961 Hearings — Part 2, supra* note 139, at 406-12.
185 *Id.* at 330.
186 A similar problem was found occasionally in civil disputes. A merchant, for example, could not compel an Indian on the reservation to pay a debt or to relinquish property through a non-Indian court. In practice, however, this problem has been minimized by the willingness of many tribal authorities to intervene on the merchant's behalf to avoid refusal of credit to all Indians. Moreover, some tribes have provided for concurrent state and tribal court jurisdiction in such cases, but the validity of these arrangements is in doubt unless they are preceded by tribal referendum and by state authorization under Public Law 280. See text at notes 316-17, *infra.*

difficulty, claiming that when tribal police apprehended whites for crimes such as rape, murder, and assault committed on the reservation and delivered them to New Mexico authorities for trial, the state disclaimed jurisdiction and released the prisoners.[187]

Extradition posed a related problem. Many tribes were found not to enjoy reciprocal agreements with the states, or even with other tribes. The Mescalero Apache testified that an Indian might commit an offense off the reservation, then find sanctuary on the reservation if tribal officials were not inclined to arrest and deliver him.[188] The Papago claimed that such difficulties had arisen with defendants finding refuge on other California reservations.[189]

Many of the problems of extradition, "no man's lands," and the failure of law enforcement in states extending jurisdiction over the reservations under Public Law 280 had their roots in the unwillingness of the states to accept the entire burden of law enforcement on the reservations. In addition, the assumption of jurisdiction by the state created a great deal of confusion, as, virtually overnight, tribal councils were rendered powerless to legislate and members of the tribe were required to conform to a "foreign" legal system. Arrangements for a "piecemeal" transfer of jurisdiction, by negotiation between state and tribe, with careful groundwork laid prior to each transfer of a specific function, offered a better solution. One state tried this alternative. In 1963, Idaho assumed jurisdiction over some formerly Indian responsibilities including school attendance, youth rehabilitation, public assistance, and domestic relations; but it refrained from further extension until each tribe affected gave its consent.[190]

When the field hearings ended in 1963, nearly 1100 pages of testimony had been recorded and nearly 2500 questionnaires distributed in the field had been returned. Expressions of Indian

---

187 *1963 Hearings, supra* note 133, at 856-57. Authority of New Mexico courts to try persons of crimes committed on the Navaho reservation had been established in State v. Warner, 71 N.M. 418, 379 P.2d 66 (1963). However, a recent decision in the Ninth Circuit, State *ex rel.* Merrill v. Turtle, 413 F.2d 683 (1969), held that Arizona authorities could not enter the Navaho reservation to arrest an Indian. This decision is criticized in Comment, *The "Right to Tribal Self-Government" and Jurisdiction of Indian Affairs,* 1970 UTAH L. REV. 291.

188 *1961 Hearings — Part 2, supra* note 139, at 491.

189 *Id.* at 393.

190 IDAHO CODE §§ 67-5101 to 5103 (Supp. 1969).

discontent focused on the violation of constitutional rights by tribal courts and councils, the inadequate support of tribal legal systems by the BIA, and the violation of constitutional rights by non-Indian authorities off the reservation or the failure of these authorities to provide law enforcement services on the reservation when empowered to do so. As these issues emerged, the interested parties began to take sides. Indian tribes, the Department of the Interior, other federal agencies, members of Congress, various associations of non-Indians, and state governments advocated positions on issues affecting their interests. At the hub of the controversy was Senator Ervin. His self-assigned task was to sift the information and to examine the positions of the parties in order to formulate a complete and sensible response.

C. *Proposed Legislation and the Washington Hearings*

In 1965, Senator Ervin introduced bills S. 961-968 and S.J. Res. 40, to provide a frame of reference for the hearings convened in Washington in June of that year.[191] The open-ended inquiry of 1961 through 1963 had produced a broad overview of and sufficient data on the Indian rights problem; it was, therefore, time to focus the attention of the interested parties on the specific provisions of tentative legislation.

The legislation Senator Ervin initially proposed reflected his personal interests. The first four bills affirmed his conviction that tribal systems of justice should not be allowed to operate outside the Constitution. Each measure displayed Senator Ervin's intention to bring the tribes more fully into the nation's legal mainstream, establishing the uniformity he had known in North Carolina. The bills were addressed primarily to bringing the Constitution to the reservations, integrating tribal systems into the overall legal system of the country, and protecting the principle of consent of the governed. But the legislation avoided harder, less abstract questions: how to control the sometimes arbitrary and unresponsive BIA, how to more adequately fund tribal systems

---

191 111 CONG. REC. 1784 (1965). Senator Ervin had introduced the same bills as S. 3041-48 and S.J. Res. 188 in 1964. At that time he cautioned that the bills were "not to be interpreted as final solutions" and acknowledged that "the language . . . . may be revised and concepts clarified as the Senate deliberates these matters." 110 CONG. REC. 17326 (1964).

of justice, how to halt violations of Indian rights by state and local officials. The hearings had revealed that the Indians were more concerned about these questions than they were about any others. These questions did not, however, present the theoretical constitutional dimensions to capture Senator Ervin's interest; the only mundane matters to which he responded were lawyers' contracts and the availability of legal research materials.

1. S. 961

S. 961 provided that any tribe exercising its powers of self-government would be subject to the same limitations and restraints as imposed upon the federal government by the Constitution. Senator Ervin's only concession to the special nature of Indian tribes was a recognition of their ethnic character; S. 961 would not have subjected them to the "equal protection" requirement of the fourteenth amendment, which applied only to states.

Indian reaction to S. 961 varied considerably. The Hopi claimed to be unaffected, since their constitution was already "in accordance with the U.S. Constitution."[192] Most tribes, however, echoed the sentiments of the Mescalero Apaches who were sympathetic to the purposes of the bill but deemed it "premature" because the tribes were not psychologically or financially prepared for it.[193] At the other extreme were the Pueblos, who were determined to maintain their closed, traditional societies. Their position was clear and unyielding:

> We have long held to our tradition of tribal courts and we have our own codes. Naturally, we are most familiar with the special conditions existing in our various communities, and the status of sovereignty which we have always enjoyed has made us dedicated to the task of preserving it.[194]

For the Crow tribe the question remained open: "We, at the Crow Indian Reservation, cherish the opportunity of selecting our own form of government. . . . [W]e mean the action of the Crow Tribal Council shall continue to remain as it is today. . . . [W]e are confident that the people are satisfied with the present

---

192 *1965 Hearings, supra* note 72, at 325.
193 *Id.* at 340-41.
194 *Id.* at 352.

system."[195] While such statements occasionally betrayed the hint of self-interest which was to be expected of tribal leaders with a stake in the existing order, a valid point was expressed nonetheless. American Indian tribes were many and various, and each had its unique problems; they were not equally prepared or willing to accommodate themselves to the structures of the Constitution.

A number of attorneys acknowledged this point and recommended that certain enumerated rights be protected by legislation rather than by imposing constitutional government in full.[196] The Department of the Interior and BIA also agreed that the blunt insertion of all constitutional guarantees into tribal systems would produce disorder and confusion. But the Department adamantly maintained that "Indian citizenship and tribal freedom from constitutional restraint have been incompatible."[197] Accordingly, the Department of Interior offered a substitute for S. 961 which was limited to the following guarantees: the privilege of writ of habeas corpus by order of a federal court; the right to jury trial with six-member panels in certain criminal cases; first amendment rights, excluding the prohibition of establishment of religion; fourth amendment protection against illegal search and seizure; fifth amendment rights, excluding the right to grand jury indictment; sixth amendment rights to fair trial, excluding the right to jury trial except as otherwise provided but including the right to counsel at the defendant's own expense; protection against excessive bail or fines; prohibition of ex post facto laws or bills of attainder; and the right of each member of a tribe to equal protection of its laws.[198]

Among the constitutional rights not included in the Department of the Interior's substitute which would have been guaranteed by blanket provision in S. 961 were the right to a grand jury indictment and to a jury panel in all criminal prosecutions and in all civil disputes involving more than twenty dollars, and the right to the assistance of counsel.[199] In each instance the cost which

---

195 *Id.* at 234.

196 *Id.* at 222.

197 *Id.* at 317.

198 *Id.* at 318-19.

199 Other exclusions created no controversy. The rights to bear arms and to refuse housing to soldiers were omitted on the theory that Indian tribes were not

the guarantee would impose on the already impoverished tribes was a major reason for its exclusion. In addition, the rights to a grand jury indictment and to a jury panel in civil cases were considered to be of questionable contemporary merit.

The Department of the Interior's response to the issue of the right to defense counsel revealed, however, its insensitive attitude that the Indians had testified about in the earlier hearings. The Solicitor recommended that defendants have the right to counsel but only at their own expense. He claimed that the alternative was to obtain appropriations from Congress to pay lawyers appointed by the tribal courts and, in order to maintain a balance, also to provide prosecutors for the courts. If the problem was one of maintaining a balance, there was no reason to accord the wealthy defendant a special advantage. Rather, it appeared that the BIA was reluctant to assume the initiative to obtain extra appropriations from Congress,[200] as it had similarly failed to request adequate funds to maintain tribal libraries and other facilities. In view of the Bureau's past performance, it was not surprising that it presented the choice essentially as one between the right to counsel at the defendant's expense or no right to counsel at all, instead of being prepared to seek funds for a balanced, professional tribal court system.

Wisely, the Department's substitute for S. 961 deleted fifteenth amendment protection because the tribes, as ethnic units, were required to restrict voting to an ethnically determined, rather than to a geographically defined, community. For the same reason, equal protection of the laws was guaranteed only to members of the tribe, in order that non-Indians on reservations could not claim benefits of tribal membership. Finally, laws respecting the estab-

---

authorized to maintain troops. No reason was given for exclusion of thirteenth amendment protection against involuntary servitude, but it may have had something to do with the fact that, in accord with established custom, courts of Indian offenses were authorized in civil cases to require performance of assigned duties for individuals or for the tribe in lieu of monetary restitution. 25 C.F.R. § 11, 24 (1971).

200 Another example of the Bureau's delinquency in acquiring funds for Indians had become manifest when health functions were transferred in 1955 from the BIA to the Public Health Service. Appropriations instantly increased and stood in 1969 at four times their 1955 level. A sweeping change in attitude was noted by one Bureau of the Budget official: "The difference between the aggressive presentation of the PHS and the defensive supplications of the BIA is really something to see." CAHN, *supra* note 80, at 59.

lishment of religion were not prohibited, because such prohibition would have dissolved the social and political fabric of the theocratic Pueblos. The Department of the Interior and the BIA did not express long-term support for theocratic forms of government, but they did acknowledge the immediate need to maintain the social cohesion of the Pueblos during a period of transition.

The Interior-BIA position on S. 961 was thus a combination of a sound historical sense and a reluctance to do more to support the reservation court systems than had been done in the past. When sensitivity to Indian problems could be expressed without a commitment, the Department and the Bureau were sensitive; but when a commitment was required, even to the relatively innocuous matter of submitting a new appropriations request, they demurred.

2. S. 962

S. 962 authorized appeals of criminal convictions from tribal courts to federal district courts, with trials de novo on appeal. Senator Ervin thus recommended a solution to the appeals problem beyond that established by the Ninth Circuit in 1965. In *Colliflower v. Garland*,[201] the court had held that courts of Indian offenses functioned in part as federal agencies since they were

---

201 342 F.2d 369 (9th Cir. 1965). Lauded by Senator Ervin as "forward looking," *Colliflower* was something of a surprise, following refusal of a federal district court in Montana to issue a writ of habeas corpus on grounds that the Constitution afforded protection of due process and right to counsel only as against the federal or state governments. Glover v. United States, 219 F. Supp. 19 (D. Mont. 1963). The point of distinction appeared to be that the Montana case involved a tribal court, created by the tribe and governed by a tribal code, which could not be termed a federal agency. *Colliflower* appeared to authorize the issue of writs of habeas corpus only in criminal cases tried by courts of Indian offenses, although there was little qualitative difference between the functions of such courts and those of tribal courts.

In Settler v. Yakima Tribal Court, 419 F.2d 486 (9th Cir. 1969), *cert. denied*, 398 U.S. 903 (1970), the court held that the power of federal district courts established in *Colliflower* to issue writs of habeas corpus applied to tribal courts as well as to courts of Indian offenses. The court found no functional basis for distinguishing between the two types of courts. The Ninth Circuit also held that writs of habeas corpus may issue even if the petitioner has been punished by fine rather than by detention. In a companion case, Settler v. Lameer, 419 F.2d 1311 (9th Cir. 1969), *cert. denied*, 398 U.S. 903 (1970), the court ruled that the writ may issue when the punishment is detention even when the petitioner is free on bail. In the latter case, an appeal was still pending within the Yakima system. The Ninth Circuit apparently rejected a contention that the tribes, like states, have a legitimate interest in freedom from premature federal court intervention and took a major step toward relegating tribal courts to the screening function Senator Ervin originally had envisioned.

creations of the BIA and were governed by the BIA's model code.[202] As federal agencies, their decisions, therefore, were subject to limited review under the federal habeas corpus statute.[203] The Ervin bill made tribal court decisions similarly reviewable and expanded the scope of the review of all Indian court decisions by providing for trial de novo. S. 962 integrated criminal justice on the reservations directly into the existing federal system and reduced the Indian courts to a screening role. Senator Ervin noted that the North Carolina magistrate system operated in this way and that it had "worked very well for one hundred years."[204]

Many tribes, while not opposed to S. 962's authorization of appeals of criminal convictions from tribal courts to federal district courts, objected to the bill's provision for trial de novo in the district court because it would severely restrict the functions of the tribal courts. The Pima-Maricopa claimed that law enforcement on the reservation would suffer as a result.[205] The United Sioux Tribes expressed opposition because Indians could not afford to pay for the legal representation needed in federal court,[206] and the American Civil Liberties Union called for absolute right to appointed counsel not provided by the 1964 Criminal Justice Act.[207] The Mescalero Apache suggested that cases be remanded to the tribal courts upon a finding of error.[208] The Fort Belknap attorney concurred, urging that this procedure would serve as a training device and improve the quality of the tribal courts. The attorney warned, however, that S. 962, like S. 961, would impose an impossible financial burden; for review by federal courts almost certainly would require the tribes to keep fuller court records, use proper procedures, and hire prosecutors.[209]

The Department and the BIA were opposed to S. 962. The Department had appellate jurisdiction over courts of Indian offenses and was unwilling to surrender it. It suggested that the district courts should be empowered to review reservation court

---

202 25 C.F.R. § 11 (1969).
203 28 U.S.C. § 2241 (1970).
204 *1965 Hearings, supra* note 72, at 91.
205 *Id.* at 328.
206 *Id.* at 148.
207 *Id.* at 224. The Criminal Justice Act of 1964, 18 U.S.C. § 3006A (1970).
208 *Id.* at 341.
209 *Id.* at 337.

decisions only upon the full exhaustion of the administrative remedy.[210] But the Department's insistence on retaining a role in the tribal justice system contradicted its earlier testimony to the effect that the Solicitor's office had received no appeals from courts of Indian offenses.[211] It became clear to Subcommittee counsel that the Department was fighting for a nominal power only, and had never regarded its appellate role with commitment.

3. S. 963

S. 963 authorized the Attorney General to investigate Indian claims of violations of their civil rights. This bill served as Senator Ervin's response to the flood of testimony about the arbitrary treatment by the BIA and the occasional brutality and discrimination by state and local officials. The bill appeared to be a broad commitment to the protection of Indian rights in general, but its breadth was circumscribed by Senator Ervin's opposition to any further growth in the investigatory function of the federal government. In any event, S. 963 was diluted in significance by its partial redundancy with authority granted to the Attorney General by previous legislation,[212] by its failure to authorize funds, and by its inappropriate reliance on the Attorney General's office to challenge arbitrary practices in another federal agency, the BIA.

Although S. 963 was considered a token gesture, it nevertheless won the support of many tribes, who welcomed any additional pressure on the federal government to investigate civil rights complaints. But the leaders of some tribes, including the Pueblos, opposed the bill, explaining, "[w]e understand, better than non-Indians, the background and traditions which shape Indian conduct and thinking, and we do not want so important a matter to be tried by those who are not familiar with them."[213] Thus, while some Indian leaders welcomed the investigation of non-Indian

---

210 This position varied from that expressed by the Assistant Secretary in 1961, when he opposed any kind of institutionalized review of reservation court decisions on the ground that such a review structure might tend to make these courts permanent, while he believed that they should eventually disappear, as all other vestiges of Indian "separateness" from the rest of society should disappear. *1961 Hearings — Part 1, supra* note 116, at 12, 26.

211 *Id.* at 115.

212 18 U.S.C. § 241 (1970).

213 *1965 Hearings, supra* note 72, at 352-53.

courts, police, and officials, they protested being subjected to that scrutiny themselves.

S. 963 also met with the opposition of the Department of the Interior. The Solicitor asserted that many of the complaints of such violations were made to the Department and were already forwarded. The Department wanted to retain its power to screen complaints before they were forwarded to the Justice Department. Indeed, it suggested substitute legislation which would have channeled all complaints pertaining to the tribal councils through the Secretary.[214] The Department's concern over the disposition of Indian complaints of interference or mistreatment appeared to be largely self-interested. Testimony which revealed that of 79 complaints screened and forwarded to the Justice Department since 1962 no convictions had been obtained cast doubt on the Department's sense of follow-up responsibility to the Indian complainants.[215] Of course, it also caused skepticism that giving new investigative and prosecutorial authority to Justice would produce impressive results.

4. S. 964

S. 964 directed the Secretary of the Interior to recommend to Congress a new model code for the courts of Indian offenses, which would serve as a guide for the tribal courts. It also provided for the establishment of special training classes for all tribal judges. The purpose of this measure was unclear. In light of S. 961 and 962, a new model code appeared to be superfluous. And although the further education of tribal judges would be helpful, there seemed little likelihood that it would bring immediate results, since most of the infringements of right in tribal courts seemed to be the result of financial restraints. None of Senator Ervin's bills authorized appropriations to remedy this basic problem.[216]

S. 964's provision for the training of tribal judges won Indian

---

214 *Id.* at 318-19.

215 *Id.* at 27.

216 The subsequent creation of the Law Enforcement Assistance Administration has partially alleviated the funding problem, since some assistance grants have been channeled to tribes. *See, e.g.,* COURT REV., Oct., 1971, at 1 (a publication of the North American Judges Association).

support, but the tribes did not agree about its provisions for a model code. Some tribes, such as Pyramid Lake Paiute and Turtle Mountain Chippewa, expressed unqualified support.[217] Many others, however, shared the Department of the Interior's criticism that the bill might effectively impose the model code on the tribes. As long as the code remained a model, cautioned the Hopi and Apache, it would be useful.[218] The Pueblos predictably were opposed, and the Chairman of the All-Pueblo Council requested that the drafting of codes be left to the tribes.[219]

The Department of the Interior objected weakly to the work that proposing the new model code would require. It claimed that the necessary allowance for variations in tribal culture and conditions would render the code meaningless, or the failure to make such an allowance would destroy many tribes as surely as would S. 961 in the form Senator Ervin had proposed. Had the Department been fully convinced of its own argument, it would have resisted S. 964 as vigorously as it resisted S. 961. Instead, the Solicitor remarked, "Let me say I do not feel very strongly about this. In fact, the Department does not take a position that this is any disaster."[220] Moreover, while it was claimed that the tribes would be deprived of valuable drafting experience if they were just handed a model code, the Solicitor expressed his belief that the tribes would use the model much as states use proposed model codes, *i.e.*, as the basis for hearings and debates. In fact, he admitted, the Department had long recommended the old model code to the tribes, and the concept of a model was not unfamiliar to them.[221]

5.   S. 965, S. 966, and S. 967

While the first four bills were intended to protect individual rights, Senator Ervin's next three proposals were addressed to the problems of inadequate law enforcement, especially in those states that assumed jurisdiction over Indians in accordance with Public

---

217 *1965 Hearings, supra* note 72, at 348-49.
218 *Id.* at 326, 343.
219 *Id.* at 191.
220 *Id.* at 28.
221 *Id.* at 28-29.

Law 280.[222] In order to eliminate "no man's lands," S. 965 provided for the extension of federal jurisdiction over crimes committed by non-Indians on the reservation, if a state failed to exercise its jurisdiction.[223] Senator Ervin's provision for federal rather than tribal jurisdiction again illustrated his determination to bring the reservations within the federal system. This measure might also have mitigated the extradition problem, since such agreements exist between state and federal authorities. It would not, however, have solved extradition problems among tribes or between tribes and the states.

With S. 966, Senator Ervin went to the heart of the jurisdiction issue. While Public Law 280 had provided for the transfer of complete jurisdiction, testimony had revealed that some states were unwilling to immediately assume the total burden; hence, these states left the tribes in confusion. The result, said Senator Ervin, was "a breakdown in the administration of justice to such a degree that Indians are being denied due process and equal protection of the law."[224] He also expressed the conviction that Public Law 280 violated the principle of government by consent of the governed. Accordingly, S. 966 provided for the repeal of those sections of Public Law 280 which authorized the extension of state jurisdiction without the consent of the tribes involved. It made consent a prerequisite for the extension of jurisdiction, and it authorized the United States to accept the retrocessions of jurisdiction from states who wished to be free of the burdens that they had previously assumed. These revisions of Public Law 280 left the states free to experiment with "piecemeal" extensions of jurisdiction; but they did not authorize the tribes to initiate such agreements or arrangements.[225]

S. 967 filled a gap in the Seven Major Crimes Act by extending

---

222 See text between notes 71 and 72, *supra.*

223 The Assimilative Crimes Act of 1948, 18 U.S.C. § 13 (1970), incorporates state law into federal law in areas under exclusive federal jurisdiction. Thus, S. 965 was redundant in all but Public Law 280 states or others in which reservations were not exclusively under federal control.

224 *1965 Hearings, supra* note 72, at 4.

225 Similar legislation had been introduced in both houses by the Montana delegation in the previous session, but had died in the Interior Committees. 109 CONG. REC. 192, 568 (1963).

federal jurisdiction to cover "aggravated assault." Senator Ervin's attention apparently had been attracted by the testimony of a Hualapai judge who had told of a case in which one Indian had caused permanent injury to another Indian by pouring five gallons of boiling water on him. Because the crime was not interpreted as "assault with a deadly weapon," the federal government disclaimed jurisdiction. As a result, the offender was convicted in tribal court, which was limited by code to sentences of six months or less.[226]

The bills to alleviate the jurisdictional problems of law enforcement on the reservations received the overwhelming support of the Indians. Not even the Pueblos objected to S. 965 or S. 967. The tribal attorney from Fort Belknap claimed, however, that S. 965 was "not worth the weight of its paper."[227]

S. 966 was also favorably received. Vine Deloria, Jr., then serving as Executive Director of the National Congress of American Indians, voiced the mood of the Indians in support of gradualism and consent: "Not only will we have consent of the governed if we get S. 966 passed, but we can have the opportunity then to be released from this psychological fear on the reservation of having the whole culture run over."[228] The bill's provision for "piecemeal" agreements did, however, receive some criticism. The Mescalero Apache and the Yakima, among others, argued that if difficulties arose tribes should be able to withdraw their consent to such arrangements on reasonable notice to the states. They also asked that the tribes be able to initiate retrocessions of jurisdiction from the states — in effect, to make the consent provision retroactive.[229]

The bills Senator Ervin proposed to deal with the problems of

---

226 *1961 Hearings — Part 2, supra* note 130, at 384.

227 *1965 Hearings* at 337.

228 *Id.* at 198. Other testimony demonstrated that there were adequate grounds for this fear. The United Sioux claimed that South Dakota refused to require Indian consent in its 1963 act extending jurisdiction — an act later defeated by referendum after a vigorous Sioux campaign. Said one leader: "We begged the State committee to put in a consent clause. We pointed out that if State law was good, the Indians would take it. The answer was: 'State law is so good for you we are afraid to let you vote on it because you might turn it down.'" *Id.* at 149. Spokesmen for the Seminole of Florida and Nez Perce of Idaho spoke of the better approach of their respective states which extended jurisdiction only after full consultation and tribal consent. *Id.* at 347, 350.

229 *Id.* at 342, 344.

state jurisdiction on reservations posed no troublesome issues to the Department of Interior as its interests were not involved. Accordingly, it agreed with the positions taken by the Department of Justice. The Justice Department predictably opposed the passage of S. 965, since that bill would have thrust upon federal law enforcement authorities the responsibility for monitoring the performance of the states and assuming jurisdiction on reservations whenever the states failed to perform their duties. The Interior Department favored the consent requirement of S. 966 even though it had supported Public Law 280 when it had been adopted; but it aligned itself with the Justice Department, warning that "piecemeal" arrangements might create "unnecessary confusion in the enforcement of criminal statutes and in the administration of Indian affairs."[230] The Department of Interior offered no opinion on S. 967, pending analysis by the Justice Department of a similar bill. The Interior Department's deference to the Justice Department on these measures reinforced the impression that it responded in an accommodating fashion when no commitment of its own was required.

6.   S. 968 and S.J. Res. 40

Senator Ervin's last bill and his proposed resolution were intended to halt two troublesome administrative practices of the Department of the Interior. S. 968 provided that any attorney contract submitted by a tribe for BIA approval would automatically be approved at the end of 90 days, unless contrary action were taken prior to that time. Senator Ervin considered that the long delays in the approval of attorney contracts were particularly intolerable because "no group in the United States has more problems requiring expert legal assistance than the American Indians."[231]

For the same reason, Senator Ervin urged the adoption of S.J. Res. 40 which would direct the Secretary of the Interior to revise, update, and consolidate legal materials pertaining to the Indians. The disorganized manner in which treaties, laws, executive orders, regulations, Solicitor's opinions, and other relevant documents had been complied and distributed had impeded research on In-

---

230 *Id.* at 321.
231 *Id.* at 4.

dian rights. Moreover, testimony in earlier hearings had shown that in many instances, tribal libraries had ben inadequately supplied with such materials.[232]

As expected, S. 968 and S.J. Res. 40 met little resistance from the tribes. Most favored compelling the Department of the Interior to pass on attorney contracts more rapidly,[233] and all of them favored any measure which would help them to maintain more complete law libraries for use by their courts and councils.

The Department of the Interior's reaction to S. 968 and S.J. Res. 40 illustrated its attitude whenever pressed for a concrete commitment of its own resources. The Department opposed S. 968, arguing that the problem of delays in contract review had been solved by delegating approval authority to area directors and that it would feel compelled by any automatic deadline to issue premature notices of disapproval whenever evaluation became protracted. The Department's actual objection probably was to the limiting of its discretionary authority. Questioned by Subcommittee counsel why more than 90 days should be required to review attorney contracts, the Solicitor suggested that if Congress was dissatisfied with Interior's performance it should find another agency to review tribe-attorney contracts.[234] Of course, no other agency would, in fact, have been appropriate. The Department seemed in effect to be saying that it would rather allow contracts to go unreviewed than to commit itself to a deadline requirement.

Finally, the Department had no objection to S.J. Res. 40 insofar as it required its personnel to compile treaties, laws, and executive orders.[235] It objected, however, to having to compile regulations and all the Solicitor's opinions. The Department acknowledged that many opinions were not distributed, yet were cited as authoritative and frequently guided policy throughout the country. Assuring the Subcommittee that a central file of opinions was maintained in Washington, the Department declared, "We believe

---

232 See text at note 159, *supra.*

233 A spokesman for the Crow of Montana disagreed, citing an instance in which the tribe was charged a $279,000 fee under its attorney contract, which it felt was too high. He asserted that more complete contract review might have avoided such a situation. *1965 Hearings, supra* note 72, at 236.

234 *Id.* at 45.

235 Treaties had long been compiled, so no additional effort was required in this area. See note 15, *supra.*

that the system makes the opinions readily available to persons who have a need for them."[236] In this instance, the Department appeared willing to risk sheer unbelievability in order to prevent a commitment of personnel time and, perhaps, also to avoid wide circulation of what it had come to regard as "in-house" documents.

7. Summary

In summary, then, Indian reaction to Senator Ervin's bills was of four basic types. The first was no reaction at all. While the records of the hearings indicated that the Subcommittee received some expression of opinion from 70 to 80 tribes, most of the 247 organized tribes did not participate in the hearings, probably through no fault of the Subcommittee. A second type of reaction was that of blanket endorsement of the Subcommittee's work, often accompanied by an expression of surprised delight that so much attention was being paid to Indians.

Most of the tribes testifying exhibited a third pattern of reaction: they were sympathetic to the purposes of the legislation and amenable to the eventual merger of the Indian and non-Indian systems of justice. They were cautious, however, about taking large steps beyond their psychological preparedness or financial capability. Consultation with these tribes usually produced areas of agreement. A fourth reaction was shown principally by the Pueblos, who had always considered themselves different from and in some ways superior to the other tribes.[237] The old, stable, and very traditional Pueblo communities were in no way convinced that the values which their system embodied were inferior to those of white America. They resisted measures which threatened their culture or the structure of their authority. When not threatened, the Pueblos were cooperative; when faced with the possibility of change imposed from the outside, they were obstinate.

Throughout the debate sparked by Senator Ervin's proposals, the attitude of the Department of the Interior and of the BIA remained consistent. When vital organizational interests, such as reputation and control, were not involved, and when a commitment of resources was not required, they proved to be cooperative.

---

236 *1965 Hearings, supra* note 72, at 323.
237 *Id.* at 352.

But when confronted with the limitation of their responsibilities or influence or when pressed for a commitment to additional tasks, they resisted, even if the interests of the Indian people were compromised.

III. MAKING INDIAN LAW

A. *The Drafting of S. 1843 and its Companions*

Senator Ervin was not under immediate pressure from an assertive constituency to proceed with Indian rights legislation. It had become a labor of love to which he could allocate his energies as he chose. Some time elapsed before the revised legislation made its appearance. On May 23, 1967, the Senator introduced bills S. 1843 through 1847 and S.J. Res. 87.[238] Although S. 961 through 968 and S.J. Res. 40 had been only tentative legislation, they had largely withstood the scrutiny of the interested parties, and the new bills were generally quite similar to the ones introduced in 1965. S. 1843 revised S. 961 and 962 to provide only enumerated constitutional rights[239] and appeals to the federal courts by writ of habeas corpus instead of by trial de novo.[240] S. 1844 contained the order to draft a model code and the judge training provisions. In S. 1845 Senator Ervin maintained his resolve to repeal section 7 of Public Law 280 and added the requirement that tribal consent had to be demonstrated by referendum. Because it had been felt that "aggravated assault" did not adequately describe the type of conduct Senator Ervin was trying to include, S. 1846 proposed addition of "assault resulting in serious bodily injury" to the Seven Major

---

238 113 CONG. REC. 13473-78 (1967).

239 In the main, Senator Ervin had re-drafted S. 961 according to the recommendations of the Interior Department, but on one critical point he deviated from them. Interior originally worded its "equal protection" provision in such a way as to limit its application to *members of the tribe* located within its jurisdiction. Senator Ervin's revision, however, guaranteed equal protection to *any person* within the tribe's jurisdiction. The significance of the altered wording was that it might be construed to extend equal benefits of tribal affiliation to non-Indians residing, leasing, or owning property on reservations, and subject to regulations established by the tribal councils.

240 Senator Ervin apparently was convinced by the arguments of many tribal attorneys and United States attorneys that tiral de novo under S. 962 would put an intolerable strain on the district courts, already suffering from a chronic overload of cases. As incorporated into S. 1843, S. 962 did little more than to confirm *Colliflower.* See discussion in note 201 and in text at note 201, *supra.*

Crimes Act. Apparently unmoved by the explanations of the Interior Department, Senator Ervin's S. 1847 retained the 90-day attorney contract review deadline and his S.J. Res. 87 instructed Interior to compile and update legal materials.

Senator Ervin did, however, retreat on S. 963 which had proposed authorizing the Attorney General to investigate and prosecute cases in which Indian civil rights were involved, and on S. 965, which had suggested providing concurrent federal jurisdiction over certain crimes when the states failed to perform their law enforcement duties. Since S. 963 had met with opposition both from the Department of the Interior and tribal leadership,[241] Senator Ervin let it die quietly. S. 965, which had not provoked a particularly substantial amount of debate,[242] was apparently felt to be largely superfluous. In states not covered by Public Law 280 federal jurisdiction already existed by virtue of the Assimilative Crimes Act.[243] Since S. 1845 provided authority for Public Law 280 states to retrocede jurisdiction to the federal government when convinced that the original extension of jurisdiction had been unwise, S. 965 appeared to be relevant only when a state simply refused either to exercise jurisdiction or to retrocede it. Apparently, Senator Ervin felt that it was more prudent to await such a situation than to anticipate it, and he quietly buried the bill.

Because the Indian rights project raised a broad range of complex constitutional issues and had produced a ponderous volume of information, the only member of the Senate who fully understood it was Sam Ervin. Furthermore, since senators are specialists by committee assignment and must rely upon the understanding and good will of their colleagues, Senator Ervin had virtually full control over the destiny of the bills in the Senate. Indeed as a senatorial courtesy and as a matter of legislative diplomacy, no senator, even if he had entertained an objection, would have sought to prevent Senator Ervin from enjoying the fruit of six years' labor. Objections, if any, would have to be raised in House debate. But Senator Ervin enjoyed the luxury of allowing the bills to rest in subcommittee, able to order them reported to the floor

---

241 See part II C 3 of this article, *supra.*
242 See part II C 5 of this article, *supra.*
243 See note 223, *supra.*

when the occasion suited him. Meanwhile, to gauge the proper timing, Senator Ervin was closely studying the possibility of mixing red with black in another civil rights storm engulfing Congress.

B.   *Tactics of Enactment*

Although it is beyond the scope of this study to examine in detail the machinations in Congress which produced the Civil Rights Act of 1968, some relevant parts of that intriguing story may be sketched. In 1967, as part of a broader civil rights package designed primarily to protect persons exercising rights guaranteed them by previous legislation, President Johnson submitted an open housing measure[244] similar to the one that had failed in 1966.[245] The House Judiciary Committee held hearings on the civil rights bill, H.R. 2516, but ignored the open housing measure. Conservatives and others seeking passage of anti-riot legislation introduced a separate measure, H.R. 421, which also was assigned to the Judiciary Committee. Chairman Emanuel Celler bottled up H.R. 421 until Representative Colmer, a bulwark of the Mississippi Old Guard and Chairman of the House Rules Committee, threatened to hold separate hearings on the anti-riot bill.[246]

Since Chairman Celler hoped to garner borderline votes for the civil rights bill by reporting it out of committee in tandem with the anti-riot legislation, he gave in to Congressman Colmer and lent his qualified support to H.R. 421. Representative Celler then added a series of provisions protecting Negroes and others from force or violence while engaged in lawful civil rights activities,[247] and persuaded Representative Colmer to cooperate in sending the rights bill to the floor.[248] On July 11, Representative Colmer's Rules Committee cleared the anti-riot bill,[249] which the House

---

244 S. 1358, 90th Cong., 1st Sess. (1967).

245 In 1966, the House had approved an Administration open housing bill, H.R. 14765, sending it to the Senate by a vote of 259 to 157. 112 CONG. REC. 18740 (1966). Although the House measure had exempted small boarding houses and had allowed home-owners to instruct realtors to discriminate in finding buyers for their dwellings, it could not generate enough support in the Senate to survive an intense filibuster. After two unsuccssful attempts at cloture, the bill died. 23 CONG. Q. ALMANAC 773 (1967).

246 23 CONG. Q. ALMANAC 782 (1967).

247 N.Y. Times, June 23, 1967, at 1, col. 2.

248 *Id.*, June 28, 1967, at 23, col. 2.

249 *Id.*, July 12, 1967, at 23, col. 2.

passed eight days later by a resounding vote of 347 to 70.[250] Keeping faith with Representative Celler, Representative Colmer dutifully forwarded the civil rights bill to the floor where it was overwhelmingly endorsed, 326 to 93.[251]

When the anti-riot bill reached the Senate, Senator Ervin charged that it would compromise rights belonging to the states.[252] Senator James Eastland, Chairman of the Senate Judiciary Committee, apparently was so alarmed at the remarks of his maverick southern colleague that he retained jurisdiction of the bill at the full committee level, fearing that Senator Ervin's subcommittee would hold hearings to delay its passage.[253] However, Senator Eastland allowed the civil rights bill to go to Senator Ervin's subcommittee, but added an open housing provision that he predicted would kill it.[254]

Senator Ervin also was troubled by the House version of the civil rights bill. Although generally in favor of protecting constitutional rights, he had his southern constituency to consider. Moreover, as a southerner, he shared the distaste of many in his region at northern hegemony and northern hypocrisy on questions of civil rights. He complained that H.R. 2516, established a new basis of federal jurisdiction — "diversity of color" — by making interference with the exercise of civil rights by members of minority groups a federal offense. He resented the implication that non-whites could not receive justice outside the North. In subcommittee he offered a substitute to H.R. 2516, grounded on the commerce clause rather than on the fourteenth amendment, eliminating "diversity of color" and making it a federal offense for any person to interfere with the exercise of civil rights.[255] The Ervin measure also extended protection for working men exercising rights under section 7 of the National Labor Relations Act[256] and provided Indians those rights which had been included in S. 1843 through 1847 and in S.J. Res. 87. In short, Senator Ervin's goal

---

250 *Id.*, July 20, 1967, at 1, col. 6.
251 *Id.*, Aug. 17, 1967, at 1, col. 8.
252 *Id.*, July 21, 1967, at 35, col. 3.
253 *Id.*, July 27, 1967, at 1, col. 7.
254 *Id.*, Aug. 26, 1967, at 23, col. 2.
255 *See, e.g.*, 114 Cong. Rec. 329-34 (1968).
256 29 U.S.C. § 158 (1970).

was either to amend the Civil rights bill into defeat or to have it pass with his Indian rights provisions attached.

Senator Ervin's tactic was based on the axiom that in some circumstances clusters of bills may be more difficult to enact than the same bills considered separately. If bill "A" could pass the Senate by a 60 to 40 vote and bills "B" and "C" each by margins of 90 to 10, and if half those opposing "B" and "C" came from the ranks of those supporting "A", then "A" with "B" and "C" appended might fail to win a majority. It was not likely that many senators would oppose Senator Ervin's Indian bill openly, but influential western congressmen in the House could be expected to resist H.R. 2516 if it returned with the Indian rights rider. These congressmen were essential to Senator Ervin's strategy.

The Indian Affairs Subcommittee of the House Interior and Insular Affairs Committee had given birth to Public Law 280 in 1953; and it was this body which had declared its intention "to get out of the Indian business."[257] The Subcommittee's membership then included Representative Aspinall, a Democrat from Colorado, and it had been chaired by Representative Berry, a Republican from South Dakota. In 1967, these two legislators remained senior authorities in their respective parties on Indian affairs legislation. Moreover, by virtue of successive Democratic administrations, Representative Aspinall had ascended to chairmanship of the full committee. Both of these congressmen had deep personal and philosophical stakes in Public Law 280.

Representative Aspinall's policy had been to remain professedly neutral on Indian legislation but far from neutral on land and water resources policy.[258] He had been a strong proponent of private and state ownership of resources currently under federal jurisdiction,[259] and Indian reservations were among the vast acreages of federally controlled land in western states. Public Law 280 had provided a simple means by which to replace federal jurisdiction with state jurisdiction in those areas. Although such a transfer did

---

257 Statement by Representative Saylor, *supra* note 68.

258 *See* CAHN, *supra* note 80, at 167.

259 Representative Aspinall had used the weight of his chairmanship to oppose the Wilderness Act of 1963 "because he believed the act would 'tie up' portions of federal lands from economic development." Henning, *The Public Land Law Review Commission,* 7 IDAHO L. REV. 77, 78 (1970).

not immediately effect a change in land ownership, it did encourage non-Indians to invest in reservation businesses and to develop reservation resources under lease agreements. In Public Law 280 states, non-Indians were not subject to the regulations of tribal councils or to the decisions of tribal courts; in any disputes, they could protect their interests in the more friendly state legislatures and tribunals.

As subcommittee chairman, Representative Berry had been instrumental in passing Public Law 280. He, too, felt it would open the reservations to economic development. His approach had always been that of the assimilationist — to bring the Indian into the American cultural and economic mainstream. Representative Berry had also played an active part in the termination legislation of 1954. He even claimed to have obtained the Indians' consent to such legislation, although at least some Indians insisted that they had not been consulted.[260] As recently as 1961, when the termination movement was all but dead, Representative Berry continued to call for evaluation and categorization of tribes to ascertain which could be terminated most expeditiously.[261]

Senator Ervin had every reason to be confident a conflict would emerge on the House floor if H.R. 2516 were amended with his Indian rights measures. The Ervin legislation would repeal the section authorizing further extensions of jurisdiction by states without tribal consent and would authorize retrocession of jurisdiction already extended. Representatives Aspinall and Berry, however, regarded Public Law 280 as so essential to the development of reservation resources and to the assimilation of the tribes that they wanted it implemented as soon as the *states* were ready. In Senator Ervin's view, the law was not so needed that it should deprive Indians of due process and fail to receive their consent; rather, he believed it should be implemented when the *tribes* were ready. The split was deep. Thus, even if the civil rights bill were to clear the Senate, resistance in the House to its changed form might force the bill back to committee or into conference.

However, Senator Ervin was not simply exploiting the Indian project to deter black civil rights legislation. Even if the House

---

260 *See, e.g.,* N.Y. Times, June 19, 1955, at 76, col. 1.
261 107 CONG. REC. 2622 (1961).

failed to approve H.R. 2516 with the Indian rights amendment, the Indian bills would be in no more disadvantageous a position than if they had been passed separately by the Senate and forwarded to the House in routine manner. The bills would go to Representative Aspinall's committee and receive the same opposition they would receive on the floor as part of H.R. 2516. On the other hand, the bleak future of the bills in committee made the amendment tactic especially attractive as a positive way to secure enactment of the Indian rights legislation. If the House were determined to accept the Senate bill in toto, the Indian provisions would bypass committee, becoming law despite the objections of powerful men.

It is quite plausible that Senator Ervin had planned such a move far in advance. Undoubtedly, he was aware of the House Interior Committee's hostility to sections of his legislation amending Public Law 280. Yet he had drafted those provisions at least three years before and had remained loyal to them. They formed essential parts of his legislative package and clearly were expressions of personal conviction. While it is difficult to imagine why Senator Ervin had allowed six years' work to languish, he may have been waiting for the right opportunity to push his Indian bills.

Senator Ervin's substitute for H.R. 2516 moved through his subcommittee with little difficulty.[262] But it failed in the full committee by a single vote.[263] Senator Eastland quietly allowed H.R. 2516 to reach the floor, but only when he became confident that the bill would not be put on the calendar for 1967. Defeat in the full committee forced Senator Ervin to call his substitute to the floor in competition with H.R. 2516. Success along this route seemed unlikely; thus he faced the prospect of having to introduce provisions of the substitute as amendments. Voting on the civil rights bill would almost certainly occur under restriction of cloture rule XXII.[264] If the Parliamentarian ruled that the Indian rights amendments were not germane, the amendments would not be voted — unless supporters could convince the Senate to set aside the ruling.

One argument for the Senate's approving the Indian rights

---

262 N.Y. Times, Oct. 10, 1967, at 22, col. 1.

263 *See* 114 Cong. Rec. 230 (1968) (remarks of Senator Ervin).

264 Senate Manual 24-25 (1971).

amendments was that Indian rights legislation would otherwise die in committee in the House. The past record of the Aspinall committee, which had buried every other bill that inserted a consent clause into Public Law 280, lent weight to this contention.[265] Senator Ervin acted to underscore the Aspinall committee's opposition and allay suspicions of his own motives; he consolidated S. 1843 through 1847 and S.J. Res. 87 into one bill, S. 1843 as amended, and had the Judiciary Committee report the bill. It passed the Senate without opposition and was directed to the Aspinall committee. Each day the committee allowed to pass without action on the bill emphasized the need to pass the Indian rights measure as an amendment to H.R. 2516.

Just prior to the close of the First Session of the Ninetieth Congress, on a sparsely populated senate floor, Majority Leader Mike Mansfield requested and obtained unanimous consent to put H.R. 2516 on the calendar for the next session starting in 1968. Senator Ervin subsequently called up his substitute bill, but Congress encountered new pressure from the President to pass the committee bill. Senate liberals attacked Senator Ervin's measure. The liberals tested their strength when the Senate tabled the Ervin substitute on February 6, 1968, by a vote of 54 to 29.[266]

Gambling that this vote was a bellwether of senate opinion on civil rights generally, Senators Brooke and Mondale introduced an open housing amendment to H.R. 2516. To mollify borderline senators, President Johnson proposed an anti-riot act, directed at those who crossed state lines to incite riots. Events of the summer of 1967 and the action taken in the House had made it clear that Congress would pass such an act, with or without Administration support. The President's statement appeared to authorize Senators Hart, Tydings, and others managing the Administration's civil rights package to use the assurance of tough anti-riot legislation to "firm up" wavering commitments to open housing. However, when Senator Mansfield delivered the first cloture petition on the civil rights bill, some senators remained wary and provided the key votes to defeat cloture by a vote of 55 to 37 on February 20.[267] The cloture vote left the Senate's stand on open housing unclear;

---

265 See note 73, *supra.*
266 N.Y. Times, Feb. 7, 1968, at 23, col. 1.
267 *Id.,* Feb. 21, 1968, at 1, col. 2.

no one knew how that issue had affected the balloting. But when Senator Mansfield moved to table the Brooke-Mondale amendment, ostensibly because it could endanger the rest of the legislation,[268] the result was a 58 to 34 straw-vote victory for civil rights and open-housing supporters.[269]

Although a second cloture vote failed soon thereafter, the straw vote appeared to move Senator Dirksen[270] to support the Brooke-Mondale amendment with "certain exceptions." A Dirksen compromise bill reached the floor on February 28. The Senate voted that same day to table the Brooke-Mondale amendment.[271] The Dirksen bill, in the form of a substitute, paralleled Brooke-Mondale in its exemption of "Mrs. Murphy;" the Dirksen bill further exempted owners of single-family dwellings selling without a broker's assistance.

After some confusion in a third unsuccessful cloture vote, the Senate finally agreed to limit debate on the civil rights package.[272] Some 80 amendments to the Dirksen substitute had been filed prior to cloture, and each now had to be read, debated, and voted on. Among the amendments rejected were several offered by Senator Ervin.[273] However, Senator Ervin's Indian rights amendment, number 430, a duplicate of the consolidated version of S. 1843 which still languished in Representative Aspinall's committee, fared better.

Amendment 430 caused considerable consternation at the White House and among senate civil rights proponents. As a friend of disadvantaged minorities, President Johnson felt compelled to support Indian rights legislation. The President included an endorse-

---

268 24 Cong. Q. Almanac 158 (1968).

269 N.Y. Times, Feb. 22, 1968, at 1, col. 2.

270 Undoubtedly a prime factor in Senator Dirksen's decision to support some form of open housing legislation, even though he had opposed the 1966 bill on constitutional grounds, was the erosion of Republican resistance to cloture. In 1966, two cloture votes had produced 10 and 12 Republican votes in favor, with 21 and 20 opposed. In 1968, however, the vote was split at 18 each on the first two votes. Fully half of Senator Dirksen's party had voted against him, and even more "yea" votes might have been cast had he not openly opposed cloture. 24 Cong. Q. Almanac 157 (1968). Senator Dirksen had taken great pride in being the voice of the party on Capitol Hill and in the party conventions. A change of position was required if he was not to lose his footing as the party shifted under him.

271 N.Y. Times, Feb. 29, 1968, at 20, col. 3.

272 114 Cong. Rec. 4960 (1968).

273 *Id.* at 5813, 5822, 5825, 5834.

ment of the amendment in his message to Congress on March 6.[274] The Johnson message may have diminished resistance to the Ervin amendment, since those torn between favoring constitutional rights for Indians and protecting the President's civil rights package could support Senator Ervin without directly opposing the White House.

Issues of Indian law became embroiled in parliamentary maneuvers. Senator Mansfield suggested a quorum was lacking,[275] perhaps in order to provide time for consultation. When the resulting order for a quorum was rescinded, Senator Mansfield assured Senator Ervin that Senator Burdick had been in contact with the House Indian Affairs Subcommittee and had learned that there was no substantial opposition to S. 1843. But pressed by Senator Ervin, Senator Burdick impeached his own sources and suggested that the Subcommittee had taken no action thus far simply because it suffered an overload of proposed legislation. Senator Ervin suggested that if the Subcommittee did not have time to report legislation it favored, the Senate should perform a service by passing the amendment so that the Indian rights bill would circumvent the Subcommittee.[276] Senator Mansfield then "reluctantly" made the point of order on germaneness. Senator Spong, serving as President Pro Tem, acquiesced in the opinion of the Parliamentarian and ruled the amendment out of order. Senator Ervin succeeded, 54 to 28, in overturning the ruling of the chair.[277] Following the vote, Senator Hart rose to support the amendment, which subsequently was approved, 81 to 0. Almost anti-climactically, the Senate then approved the Dirksen substitute, as amended, 61 to 19.[278] Three days later, on March 11, the Senate voted 71 to 20 to send H.R. 2516, as amended back to the House.[279]

On March 13, House Speaker McCormack emerged from a White House conference to announce his intention to ask the House to accept the Senate's version of H.R. 2516 in toto.[280] How-

---

274 *Id.* at 5520 (1968).
275 *Id.* at 5834.
276 *Id.* at 5837-38.
277 *Id.* at 5838.
278 *Id.* at 5839.
279 *Id.* at 5992.
280 N.Y. Times, Mar. 14, 1968, at 1, col. 7.

ever, when Representative Colmer's Rules Committee convened, it voted to postpone action on the bill until April 9 and to conduct hearings in the interim. That decision provided time for Representative Aspinall to mount a last-minute campaign against the Indian rights provisions.[281] On March 19, in the absence of his subcommittee chairman, Representative Aspinall himself convened a hearing on S. 1843.[282] Eight witnesses testified in opposition to the legislation, and three in favor.

While the one-day hearing raised no new issues and few new facts, it did generate concern that H.R. 2516 should not be passed precipitously. The hearing had provided concrete testimony both on the need to retain Public Law 280 as a tool the states could use to promote urban growth in the Southwest and on the opposition of some Indians to the enumerated rights and model code sections of the legislation. With this evidence Representative Aspinall appealed to the Rules Committee to send the Indian amendment to H.R. 2516 to committee for further study. Representative Reifel of South Dakota, the only American Indian serving in Congress and one of the Indians who supported the Ervin amendment, objected and opposed further delay of the civil rights and open housing provisions of H.R. 2516. Questioned about the Pueblos' opposition, Representative Reifel said, in effect, that he considered their objections to be ill-founded and accorded them little weight.[283]

As the Rules Committee hearings continued, Minority Leader Ford and other senior House Republicans agreed to a conference, pledging to accept the Senate version of H.R. 2516 if the conferees failed to reach agreement within ten days.[284] President Johnson exerted his influence in characteristic fashion, urging Congress to quit "fiddling and piddling" with his civil rights bill.[285]

Then, on the fourth day of April, Martin Luther King was killed.

---

281 Representative Colmer's move was also interpreted as an attempt to afford the national real estate lobby time to bring effective pressure against the open housing provisions. *See* 24 CONG. Q. ALMANAC 165 (1968).

282 *Hearings on Rights of Members of Indian Tribes Before the Subcomm. on Indian Affairs of the House Comm. on Interior and Insular Affairs,* 90th Cong., 2d Sess. 1 (1968).

283 114 CONG. REC. 9110-12 (1968).

284 N.Y. Times, Mar. 21, 1968, at 28, col. 1.

285 24 CONG. Q. ALMANAC 165 (1968).

The President somberly reviewed the legislation with House leaders. Representative Ford hinted that he might be changing his position.[286] As April 9 approached, civil rights forces lobbied intensely for passage of H.R. 2516 as a tribute to their assassinated leader. On the critical day, the Rules Committee defeated by one vote a motion directing H.R. 2516 to conference.[287] A resolution concurring in the Senate amendments was reported to the floor as Chairman Colmer, taking note of the disorders in Washington following the King murder, accused his fellow committeemen of legislating "under the gun."[288]

The debate on the floor on April 10 generally appeared to center on whether H.R. 2516 had been so radically altered by the Senate that its passage without further delay would impugn the integrity of the House as a deliberative body. Discussion of the Indian provisions was more specific, touching on the merits and faults of particular sections of the Ervin legislation. Several congressmen participated, but Representatives Aspinall and Reifel remained the principal figures. Representative Aspinall argued that his hearing had revealed the spectre of treaty rights in jeopardy and that by passing H.R. 2516 Congress might be destroying the rights of one minority (Indians) to aid another (blacks). He charged that certain procedural requirements in title I, such as trial by jury, could destroy the tribal courts. Predictably, he attacked the amendment's alterations of Public Law 280, focusing on the possible confusion caused by states extending or withdrawing jurisdiction over reservations.[289] In rebuttal, Representative Reifel routinely explained the amendment's provisions and assured the House that the Ervin legislation would relieve the oppressiveness of tribal governments and errors of Public Law 280.[290] Representative Reifel's efforts may well have been crucial. The House voted 229 to 195 to consider the resolution to accept H.R. 2516; and by a vote of 250 to 171, the bill was approved. The President signed

---

286 N.Y. Times, Apr. 7, 1968, at 57, col. 7.

287 The key "nay" vote was cast by Representative Anderson of Illinois who may have been encouraged by the timely adoption of an open housing ordinance by a city in his home district. 24 CONG. Q. ALMANAC 168 (1968).

288 N.Y. Times, Apr. 10, 1968, at 31, col. 4.

289 114 CONG. REC. 9614-15 (1968).

290 *Id.* at 9552-53 (1968).

it the following day.[291] In the angry clash of black and white,
North and South, Indian law was made.

IV. THE IMPACT OF THE 1968 ACT ON INDIAN LAW

Even after the 1968 Civil Rights Act was passed, the Pueblos
sought exemption from its Indian rights provisions. In response to
their political agitation, members of the New Mexico congressional
delegation introduced bills to that effect,[292] and Senator Ervin
returned to New Mexico to hold a special hearing of his subcommittee. In it the Pueblos reiterated a familiar theme:

> Our whole value structure is based on the concept of harmony
> between the individual, his fellows, and his social institutions.
> For this reason, we simply do not share your society's regard
> for the competitive individualist. In your society, an aggres-
> sive campaigner is congratulated for his drive and political
> ability. In Pueblo society, such behavior would be looked
> down upon and distrusted by his neighbors. Even the offices
> themselves, now so respected, would be demeaned by sub-
> jecting them to political contest. The mutual trust between
> governors and governed, so much a part of our social life,
> would be destroyed.[293]

More specifically, the witnesses voiced concern about extending
equal protection to non-Indians in their communities and about
the bill of attainder problems created in tribal systems where the
same body often served as the tribal council and court.

Senator Ervin's response was limited. When he returned to
Washington, he introduced S. 2172 and S. 2173.[294] The first of
these bills restricted the meaning of "any person" in title II to
"American Indians" and provided that non-Indians on the reservations were not entitled to the equal protection of tribal laws. But

---

291 On November 21, 1968, President Johnson issued Exec. Order No. 11435,
authorizing the Secretary of the Interior to accept states' retrocessions of jurisdiction over Indian country, pursuant to the Act. That order appears with title IV
of the Act, at 25 U.S.C.A. § 1321-26. See Appendix for the language of the Ervin
legislation as it finally appeared, as Titles II-VII of the Civil Rights Act of 1968.

292 S. 3470 and H.R. 17040, 91st Cong., 1st Sess. (1969).

293 *Hearings on S. 211 Before the Subcomm. on Constitutional Rights of the
Senate Comm. on the Judiciary*, 91st Cong., 1st Sess. (1969) (reproduced in part in
2 AM. INDIAN L. NEWSLETTER 94, 95 [1969]).

294 115 CONG. REC. 12532 (1969).

Senator Ervin qualified his support for the bill by remarking that he introduced it in order "to afford Congress an opportunity to consider the advisability of such an amendment."[295] After being placed under advisement in the Senate, S. 2172 quietly disappeared. The second bill, S. 2173 provided that the model code which the Department of the Interior was instructed to draft under title III would serve as no more than a model and would not be imposed by Congress. Because fear of the title III had diminished as the BIA moved slowly to draft a new code, the bill was really addressed to a less than urgent issue. It did, however, pass the Senate on July 11, 1969;[296] but after being sent to the House of Representatives, it died in the Indian Affairs Subcommittee. The new bills Senator Ervin introduced did not respond effectively to any of the Pueblo problems because no proposal was made on the equal protection controversy or on the problem of the separation of powers. Instead, Pueblo leaders learned that their communities were expected to conform to the 1968 legislation.

That lesson has not been lost on other major tribes, who have begun to make the necessary adjustments, but "to date there has been no dramatic overall change."[297] The factors prolonging the period of transition include the need for funding (which is being met in part by the Law Enforcement Assistance Administration), the high turnover and inadequate training of tribal judges, the blurred separation of executive and judicial powers in a number of tribal governments, and the continued resistance by some tribes to congressional intrusion into their internal affairs.[298] It has been further noted that "as long as the Bureau of Indian Affairs has not changed the Code of Indian Offenses as directed by Congress, the chances are slim that the tribes having their own codes will assume any new burdens."[299]

A questionnaire to which 16 of the largest tribes responded[300]

---

295 *Id.* at 12555.

296 *Id.* at 19239.

297 Letter from William F. Meredith, Project Director, National American Indian Court Judges Association, to the author, April 29, 1971, on file at the office of the Harvard Legislative Research Bureau.

298 *Id.*

299 Letter from Arthur Lazarus, Jr., general counsel to the Association on American Indian Affairs, to the author, April 5, 1971, on file at the office of the Harvard Legislative Research Bureau.

revealed that while only seven had permitted professional, non-Indian attorneys to represent criminal defendants in tribal courts prior to 1968, 11 tribes now do, while four have expressed no policy. The only tribe which stated that it continued to bar non-Indian attorneys was later compelled to admit them by a federal district court.[301] The tribes reported a difficulty, however, in funding prosecutor's offices. Ten of the 12 tribes which lacked prosecutors prior to 1968 continue to operate without them. This financial inability to formalize tribal court proceedings has led one observer to warn that a disproportionate number of habeas corpus proceedings arising from detention by tribal authorities may require new evidentiary hearings in federal district courts, thus in part creating the system of trial de novo which Senator Ervin originally had intended to establish.[302]

In other areas where reform requires money, little change has occurred. Five of the six tribes which did not protect the defendant's right to silence (apparently in order to compensate for inadequate investigative facilities) still do not do so, or at least have no standing policy of protection. Before 1968 two tribes made no provision for trial by jury, and the same number today continue to refuse as a matter of policy to express the right, although neither tribe actually denies trial by jury to all defendants. Fifteen tribes had institutionalized appellate structures[303] prior to 1968; the number does not appear to have changed.[304]

---

300 The tribes responding were the Shoshone-Bannock, Blackfeet, Cheyenne River Sioux, Colorado River tribes, Fort Belknap, Flathead, Hopi, Jicarilla Apache, Navaho, Northern Cheyenne, Pierre (Crow Creek and Lower Brule), Rosebud Sioux, Standing Rock Sioux, Warm Springs Confederation, Wind River, and Yakima. The author mailed the questionnaires in the spring of 1971 and received replies throughout that summer. The questionnaires which support the factual propositions in the text between notes 304 and 308 are on file at the office of the Harvard Legislative Research Bureau. More detailed information on particular tribes has been compiled by the National American Indian Court Judges Association, 1345 Connecticut Avenue, N.W., Washington, D.C. 20036.

301 Towersap v. Fort Hall Indian Tribal Court, Civ. No. 4-70-37 (D. Idaho, Dec. 28, 1971). See text at note 315, *infra.*

302 *See* Note, *Criminal Procedure: Habeas Corpus as an Enforcement Procedure under the Indian Civil Rights Act of 1968*, 46 Wash. L. Rev. 541, 547-50 (1971).

303 The existence of a structure does not always signify an *operating* appeals system. Meredith, *supra* note 297.

304 This conclusion necessarily reflects the author's interpretation of the significance of failure in some instances to respond directly to a particular question. This evaluation is based on comments appended to the questionnaires and on earlier testimony in the Ervin hearings.

The federal judiciary may have the most important role in administering change in the tribal justice systems. These courts, especially at the district level, will determine how broadly the 1968 legislation will affect traditional practices. In construing the statute, the federal courts should look closely at the legislative history.

The legislative history of title II appears to reflect Senator Ervin's change from an approach of imposing on the tribes the constitutional limitations applicable to the federal government to an approach (suggested by the Department of the Interior and many of the tribes) of extending certain specified protections to members of the tribes as individuals. This change was the product of a philosophical compromise between Senator Ervin's apparent view that the scope of public authority should be strictly defined by the individual's need for protection and essential services, and the view, expressed in extreme form by the Pueblos, that the scope of individual liberty should be strictly limited by the community's traditional need for harmony. While S. 961 had been rooted in a theory of government with enumerated powers, title II provided members of tribes with enumerated rights.

For the federal courts, the practical meaning of this accommodation is that title II requires a limited construction which takes an informed account of its development. It does not authorize the court to apply broadly such elusive and expanding concepts as due process, equal protection, or unreasonable search and seizure without a sensitive regard for their impact on tribal structures and values. Because this point is fully revealed only by tracing seven years of legislative history, there is a danger that it may be missed and that an unlimited construction of title II will exacerbate the tribes' difficulties adjusting to its requirements.

Three federal district court decisions illustrate this danger. In 1968, an outspoken and reportedly abrasive non-Indian attorney directing the Navaho legal aid agency was ordered expelled from the reservation by the tribal council. In an action to enjoin enforcement of the order, the attorney challenged the power of the council to enter such an order after the enactment of title II. In *Dodge v. Nakai*,[305] the federal district court held that it had pendent jurisdiction to hear the case despite the failure to exhaust a

---

305 298 F. Supp. 17 (D. Ariz. 1968).

remedy available in the tribal system because not all of the issues or parties involved were cognizable in the tribal courts. It also based jurisdiction to hear the non-Indian's complaint against the tribal council on the language of title II, guaranteeing equal protection of tribal laws to "any person." The court subsequently enjoined enforcement of the order, finding that it not only denied due process but also constituted a bill of attainder.[306]

In 1969, a district court in Montana held that title II did not directly authorize civil actions for damages against individuals who in their official capacities violated enumerated rights. The court did rule, however, that it had pendent jurisdiction to adjudicate such a claim if it was coupled with an action against the tribe for equitable or habeas corpus relief with which it shared a "common nucleus of operative fact."[307]

A federal court in New Mexico expanded the reasoning of these cases in a civil action for personal injuries allegedly inflicted by a Zuni Pueblo police officer upon the plaintiff in his custody.[308] The Court noted that the applicable provisions of title II bore a "striking" resemblance to the fourth and fifth amendments and said:

> The similarity of language and the legislative history of the Act establish that Congress intended these provisions to limit tribal governments as the Fourth and Fifth Amendments limit the federal government. . . . The analogy of the Indian Civil Rights Act to the Amendments is appropriate and the law governing actions against individuals for damages under the Fourth and Fifth Amendments should be applied to the Act.[309]

Thus, in a series of decisions, district courts have built upon notions of pendent jurisdiction and analogies to constitutionally protected right to extend the power of the federal judiciary. The 1968 legislation has been interpreted to empower federal courts to decide cases not previously heard by the tribal courts or brought

---

306 Dodge v. Nakai, 298 F. Supp. 26 (D. Ariz. 1969).

307 Spotted Eagle v. Blackfeet Tribe, 301 F. Supp. 85 (D. Mont. 1969). The court relied heavily on an analogous Supreme Court case, United Mine Workers v. Gibbs, 383 U.S. 715 (1966), holding that federal courts exercised pendent jurisdiction in damage claims arising under state law coupled with federal claims sharing a "common nucleus of operative fact."

308 Loncassion v. Leekity, 334 F. Supp. 370 (D.N.M. 1971).

309 *Id.* at 374.

to federal courts by habeas corpus, to apply developing fourth and fifth amendment concepts, and to allow damage actions not authorized by the statute. The "legislative history" to which the *Loncassion* court referred and on which the decision was said to have rested, has really received no consideration.

In a recent decision, the Tenth Circuit declined to follow the examples set by these three district courts and affirmed the action of the District Court for Wyoming. The lower court had held that title II did not extend federal jurisdiction to hear complaints of discriminatory practices in admission to tribal membership.[310] On appeal, the court assumed that the application of standards for tribal membership might raise equal protection or due process problems, but held that the pleadings disclosed no such issues.[311] Moreover, it recalled its holding in a previous case[312] that title II did not impose broad due process requirements which conflicted with a statutory system of appointing rather than electing a tribal chief. The Tenth Circuit stressed that "the Indian Bill of Rights was concerned primarily with tribal administration of justice and the imposition of tribal penalties and forfeitures and not with the specifics of tribal structure or office-holding."[313] Had the court fully examined the legislative history of title II, its analysis (more persuasive than that of the three interventionist lower courts) would have found additional support.

This tension between restraint and intervention should not arise, however, when the courts apply the various specific commands and prohibitions of the Act. The express provision for representation by defense attorneys, for example, has been strictly applied by district courts in Montana[314] and Idaho,[315] which have ordered tribal courts to permit non-Indian lawyers to represent

---

310 Pinnow v. Shoshone Tribal Council, 314 F. Supp. 1157 (D. Wyo. 1970).

311 Slattery v. Arapahoe Tribal Council, 453 F.2d 278 (10th Cir. 1971).·

312 Groundhog v. Keeler, 442 F.2d 674 (10th Cir. 1971).

313 Slattery, 453 F.2d at 282. *Accord* Lefthand v. Crow Tribal Council, 329 F. Supp. 728 (D. Mont. 1971); *but cf.* Solomon v. LaRose, 335 F. Supp. 715 (D. Neb. 1971).

314 Spotted Eagle v. Blackfeet Tribe, Civ. No. 2780; Rafalsky v. Blackfeet Tribe, Civ. No. 2849; Regan v. Blackfeet Tribal Court, Civ. No. 2850 (D. Mont., July 7, 1969).

315 Towersap v. Fort Hall Indian Tribal Court, Civ. No. 4-70-37 (D. Id., December 28, 1971).

Indian defendants. In the Idaho case, the court rejected the contention of the Shoshone-Bannock that the phrase "assistance of counsel" in title II should be construed to mean only the aid of a friend within the tribe, a practice traditionally permitted by the tribal court. While the policy of allowing professional counsel in tribal courts at the defendant's expense may be subject to criticism, there is little doubt that in adhering to the plain language of the statute the court implemented the intent of the drafter of the provision.

The meaning of title IV language is generally clear and may usually be applied strictly. In *Kennerly v. District Court of the Ninth Judicial District of Montana*,[316] the United States Supreme Court invalidated a Blackfeet tribal ordinance granting Montana courts concurrent jurisdiction over civil actions against members of the tribe on the ground of its failure to conform to express title IV requirements. In so doing, the Court pointed out that Montana had not taken legislative action to extend jurisdiction under Public Law 280 and that the tribe had failed to evidence the consent of its members through referendum.[317] While this decision apparently was in accord with Senator Ervin's strong feelings about the need for consent of the governed through a vote of the members of the tribe, the Court's opinion did not fully examine the legislative history of title IV but relied mainly on surface statutory construction.

Construing merely the words of the statute is proper when they are unambiguous. The necessity for using legislative history, however, was demonstrated by the Nebraska District Court's effort to decide whether title IV required the federal government to accept all jurisdiction retroceded by Nebraska or whether the state could retain part of the jurisdiction assumed under Public Law 280.[318] The extent of the court's historical analysis was to conclude from statutory language itself that title IV was enacted to benefit the

---

316 400 U.S. 423 (1971).

317 *Compare* Annis v. Dewey County Bank, 335 F. Supp. 133 (D.S.D. 1971); Martin v. Denver Juvenile Court, 493 P.2d 1093 (Colo. 1972); Crow Tribe of Indians v. Deernose, 487 P.2d 1133 (Mont. 1971) *with* Makah Indian Tribe v. State, 76 Wash. 2d 485, 457 P.2d 590 (1969), *appeal dismissed sub nom.* Makah Indian Tribe v. Washington, 397 U.S. 316 (1970) (the cause of action had arisen prior to 1968).

318 United States v. Brown, 334 F. Supp. 536 (D. Neb. 1971).

Indians.[319] Since the tribe in question had expressed a preference to remain under state jurisdiction after title IV had been enacted, the court held that the federal government could accept a partial retrocession. The legislative history treated in this article reveals that the hearings highlighted the need for piecemeal transfers of jurisdiction by negotiation between state and tribe in order to avoid problems of extradition, "no man's lands," and inadequate law enforcement caused by "lump sum" transfers of jurisdiction.[320] In response, Senator Ervin had introduced S. 966 and maintained its provisions intact until enactment as title IV. S. 966 had authorized piecemeal transfers, but had provided that such transfers could be initiated only by the states. Although the latter provision was criticized by several tribal spokesmen, Senator Ervin retained it, apparently to assure the states that they would be affected by this repeal of section 7 of Public Law 280 only at their own option. Consequently, the language authorizing piecemeal transfers of jurisdiction was not intended solely to benefit the Indians. The partial retrocession approved in *Brown* could have been grounded more firmly in a power reserved to the states, had the legislative history been fully examined.

V. CONCLUSION

Each of the decisions discussed reveals a need for a closer analysis of legislative history of the Indian rights provisions. In the future the federal courts will again be asked to construe the 1968 Act in manners inconsistent with its plain language or its history. Advocates of further federal intervention into tribal criminal justice systems may seek to broaden the meaning of the due process, equal protection, or search and seizure provisions in title II, converting the enumerated rights section into what Senator Ervin had originally suggested but later rejected in S. 961. Opponents of the philosophical foundations of the legislation may argue for the special construction of particular protections or prohibitions in order to bring them into closer correspondence with tribal practices before 1968. The federal judge should refrain from exer-

---

319 *Id.* at 541-42.
320 See part II C 1 of this article, *supra.*

cising a broad power to establish policy when plenary power over Indian affairs rests with Congress. The judge may believe that he perceives what is best for the tribes within the court's jurisdiction; but the Indians have suffered from a surfeit of patrons in all branches of government. Given adequate resources, the tribes may best adjust to the new legislation in a judicial milieu of sensitive, restrained construction. In this difficult period of transition, the judge who seizes opportunities to demand more of the tribes than required by the letter and history of the Act might become a contemporary analogue to the BIA agent of an earlier period, who imposed tenets of personal conviction through the power of the white conqueror.

Appendix

Civil Rights Act

Public Law 90-284
90th Congress, H.R. 2516
April 11, 1968
An Act

To prescribe penalties for certain acts of violence or intimidation, and for other purposes.

•   •   •   •   •   •

Title II — *Rights of Indians*

Definitions

Sec. 201. For purposes of this title, the term —

(1) "Indian tribe" means any tribe, band, or other group of Indians subject to the jurisdiction of the United States and recognized as possessing powers of self-government;

(2) "powers of self-government" means and includes all governmental powers possessed by an Indian tribe, executive, legislative, and judicial, and all offices, tribes, and tribunals by and through which they are executed, including courts of Indian offenses; and

(3) "Indian court" means any Indian tribal court or court of Indian offense.

Indian Rights

Sec. 202. No Indian tribe in exercising powers of self-government shall —

(1) make or enforce any law prohibiting the free exercise of religion, or abridging the freedom of speech, or of the press, or the right of the people peaceably to assemble and to petition for a redress of grievances;

(2) violate the right of the people to be secure in their persons, houses, papers,

and effects against unreasonable search and seizures, nor issue warrants, but upon probable cause, supported by oath or affirmation, and particularly describing the place to be searched and the person or thing to be seized;

(3) subject any person for the same offense to be twice put in jeopardy;

(4) compel any person in any criminal case to be a witness against himself;

(5) take any private property for a public use without just compensation;

(6) deny to any person in a criminal proceeding the right to a speedy and public trial, to be informed of the nature and cause of the accusation, to be confronted with the witnesses against him, to have compulsory process for obtaining witnesses in his favor, and at his own expense to have the assistance of counsel for his defense;

(7) require excessive bail, impose excessive fines, inflict cruel and unusual punishments, and in no event impose for conviction of any one offense any penalty or punishment greater than imprisonment for a term of six months or a fine of $500, or both;

(8) deny to any person within its jurisdiction the equal protection of its laws or deprive any person of liberty or property without due process of law;

(9) pass any bill of attainder or ex post facto law; or

(10) deny to any person accused of an offense punishable by imprisonment the right, upon request, to a trial by jury of not less than six persons.

Habeas Corpus

Sec. 203. The privilege of the writ of habeas corpus shall be available to any person, in a court of the United States, to test the legality of his detention by order of an Indian tribe.

TITLE III — *Model Code Governing Courts of Indian Offenses*

Sec. 301. The Secretary of the Interior is authorized and directed to recommend to the Congress, on or before July 1, 1968, a model code to govern the administration of justice by courts of Indian offenses on Indian reservations. Such code shall include provisions which will

(1) assure that any individual being tried for an offense by a court of Indian offenses shall have the same rights, privileges, and immunities under the United States Constitution as would be guaranteed any citizen of the United States being tried in a Federal court for any similar offense,

(2) assure that any individual being tried for an offense by a court of Indian offenses will be advised and made aware of his rights under the United States Constitution, and under any tribal constitution applicable to such individual,

(3) establish proper qualifications for the office of judge of the court of Indian offenses, and

(4) provide for the establishing of educational classes for the training of judges of courts of Indian offenses. In carrying out the provisions of this title, the Secretary of the Interior shall consult with the Indians, Indian tribes, and interested agencies of the United States.

Sec. 302. There is hereby authorized to be appropriated such sum as may be necessary to carry out the provisions of this title.

TITLE IV — *Jurisdiction Over Criminal and Civil Actions*

Assumption by State

Sec. 401. (a) The consent of the United States is hereby given to any State not having jurisdiction over criminal offenses committed by or against Indians in the areas of Indian country situated within such State to assume, with the consent of the Indian tribe occupying the particular Indian country or part thereof which could be affected by such assumption, such measure of jurisdiction over any or all of such offenses committed within such Indian country or any part thereof as may be determined by such State to the same extent that such State has jurisdiction over any such offense committed elsewhere within the State, and the criminal laws of such State shall have the same force and effect within such Indian country or part thereof as they have elsewhere within that State.

(b) Nothing in this section shall authorize the alienation, encumbrance, or taxation of any real or personal property, including water rights, belonging to any Indian or any Indian tribe, band, or community that is held in trust by the United States or is subject to a restriction against alienation imposed by the United States; or shall authorize regulation of the use of such property in a manner inconsistent with any Federal treaty, agreement, or statute or with any regulation made pursuant thereto; or shall deprive any Indian or any Indian tribe, band, or community of any right, privilege, or immunity afforded under Federal treaty, agreement, or statute with respect to hunting, trapping, or fishing or the control, licensing, or regulation thereof.

Assumption by State of Civil Jurisdiction

Sec. 402. (a) The consent of the United States is hereby given to any State not having jurisdiction over civil causes of action between Indians or to which Indians are parties which arise in the areas of Indian country situated within such State to assume, with the consent of the tribe occupying the particular Indian country or part thereof which would be affected by such assumption, such measure of jurisdiction over any or all such civil causes of action arising within such Indian country or any part thereof as may be determined by such State to the same extent that such State has jurisdiction over other civil causes of action, and those civil laws of such State that are of general application to private persons or private property shall have the same force and effect within such Indian country or part thereof as they have elsewhere within that State.

(b) Nothing in this section shall authorize the alienation, encumbrance, or taxation of any real or person [sic] property, including water rights, belonging to any Indian or any Indian tribe, band, or community that is held in trust by the United States or is subject to a restriction against alienation imposed by the United States; or shall authorize regulation of the use of such property in a manner inconsistent with any Federal treaty, agreement, or statute, or with any regulation made pursuant thereto; or shall confer jurisdiction upon the State to adjudicate, in probate proceeding or otherwise, the ownership or right to possession of such property or any interest therein.

(c) Any tribal ordinance or custom heretofore or hereafter adopted by an Indian tribe, band, or community in the exercise of any authority which it may possess shall, if not inconsistent with any applicable civil law of the State be given full force and effect in the determination of civil causes of action pursuant to this section.

Retrocession of Jurisdiction by State

Sec. 403. (a) The United States is authorized to accept a retrocession by any State of all or any measure of the criminal or civil jurisdiction or both, acquired by such State pursuant to the provisions of section 1162 of title 18 of the United States Code, section 1360 of title 28 of the United States Code, or section 7 of the Act of August 15, 1953 (67 Stat. 588), as it was in effect prior to its repeal by subsection (b) of this section.

(b) Section 7 of the Act of August 15, 1953 (67 Stat. 588), is hereby repealed but such repeal shall not affect any cession of jurisdiction made pursuant to such section prior to its repeal.

Consent to Amend State Laws

Sec. 404. Notwithstanding the provisions of any enabling Act for the admission of a State, the consent of the United States is hereby given to the people of any State to amend, where necessary, their State constitution or existing statutes, as the case may be, to remove any legal impediment to the assumption of civil or criminal jurisdiction in accordance with the provisions of this title. The provisions of this title shall not become effective with respect to such assumption of jurisdiction by any such State until the people thereof have appropriately amended their State constitution or statutes as the case may be.

Actions Not to Abate

Sec. 405. (a) No action or proceeding pending before any court or agency of the United States immediately prior to any cession of jurisdiction by the United States pursuant to this title shall abate by reason of that cession. For the purposes of any such action or proceeding, such cession shall take effect on the day following the date of final determination of such action or proceeding.

(b) No cession made by the United States under this title shall deprive any court of the United States of jurisdiction to hear, determine, render judgment, or impose sentence in any criminal action instituted against any person for any offense committed before the effective date of such cession, if the offense charged in such action was cognizable under any law of the United States at the time of the commission of such offense. For the purposes of any such criminal action, such cession shall take effect on the day following the date of final determination of such action.

Special Election

Sec. 406. State jurisdiction acquired pursuant to this title with respect to criminal offenses or civil causes of action or with respect to both, shall be applicable in Indian country only where the enrolled Indians within the affected area of such Indian country accept such jurisdiction by a majority vote of the adult Indians voting at a special election held for that purpose. The Secretary of the Interior shall call such special election under such rules and regulations as he may prescribe, when requested to do so by the tribal council or other governing body, or by 20 per centum of such enrolled adults.

TITLE V — *Offenses Within Indian Country*
Amendment

Sec. 501. Section 1153 of title 18 of the United States Code is amended by inserting immediately after "weapon," the following: "assault resulting in serious bodily injury,".

TITLE VI — *Employment of Legal Counsel*
Approval

Sec. 601. Notwithstanding any other provision of law, if any application made by an Indian, Indian Tribe, Indian council, or any band or group of Indians under any law requiring the approval of the Secretary of the Interior or the Commissioner of Indian Affairs of contracts or agreements relating to the employment of legal counsel (including the choice of counsel and the fixing of fees) by any such Indians, tribe, council, band, or group is neither granted nor denied within ninety days following the making of such application, such approval shall be deemed to have been granted.

TITLE VII — *Materials Relating to Constitutional Rights of Indians*
Secretary of Interior to Prepare

Sec. 701. (a) In order that the constitutional rights of Indians might be fully protected, the Secretary of the Interior is authorized and directed to —

(1) have the document entitled "Indian Affairs, Laws, and Treaties" (Senate Document Numbered 319, volumes 1 and 2, Fifty-eighth Congress), revised and extended

to include all treaties, laws, Executive orders, and regulations relating to Indian affairs in force on September 1, 1967, and to have such revised document printed at the Government Printing Office;

(2) have revised and republished the treatise entitled "Federal Indian Law"; and

(3) have prepared, to the extent determined by the Secretary of the Interior to be feasible, an accurate compilation of the official opinions, published and unpublished, of the Solicitor of the Department of the Interior relating to Indian affairs rendered by the Solicitor prior to September 1, 1967, and to have such compilation printed as a Government publication at the Government Printing Office.

(b) With respect to the document entitled "Indian Affairs, Laws and Treaties" as revised and extended in accordance with paragraph (1) of subsection (a), and the compilation prepared in accordance with paragraph (3) of such subsection, the Secretary of the Interior shall take such action as may be necessary to keep such document and compilation current on an annual basis.

(c) There is authorized to be appropriated for carrying out the provisions of this title, with respect to the preparation but not including printing, such sum as may be necessary.

TITLE II OF THE 1968 CIVIL RIGHTS ACT:
AN INDIAN BILL OF RIGHTS

ARTHUR LAZARUS, JR*

One hundred years after adoption of the fourteenth amendment, forty-four years after all native-born American Indians were declared to be citizens of the United States,[1] and eleven years after the Constitution followed the flag overseas,[2] the Bill of Rights finally came to Indian reservations.

Title II of the 1968 Civil Rights Act[3] provides, in substance, that no Indian tribe in exercising its powers of local self-government[4] may engage in action, with certain important exceptions, which the federal or state governments are prohibited from undertaking by the first ten and fourteenth amendments to the Constitution. Significantly, the legislative forerunner of Title II, as originally drafted, would have required that "any Indian tribe in exercising its powers of local self-government shall be subject to [exactly] the same limitations and restraints as those which are imposed on the Government of the United States by the United States Constitution."[5] In response to testimony that such general language could cause a host of legal and practical problems in the administration of justice on Indian reservations,[6] and at the suggestion

---

* Member, Strasser, Spiegelberg, Fried, Frank & Kampelman, Washington, D. C.; A.B., Columbia University (1946); LL.B., Yale University (1949). Mr. Lazarus is Chairman of the American Bar Association Committee on Indian Affairs, and represents a number of Indian tribes.

1. Act of June 2, 1924, 43 Stat. 253, now codified in 8 U.S.C. § 1401(a)(2) (1964). Prior to the Citizenship Act of 1924, approximately two-thirds of the Indians of the United States already had acquired citizenship by treaty or statute. U.S. DEP'T OF THE INTERIOR, FEDERAL INDIAN LAW 517-520 (1958), derived from F. COHEN, HANDBOOK OF FEDERAL INDIAN LAW (G.P.O. 4th ed., 1945).

2. Reid v. Covert, 354 U.S. 1 (1957); Kinsella v. United States ex rel. Singleton, 361 U.S. 234 (1960).

3. Act of April 11, 1968, 82 Stat. 77, 25 U.S.C. §§ 1301-1303.

4. In section 201(2) of the 1968 Act, "powers of self-government" are defined to mean and include "all governmental powers possessed by an Indian tribe, executive, legislative, and judicial, and all offices, bodies, and tribunals by and through which they are executed, including courts of Indian offenses; * * *."

5. S. 961 of the 89th Congress, reprinted in *Hearings on S. 961 etc. Before the Subcommittee on Constitutional Rights of the Senate Comm. on the Judiciary*, 89th Cong., 1st Sess. 5 (1965) [hereinafter cited as *Hearings*].

6. *Hearings* at 16, 64-65, 130-131, and elsewhere. As summarized in STAFF OF SUBCOMM. ON CONSTITUTIONAL RIGHTS OF THE SENATE COMM. ON THE JUDICIARY, 89th Cong., 2nd Sess., SUMMARY REPORT OF HEARINGS AND INVESTIGATIONS ON THE CONSTITUTIONAL RIGHTS OF THE AMERICAN INDIAN 9 (Comm. Print 1966) [hereinafter cited as SUMMARY REPORT]:

> The most serious objections to S. 961 took the form neither of objection to the purposes of the bill nor quarrel with the sundry allegations of the practice of [sic] possibility of denial of rights by tribal governments. Instead, as numerous witnesses pointed out, the peculiarities of the Indian's economic

of the Department of the Interior,[7] the proposed legislation was rewritten in order to select and specify the constitutional protections American Indians were to possess in their relations with tribal governments.[8]

The idea that Congress in 1968 had to bring the Bill of Rights to Indian reservations by statute, and that Congress could pick and choose which constitutional safeguards to extend, is alien to popular concepts of American jurisprudence. Before examining the historical and legal precedents which led to this anomaly, a brief review of how Title II compares with the first ten amendments would seem in order.

Section 202(1) of the 1968 Civil Rights Act provides that no Indian tribe[9] shall "make or enforce any law prohibiting the free exercise of religion, or abridging the freedom of speech, or of the press, or the right of the people peaceably to assemble and to petition for a redress of grievances." This language, of course, is taken virtually word for word from the first amendment, with the omission of the clause prohibiting "establishment of religion." Deletion of the establishment clause was deliberate, in recognition of the theocratic nature of many tribal governments.[10]

Section 202(2) paraphrases the fourth amendment by requiring that Indian tribes shall not "violate the right of the people to be

---

and social condition, his customs, his beliefs, and his attitudes, raised serious questions about the desirability of imposing upon Indian cultures the legal forms and procedures to which other Americans had become long accustomed.

7. *Hearings* at 317-319.

8. SUMMARY REPORT at 25. The revised bill was introduced as S. 1843 of the 90th Congress on May 23, 1967. 113 CONG. REC. S 7214 (daily ed. May 23, 1967). S. 1843 subsequently was combined with other bills affecting Indians under consideration by the Subcommittee on Constitutional Rights, and, as so amended, was favorably reported on December 6, 1967, by the Senate Committee on the Judiciary. S. REP. No. 841, PROTECTING THE RIGHTS OF THE AMERICAN INDIAN, 90th Cong., 1st Sess. (1967) [hereinafter cited as SENATE REPORT]. The Senate passed the bill by unanimous vote on December 7, 1967 (113 CONG. REC. S 18156 (daily ed. Dec. 7, 1967), but the House Committee on Interior and Insular Affairs, to which S. 1843 was referred, took no action to move the legislation.

On March 8, 1968, Senator Sam J. Irvin, Jr., (D., N.C.), Chairman of the Senate Subcommittee on Constitutional Rights, offered the complete final text of S. 1843 as an amendment to H.R. 2516, the House-passed civil rights bill, and, after some procedural debate as to whether the proposal was germane under the cloture rule then in force, the Senate approved the amendment by a vote of 81-0. 114 CONG. REC. S 2459 *et seq.* (daily ed. March 8, 1968). A few days later, the Senate passed H.R. 2516, which was referred for consideration back to the House of Representatives and ultimately was approved without further amendment. 114 CONG. REC. H 2825-2826 (daily ed. April 10, 1968).

The story of how the Indian Bill of Rights, apparently blocked from passage on its own merits in the House of Representatives, became law as part of the 1968 Civil Rights Act is a subject worthy of the political scientist—a fascinating tale in the fine art of legislative strategy.

9. An Indian tribe is defined in section 201(1) to mean "any tribe, band or other group of Indians subject to the jurisdiction of the United States and recognized as possessing powers of self-government."

10. Report of the Department of Justice on S. 1843, dated March 29, 1968, printed in *Hearings on H.R. 15419 and Related Bills Before the Subcomm. on Indian Affairs of the House Comm. on Interior and Insular Affairs*, 90th Cong., 2nd Sess. 26 (1968). [hereinafter cited as *House Hearings*], see Statement on H.R. 2516 by Congressman Ben Reifel (R., S.D.)—the only member of Congress also enrolled as a member of an Indian tribe—before the House Committee on Rules, published as an Extension of Remarks of Congressman Ray J. Madden (D., Ind.) [hereinafter cited as Reifel Statement], 114 CONG. REC. E 2741-2742 (daily ed. April 4, 1968).

secure in their persons, houses, papers, and effects against unreasonable search and seizures, nor issue warrants, but upon probable cause, supported by oath or affirmation, and particularly describing the place to be searched and the person or thing to be seized." Perhaps mindful of the nineteenth century Sioux and Apache campaigns, Congress in Title II did not restate the second amendment right of the Indian people to keep and bear arms.

Sections 202 (3) - (5), inclusive, make applicable to Indian tribes the restraints upon double jeopardy, self-incrimination and the taking of private property without payment of just compensation respectively, imposed upon the federal and state governments by the fifth and fourteenth amendments. The fifth amendment right to indictment by a grand jury in capital cases, on the other hand, is omitted in view of the limited criminal jurisdiction of tribal courts.

Section 202(6) provides that no Indian tribe shall "deny to any person in a criminal proceeding the right to a speedy and public trial, to be informed of the nature and cause of the accusation, to be confronted with the witnesses against him, to have compulsory process for obtaining witnesses in his favor, and at his own expense to have the assistance of counsel for his defense." This language is taken virtually word for word from the sixth amendment, with the omission of the right to trial "by an impartial jury," which is covered under section 202 (10), and the addition of the qualification that an Indian criminal defendant in tribal court has a right to counsel only "at his own expense." In commenting upon the latter limitation on a civil right of growing prominence,[11] the Justice Department explained:[12]

> The fact that this is a departure from recent United States case law requiring free counsel for indigents does not necessarily mean it is repugnant to modern judicial standards when viewed in the context of Indian court practices. In most Indian tribes there is no organized bar association. Thus, attorneys are not generally available to repre-

---

11. Gideon v. Wainwright, 372 U.S. 335 (1963); Escobedo v. Illinois, 378 U.S. 478 (1964); Miranda v. Arizona, 384 U.S. 436 (1966).

12. *House Hearings* at 26-27; *see* Remarks of Interior Department Solicitor Edward Weinberg before the Indian Law Committee, Federal Bar Association 2-3 (Sept. 13, 1968) (unpublished):

> [I]f the right to professional counsel without charge were construed as applicable to criminal proceedings in tribal courts, such courts would practically have to cease functioning because they have no bars of professional lawyers associated with them from which they could appoint counsel to represent indigent defendants. Hence, the right to professional counsel guaranteed by the Indian Bill of Rights is conditional upon the defendant's providing such counsel for himself.

As a general rule, professional attorneys have not heretofore been permitted to practice in tribal courts. JUSTICE, U.S. COMM. ON CIVIL RIGHTS REPORT No. 5 145 (1961) [hereinafter cited as CIVIL RIGHTS REPORT]. The regulation preventing attorneys from appearing in Courts of Indian Offenses under the control of the Secretary of the Interior, however, was revoked on May 16, 1961. 25 C.F.R. § 11.9.

sent defendants. In addition, the prosecution in tribal courts is often informal and may be presented without the assistance of professional attorneys. Finally, the tribal cases generally deal with traditional and customary law where the expertise of trained counsel is not essential.

Section 202 (7) ordains that Indian tribes shall not "require excessive bail, impose excessive fines, inflict cruel and unusual punishments, and in no event impose for conviction of any one offense any penalty or punishment greater than imprisonment for a term of six months or a fine of $500, or both." The first part of this text obviously is taken from the eighth amendment, while the latter part essentially codifies existing practice under the various tribal law and order codes. Section 202 (9) carries over to Indian tribes the prohibition in article I, section 10, against passage by Congress of any bill of attainder or ex post facto law.

Section 202 (10) provides that no Indian tribe shall "deny to any person accused of an offense punishable by imprisonment the right, upon request, to a trial by jury of not less than six persons." This modification of the sixth amendment right to trial by a twelve-man jury in criminal cases was deemed appropriate in light of the relatively informal nature of tribal court proceedings, while the omission of the seventh amendment right to a trial by jury in civil cases at common law where the value in controversy exceeds $20 also permits continued flexibility in the tribal court systems.[13]

Secton 202 (8) , reflecting the fourteenth amendment, directs that no Indian tribe shall "deny to any person within its jurisdiction the equal protection of its laws," and, reflecting the fifth amendment, further directs that Indian tribes shall not "deprive any person of liberty or property without due process of law." Section 203, reflecting article I, section 9, provides that the "privilege of the writ of habeas corpus shall be available to any person, in a court of the United States, to test the legality of his detention by order of an Indian tribe." As the following discussion will show, sections 202 (8) and 203 undoubtedly will have a greater impact upon the operations of tribal governments, and are more likely to be the subject or basis of future litigation, than any of the other provisions of Title II.

TRIBAL SOVEREIGNTY AND THE BILL OF RIGHTS BEFORE TITLE II

From the earliest days of our Nation, Indian tribes have been recognized, in the words of Chief Justice Marshall, as "distinct,

---

13. *House Hearings* at 27.

independent, political communities,"[14] and, as such, authorized to exercise powers of local self-government. In a more recent restatement of the controlling rule of law, the Supreme Court of Arizona observed:

> The whole course of judicial decision on the nature of Indian tribal powers is marked by adherence to three fundamental principles; (1) An Indian tribe possesses, in the first instance, all the powers of any sovereign state. (2) Conquest renders the tribe subject to the legislative power of the United States and, in substance, terminates the external powers of sovereignty of the tribe, e.g., its power to enter into treaties with foreign nations, but does not by itself affect the internal sovereignty of the tribe, i.e., its powers of local self-government. (3) These powers are subject to qualification by treaties and by express legislation of Congress, but, save as thus expressly qualified, full powers of internal sovereignty are vested in the Indian tribes and in their duly constituted organs of government.[15]

A striking affirmation of the foregoing principles in particular relation to the Bill of Rights is found in the case of *Talton v. Mayes*, 163 U.S. 376 (1896). The question there presented was whether a law of the Cherokee Nation authorizing a jury of five persons to institute criminal proceedings violated the fifth amendment requirement of indictment by a grand jury. The Supreme Court held that the fifth amendment applies only to the acts of the federal government, that the sovereign powers of the Cherokee Nation, although recognized by the United States, were not created by the United States, and that the judicial authority of the Cherokees was, therefore, not subject to the limitations imposed by the fifth amendment.

The *Talton* holding actually stands only for the proposition that a tribal government, absent any federal action, is not required to grant Indians a *remedial* right — a right concerning the form and manner in which the power of government is exercised — conferred by the Constitution.[16] Left open by the holding, and never decided by the Supreme Court, was whether a tribal government, again absent any federal action, may deny its members a *fundamental* right — an inviolable and personal liberty — under the Constitution, such as freedom of religion.[17] The lower federal

---

14. Worcester v. Georgia, 31 U.S. (6 Pet.) 515, 559 (1832).
15. Begay v. Miller, 70 Ariz. 380, 222 P.2d 624, 627 (1950), quoting from F. Cohen, Handbook of Federal Indian Law, *supra* note 1 at 123; *see* Iron Crow v. Oglala Sioux Tribe, 231 F.2d 89, 92-93 (8th Cir. 1956).
16. The Talton decision is correctly cited in The Edgewood, 279 F. 348 (3rd Cir. 1922), in support of the principle that presentment by a grand jury is not a fundamental constitutional right. *See* Hawaii v. Mankichi, 190 U.S. 197 (1903), and Soto v. United States, 273 F. 628, 633 (3rd Cir. 1921).
17. The flat prohibition against slavery in the thirteenth amendment has been held applicable to Indian tribes. *In re* Sah Quah, 31 F. 327 (D. Alas. 1886).

courts, though, in a series of decisions withholding basic Bill of Rights protections, eventually filled that gap.

In *Martinez v. Southern Ute Tribe of Southern Ute Res.*, 249 F.2d 915 (10th Cir. 1957), *cert. denied*, 356 U.S. 960 (1958), for example, the court ruled that the due process clause did not apply to the acts of an Indian tribe in denying an individual Indian the benefits of tribal membership. In *Barta v. Oglala Sioux Tribe of Pine Ridge Reservation*, 259 F.2d 553 (8th Cir. 1958), *cert. denied*, 358 U.S. 932 (1959), the court ruled that neither the due process clause of the fifth amendment nor the equal protection clause of the fourteenth amendment applied to the act of an Indian tribe in imposing a tax only on non-members for the use of Indian trust lands. In *Native American Church v. Navajo Tribal Council*, 272 F.2d 131 (10th Cir. 1959), the court ruled in rejecting a first amendment attack upon a criminal conviction under tribal law for the ritual use of peyote.[18]

> The First Amendment applies only to Congress. It limits the powers of Congress to interfere with religious freedom or religious worship. It is made applicable to the States only by the Fourteenth Amendment. Thus construed, the First Amendment places limitations upon the action of Congress and of the States. But as declared ¯in the decisions hereinbefore discussed, Indian tribes are not states. They have a status higher than that of states. They are subordinate and dependent nations possessed of all powers as such only to the extent that they have expressly been required to surrender them by the superior sovereign, the United States. The Constitution is, of course, the supreme law of the land, but it is nonetheless a part of the laws of the United States. Under the philosophy of the decisions, it, as any other law, is binding upon Indian nations only where it expressly binds them, or is made binding by treaty or some act of Congress. No provision in the Constitution makes the First Amendment applicable to Indian nations nor is there any law of Congress doing so.[19]

The doctrine that Indian tribes are not federal instrumentalities for purposes of invoking the Bill of Rights or states within the meaning of the fourteenth amendment also has found expression in the district courts. Thus in *United States v. Seneca Nation of*

---

18. Forty years ago, the validity of a State anti-peyote ordinance was upheld. State v. Big Sheep, 75 Mont. 219, 243 P. 1067 (1926). More recently, State prosecutions of members of the Native American Church for the use or possession of peyote outside a reservation uniformly have been dismissed on first amendment grounds. People v. Woody, 61 Cal.2d 889, 394 P.2d 813, 40 Cal. Rptr. 69, (1964); Arizona v. Attakai, Criminal Cause No. 4098, Coconino Cty. (1960); Colorado v. Pardeahtan, Criminal Action No. 9454, Denver Cty. (1967); Texas v. Clark, Criminal Action No. 12, 879, Webb Cty. (1968).

19. 272 F.2d at 134-135. As stated by the court (272 F.2d at 132), the Native American Church case also involved a claim of illegal search and seizure under the fourth amendment, but this argument is not discussed in the opinion.

New York Indians, 274 F. 946 (W.D. N.Y. 1921), the court dismissed for lack of jurisdiction a claim based upon the alleged unlawful taking of private property by a tribal government. *Glover v. United States*, 219 F. Supp. 19 (D. Mont. 1963), held that a criminal defendant in tribal court has no right to counsel under the sixth amendment. A non-Indian doing business on, but evicted from, an Indian reservation was denied protection under the fourteenth amendment. *United States v. Blackfeet Tribal Court*, 244 F. Supp. 474 (D. Mont. 1965). And, in a frequently noted case, *Toledo v. Pueblo de Jemez*,[20] a suit under the old Civil Rights Act, 8 U.S.C. §43, by a Protestant minority, refused the right to build a church or use a tribal cemetery, was dismissed on the ground that the conduct of an Indian tribe is not State action.

Notwithstanding its firm foundation in legal and historical precedents, however, the continuing vitality of the *Talton* rule was by no means assured in this era of changing constitutional interpretation.[21] The more often claimed violations of fundamental rights were litigated, the more likely some court would find a rationale for holding Indian tribes subject to the Bill of Rights — and finally one did. In *Colliflower v. Garland*, 342 F.2d 369 (1965), the Court of Appeals for the Ninth Circuit, on the newly stated premise that tribal courts "function in part as a federal agency," held that the District Court had jurisdiction "in a habeas corpus proceeding to inquire into the legality of the detention of an Indian pursuant to an order of an Indian court."[22]

The *Colliflower* decision required fancy judicial footwork.[23] Although the ruling expressly was confined "to the courts of the Fort Belknap reservation,"[24] no meaningful difference really exists between the Fort Belknap Tribal Court and, as one example, the Oglala Sioux Tribal Court which the Court of Appeals for the Eighth Circuit found not to be a federal instrumentality in *Iron Crow v. Oglala Sioux Tribe of Pine Ridge Res.*, 231 F.2d 89, 94-98

---

20. 119 F. Supp. 429 (D. N.M. 1954); *see*: 7 STAN. L. REV. 285 (1955); *The Constitutional Rights of the American Tribal Indian*, 51 VA. L. REV. 121, 132 (1956); 51 IOWA L. REV. 654, 665 n. 79 (1966).

21. Actually, spadework for the burial of Talton already had started. In Elk v. Wilkins, 112 U.S. 94 (1884), a relatively contemporaneous case, the Supreme Court declared that: "[G]eneral acts of Congress did not apply to Indians, unless so expressed as to clearly manifest an intention to include them." 112 U.S. at 100. The Supreme Court, though, repudiated this statement from Elk in Federal Power Comm'n v. Tuscarora Indian Nation, 362 U.S. 99 (1960) at 116, and, as the Court of Appeals for the District of Columbia Circuit observed, Elk v. Wilkins, "whatever its present day significance, certainly does not operate to remove 'Indians and their property interests' from the coverage of a general statute." Navajo Tribe v. NLRB, 288 F.2d 162, 165 n. 4 (D.D.C. 1961), *cert. denied*, 366 U.S. 928 (1961). The death of Elk clearly signaled the ultimate demise of Tatlon.

22. Colliflower v. Garland, 342 F.2d 369, 379 (9th Cir. 1965).

23. The opinion was both criticized (79 HARV. L. REV. 436 (1965)), and praised (26 MONT. L. REV. 235 (1965)).

24. *Supra* note 22, at 379.

(1956).[25] Moreover, although passing reference was made to a possible distinction between fundamental and remedial rights under the Constitution,[26] the Ninth Circuit established no standards for determining which constitutional restrictions should apply to tribal courts and, indeed, affirmatively indicated that the fourteenth amendment might not apply at all.[27] What emerges from a close reading of *Colliflower*, therefore, is not a cohesive new theory of constitutional law, but rather the distinct impression that the Court of Appeals found a gross injustice to have been perpetrated[28] and simply decided to stop it.[29]

In addition to judicial concern, Congress and the executive agencies, and that fourth branch of government, the private foundation, devoted ever-increasing attention through the 1960's to controlling possible violations of constitutional rights in the operations of Indian tribes. Whereas a Special Task Force on Indian Affairs in 1961 recommended to the Secretary of the Interior only that tribes be encouraged to protect civil liberties by their own ordinances,[30] President Lyndon Johnson urged Congress in 1968 to enact a statutory Indian Bill of Rights.[31] A Commission on the Rights, Liberties, and Responsibilities of the American Indian, established by the Fund for the Republic, in 1961 declared that the immunity of Indian governments from Bill of Rights restraints jeopardizes "the very assumptions on which our free society was established."[32] Most important, beginning in 1961 the Senate Subcommittee on Constitutional Rights began the public hearings[33] which ultimately led to the inclusion of Title II in the 1968 Civil Rights Act.

---

25. To the same general effect with respect to the Navajo Tribal Court is Oliver v. Udall, 306 F.2d 819 (D.C. Cir. 1962), *cert. denied*, 372 U.S. 908 (1963).

26. 342 F.2d at 379, referring to the so-called "Insular Cases": Hawaii v. Mankichi, *supra* note 16; Downes v. Bidwell, 182 U.S. 244 (1901); Dorr v. United States, 195 U.S. 138 (1904); and Talton v. Mayes. Whether the fundamental-remedial right distinction established in the Insular Cases would be extended to cases involving tribal sovereignty is questionable in view of the Supreme Court's statement with respect to the former that "it is our judgment that neither the cases nor their reasoning should be given any further expansion." Reid v. Covert, *supra* note 2, at 14.

27. *Supra* note 22, at 379.

28. As stated by the court (342 F.2d at 370-371), the record seems clearly to support Mrs. Colliflower's claim that she was not afforded the right to counsel, was not confronted by any witnesses against her and, for all practical purposes, was not afforded any trial.

29. The district court, on remand, took the hint. Citing only the court of appeals decision as authority, and after a brief statement of the facts, Judge Jameson concluded "that there was a lack of due process under the fifth amendment," granted petitioner's motion for summary judgment, and discharged Mrs. Colliflower from custody. Colliflower v. Garland, Civil No. 2414 (D. Mont., Aug. 19, 1965).

30. *Report to the Secretary of the Interior by the Task Force on Indian Affairs* 31-32 (July 10, 1961).

31. *House Hearings* at 24.

32. COMM. ON THE RIGHTS, LIBERTIES, AND RESPONSIBILITIES OF THE AMERICAN INDIAN, A PROGRAM FOR INDIAN CITIZENS 24 (1961), expanded and restated in W. BROPHY & S. ABERLE, THE INDIAN: AMERICA'S UNFINISHED BUSINESS 44 (1966).

33. The complete history of these hearings is summarized in the SENATE REPORT, *supra* note 8, at 5, as follows:

> In 1961, the subcommittee began its preliminary investigation of the legal status of the Indian in America and the problems Indians encounter when as-

Tribal Sovereignty and the Bill of Rights—
An Attempted Reconciliation

In their relations with the federal and state governments, Indians are entitled to the same rights, privileges and immunities as any other citizens.[34] As the cases previously cited would indicate, however, the Senate Subcommittee on Constitutional Rights confirmed during the course of its hearings that Indians in their relations with tribal governments are not always accorded those same rights, privileges and immunities[35]—a situation the Subcommittee members found intolerable. Congress, unlike the courts, had clearcut authority to make constitutional protections applicable to Indian tribes,[36] and the ultimate question presented to the Subcommittee, therefore, was not whether to act, but rather how far and how fast to proceed. Consistent with the long history of dealings between the United States and Indian tribes, any extension of the Bill of Rights to Indian reservations, in order to become practically as well as legally effective, would require agreement from the Indians, and such consent in turn required respect for tribal sovereignty.

For Indians, tribal sovereignty is not an abstract concept, a cultural relic, or even a vanishing institution. On their reservations,

---

serting constitutional rights in their relations with State, Federal, and tribal governments. Approximately 2,000 questionnaires, addressed to a broadly representative group of persons familiar with Indian Affairs, comprised an important segment of this investigation. The preliminary research, the first such study ever undertaken by Congress, demonstrated a clear need for further congressional inquiry. Accordingly, hearings were commenced in Washington in August 1961, and moved to California, Arizona, and New Mexico in November. The following June, hearings were held in Colorado and North and South Dakota and finally concluded in Washington during March of 1963. These hearings and staff conferences were held in areas where the sub-committee could receive the views of the largest number of Indian tribes. During this period, representatives from 85 tribes appeared before the subcommittee.

S. 961 through S. 968 and Joint Resolution 40 of the 89th Congress were introduced in response to the findings of the subcommittee based on these hearings and investigations.

On June 22, 23, 24, and 29, 1965, the subcommittee, meeting in Washington, received testimony relative to these measures. Additional statements were filed with the subcommittee before and following the public hearings. In all, some 79 persons either appeared before the subcommittee or presented statements for its consideration. These persons included representatives from 36 separate tribes, bands or other groups of Indians located in 14 States. Four national associations representing Indians, as well as three regional, federated Indian organizations, presented their views. Members of Congress, State officials, and representatives from the Department of the Interior also submitted opinions on this legislation.

The 1965 hearings revealed the necessity of revising some of the orginal measures, combining two of them into title I, and deleting two proposals from the legislative package. The six titles of S. 1843, as amended, are products of the recommendations of the Subcommittee on Constitutional Rights as reported in its 'Summary Report of Hearings and Investigations on the Constitutional Rights of the American Indian, 1966'.

34.   U.S. Const. amend. XIV, § 1; Montoya v. Bolack, 70 N.M. 196, 372 P.2d 387 (1962); Harrison v. Laveen, 67 Ariz. 337, 196 P.2d 456 (1948); Senate Report at 7; Civil Rights Report, supra note 12, at 131-132, 160.

35.   Senate Report at 6-9; Summary Report, supra note 6, at 3.

36.   United States v. Kagama, 118 U.S. 375 (1886); U.S. Dept. of the Interior, Federal Indian Law 24-33 (1958); see cases cited supra note 15.

the tribe represents to its members not only the local government,[37] but also a dominant force in their economic and social lives. Indeed, in 1934, after pursuing a contrary policy for generations, Congress itself recognized that strong, independent tribal organizations are fundamental to reservation development (for humans as well as natural resources), and granted to the tribes new powers in the management of their political and business affairs.[38] Moreover, through the years, tribal institutions, including the tribal courts, though handicapped by lack of funds and experience,[39] have worked unusually well in protecting the rights and promoting the interests of the Indian people. Small wonder, therefore, that Indians could be expected to resist any change in the law, no matter how attractive otherwise, which threatened the underlying powers or independence of tribal governments.

The legislative history of Title II makes clear that Congress viewed extension of the Bill of Rights to Indian reservations as a tool for strengthening tribal institutions and organizations, not as a weapon for their destruction.[40] The omission of the first amend-

---

37. Congress has shifted jurisdiction over major crimes, such as murder, manslaughter, rape, arson, burglary, etc., from the tribal courts to the federal district courts by statute (18 U.S.C. §1153), but the tribal courts retain jurisdiction over lesser offenses and, generally, in civil actions between Indians. The scope of tribal self-government is summarized in U.S. DEPT. OF THE INTERIOR, FEDERAL INDIAN LAW 395 (1958) as including the powers

> . . . to define conditions of tribal membership, to regulate domestic relations of members, to prescribe rules of inheritance, to levy taxes, to regulate property within the jurisdiction of the tribe, to control the conduct of members by municipal legislation, and to administer justice.

38. Indian Reorganization Act of June 18, 1934, 48 Stat. 984, 25 U.S.C. §461-79 (1964).
39. SUMMARY REPORT, at 24: "These denials [of constitutional rights] occur, it is also apparent, not from malice or ill will, or from a desire to do injustice, but from the tribal judges' inexperience, lack of training, and unfamiliarity with the traditions and forms of the American legal system." CIVIL RIGHTS REPORT, at 146: "Indian courts are said to render a good brand of justice except, perhaps, where offenders require treatment rather than punishment, as in the case of many juvenile delinquents and some adults. Most Indian courts have neither the personnel nor the resources to cope with offenders of this sort." *Report to the Secretary of the Interior by the Task Force on Indian Affairs* 28 (July 10, 1961):

> The size and effectiveness of local forces of law and order are highly variable. Thus, the Navajos have a tribal court with seven judges, spend more than $1 million in tribal funds annually for law and order activities, equip their Indian police force with squad cars and two-way radios, and have built modern and well-equipped jails which would be the envy of many county sheriffs. But, at the other end of the scale, there are tribal courts established in Indian country where, due to inadequate tribal funds, there is only one judge, untrained, no police force, and an outworn building for detention purposes.

40. *House Hearings, supra* note 10, at 26; Reifel Statement, *supra* note 10; Remarks of Edward Weinberg, *supra* note 12, at 2, in describing the Interior Department's "selective" approach, which the Subcommittee adopted: "we were concerned that certain of the limitations placed by the Constitution upon the powers of the Federal Government, if imposed upon tribal governments, would be disruptive of those governments out of all proportion to the protection they would afford individuals." *See* W. BROPHY & S. ABERLE, THE INDIAN: AMERICA'S UNFINISHED BUSINESS 44 (1966), and recommendations in the *Report to the Secretary of the Interior by the Task Force on Indian Affairs* 31 (July 10, 1961):

> The Task Force is guided in thinking by the conviction that the protection of life and property, the preservation of civil rights, and the development of clearly defined civil and criminal codes is essential to rapid economic growth in the Indian country, and this, in turn, is fundamental to the

ment establishment clause, in deference to the theocratic nature of some Indian tribal governments, and the limitations placed upon a criminal defendant's right to counsel, in deference to the unmanageable administrative burdens an absolute right to counsel would place upon tribal court systems, already have been mentioned. In addition, although the Subcommittee staff urgently recommended in 1966 that individual Indians be granted a right of appeal from an adverse decision in a tribal court and a trial *de novo* in the federal district court in criminal cases where a denial of constitutional rights may have occurred,[41] and although the bill which ultimately became Title II contained such language when originally introduced in 1967,[42] the appellate provisions of the legislation were completely eliminated before S. 1843 was reported by the Senate Committee on the Judiciary.[43] Again, the Subcommittee agreed to delete a proposed new legal safeguard — even one strongly endorsed by its Chairman[44]—on the ground that an appeal and trial *de novo* in federal court would cause too serious a disruption of tribal self-government.

A Congressional intent to preserve tribal sovereignty under the 1968 Civil Rights Act is vividly illustrated by the provisions of Title IV. In 1953, when the most serious effort in modern times to terminate the special relationship between the federal government and Indian tribes was reaching its peak, Congress passed an act[45] which authorized a number of western states, not previously possessed of that right, unilaterally to amend their constitutions or statutes in order to extend state civil or criminal jurisdiction over Indian reservations and, in effect, to wipe out tribal jurisdiction. In response to fifteen years of Indian protests against this ever-present threat to their powers of local self-government, Title IV amends the 1953 Act to require "the consent of the Indian tribe occupying the particular Indian country or part thereof which could be affected by such assumption" before any extension of state jurisdiction would become operative.

The legal background, legislative history and actual text of the 1968 Civil Rights Act thus show that Congress there intended affirmatively and sensitively to reconcile application of the Bill of Rights on Indian reservations with continued control by Indians over

---

rapid rise of the standard of living on the reservations which is necessary to Indian well-being.

For the view that Title II weakened tribal sovereignty, on the other hand, *see The Indian: The Forgotten American,* 81 HARV. L. REV. 1818, 1822 (1968).

41. SUMMARY REPORT at 25-26.

42. S. 1843 of the 90th Congress, reprinted at 113 CONG. REC. S 7214 (daily ed. May 23, 1967).

43. SENATE REPORT at 1-2, 14.

44. SUMMARY REPORT at 13-14; *Hearings, supra* note 5, at 91.

45. Act of Aug. 15, 1953, 67 Stat. 588, 18 U.S.C. § 1162 (1964), 28 U.S.C. § 1360 (1964).

their own affairs.[46] In attempting this reconciliation, Congress undertook to solve a legal problem which, realistically, the courts appeared ill-equipped to handle. Specifically, given current trends of judicial decision, the exclusion of reservation Indians from the enjoyment of many rights conferred by the Constitution was not likely much longer to endure. At the same time, however, applying every limitation in the Bill of Rights to the acts of Indian tribes could destroy tribal self-government, while the economic and social advancement of reservation Indians clearly is tied to the maintenance of strong tribal institutions. In a way which the courts might not have found possible, Congress in the 1968 Civil Rights Act sought to balance these interests — freedom for the individual, yet respect for tribal sovereignty. The measure of its initial success is evident in the almost unanimous support which Indians gave Title II, notwithstanding the trepidation with which they had viewed earlier versions of the same legislation.[47]

FUTURE ENFORCEMENT OF TITLE II

Title II has not yet been judicially construed.[48] As in the case of constitutional rights generally, the Indian Bill of Rights presents a limitless potential for litigation. Even in the absence of guiding precedents, however, some conclusions reasonably may be reached in answer to the two key questions: how far do the rights created by the statute extend,[49] and in what court can those rights be enforced?

---

46. CIVIL RIGHTS REPORT, *supra* note 12, at 133: "Whether and to what extent such limitations [Bill of Rights restraints] are desirable involves (as in so many Indian affairs) a delicate balancing of values—between civil rights and liberties on the one hand, and the benefits of tribal autonomy on the other." *Compare* 51 VA. L. REV. 121 at 135 (1965).

47. Endorsements of S. 1843 by numerous Indian tribes and Indian-interest organizations appear at 113 CONG. REC. S 18157 *et seq.* (daily ed. Dec. 7, 1967). In the final stages of the legislative process, only the more traditional Pueblo groups in New Mexico actually objected to Title II. *House Hearings* at 37 *et seq.*; Reifel Statement, *supra* note 10, at E 2742. By contrast, representatives of many tribes opposed predecessor bills during the 1965 hearings of the Senate Subcommittee on Constitutional Rights. *Hearings, supra* note 5, *passim.*

48. At least two cases have been instituted under the 1968 Act, one in the federal district court in Arizona to upset the eviction of the head of the OEO-supported Navajo legal service from the Navajo Reservation, and the second in the federal district court in Montana to change practices in the Blackfeet Tribal Court; but neither had progressed to final decision as of the date of this writing; in the former case, Judge Walter E. Craig on December 16, 1968 did deny defendant's motion to dismiss for lack of jurisdiction in part on the basis of Title II, Dodge v. Nakai, Civ. No. 1209 Pct.

49. The proposition that Title II is "selective" in making Indian tribes subject to constitutional restraints seems beyond dispute. SENATE REPORT at 10-11; SUMMARY REPORT at 25; Remarks of Edward Weinberg, *supra* note 12, at 1-3; Vol. VII, No. 5 ALBUQUERQUE L. J. 5-11 (1968); M. Price, *The Civil Rights Act of 1968: An Analysis for Discussion,* Vol. 1, No. 4 *Am. Indian L. Newsletter* 4 (May 24, 1968). The issue which the courts must face is what was selected in and what was selected out.

Significantly, Title III of the 1968 Civil Rights Act, under which the Secretary of the Interior is directed to recommend to Congress "a model code to govern the administration of justice by courts of Indian offenses on Indian reservations," provides that such code shall assure that a criminal defendant "shall have the same rights, privileges, and immunities under the United States Constitution as would be guaranteed any citizen of the

1. *Forum*: With respect to the review of criminal proceedings in tribal courts, section 203 of Title II expressly provides that the privilege of the writ of habeas corpus shall be available to any person, in a court of the United States, to test the "legality of his detention" by order of an Indian tribe. Although the statute speaks only in terms of "detention," the federal district courts in all likelihood will (and should) extend their habeas corpus review of criminal convictions in tribal courts to include cases where the defendant is released on probation, which still involves restraint upon his person, or where the defendant merely is fined, which usually is an alternative to, or substitute for, actual imprisonment.[50] Furthermore, although the term "legality" is not defined, the only interpretation of that word consistent with the purposes of the statute would be that the federal district courts are authorized to inquire into the question of whether a defendant's rights under section 202 may have been violated, but are not authorized to inquire into whether he may have been denied some other right under either the Constitution or tribal law. Even as so limited, section 203 provides ample opportunity for the federal courts to insure that tribal criminal proceedings are basically fair and that the constitutional rights of Indian criminal defendants, as specified by Congress, are fully protected.

Title II, of course, does not provide for an appeal to the federal courts or other review of decisions by tribal courts in civil cases. More important, the 1968 Act does not designate any court in which the legality of tribal executive or legislative action, which allegedly conflicts with the Bill of Rights, can be tested. In the absence of a statutory direction, the choice of the appropriate forum for an adjudication of these rights is further complicated by the well-settled rule that Indian tribes enjoy sovereign immunity from suit, which may not be waived without the consent of Congress.[51]

Where executive or legislative activities are subject to Secretarial review — as frequently is the case under tribal constitutions, particularly with respect to the management of trust lands and the expenditure of trust funds — the Secretary of the Interior will have the power, which an aggrieved party by appeal may request that he invoke,[52] to determine whether such tribal action is in accordance

---

United States being tried in a Federal court for any similar offense." Congress intended a difference between the two titles of the 1968 Act. Unlike tribal courts, which are run by the tribes, courts of Indian offenses are controlled by the Secretary. 25 C.F.R. §11.1.

50. *See* W. Canby & W. Cohen, *The Professional Attorney and the Civil Rights Act,* Vol. 1, No. 28 *Am. Indian L. Newsletter* 7 (Dec. 16, 1968).

51. United States v. United States Fidelity & Guaranty Co., 309 U.S. 506 (1940), and cases therein cited; Maryland Casualty Co. v. Citizens Nat. Bank, 361 F.2d 517, 520 (5th Cir. 1966), *cert. denied,* 385 U.S. 918 (1966); Green v. Wilson, 331 F.2d 769 (9th Cir. 1964); Haile v. Saunooke, 246 F.2d 293 (4th Cir. 1957), *cert. denied sub nom.* Haile v. Eastern Band of Cherokee Indians, 355 U.S. 893 (1957).

52. 25 C.F.R. §2.3.

with Title II, and his determination can be reviewed in the federal courts pursuant to the Administrative Procedure Act.[53] Where tribal executive or legislative activities are not subject to Secretarial review, as generally is the case with respect to political affairs, the logical forum for testing the validity of such tribal action is the tribal court.[54] As noted above, however, no appeal is available to the federal or state courts in the event the tribal court refuses to take jurisdiction over the dispute.

Assuming the formidable sovereign immunity hurdle can be overcome,[55] a suit to enforce rights recognized and protected under Title II probably will lie in the state court of general jurisdiction, where the state possesses jurisdiction on Indian reservations in accordance with Public Law 280 of the 83rd Congress,[56] and in the federal district court, where the amount in controversy exceeds $10,000.[57] The bulk of all civil cases arising on Indian reservations in which a violation of section 202 rights is alleged, though, will not fall within either of these categories.[58] The conclusion necessarily follows that, at least in some classes of cases, Title II may have provided a right without an effective remedy.

2. *Substantive Law*: Passage of the 1968 Civil Rights Act undoubtedly has postponed the day when the Supreme Court must decide whether *Talton v. Mayes, supra,* still is good law.[59] Assuming (as the cases so far hold) that the principles of *Talton* and derivative

---

53. 5 U.S.C. §§ 702-06 (Supp. II 1966). If the ordinance under attack has long previously been approved by the Secretary, laches may defeat an administrative or judicial appeal. In such cases, an action for a declaratory judgment would seem more appropriate. 28 U.S.C. §2201 (1964). *But see* Oliver v. Udall, *supra* note 25.

54. *Cf.* Williams v. Lee, 358 U.S. 217 (1969); Kain v. Wilson, —S.D.—, 161 N.W.2d 704 (1968).

55. *See* Remarks of Edward Weinberg, *supra* note 12, at 7: "This fact [tribal immunity from suit] would not seem to pose any particular problem to a suitor because he seemingly could proceed against the tribal officers responsible for the challenged action, as individuals, under the familiar doctrine that the cloak of immunity does not cover officers whose acts are beyond their authority." *But see* Green v. Wilson, *supra* note 51.

56. Act of August 15, 1953, 67 Stat. 588, 18 U.S.C. § 1162 (1964), 28 U.S.C. § 1360 (1964).

57. 28 U.S.C. § 1331, (1964) granting jurisdiction to the District Courts where an issue arises under the Constitution, laws, or treaties of the United States. Under the Act of October 10, 1966, 80 Stat. 880, 28 U.S.C. § 1362 (Supp. II 1966), the jurisdictional amount was dropped for suits involving a federal question brought by Indian tribes, but no such waiver exists for suits by individual Indians.

58. Another potential statutory source for the review of tribal action in the light of Title II is 28 U.S.C. § 1343 (1964), which provides in part:

> The district courts shall have original jurisdiction of any civil action authorized by law to be commenced by any person:
>
> * * *
>
> (4) To recover damages or to secure equitable or other relief under any Act of Congress providing for the protection of civil rights . . . .

The 1968 Civil Rights Act clearly qualifies as a law "for the protection of civil rights," but Title II on its face does not authorize the filing of any civil action and, therefore, the courts more probably than not will dismiss suits based upon 28 U.S.C. § 1343 (1964) alone for lack of jurisdiction.

59. If the Talton rule no longer is valid, and the Bill of Rights limits tribal action under the Constitution absolutely, then enactment of Title II becomes a grand, but empty gesture.

decisions remain controlling, and thus that Congress has the power to select which Bill of Rights protections shall apply to the acts of Indian tribes, the central substantive issue that the courts now will face is whether Title II should be strictly or liberally construed. The historical and legal background of Title II, as well as the manifest Congressional intent in the 1968 Act to preserve, if not enhance, tribal sovereignty, all point to a strict construction of its language.

Section 202(6), for example, provides that a criminal defendant in tribal court shall have the right "at his own expense" to have the assistance of counsel for his defense. This right to counsel logically extends to attorneys who are willing to serve at no cost to the defendant because he is poor. The legislative history of Title II makes clear, on the other hand, that the tribal court has no statutory obligation to appoint counsel for an indigent defendant,[60] and any judicial extension of the right to counsel to impose such a burden upon the tribal court would seem wholly unwarranted.[61] Similarly, under the doctrine of *expressio unius est exclusio alterius*,[62] a party to a civil suit in tribal court apparently is not entitled as a matter of right to the assistance of a professional attorney of his own choice.

The requirements of section 202(8) that an Indian tribe not "deny to any person within its jurisdiction[63] the equal protection of its laws or deprive any person of liberty or property without due process of law" pose more difficult problems of statutory interpretations. Here again, in order to carry out the twin purposes of the 1968 Act—protection for the individual, yet respect for tribal sovereignty—the courts properly should exercise restraint before striking down long-standing tribal practices which reasonably can be justified. Thus, under Title II, a continuing violation of the "one man, one vote" principle[64] in a tribal election code probably could and should be subject to judicial correction. The Iroquois custom that tribal membership and inheritance rights with respect to land descend only through the female line, on the other hand, is not so repugnant to ordinary standards of fair play as to dictate its abolition by the courts.[65] Moreover, to cite other examples in the field of

---

60. Citations *supra* note 12.
61. *Supra* note 11. The Supreme Court never has ruled that a right to counsel exists in cases of petty offenses, the general area of tribal court criminal jurisdiction.
62. 50 Am. Jur. *Statutes* §§ 244, 429 (1944).
63. Although a serious question exists as to whether non-Indians come within a tribe's jurisdiction as a matter of law, Congress obviously intended to establish "rights for all persons who may be subject to the jurisdiction of tribal governments, whether Indians or non-Indians." Summary Report at 10. In view of the actual text of section 202(8), a subsidiary question exists as to whether non-Indians are entitled to due process, or only to the equal protection of the law.
64. Baker v. Carr, 369 U.S. 186 (1962); Reynolds v. Sims, 377 U.S. 533 (1964); Avery v. Midland County, 36 U.S.L.W. 4257 (April 2, 1968); *but see* Sailors v. Board of Educ., 387 U.S. 105 (1967), and Dusch v. Davis, 387 U.S. 112 (1967).
65. In conferring civil jurisdiction over Indian reservations within that state upon the

economic regulation, ample factual justification exists for sustaining even as against a due process or equal protection attack the right of a tribe to grant its members a preference in the allocation of reservation grazing privileges or to assess a tax only upon nonmembers doing business on the reservation.[66]

In the final analysis, though, how the courts will construe Title II and, in particular, section 202(8) is a story yet to be told. Perhaps the safest conclusion is that, over the years, the 1968 Civil Rights Act will prove another landmark statute both in the protection of individual Indian rights and in the progressive development of tribal resources and institutions.

New York courts, Congress specifically recognized and gave effect to "those tribal laws and customs which they [the Indians] desire to preserve . . . ." Act of September 13, 1950, 64 Stat. 845, 25 U.S.C. § 233 (1964).

66. Morris v. Hitchcock, 194 U.S. 384 (1904) ; *see* Travelers' Insurance Co. v. Connecticut, 185 U.S. 364 (1902) ; Carmichael v. Southern Coal & Coke Co., 301 U.S. 495 (1937) ; Madden v. Kentucky, 309 U.S. 83 (1940).

INDIAN RIGHTS UNDER THE
CIVIL RIGHTS ACT OF 1968

G. Kenneth Reiblich[*]

Titles II-VII of the Civil Rights Act of 1968 established new and far reaching changes in federal Indian policy: Title II, easily the most controversial of the six titles, gives tribal members certain protections, similar to Bill of Rights guarantees, against tribal action. Title III directs the Secretary of the Interior to recommend to the Congress a model code for courts of Indian offenses. Title IV requires tribal consent before those states without jurisdiction over Indian country may assert it; Title V adds the crime of "assault resulting in serious bodily injury" to the Major Crimes Act. Title VI deals with tribal employment of legal counsel; and Title VII directs the Secretary of the Interior to update certain material relating to Indian law.[1] Although it is too early to fully appraise the impact of this legislation, this article proposes to consider the Act in relation to: the legislative history; previous federal Indian policy; and the accomplishment of the desirable purpose of integrating the American Indian into our system of government without breaking faith with the historical semi-sovereign power of internal government assured to many Indian tribes by treaties and other dealings with them.[2]

Attached by the Senate as a rider to House Resolution 2516, which was originally aimed at expanding protections established by federal legislation for civil rights, Titles II-VII passed the House of Representatives on April 10, 1968[3] (the day after the funeral of Dr. Martin Luther King), and was signed by the President on April 11. Titles II-VII include the same provisions as Senate bill 1843, which had passed the Senate on December 7, 1967 and was pending before the Subcommittee on Indian Affairs of the House Committee on Internal and Insular Affairs when House Resolution 2516 came directly to the floor of the House.

On the day of the statute's passage, Wayne N. Aspinall, Repre-

---

[*] Professor of Law, University of Arizona. A.B. 1925, Ph.D. 1928, The Johns Hopkins University; J.D. 1929, New York University; LL.M. 1937, Columbia University. The author extends his appreciation to Fredrick D. Palmer, the Symposium Editor, for his contribution to this article by supplying discussion of the nature of Indian property rights in relation to eminent domain and making many other helpful suggestions.

[1] 25 U.S.C.A. §§ 1301-41 (Supp. 1969). See Appendix I for the full text of Titles II-VII.

[2] See generally Kelly, *Indian Adjustment and the History of Indian Affairs*, p. 559 supra.

[3] H.R. Res. 2516, 90th Cong., 2d Sess., 114 Cong. Rec. 2825-26 (1968).

sentative from Colorado, and Chairman of the House Committee on Interior and Insular Affairs, opposed passage of the proposed legislation on the ground that the House committee had not had time to fully consider the merits of the proposals relating to Indians, and stated:

> Mr. Speaker, there is a grave danger that by giving our approval to H.R. 2516, as it comes to us from the other body, we may, in fact, *be destroying Indian treaty rights in the name of so-called civil rights — in trying to aid one minority we are destroying rights of another minority.* . . .

> . . . .

> . . . While this is not the time to discuss the merits or defects of titles II through VII or H.R. 2516, I have satisfied myself that they contain provisions that merit careful evaluation before they are accepted by the Members of this House. *The Interior and Insular Affairs Committee has received from some Indian tribes expressions of alarm and requests for amendments.* Those Indian groups are entitled to be heard. Without in any way expressing an opinion regarding the merits of the objections because I believe the formulation of an opinion would be premature, I can mention a few of them as illustrative:

> First. One provision of title II provides that in an Indian tribal court a defendant in a criminal case shall be entitled to the assistance of counsel. In an ordinary court of law this would, of course, be a highly desirable provision. A tribal court, however, is not an ordinary court. Neither the judges nor the prosecutors are attorneys. They function in a most informal manner. The fear expressed, which I believe should be evaluated, is that a defense lawyer in that kind of court would so confuse the lay judges with formalistic demands that the system might collapse. That fear may or may not be well founded. We should find out.

> . . . .

> Third. Trial by jury, although embedded in our common law, is foreign to the customs of many tribes. Before imposing this requirement in tribal courts, the probable results should be considered.[4] (emphasis added).

These remarks, plus others of like character,[5] provide the impetus for the detailed consideration of Titles II-VII which follows and suggest that Title II is not the unmitigated blessing to Indians that was urged in support of its passage. Titles III-VII represent a sound approach to Indian policy for the future.

Titles II-VII stem from legislation first introduced in the 89th Congress as Senate bills 961-68 and Senate Joint Resolution 40, promulgated after several years of hearings by the Subcommittee on Constitutional Rights of the Judiciary Committee of the Senate under the Chairman-

---

[4] *Id.* at 2819-20 (1968) (remarks of Representative Aspinall). *See Id.* at 2761, 2791 and 2807 for comparable statements of other congressmen.
[5] See note 4 *supra.*

ship of Senator Ervin (which has caused this Indian rights legislation to be referred to as the "Ervin Bill"). The subcommittee conducted hearings in nine states — Arizona, California, Colorado, Idaho, Nevada, New Mexico, North Carolina, North Dakota and South Dakota — received testimony from 79 witnesses including members of Congress, state officials, representatives from the Department of Justice, the Department of the Interior, 89 Indian tribes, and several national associations representing Indians.[6] The subcommittee unanimously recommended to the 90th Congress the passage of Senate Bill 1843. When the Senate Judiciary Committee gave House Resolution 2516 a favorable report without appending the provisions relating to Indians, which had already been passed as Senate bill 1843, Senator Ervin in a strong minority report successfully supported the inclusion of the protections of Indian rights in House Resolution 2516, emphasizing that the Indian rights bills were supported by

> [t]he National Congress of American Indians; the Association of the Bar of the City of New York; the Department of the Interior; the Indian Rights Association; the American Civil Liberties Union; the National Council of Churches of Christ; and Indian tribes throughout the United States.[7]

President Johnson in a special message to Congress also supported passage of the legislation protecting Indian rights.[8]

In view of such powerful support, it is easy to conclude that legislation passed after such long and careful deliberation is of necessity sound. However, considering the general enthusiasm developed during the last several years concerning civil rights, Congress in enacting Title II may have overlooked some aspects of Indian history and culture that distinguish the Indian on his reservation from other ethnic groups which are mingled with the general population. Indeed, there is a very real difference in the position of the American Negroes, freed from slavery and immediately cast into the maelstrom of the political, economic, and social organization of the states where they sought (and continue to seek) full citizenship and all the constitutional protection it offers, and the American Indians who have been asked (or compelled) to surrender a simple free existence under tribal or family government on land they were free to roam at will for a way of life which they have never sought, nor accepted, as better than their own.[9]

---

[6] *Hearings on S. 961-68 and S.J. Res. 40 Before the Subcomm. on Constitutional Rights of the Senate Comm. on the Judiciary,* 89th Cong., 1st Sess. 1 (1965) [hereinafter cited as *Senate Hearings on Constitutional Rights*].

[7] S. Ervin, Interference With Civil Rights, S. Rep. No. 721, 90th Cong., 1st Sess. 29-33 (1967).

[8] Bureau of Indian Affairs, Indian Record, Special Issue — President Johnson Presents Indian Message to Congress — The Forgotten American 13 (1968).

[9] Fretz, *The Bill of Rights and the American Indian Tribal Government,* 6 Natural Resources J. 581, 586-87 (1966).

There can be little doubt as to Congress' power by statute to limit Indian control over internal Indian tribal government,[10] but Congress has not always exercised its power judiciously. Although it would seem unwise to generalize as to fluctuating federal Indian policy, without further discussion of the details of the different policies, such studies of Indian culture and development as have been reviewed in preparation of this article and the testimony before subcommittees of Congress inquiring into Indian affairs since 1961, indicate that the process of gradual education, encouragement and assistance to Indians has worked better than flat imposition of new rules with which Indians are unfamiliar, or of new ways of life for which they have not been adequately prepared.[11]

Titles III-VII, standing alone, do little to infringe on the treaty recognized, semi-sovereign character of Indian tribes.[12] Indian sovereignty should not be pushed aside without Indian consent, on the argument that Title II gives the Indian the same rights as other Americans, without a stronger showing than has yet been made that Title II is a feasible and helpful protection to individual Indians. We should

---

[10] Village of Kake v. Egan, 369 U.S. 60 (1962); United States v. Kagama, 118 U.S. 375 (1886).

[11] *See* W. Brophy & S. Aberle, The Indian — America's Unfinished Business (1966) [hereinafter cited as The Indian]; Kelly, *Indian Adjustment and the History of Indian Affairs*, p. 559 *supra*. Arthur Lazarus, Jr., General Counsel of the Association of American Indian Affairs, Inc., made the following statement before the Ervin subcommittee:

Perhaps the major problem posed by S. 961 . . . is the attempt in this legislation to impose upon all Indian communities at one fell swoop a sophisticated legal system which has been developing in our society over a period of centuries. I suggest that Indian tribes vary — each having different resources, customs, size, degree of education or assimilation, etc. — and that the proposed establishment of one set of legal rules for all tribes is unworkable and unwise. I further suggest that it is not realistic to expect Indians (or any other nation) to learn respect for our constitutional principles when their application is required by legislative direction from outside and does not grow out of the actual operations of tribal government. *Senate Hearings on Constitutional Rights, supra* note 6, at 65.

[12] Worcester v. Georgia, 31 U.S. (6 Pet.) 515, 559-60 (1832), where Mr. Chief Justice Marshall stated:

The Indian nations had always been considered as distinct, independent political communities, retaining their original natural rights, as the undisputed possessors of the soil from time immemorial, with the single exception of that imposed by irresistible power, which excluded them from intercourse with any other European potentate than the first discoverer of the coast of the particular region claimed: and this was a restriction which those European potentates imposed on themselves, as well as on the Indians. The very term 'nation,' so generally applied to them, means 'a people distinct from others.' The Constitution, by declaring treaties already made, as well as those to be made, to be the supreme law of the land, has adopted and sanctioned the previous treaties with the Indian nations, and consequently admits their rank among those powers who are capable of making treaties The words 'treaty' and 'nation' are words of our own language, selected in our diplomatic and legislative proceedings, by ourselves, having each a definite and well understood meaning. We have applied them to Indians, as we have applied them to other nations of the earth. They are applied to all in the same sense.

For the view that this idea of a primordial tribal right to self-government is completely out-dated and should be discarded, see Schaab, *Indian Industrial Development and the Courts*, 8 Natural Resources J. 303, 308 (1968).

heed the admonition of Mr. Justice Black, joined in dissent by Mr. Chief Justice Warren and Mr. Justice Douglas, in *Federal Power Comm'n v. Tuscarora Indian Nation* that, "Great nations, like great men, should keep their word."[13]

TITLE II — RIGHTS OF INDIANS

Title II, as first proposed in Senate bill 961, provided that "any Indian tribe in exercising its powers of local government shall, with certain exceptions, be subject to the same limitations and restraints as those which are imposed on the government of the United States by the Constitution."[14] This original proposal stemmed in part from the belief that, absent imposition by statute, even fundamental guarantees of the Constitution do not protect Indians in relations with their tribes, and that Congress should cure by statute the lack of Indian civil rights under the Constitution.[15] During the hearings on the proposed legis-

---

[13] 362 U.S. 99, 142 (1960). Dissenting from a majority opinion which sustained the right of the Federal Power Commission to confiscate Tuscarora homelands found by the majority to be outside exempt reservation lands within the meaning of the authorizing statute, Mr. Justice Black said:

> These Indians have a way of life which this Government has seen fit to protect, if not actually to encourage. Cogent arguments can be made that it would be better for all concerned if the Indians were to abandon their old customs and habits, and become incorporated in the communities where they reside. The fact remains, however, that they have *not* done this and they have continued their tribal life with a trust in a promise of security from this Government.
>
> . . . .
>
> It may be hard for us to understand why these Indians cling so tenaciously to their lands and traditional tribal way of life. The record does not leave the impression that the lands of their reservation are the most fertile, the landscape the most beautiful, or their homes the most splendid specimen of architecture. But this is their home — their ancestral home. . . .
> . . . I regret that this Court is to be the governmental agency that breaks faith with this dependent people. Great nations, like great men, should keep their word. (emphasis original). *Id.* at 141-42.

It might be noted that the first judicial opinion applying Title II, Dodge v. Nakai, Civil No. 1209 (D. Ariz., Feb. 28, 1969), held that Title II was a legitimate exercise of Congress' power to modify the autonomy reserved to the Navajo Tribe in its 1868 treaty with the United States.

[14] *Senate Hearings on Constitutional Rights, supra* note 6, at 1-6.

[15] *Id. See also Hearings on H.R. 15419 and Related Bills Before the Subcomm. on Indian Affairs of the House Comm. on Interior and Insular Affairs,* 90th Cong., 2d Sess. 16, 17 (1968) [hereinafter cited as *House Subcomm. on Indian Affairs*]. Although this article does not explore the applicability of basic guarantees of the Constitution to Indian tribal action, the recent case of Colliflower v. Garland, 342 F.2d 369 (9th Cir. 1965) suggests the Constitution may be applicable to tribal action. Only one Supreme Court decision, Talton v. Mayes, 163 U.S. 376 (1896), dealing with the non-fundamental right to a grand jury trial, stands as authority contrary to *Colliflower.* Although there are several decisions in the lower federal courts which have relied on *Talton, e.g.* Native American Church v. Navajo Tribal Council, 272 F.2d 131 (10th Cir. 1959); Glover v. United States, 219 F. Supp. 19 (D. Mont. 1963), as a basis for refusing to extend constitutional guarantees to tribal action against tribal members, it can be argued that the current Supreme Court might overrule, or distinguish *Talton* if called upon to do so. *See generally* Fretz, *supra* note 9; Note, *The Constitutional Rights of the American Tribal Indian,* 51 VA. L. REV. 121 (1965). Attorney General Kennedy, when asked by Senator Ervin about his views concerning the constitutional rights of Indians, replied:

lation, however, numerous witnesses pointed out that the peculiarities of the Indians' economic and social condition, his customs, his beliefs, and his attitudes, raised serious questions about the desirability of imposing upon Indian cultures the legal forms and procedures to which other Americans had become accustomed.[16] Mr. Frank J. Barry, Solicitor of the Department of Interior summarized this argument stating:

> [T]he Constitution of the United States was adopted by a people whose philosophical and political roots were deeply embedded in the history of England and of Western Europe. Many of the restraints and limitations on the United States contained in the U.S. Constitution were an outgrowth of that history. On the other hand, the people of Indian tribes have their roots in an entirely different culture and it may be that the devices which appropriately protected the interests of the Anglo-American of the late 18th century may not be appropriate to protect the Indian tribal member of the middle 20th century.[17]

Solicitor Barry, on behalf of the Department of Interior, offered a substitute bill spelling out in specific terms the rights Indians would possess in their relationships with their tribal governments. The substitute bill was substantially the same as that finally adopted in Title II.

Also opposing blanket imposition of all the guarantees of the Constitution, Mr. Albert Lazarus, Jr., General Counsel of the Association on American Indian Affairs, argued that:

> A full and direct application of the Federal Bill of Rights . . . would require tribal courts to hold trials by a jury of 12 men in all criminal cases . . . and in civil cases involving more than $20, . . . even though State governments are not made subject to the same limitations. . . . [T]here seems to be no justification for holding Indian tribes to a higher standard of conduct than States must observe under the 14th amendment.[18]

The Senate subcommittee, in accepting Solicitor Barry's alternate proposal, concluded that adoption would:

> avoid both the alleged inappropriateness of restraint of Indian governments by full application of the U.S. Constitution, as well as the dislocations inherent in too swift subjection of those governments to a sophisticated legal structure . . . .[19]

All the constitutional guarantees apply to the American Indians in their relations with the Federal Government, or its branches, and the State governments to the same extent that they apply to other American citizens. It is not entirely clear to what extent the constitutional restrictions applicable to the Federal Government, or its branches, and to the State governments are applicable to tribal governments, but the decided cases indicate there are large areas where such restrictions are not applicable. *Senate Hearings on Constitutional Rights, supra* note 6, at 1-6.

[16] *Senate Hearings on Constitutional Rights, Summary Report*, 89th Cong., 2d Sess. 9 (1966).

[17] *Id.*

[18] *Id.* at 9-10. (omissions original). *Cf.* remarks of Mr. Lazarus, *supra* note 11.

[19] *Id.* at 10.

Although the statements of Solicitor Barry, Mr. Lazarus, and the subcommittee, were advanced as reasons why the committee should propose the substitute bill offered by the Department of Interior, instead of the originally proposed application of *all* protections of the Constitution, the statements would seem to cut as effectively against the restrictions imposed on the Indian tribes by Title II. Each of the provisions of Title II constitutes a statutory intrusion upon the semi-sovereign right of the tribes to govern themselves,[20] and since imposed by congressional fiat, they would seem to be more hazardous to the maintenance of Indian self-respect and orderly control of the tribe's affairs than would a case-by-case judicial application of particular constitutional protections as might be appropriate under the circumstances of each case and the particular tribal action involved.[20a]

Paragraph (1) of Title II essentially incorporates the protections of the first amendment, excluding the prohibition against establishment of religion.[21] There is excellent reason for omitting the establishment clause since many Indian tribes are essentially theocracies.[22] Accordingly, a prohibition against establishment of religion could seriously impair the entire basis of some tribal governments. In explaining the omission from the Department of Interior's proposal, Solicitor Barry stated to the subcommittee:

> we did not include in the constitutional guarantees that we proposed be extended to Indians that they be deprived of their right to pass laws affecting the establishment of religion. Because religion is so deeply rooted in their system that it might be destructive of their government and we raise a problem which would set us back 10 years instead of advancing us a step.[23]

If the original version of the bill extending all the protections of the Constitution had been recommended and passed, however, the Supreme Court in a proper case could have found that the first amendment's prohibition against the establishment of religion *by Congress* has no effect on *Indian tribes.*

Paragraph (1) does, however, prohibit Indian tribes from abridging "freedom of speech, or of the press, or the right of the people peaceably to assemble and to petition for a redress of grievances." The wisdom of affording this protection to dissident members of closely knit tribes is questionable. Indian tribes being more like families than govern-

---

[20] *See* Worcester v. Georgia, 31 U.S. (6 Pet.) 515 (1832).
[20a] *Cf.* Note, *The Indian Bill of Rights and the Constitutional Status of Tribal Governments*, 82 HARV. L. REV. 1343 (1969).
[21] Appendix I.
[22] Fretz, *supra* note 9, at 611-13.
[23] *Senate Hearings on Constitutional Rights, supra* note 6, at 26. *See also* Fretz, *supra* note 9, at 612; 7 ALBUQUERQUE BAR J. No. 5, 5-11 (1968).

mental units, the risk exists that barriers raised against "intra-family" discipline could well lead to a further breakdown of tribal society, to a higher crime rate, and to increased alcoholism, a thesis supported by more than one anthropologist.[24]

What is more likely is that paragraph (1) will serve as a buffer for those bent on remaking the tribal social order. The recent case of *Dodge v. Nakai*[25] supports this conclusion. In that case, Ted Mitchell, director of Dinebeiina Nahiilna Be Azaditahe, Inc. (DNA), the Office of Economic Opportunity's legal aid program on the Navajo Reservation, was ordered off the reservation by the Advisory Committee of the Navajo Tribal Council because of Mitchell's allegedly improper operation of the DNA program, and public disrespect shown the tribal council. An injunction was issued by the United States District Court for the District of Arizona, restraining the tribal council from carrying out its exclusion order. The court held, among other things, that the action by the advisory committee constituted an abridgement of free speech (in violation of paragraph (1))

> on the Navajo Reservation, both the freedom of speech of the lawyer who is representing his client . . . and the freedom of speech of the clients who seek out that lawyer to act as their spokesman in the community.[26]

No provisions similar to the second and third amendments are found in Title II. There is obviously no need for Indian tribes to have a statutory right "to a well-regulated militia" or "to keep and bear arms." Nor is there any apparent reason for tribes to be protected against the quartering of troops. Had the original inclusion of all the constitutional protections been accepted, it is doubtful if any of these protections would ever have been applied judicially.

Paragraph (2) is a repetition of the language of the fourth amendment and is apparently intended to extend the full protection of that amendment against the action of tribal officials or agents.[27] Recent changes and expansion of fourth amendment protections as part of the fourteenth amendment's due process safeguard against state action,[28] the difficulties state police departments assert they face as the Supreme Court changes the law, and congressional objections to requiring the

---

[24] La Farge, *Termination of Federal Supervision: Disintegration and the American Indians,* 311 ANNALS 41, 41-43 (1957); Simpson & Yinger, *Integration of Americans of Indian Descent,* 311 ANNALS 158, 161 (1957).
[25] Civil No. 1209 (D. Ariz., Feb. 28, 1969).
[26] *Id.* at 14. *But see* Note, *supra* note 20a, at 1364.
[27] See Appendix I.
[28] Sibron v. New York & Peters v. New York, 392 U.S. 40 (1968); Terry v. Ohio, 392 U.S. 1 (1968); Berger v. New York, 388 U.S. 41 (1967); Katz v. United States, 389 U.S. 347 (1967); Ker v. California, 374 U.S. 23 (1963); Mapp v. Ohio, 367 U.S. 643 (1961). For two recent fourth amendment cases, see Spinelli v. United States, 89 S. Ct. 584 (1969); Alderman v. United States, 89 S. Ct. 961 (1969).

federal system to meet some of the newer Supreme Court tests,[29] raise doubts as to the wisdom of statutory imposition of the full panoply of fourth amendment uncertainty upon Indian police who are uneducated in even the rudimentary concepts of Anglo-Saxon due process, particularly when tribal courts are limited to imposing a punishment of six months imprisonment along with a $500 fine, which may well delineate the outer limit of petty offenses.[30]

Paragraphs (3), (4), and (5) include portions of the fifth amendment (double jeopardy, the privilege against self-incrimination, and the eminent domain clause).[31] The grand jury requirement has been omitted however,[32] and this would seem wise. The requirement has been held not to be applicable to the states,[33] a sufficient reason for omitting it here. Better reasons would be its incompatibility with traditionally informal Indian procedures for dealing with Indian criminal behavior, and the unreasonable burden that would be imposed by requiring indictment by a panel of Indians when very few may live within a 20 mile radius.

Similar reasons suggest that statutory imposition of the double jeopardy requirement and the privilege against self-incrimination are equally undesirable. Fifth amendment double jeopardy has been held not to be applicable to the states,[34] and for that reason alone could well have been omitted here. Also, its inclusion will raise problems of dual sovereignty if an Indian has been previously tried and acquitted in a federal court under the Major Crimes Act,[35] but his tribe has firm conviction that some form of Indian justice is essential to the proper maintenance of tribal order. It would seem unwise to have such an internal tribal problem complicated by imposition of the currently uncertain double jeopardy provision.[36]

---

[29] *See* Title III of the Omnibus Crime Control and Safe Streets Act of 1968, 18 U.S.C.A. § 2510 (Supp. 1969).

[30] See notes 65-66 and related text *infra*.

[31] Appendix I.

[32] The due process clause is also omitted from Par. 5, but it is included in Par. 8. See notes 70-81 and related text *infra*.

[33] Hurtado v. California, 110 U.S. 516 (1884).

[34] Palko v. Connecticut, 302 U.S. 319 (1937).

[35] 18 U.S.C. § 1153 (1964). See Comment, *Indictment Under the "Major Crimes Act" — An Exercise in Unfairness and Unconstitutionality*, p. 691 *infra*.

[36] Although the Supreme Court has held that double jeopardy does not preclude a second trial in a separate sovereignty (as between federal and state courts), Bartkus v. Illinois, 359 U.S. 121 (1959); Abbate v. United States, 359 U.S. 187 (1959), the fact that the Court in both of these cases was sharply divided, and that the dissenting justices therein have subsequently secured a majority for destroying the separate sovereignty argument in the self-incrimination area, Murphy v. Waterfront Comm'n, 378 U.S. 52 (1964), show the complicated nature of the double jeopardy defense, which presents difficult and unresolved legal problems for lawyers and courts steeped in the common law tradition. See State v. Fletcher, 36 U.S.L.W. 2727 (Ohio C.P. Cuyahoga Cty. May 15, 1968), where the Ohio Court of Common Pleas for Cuyahoga County referred to *Murphy v. Waterfront* to predict that *Bartkus* and *Palko* both will be overruled.

Only recently has the federal self-incrimination privilege with all its surrounding protections been held applicable to the states, and then over the dissenting views of four justices of the Supreme Court.[37] If the desirability of its application to the states in 1964 was that questionable, the wisdom of imposing it on the semi-sovereign Indian tribes should raise even more serious doubts. With tribal court jurisdiction as to thirteen serious crimes superseded by the Major Crimes Act,[38] with the remaining jurisdiction limited as to severity of punishment, and with Indian criminal justice directed primarily at rehabilitation of the offending Indian and compensation for the victim,[39] no great moral or practical harm would seem to result from allowing the Indian tribes to conduct their investigations and trials of petty Indian offenses against other Indians on Indian reservations as Indian custom and practice would permit. Indian witnesses before the subcommittee attempted to establish why this was desirable by pointing out the recognized responsibility of the tribe to treat defendants fairly and the burden that would be imposed on tribal courts by requiring adherence to unfamiliar procedure.[40]

The desirability of heeding such Indian pleas is emphasized by the *Miranda* requirements of warnings and counsel the moment police take a suspect into custody.[41] Questions can be raised as to whether *Miranda* requirements apply to petty offenses prosecuted in the state and federal courts,[42] and hence it is possible that they would have no application to offenses within the jurisdiction of the Indian courts. Until problems of this character have been more satisfactorily resolved, it seems unnecessary to complicate Indian proceedings with such problems which under Title II will undoubtedly be raised by legal counsel before the informal Indian courts.[43]

In this respect, it should be noted that the same Congress that

---

[37] Malloy v. Hogan, 378 U.S. 1 (1964), *overruling* Adamson v. California, 332 U.S. 46 (1947), *and* Twining v. New Jersey, 211 U.S. 78 (1908).

[38] See note 131 *infra*.

[39] Fretz, *supra* note 9, at 606.

[40] *Hearings on S.R. 58 Before Senate Subcommittee on Constitutional Rights*, 88th Cong., 1st Sess. 872-77 (1964); *Senate Hearings on Constitutional Rights*, *supra* note 6, at 90, 136, 138-39, 190-91, 193-94, 218; *Senate Hearings on Constitutional Rights*, 90th Cong., 2d Sess. 35-70 (1968).

[41] Miranda v. Arizona, 384 U.S. 436 (1966). For the latest development in the *Miranda* area see Orozco v. Texas, 37 U.S.L.W. 426 (March 25, 1969).

[42] *Miranda*, like its forerunner Escobedo v. Illinois, 378 U.S. 478 (1964), involved serious crimes ranging from kidnapping and rape to murder. Recently, the Court has limited the sixth amendment's guarantee of jury trial as applied to the states through the fourteenth amendment to offenses punishable by more than six months' imprisonment. Duncan v. Louisiana, 391 U.S. 145 (1968), Bloom v. Illinois, 391 U.S. 194 (1968), and Dyke v. Taylor Implement Mfg. Co., 391 U.S. 216 (1968). It remains to be seen whether this will be the dividing line for other guarantees. *But see* Mathis v. United States, 391 U.S. 1 (1968) requiring that *Miranda* warnings be given by several agents questioning prisoner in a state jail concerning his tax returns.

[43] *See* authorities cited note 40 *supra*; Fretz, *supra* note 9, at 602, 606.

adopted Title II has sought to "repeal" or at least alleviate, by the Omnibus Crime Control and Safe Streets Act of 1968,[44] what it must have considered to be the harmful effects of *Miranda* in the confessions area. Also, some states are apparently proceeding toward similar legislation.[45] It is difficult to believe that the administration of Indian justice will be helped or improved by the sudden imposition on Indian police and courts of procedures which are seriously questioned for federal and state courts.

The eminent domain clause, which prohibits the taking of private property for public use without just compensation, could also present difficult problems. Most Indian land is owned by the tribes, with the fee held in trust by the United States.[46] Occupancy of tribal land by members does not create vested rights in the occupant as against the tribe,[47] nor can a tribe vest title in a member without congressional authorization.[48] But occupancy by tribal members over a period of time does give rise to a use-right which in practice does not differ greatly from ownership in fee since the holder may inherit, devise, lease or sell his right to another tribal member.[49] It is possible that a use-right would be held compensable under the eminent domain provision, but more likely tribes will be held to have plenary power over tribal lands.[50] However, even though the eminent domain provision may not limit the tribes as to extinguishment of use-rights, the due process provision of paragraph (8) can still be used to prevent the tribe from extinguishing use-rights in an arbitrary manner.[51]

Some individual Indians own land allotted to their predecessors under the General Allotment Act of 1887, with the fee held in trust by the United States.[52] Allotted land within reservation boundaries is subject to tribal control,[53] and a "taking" of such land by a tribe would now seem compensable. Whether a taking would result from a tribe's effort to change current grazing, or other limited farming use of allotted land to further the tribe's communal good is another question. It is also possible that the eminent domain provision will be important for non-Indians who have acquired rights to (or on) reservation land.

Paragraph (6) extends the basic protections of the sixth amendment with the exception of the right to jury trial (but note that para-

[44] 18 U.S.C.A. § 3501 (Supp. 1969) (Title II).
[45] S. 53, Ariz. Leg., 1969 Sess.
[46] Berger, *Indian Mineral Interest — A Potential For Economic Advancement*, p. 675 *infra*.
[47] U.S. Dep't of Interior, Federal Indian Law 440 (1958).
[48] *Id.* at 441.
[49] Fretz, *supra* note 9, at 607.
[50] *See* Federal Indian Law, *supra* note 47, 440-44.
[51] Appendix I.
[52] Berger, *Indian Mineral Interest — A Potential For Economic Advancement*, p. 675 *infra*.
[53] U.S. Dep't of Interior, Federal Indian Law 440 (1958).

graph (10) guarantees a limited right of jury trial).[54] Also, instead of fully protecting the right to assistance of counsel, paragraph (6) gives only a right to the defendant "at his own expense to have the assistance of counsel for his defense." This limited right to counsel is, of course, coincident with the constitutional right that anyone has to retained counsel in federal and state criminal proceedings.[55] However, like the recently highly-developed right to assigned counsel,[56] this right to one's retained counsel has been closely related to the formalities and technicalities of criminal procedure in state and federal courts, including the confusing rules of evidence applied therein. There is considerable doubt whether a right to retained counsel is either necessary or desirable for the informal Indian trial.[57] The Indian practice of allowing the defendant to be advised and helped by another member of the tribe, familiar with the customs, practices, and procedures of the tribe,[58] would seem to afford as great (or greater) protection to the Indian defendant than this new statutory right to retained counsel. The statutory imposition on Indian trials of the requirements of Title II will probably impel the use of counsel; but, this is an argument against rather than for the desirability of Title II.

An inherent complication exists in the fact that many proceedings in tribal courts are still conducted in the native tongue[59] and since many Indian defendants may be able to communicate only in their native language, effective use of non-Indian counsel (assuming paragraph (6) opens Indian courts to non-Indian counsel) will be possible only to the extent that skilled interpreters can be made available. This complication would seem to raise the further possibility of Indian objections as to effective assistance of counsel.

A further problem is presented by the term "counsel." Does this refer to non-Indian lawyers who are members of a state bar, or can the term be limited to mean "counsel" as defined by the various tribal councils? State governments have great leeway in setting criteria for the practice of law. Indian tribes, as quasi-sovereignties, should arguably have the same leeway in drawing rules of admission for the practice of law before their tribal courts. In fact, the Navajos are considering doing so.[60] The tribes will not be able to discriminate unreasonably

---

[54] Appendix I.

[55] Chandler v. Fretag, 348 U.S. 3 (1954).

[56] United States v. Wade, 388 U.S. 218 (1967); Miranda v. Arizona, 384 U.S. 436 (1966); Escobedo v. Illinois, 378 U.S. 478 (1964); Gideon v. Wainwright, 372 U.S. 335 (1963).

[57] *See* Fretz, *supra* note 9, at 602-04.

[58] *Id.*

[59] *Senate Hearings on Constitutional Rights, supra* note 6, at 212-13.

[60] Letter from the Office of Indian Law, Arizona State University to the University of Arizona College of Law, Nov. 1, 1968, on file in the University of Arizona Law Library.

against non-Indians, but it is at least arguable that tribes would have a rational basis for excluding from tribal courts those not versed in Indian language, procedure and tradition.[61]

To the extent that funds will be insufficient, additional problems are posed. This could possibly be an area where the OEO (or some other government financed program) is encouraged to spend substantial sums of money to provide counsel for indigent Indians where no serious need exists (except possibly for the complications introduced by Title II). The situation is further complicated by the fact that legal aid programs are often composed largely of young and substantially inexperienced counsel, and their eagerness to insure that Indian defendants get the full benefit of their newly created statutory rights may surpass their ability to handle the difficult situation presented. Hence they may seriously complicate the usually informal Indian proceedings and in the long run harm rather than help the cause of law and order in many Indian communities. Further, the due process and equal protection requirements of paragraph (8) of Title II may be invoked under *Gideon v. Wainwright*[62] and *Griffin v. Illinois*,[63] to require assigned counsel in tribal courts, now that Indian defendants are given the statutory right to supply their own counsel.[64]

The Supreme Court has not yet extended *Gideon* beyond its "felony with serious penalty" holding. The jury trial decisions of the October 1967 term, distinguishing between petty offenses carrying not more than six months imprisonment (not requiring jury trial) and major offenses carrying greater penalties (and accordingly requiring jury trial), could suggest the dividing line for the constitutional requirement of assigned counsel.[65] If the latter should become the test, the six months imprisonment limitation of paragraph (7) of Title II arguably exempts tribal courts from any requirement for assigned counsel. On the other hand,

---

[61] The Office of Indian Law, Arizona State University, takes a contra position on the ground that "a rule requiring all attorneys to be able to speak the tribal language . . . would . . . exclude professional attorneys entirely." *Id.* If one defines "professional attorneys" as non-Indians admitted to their respective state bars, this is true, but that is the very question courts will have to answer. *See* Fretz, *supra* note 9, at 602.

[62] 372 U.S. 335 (1963).

[63] 351 U.S. 12 (1956).

[64] Griffin v. Illinois, 351 U.S. 12 (1956), and its progeny establish that equal protection of the laws requires states (and fifth amendment due process requires the federal government) to furnish the poor man all the procedural protections which his wealthier brother is allowed if he pays for them. On counsel, see Douglas v. California, 372 U.S. 353 (1963), holding the *Griffin* principle applicable to require appointment of counsel in indigent appeals. *See generally* textual note in N. DOWLING & G. GUNTHER, CONSTITUTIONAL LAW 778-85 (7th ed. 1965).

From conversations with Indians this writer gets the impression that few Indians will avail themselves of the right to retained counsel (unless persuaded to do so by outside influences) partly because of the Indian's greater trust in the advice and help of his fellow tribesmen and because of his lack of funds.

[65] Dyke v. Taylor Implement Mfg. Co., 391 U.S. 216 (1968); Bloom v. Illinois, 391 U.S. 194 (1968); Duncan v. Louisiana, 391 U.S. 145 (1968).

Griffin's doctrine that due process and equal protection require that states afford to the indigent all procedural protections that are afforded to those who can afford them might well be invoked to require assigned counsel. Thus paragraph (6) may have unwittingly imposed the expense of assigned counsel which many tribes cannot afford.[66]

Paragraph (7) includes the protections of the eighth amendment (no excessive bail, no excessive fines and no cruel and unusual punishment), and adds that tribal courts may not impose a punishment greater than imprisonment for a term of six months or a fine of $500, or both.[67] It is difficult to appraise the effect of these requirements upon tribal procedures without having a substantially complete knowledge of the practices in holding (or releasing) Indian prisoners prior to trial (as to the bail problem) and in imposing punishment within the limited jurisdiction that tribal courts exercise (as to the protections against excessive fines and cruel and unusual punishment). The protection against excessive fines would not seem to present a serious problem, since the maximum fine is limited to $500. It must be remembered, however, that a $500 fine (or even a $100 fine) might well be excessive for an Indian, although it would not be for the average white man. Generally, though, Indian punishment is lenient when considered in relation to the white man's norms.[68]

A major problem could arise under paragraph (7) as to chronic alcoholism which may be a disease and not subject to punishment because of the protection against cruel and unusual punishment. Although *Powell v. Texas*,[69] sustained (by 5-4 vote) punishment for being drunk in a public place, five justices of the Supreme Court agreed that habitual alcoholism *could be* a disease not subject to punishment under the doctrine of *Robinson v. California*,[70] which held that drug addiction could not be punished. Because one of the major problems on Indian reservations is the tendency of Indians to abuse the use of alcohol,[71] tribal courts will be faced with the difficult problem of applying the law which so sharply split the Court in *Powell*.

Paragraph (8) provides for equal protection and due process for "persons within its [the tribe's] jurisdiction."[72] While there is an initial problem under paragraph (8) in determining who are persons within the tribe's jurisdiction,[73] the major difficulty will be in determining the

---

[66] *Senate Hearings on Constitutional Rights, supra* note 6, at 65, 92, 138-39, 190, 342.
[67] Appendix I.
[68] *See* Fretz, *supra* note 9, at 605-06.
[69] 392 U.S. 651 (1968).
[70] 370 U.S. 660 (1962).
[71] *Senate Hearings on Constitutional Rights*, 88th Cong., 1st Sess., 886-87 (1964). *See* A. YOUNG, THE NAVAJO YEARBOOK 280-84 (1961).
[72] Appendix I.
[73] *See* Dodge v. Nakai, Civil No. 1209 (D. Ariz., Feb. 28, 1969), where the

meaning of equal protection and due process in the Indian context. Every lawyer is aware that the Supreme Court has recognized that it would be unwise and perhaps impossible to define due process of law with clarity and finality and, consequently, has determined its scope on a case by case basis.[74] To the extent that generalization is possible, substantive due process has been treated as a matter of reasonableness with a high degree of finality accorded legislative determinations,[75] except in the area of first amendment freedoms.[76] For example, since the middle thirties, economic legislation has consistently withstood challenges based on unreasonableness.[77] In the first amendment context (speech, press, religion, association), due process has included the development of the "clear and present danger test,"[78] its partial (if not complete) demise in *Dennis v. United States*,[79] and the subsequent tendency of the Court to speak of a "balancing" approach even in the first amendment freedoms area.[80] Thus subjecting tribal laws and regulations to general due process objections could create a lawyer's paradise for litigation, and certainly allows the federal courts to play a substantial role in governing tribal affairs.

The case of *Dodge v. Nakai*,[81] illustrates the point. Along with holding the exclusion of Mitchell an abridgement of free speech, the court held that the exclusion was lacking in due process since the advisory council's reasons for so acting did not meet one of the grounds for exclusion as set forth in the Navajo Tribal Code, nothwithstanding the tribe's contention that the Treaty of 1868 gave it the absolute right to exclude non-Indians from the reservation.[82]

Equal protection objections have followed the due process pattern

---

advisory council of the Navajo Tribe's attempt to exclude the non-Indian director of the Navajo legal aid program was held to be a denial of due process. Obviously the non-Indian was a "person within [the tribe's] jurisdiction." *See also* discussion in Note, *supra* note 20a, at 1353, 1368-71.

[74] Davidson v. New Orleans, 96 U.S. 97, 104 (1877) stating that the meaning of due process must be determined only by "the gradual process of judicial inclusion and exclusion." Twining v. New Jersey, 211 U.S. 78 (1908). *See* 3 W. WILLOUGHBY, ON THE CONSTITUTION OF THE UNITED STATES § 1135 at 1685 (2d ed. 1929); Kadish, *Methodology and Criteria in Due Process Adjudication — A Survey and Criticism*, 66 YALE L.J. 319 (1957).

[75] Day-Bright Lighting, Inc. v. Missouri, 342 U.S. 421 (1952); Lincoln Fed. Labor Union v. Northwestern Iron & Metal Co., 335 U.S. 525 (1949); Nebbia v. New York, 291 U.S. 502 (1934); Jacobson v. Massachusetts, 197 U.S. 11 (1905).

[76] United States v. Carolene Prod. Co., 304 U.S. 144, 152 n.4 (1938).

[77] *See* Day-Bright Lighting, Inc. v. Missouri, 342 U.S. 421 (1952); Lincoln Fed. Labor Union v. Northwestern Iron & Metal Co., 335 U.S. 525 (1949); Nebbia v. New York, 291 U.S. 502 (1934). *See also* N. DOWLING & G. GUNTHER, CONSTITUTIONAL LAW 899 (7th ed. 1965).

[78] *See* Mendelson, *Clear and Present Danger — From Schenck to Dennis*, 52 COLUM. L. REV. 313 (1952).

[79] 341 U.S. 494 (1951).

[80] Communist Party of America v. Subversive Activities Control Bd., 367 U.S. 1 (1961); Konigsberg v. State Bar, 366 U.S. 36 (1961). *Cf.* United States v. O'Brien, 391 U.S. 367 (1968); Pickering v. Board of Educ., 391 U.S. 563 (1968).

[81] Civil No. 1209 (D. Ariz., Feb. 28, 1969).

[82] *Id.* at 12.

of allowing reasonable classification in the accomplishment of legislative controls with a high degree of finality attaching to legislative determinations.[83]   But, the equal protection requirement when applied to tribal actions raises additional problems.   For instance, does *Reynolds v. Sims*[84] mean that the "one-man, one-vote" requirement must apply in the selection of tribal councils?   How will it affect those tribes which deny women the vote and those which exclude some adult males from the selection of tribal leaders?   One recent comment states:

> The majority of the New Mexico pueblos do not elect their legislative body, the pueblo council. In the more traditional minded pueblos, the council is chosen by religious societies in a manner not fully known to the outsider. Some pueblos put basic questions of policy to a vote in a so-called "general meeting" of the members. However, the "general meeting" almost always consists of the men only and even then not all men are allowed to vote. One pueblo is governed by a constitution approved by the Secretary of the Interior which provides for an election of the pueblo governor and leaders of the council. Only male heads of households over 21 years of age are allowed to vote, the adult women and other adult males being excluded. The governor and council leaders voted into office then select the remaining council members . . . . If the standards of the reapportionment cases are applied to the . . . pueblos, considerable modification of their governmental form will have to be effected.[85]

Unquestionably, specific aspects of due process and equal protection that have developed in relation to federal and state action will require careful judicial reappraisal before being applied to tribal action.

Paragraph (9) extends to the tribes the bill of attainder and ex post facto law protections of article one of the Constitution.[86]   In addi-

---

[83] *See* Williamson v. Lee Optical Co., 348 U.S. 483 (1955); Day-Bright Lighting, Inc. v. Missouri, 342 U.S. 421 (1952); N. DOWLING & G. GUNTHER, CONSTITUTIONAL LAW 881-900 (7th ed. 1965).

[84] 377 U.S. 533 (1964). *Reynolds* was recently extended to local governments in Avery v. Midland County, 390 U.S. 474 (1968), where, in a 5-3 opinion, the Court held "that the Constitution permits no substantial variation from equal population in drawing districts for units of local governments having general governmental powers over the entire geographic area served by the body." *Id.* at 485. Testifying before the subcommittee, Marvin J. Sonosky, Esq., appearing on behalf of tribes in Montana, Wyoming, and North Dakota, stated:

> Reapportionment on the basis of one man, one vote would probably result in abolishing all districts and election of members of governing bodies at large. I hesitate to forecast the disruptive effects on stable tribal governments.
>
> We are sure the committee will appreciate that the United States cannot make Indian tribes over in its own image. Indian tribes cannot be expected to become miniature U.S. governments. The answer must fit the problem. We cannot resolve the tribal problem by imposing what we regard as the answer to our own problem; namely, the structures of the Constitution of the United States. *Senate Hearings on Constitutional Rights, supra* note 7, at 131.

[85] VII ALBUQUERQUE BAR J., No. 5, at 3-4 (1968).

[86] Appendix I.

tion to its holdings regarding free speech and due process, the court in *Dodge v. Nakai,* held that the order of exclusion constituted an unlawful bill of attainder, defined by the court as "a legislative act which inflicts punishment without a judicial trial."[87] The court did recognize that "the form of government utilized on the Navajo Reservation does not lend itself to the nice categorizations that may be made where the branches of government are more distinct," since "with respect to enforcement of the power of exclusion, the Navajo Tribal Code vests the Advisory Committee [an executive branch] with judicial powers."[88] Nevertheless, the court concluded that the advisory council here acted in a legislative capacity since the order was not based on "the interpretation and individual application of existing rules of general application," and since the exclusion constituted punishment within the meaning of *Kennedy v. Mendoza-Martinez.*[89] Given the different nature of tribal government, prediction as to the specific meaning of these protections in the tribal context will be difficult, especially in light of the difficulties the Supreme Court has had in applying them to federal action.[90]

Paragraph (10) extends the right to trial by jury of six persons in any case where imprisonment is possible.[91] It would seem questionable whether this requirement should be imposed on Indian courts, particularly since the Supreme Court in 1968 held that where imprisonment for six months or less is the maximum punishment a jury trial is not required of state courts.[92] The six months imprisonment limit also marks the petty trial jurisdiction of United States Commissioners, who act without juries. Under such circumstances, it would not seem essential that tribal courts should be required to afford juries unless tribal laws provide for them.

The discussion of Title II is not complete without noting that in the legislation proposed to the 89th Congress (Senate bills 961-68) Senate bill 962 provided for appeal to the United States District Court, with a trial de novo, from any conviction in an Indian court in which the accused was deprived of a constitutional right. Further, Senate bill 963 would have authorized and directed the Attorney General to

---

[87] Civil No. 1209 at 14 (D. Ariz., Feb. 28, 1969).
[88] *Id.* at 15.
[89] *Id.* at 16.   372 U.S. 144 (1963).
[90] *See* Fleming v. Nestor, 363 U.S. 603 (1960); United States v. Brown, 381 U.S. 437 (1965).
[91] Appendix I.
[92] Duncan v. Louisiana, 391 U.S. 145 (1968); Bloom v. Illinois, 391 U.S. 194 (1968); Dyhe v. Taylor Implement Mfg. Co., 391 U.S. 216 (1968). And note that, in holding that these decisions should have no retroactive effect, DeStefano v. Woods, 392 U.S. 631, (1968), the Court repeated its statement in *Duncan* that, "[w]e would not assert, however, that every criminal trial — or any particular trial — held before a judge alone is unfair or that a defendant may never be as fairly treated by a judge as he would be by a jury." *Id.* at 158.

investigate Indian complaints alleging deprivation of a constitutional right (whether by tribal, state, federal, or other action) and, on the basis of the investigation to bring an appropriate civil or criminal action to vindicate and secure such right.[93] Both of these procedures were omitted from the bills introduced in the 90th Congress, seemingly on the recommendation of the Department of the Interior. In the substitute bill which it proposed to the Subcommittee on Constitutional Rights, the Department substituted for the appeal to the federal courts, a provision for habeas corpus by any person under detention by order of an Indian tribe,[94] and omitted entirely the procedure of filing a complaint with the Attorney General. Earlier in the hearings Solicitor Barry had argued that the original appeals procedure would unduly burden already overburdened federal courts and that the specific provisions for complaint to the Attorney General were unnecessary in that, under existing practice of the Department of Interior, complaints of Indians were always forwarded to his Department for investigation.[95]

The Department of the Interior's recommendation may have been administratively sound, in that it doesn't divide authority or involve the possibility of the Attorney General's office being charged with investigation of complaints by Indians against the Bureau of Indian Affairs or the Interior Department. However, much of the Indian testimony before the subcommittee leaves the impression that the Indian tribes, and also individual Indians, had more justifiable grounds for complaining of deprivation of rights by the federal government, state courts and administrative officials,[96] than for concern about individual Indians being seriously hurt by tribal actions. Thus, Title II as enacted does little to alleviate the major source of the Indian's complaints.

As for the elimination of the procedure of direct appeal, which was originally provided for in Senate bill 962, there is little doubt that the provision for a de novo hearing on such appeal was a needless complication, and Senator Ervin's recommendation that the de novo feature be eliminated was sound.[97] But, it would seem equally clear that direct appeal to the federal district court in any case would provide a more effective procedure for implementing the rights conferred in Title II, than the provision for habeas corpus relief, assuming arguendo the protections Title II affords Indians against tribal action was desirable. The habeas corpus procedure allows relief only when the punishment imposed by an Indian court is imprisonment. Intrusion on Title II rights in a criminal proceeding resulting in a penalty other than confinement,

---

[93] *Senate Hearings on Constitutional Rights, supra* note 6, at 6-8.
[94] *Id.* at 18-22.
[95] *Id.*
[96] *Senate Hearings on Constitutional Rights.* 89th Cong., 1st Sess. 817-71 (1964).
[97] *Id.*

or from civil action not involving confinement, is left without remedy as far as Title II is concerned.[98]

It would appear that federal jurisdiction will be found in many situations pursuant to 28 *United States Code* section 1343(4) (1964), which states:

> The district courts shall have original jurisdiction of any civil action authorized by law to be commenced by any person . . . .
>   (4) To recover damages or to secure equitable or other relief under any Act of Congress providing for the protection of civil rights, including the right to vote.[99]

In the recent Supreme Court case of *Allen v. State Board of Elections*,[100] a declaratory judgment action was instituted by private citizens against states to compel compliance with the Voting Rights Act of 1965.[101] The Act does not expressly authorize such actions on the part of private citizens, but the Court found jurisdiction pursuant to section 1343(4), since

> [t]he Act was drafted to make the guarantee of the Fifteenth Amendment . . . a reality for all citizens [and since] [t]he achievement of the Act's laudable goal could be severely hampered . . . if each citizen were required to depend solely on litigation instituted at the discretion of the Attorney General.
>
>   . . . . .
>   . . . [A] federal statute passed to protect a class of citizens, although not specifically authorizing members of the protected class to institute suit, nevertheless implie[s] a private right of action.[102]

If fear of burdening the federal courts was a major reason for eliminating the appeal provision, it is possible that as great (or greater) burdens will be imposed by counsel seeking relief under other federal jurisdiction statutes such as the Federal Declaratory Judgments Act,[103] or the above discussed section 1343.

As to habeas corpus, Solicitor Barry, in arguing against Senate bill 962 and for the Department of the Interior's substitute, testified to the subcommittee in part:

---

[98] The normal result would be that in any claim of violation of the rights guaranteed by Title II not within the habeas corpus procedural protection, the complainant could get relief in the federal courts only if his case comes within the jurisdiction of federal courts as provided for by Congress in other statutes. *E.g.* 28 U.S.C. § 1343(4) (1964). *See* Turner v. Bank of North America, 4 U.S. (4 Dall.) 6 (1799); H. HART & H. WECHSLER, THE FEDERAL COURTS AND THE FEDERAL SYSTEM ch. IV. (1953). *See also Ex parte* McCardle, 74 U.S. (7 Wall.) 506 (1868); N. DOWLING & G. GUNTHER, CONSTITUTIONAL LAW 75-76 (7th ed. 1965).
[99] The court in Dodge v. Nakai, Civil No. 1209 (D. Ariz., Feb. 28, 1969), followed this route in granting relief to the director of the DNA.
[100] 89 S. Ct. 817 (1969).
[101] 42 U.S.C. § 1973 (Supp. I, 1965).
[102] 89 S. Ct. at 826-27.
[103] 28 U.S.C. §§ 2201-02 (1964).

I think it ought to be borne in mind that there are no offenses over which Indian tribal courts have jurisdiction which carry a penalty of more than 6 months in jail. These would be classed as misdemeanors in most jurisdictions. While it is very easy to deprive a person of his civil rights in such cases, a very large number of cases would burden the dockets of a rather small number of district courts if, as provided in the bill, S. 962, an Indian, by claiming his constitutional rights were violated, would get a trial de novo before a jury in a district court. We have proposed a substitute appellate judicial procedure which I think could be regarded as transitional. At least, it would not last any longer than the independent tribal governments would last.[104]

This reasoning of Solicitor Barry may have been sound support for the habeas corpus procedure he was proposing for Senate bill 962, but in each of its major aspects it supports the thesis that Title II might well have been left out of this legislation and reliance placed on Titles III to VII (see discussion *infra*) for the accomplishment of the legislation's asserted purposes. The argument that trials in Indian courts (because of the limit on the punishment) are too petty in character to justify the burden that would be imposed on the federal district courts by providing for appeals thereto suggests that perhaps Indian court trials are so petty in nature as not to warrant imposing on Indian tribes the requirements of Title II. The argument that the legislation will operate only for a transitional period, until complete assimilation occurs, cuts strongly in favor of not imposing unnecessary intrusions on tribal sovereignty during that period.[105]

TITLE III — MODEL CODE GOVERNING COURTS OF INDIAN OFFENSES

Title III authorizes and directs the Secretary of the Interior in consultation with the Indians, Indian tribes, and interested federal agencies, to recommend to the Congress, on or before July 1, 1968, a model code to govern the administration of justice by "*courts of Indian offenses*" so that individuals tried thereby shall have "*the same rights, privileges, and immunities under* the United States Constitution as would be guaranteed any citizen *being tried in a federal court for any similar offense.*"[106] (emphasis added). The section further requires that the code provide for: notice to defendants of their rights under the United States Constitution[107] and under applicable tribal constitutions; proper qualifica-

---

[104] *Senate Hearings on Constitutional Rights, supra* note 6, at 22.

[105] It is interesting to note, that the Pueblos of New Mexico have introduced a bill in the 90th Congress to exclude them from the provisions of Title II. H.R. 3397, 90th Cong., 2d Sess. (1968).

[106] Appendix I.

[107] Does this suggest that there are *Indian rights protected by the Constitution?* See note 17 and related text *supra*.

tions for judges in courts of Indian offenses; and for the establishment of classes for the training of such judges.[108]

At the outset, it might be noted that the deadline of July 1, 1968 was an impossible one, that Congress adjourned in 1968 without appropriating funds to carry out the direction to the Secretary of the Interior,[109] and that as of the date of preparation of this article, no model code had been prepared by the Secretary. Assuming that appropriations are provided and that the Secretary fulfills his responsibility, certain problems will arise.

It can be seen that Title III differs from Title II in that "courts of Indian offenses" are required to provide *the same* protections as prevail in the federal courts. If this requirement were applied to all tribal courts, Title II's selective application of certain protections would be negated. However, Title III would seem to apply only to those courts established by the Secretary of the Interior under 25 *Code of Federal Regulations* section 11.1 (1968).

There are three types of Indian courts.

(1) a court of Indian offenses, in which judges are Indians appointed by the Secretary of the Interior and procedural rules have been drafted by the Secretary [25 C.F.R. § 11.1 (1968)]; (2) a tribal court, in which judges are chosen under tribal law and written rules have been approved by the Secretary, and (3) a traditional court, which functions only in each of the Rio Grande pueblos, with procedures which are relatively unknown to outsiders.[110]

In its 1964 summary report, the Subcommittee on Constitutional Rights reported in part:

In 1934, Secretary of the Interior Ickes established a committee to review the status of law and order on Indian reservations. The result of this review was the present day judicial codes of the courts of Indian offenses and the tribal courts applicable to Indians living on reservations. Section 11.1 through 11.306, title 25, of the Code of Federal Regulations describe the jurisdiction and procedure of the court of Indian offenses. During the same period, the Indian Reorganization

---

[108] *Id.*

[109] Section 302 of Title III, authorizes the appropriation of "such sum as may be necessary to carry out the provisions of this Title." Appendix I. In response to inquiry of his Congressman, Morris K. Udall (Arizona), the author was informed on Dec. 17, 1968, that the Deputy Solicitor of the Interior Department had called to the attention of the appropriate congressional committee the impossibility of the target date and also that the appropriation authorized by section 302, like that authorized by section 701(c) of Title VII for updating various publications as discussed *infra*, had not been made. Apparently, the target date was the one set earlier in the statute's history and the need for change was overlooked when it quickly became a rider to the 1968 Civil Rights Act. As of Dec. 17, 1968, there was no indication as to when the directed programs for the Department of the Interior would be undertaken or completed.

[110] Fretz, *supra* note 9, at 583.

Act authorized the establishment of tribal organizations and required that formal codes of law and order be written and approved by the Secretary of Interior. Today, there are 53 tribal courts, 12 courts of Indian offenses, and approximately 19 traditional courts.

The traditional Indian courts bear little, if any, resemblance to the tribal courts and the courts of Indian offenses. As their name implies, traditional courts operate according to the dictates of tribal custom without formal machinery or written guidelines. . . .

Philleo Nash, Commissioner of Indian Affairs, describes traditional courts as having '. . . no separation; no code; no written ordinances . . . .'[111]

Assuming the above remarks describe approximately the nature of Indian courts, there would seem to be little chance the words "courts of Indian offenses" could be construed to include all tribal courts. Senator Ervin, Chairman of the Senate subcommittee, in testifying in 1968 before the House committee charged with considering the legislation, stated:

Title II would be directed only toward Courts of Indian Offenses, which are to be carefully distinguished from tribal courts. At the present time there are no more than *five* courts of Indian Offenses in existence. Therefore, even if Congress were to enact the model code to be recommended by the Secretary of the Interior, it would apply only to *five* presently existing courts, none of which has been or will be established in the Pueblo nation.

Consequently, no tribe should fear Title II, for its only purpose is to provide a model code after which Indian tribal governments might wish to pattern their own. It should be also noted that the Secretary of the Interior is directed to consult with Indians and Indian tribes in drawing up the code, and cannot, therefore, act capriciously upon his own notions.[112] (emphasis added).

The courts of Indian offenses were established by the Secretary of the Interior to handle situations where there was insufficient tribal organization (or for some other reason no effective system of judicial organization was in operation).[113] In origin and current operation, they are more directly arms of the federal government than the other Indian courts and accordingly would be more likely to be subject to the constitutional limitations imposed on federal action.[114] Under such analysis, Title III's requirement that the model code assure defendants before such courts all the rights of defendants before federal courts for similar

---

[111] *Senate Hearings on Constitutional Rights, Summary Report,* 88th Cong., 2d Sess. 15 (1964).

[112] *House Subcomm. on Indian Affairs, supra* note 15, at 136.

[113] 25 C.F.R. § 11.1 (1968). Davis, *Criminal Jurisdiction Over Indian Country In Arizona,* 1 ARIZ. L. REV. 62, 91 (1959).

[114] *See* Colliflower v. Garland, 342 F.2d 369 (9th Cir. 1965). *See also* note 15 *supra.*

offenses could be considered but statutory (and subsequently administrative) confirmation of rights already protected by the constitution. This would explain the suggestion under Title III of the imposition of *all* constitutional procedural protections currently existing in other federal courts, as distinguished from Title II's application to tribal action of only certain protections similar to constitutional guarantees.

Much of the early testimony before the Senate subcommittee indicates that the provision enabling the Secretary of the Interior to propose a model code for Indian offenses was thought of as being one for voluntary adoption of the code by Indian tribes for their tribal courts as well as a new code for the courts of Indian offenses (in lieu of the existing and outmoded provisions of Title 25 of the United States Code). As such the proposal for a model code was opposed by Solicitor Barry, speaking for the Department of the Interior. He argued that the Indian tribes are too diverse for a single code and though the Department of the Interior could prepare a "sufficiently elastic" model code, "you finally reach a point where it ceases to be a model."[115] He also stated:

> [S]ince the long-term objective of the administration of Indian Affairs is to secure the smooth assimilation of the Indian people into our society, we think that Indian codes should conform as much as possible to the substantive and procedural laws of the States in which the Indians live. Since the codes in various States differ, a uniform code for Indian tribes would frustrate this objective.[116]

One witness pointed out to the subcommittee that Title 25 of the *Code of Federal Regulations* already provides a model code.[117] However, in its reports favoring adoption of Title III, the subcommittee indicated that it felt Title 25 was out-of-date and that it needed careful revision.[118] A review of the hearings since 1961 reveals support for the subcommittee's position.[119] The reason for this support is not difficult

---

[115] *Senate Hearings on Constitutional Rights, supra* note 6, at 28. Solicitor Barry also stated: "We recommend against the enactment of this bill. Our reasons for so recommending are that the Indian tribes are widely diverse and that a code appropriate for one tribe might be wholly inappropriate for another." *Id.* at 20.

[116] *Id.* at 20.

[117] *Id.* at 104 (testimony of Emory Sekaquaptewa, Sr., Chief Judge, Hopi Reservation, Keams Canyon, Ariz.).

[118] *Senate Hearings on Constitutional Rights, Summary Report*, 88th Cong., 2d Sess. 17 (1964) states:

> The Code of Indian Offenses (which appears in the Code of Federal Regulations) is outmoded and impractical. For example, challenges for cause, as well as peremptory challenges in the selection of a jury are limited to three. A jury may render a verdict by majority vote. Witnesses answering subpoenas are paid 50 cents a day, although witnesses testifying voluntarily are, at the court's discretion, paid for their actual traveling and living expenses by the party calling them. The wide disparity between sentences in Indian courts and in Federal and State courts for identical crimes already has been noted. (footnotes omitted).

[119] *E.g., Senate Hearings on Constitutional Rights, Summary Report*, 89th Cong., 1st Sess. 16 (1965).

to ascertain. Upon completion of the model code the Interior Department's courts of Indian offenses will be subject to the same constitutional procedural requirements which are effective in the federal court system (and to a considerable degree applicable in state courts), but for all other Indian courts the code will only serve as a model for adoption by the organized Indian tribes for their tribal courts as soon as they are prepared to accept it.[120] The process of gradual education of the Indian communities affected would seem to be the most desirable way of accomplishing the desired purpose of smooth integration of Indian systems of justice into the existing surrounding state and federal systems. This approach is fully consistent with the new Indian policy expressed in Title IV, *infra,* which now requires the referendum consent of Indian governments before a state can assert jurisdiction over tribal affairs.[121] It is, of course, inconsistent with the blanket imposition of Title II.

Indeed, the need for flexibility in developing codes for the courts of Indian offenses and for the Indian tribes, as urged by Solicitor Barry in opposition to the model code would seem to be a stronger argument *against* Title II than it was against Title III. The statement of an Indian, Cato W. Valandra, President, United Sioux Tribes, St. Francis, South Dakota (supported by a number of others representing the nine Sioux Tribes), is an eloquent expression of a point of view which seems quite sound:

> I want to say at the outset, that American Indian tribes certainly support the fundamental protection given to individuals by the Constitution of the United States. I am not aware of any constitutional rights which have been taken from any member of an Indian tribe by its governing body.
>
> . . . There have been cases where Indian judges have acted beyond their authority and have deprived Indians of their liberty or other rights without a fair trial.
>
> According to the Supreme Court cases I have been reading about in the papers, the same thing happens in the white man's courts. We agree there should be some way of protecting individuals in their basic rights. But we think this can be done by the tribes themselves through the enactment of codes of justice, containing provisions which will give substantially all of the constitutional protection S. 961 would give.
>
> . . . . .
>
> . . . We believe if this is done, legislation such as S. 961 and S. 962 [for which Title II was substituted] would not be necessary.[122]

---

[120] Note that the Navajo Tribe and the Mescalero Apaches felt that responsibility for the model code should not rest with the BIA and the Department of the Interior but with an independent contractor under supervision of the American Bar Association, or with an independent study commission. *Id.* at 17.

[121] Appendix I.

[122] *Senate Hearings on Constitutional Rights, Summary Report,* 88th Cong., 2d Sess. 147-48 (1964).

TITLE IV — JURISDICTION OVER CRIMINAL AND CIVIL ACTIONS

This Title seems intended to accomplish a major and desirable change in the policy adopted by the federal government with the passage of Public Law 280 in 1953.[123] That policy was to give to certain named states, and others as they might choose, the complete authority to assert criminal and civil jurisdiction over Indian country.

During the subcommittee hearings and investigations, it was indicated that Public Law 280 had resulted in a breakdown in the administration of justice in Indian country because of the failure of states to implement their authority.[124] There was considerable evidence to show: that because Public Law 280 conferred total jurisdiction over Indian reservations, many states would need subsidies from the federal government to adequately enforce the law on the reservations;[125] that piecemeal cession of jurisdiction over Indian countries would be more feasible;[126] that the administration of justice on many reservations had completely broken down since Public Law 280 had authorized the unilateral application of state law to all tribes without their consent and regardless of their needs and special circumstances;[127] and that tribal laws were unnecessarily pre-empted by Public Law 280 and, as a consequence, tribal government could not govern their tribal communities effectively.[128]

Accepting the fact that many (if not all) of these criticisms were valid, Title IV attempts to remedy the situation by providing for future assumption of criminal and civil jurisdiction by the states over Indian reservations within their respective boundaries only with the consent of the Indian tribe, such consent to be established by majority vote at a special election held for that purpose.[129] This Title is a comprehensive effort to correct the major mistake of Public Law 280 in its provision for integrating Indian reservations without their consent into the states in which they are located. A clear preponderance of testimony before the subcommittee supports the conclusion that state assumption of criminal and civil jurisdiction has been successful only when undertaken with the consent and cooperation of the Indian tribes.[130] In requiring

---

[123] 18 U.S.C. § 1162 (1964). For a discussion of the unsatisfactory operation of Public Law 280 see, THE INDIAN, supra note 11, at 184-90.
[124] Senate Hearing on Constitutional Rights, Summary Report, 88th Cong., 2d Sess. 9-14 (1964); Senate Hearings on Constitutional Rights, Summary Report, 89th Cong., 2d Sess. 19 (1966).
[125] Senate Hearings on Constitutional Rights, Summary Report, 89th Cong., 2d Sess. 20 (1966); Senate Hearings on Constitutional Rights, supra note 6, at 11, 344.
[126] Senate Hearings on Constitutional Rights, Summary Report, 88th Cong., 2d Sess. 13 (1964).
[127] Senate Hearings on Constitutional Rights, supra note 6, at 11, 148-49.
[128] Id.
[129] Appendix I.
[130] See authorities cited notes 9-13 supra; THE INDIAN, supra note 11.

such consent for the future, and in providing the methods for correcting existing unsuccessful assimilations, Title IV is a step in the right direction.

TITLE V — OFFENSES WITHIN INDIAN COUNTRY

This Title merely adds the offense of assault resulting in serious bodily injury to the 12 other offenses already covered by the Major Crimes Act.[131] There was considerable evidence and argument before the committee that this offense should be added to the jurisdiction of the federal courts because of the failure of most Indian courts to punish severely enough.[132] While Title V represents a slight infringement on Indian sovereignty, the hearings showed no substantial criticism of the Major Crimes Act, nor of the proposed Title V. Since the Civil Rights Act sets six months imprisonment as the maximum punishment that may be imposed, it would seem proper that aggravated assault be included in the "major crimes" for prosecution in federal court.

TITLE VI — EMPLOYMENT OF LEGAL COUNSEL

During the committee's hearings, it developed that many tribes were complaining about delay in securing from the Secretary of the Interior, or the Commissioner of Indian Affairs, the required approval of contracts or agreements relating to the employment of legal counsel.[133] Title VI seeks to remedy this situation by providing that if such approval is neither granted nor denied within 90 days following the making of application for the same, such approval shall be deemed to have been granted.[134] Although the Interior Department has taken steps to remedy the long delays that were occurring some years ago in giving approval to tribal counsel, the Solicitor for the Department testified to the committee that it seemed unwise to have contracts for counsel become automatically valid if not approved (or disapproved) within 90 days.[135] The subcommittee nevertheless recommended the statute and Congress accepted the recommendation. It would seem desirable that the Interior Department comply in good faith with this requirement of timely approval, or disapproval, of Indian contracts for counsel.

---

[131] Appendix I. The Major Crimes Act, 18 U.S.C. § 1153 (1964), now provides for trial in the federal courts of any Indian committing within Indian country any of the following offenses: murder, manslaughter, rape, carnal knowledge of any female under sixteen (not his wife), assault with intent to commit rape, incest, assault with intent to kill, assault with a dangerous weapon, assault resulting in serious bodily injury, arson, burglary, robbery, and larceny. *See generally* Comment, *Indictment Under the "Major Crimes Act" — An Exercise in Unfairness and Unconstitutionality,* p. 691 *infra.*

[132] *Senate Hearings on Constitutional Rights, supra* note 6 at 68.

[133] *Id.* at 21, 39-48.

[134] Appendix I.

[135] *Senate Hearings on Constitutional Rights, supra* note 6, at 39-48. The Solicitor felt that the statute would force disapproval during the 90-day period, which could under present procedures be satisfactorily adjusted. He felt that the automatic validation through lapse of time would hinder negotiation more than it would help it.

TITLE VII — MATERIALS RELATING TO CONSTITUTIONAL RIGHTS OF INDIANS

This Title requires the Secretary of the Interior to: have the document which is entitled "Indian Affairs, Laws and Treaties" revised to date and kept annually current through publication at the Government Printing Office; have revised and republished the Department of the Interior's treatise entitled "Federal Indian Law"; and to the extent feasible, have prepared an accurate compilation of the opinions (published or unpublished) of the Solicitor of the Department of the Interior relating to Indian affairs and to have such compilation printed at the Government Printing Offices.[136] Senator Ervin submitted a statement to the House Subcommittee on Indian Affairs supporting Title VII:

> The need for adequate and up-to-date research tools in the area of Indian affairs is pronounced. If our Indian citizens are to receive benefits in full measure from their own efforts, as well as from the activities of their attorneys and of scholars working on their behalf, full and easy access must be had to relevant documentary sources. Instances of out-of-print, out-of-date and out-of-circulation materials must be corrected.[137]

Only good can come from full compliance with Title VII.

CONCLUSION

The Senate Subcommittee on Constitutional Rights of the Committee on the Judiciary, in submitting to the 89th Congress its conclusions and recommendations concerning the Senate bills which in substance were carried into the above discussed Titles of the Civil Rights Act of 1968, stated that its position was essentially that of the House Committee on Indian Affairs reporting to the 23rd Congress in 1834:

> The committee are [sic] aware of the intrinsic difficulties of the subject — of providing a system of laws and of administration, simple and economical, and, at the same time, efficient and liberal — that shall be suited to the various conditions and relations of those for whose benefit it is intended; and that shall, with a due regard to the rights of our own citizens, meet the just expectations of the country in fulfillment of its proper and assumed obligations to the Indian tribes. Yet, so manifestly defective and inadequate is our present system, that an immediate revision seems to be imperiously demanded. What is now proposed is only an approximation to a perfect system. Much

---

Abundant testimony, however, favored imposing a time limit that the Secretary should be required to meet.
[136] Appendix I.
[137] *House Subcomm. on Indian Affairs, supra* note 15, at 134.

is necessarily left for the present to executive discretion, and still more to future legislation.[138]

Revision of existing Federal Indian policy was needed and Titles III - VII, properly implemented, offer excellent possibilities for accomplishing fair and successful integration of the American Indian into his proper place in our state and federal governments. But, the desirability of imposing on tribal governments the requirements of Title II is doubtful. If this is desirable, as distinguished from having the several Indian tribes accept similar restrictions through voluntary adoption of tribal codes in response to the model code to be prepared under Title III, Congress needs to give further consideration to specifically providing for review in the federal courts of the decisions of tribal courts which deprive Indians (or others) of the protected rights. And, for reasons discussed earlier, some clarification of the statutory prescribed rights would seem desirable.

However, because of the many uncertainties which currently exist as to the scope and content of the related guarantees of the Constitution against state and federal action, because of the undesirability of tour-de-force intrusion on the semi-sovereign status accorded to date to the Indian tribes, it would seem to be sounder long range policy to repeal Title II and leave the protection of Indians against their tribal governments to develop from a process of education and cooperation. If such repeal is unlikely, as is probably the case, then it is essential that the courts be as considerate as possible in a gradual imposition on the Indian tribes of the requirements of Title II and for the Department of the Interior to be as prompt as possible in developing a model code, in educating Indian tribes to adopt it, and in helping to train tribal judges to adjust to the new requirements imposed by Title II.

---

[138] *Senate Hearings on Constitutional Rights, Summary Report*, 89th Cong., 2d Sess. 19 (1966).

APPENDIX I

CIVIL RIGHTS ACT

Public Law 90-284
90th Congress, H.R. 2516
April 11, 1968

AN ACT

To prescribe penalties for certain acts of violence or intimidation, and for other purposes.

•   •   •   •   •   •

TITLE II — RIGHTS OF INDIANS

Definitions

Sec. 201.   For purposes of this title, the term —

(1)   "Indian tribe" means any tribe, band, or other group of Indians subject to the jurisdiction of the United States and recognized as possessing powers of self-government;

(2)   "powers of self-government" means and includes all governmental powers possessed by an Indian tribe, executive, legislative, and judicial, and all offices, bodies, and tribunals by and through which they are executed, including courts of Indian offenses; and

(3)   "Indian court" means any Indian tribal court or court of Indian offense.

Indian Rights

Sec. 202.   No Indian tribe in exercising powers of self-government shall —

(1)   make or enforce any law prohibiting the free exercise of religion, or abridging the freedom of speech, or of the press, or the right of the people peaceably to assemble and to petition for a redress of grievances;

(2)   violate the right of the people to be secure in their persons, houses, papers, and effects against unreasonable search and seizures, nor issue warrants, but upon probable cause, supported by oath or affirmation, and particularly describing the place to be searched and the person or thing to be seized;

(3)   subject any person for the same offense to be twice put in jeopardy;

(4)   compel any person in any criminal case to be a witness against himself;

(5)   take any private property for a public use without just compensation;

(6)   deny to any person in a criminal proceeding the right to a speedy and public trial, to be informed of the nature and cause of the accusation, to be confronted with the witnesses against him, to have compulsory process for obtaining witnesses in his favor, and at his own expense to have the assistance of counsel for his defense;

(7)   require excessive bail, impose excessive fines, inflict cruel and unusual punishments, and in no event impose for conviction of any one offense any penalty or punishment greater than imprisonment for a term of six months or a fine of $500, or both;

(8)   deny to any person within its jurisdiction the equal protection of its laws or deprive any person of liberty or property without due process of law;

(9)   pass any bill of attainder or ex post facto law; or

(10)   deny to any person accused of an offense punishable by imprisonment the right, upon request, to a trial by jury of not less than six persons.

Habeas Corpus

Sec. 203.   The privilege of the writ of habeas corpus shall be available to any person, in a court of the United States, to test the legality of his detention by order of an Indian tribe.

TITLE III — MODEL CODE GOVERNING COURTS OF INDIAN OFFENSES

Sec. 301.   The Secretary of the Interior is authorized and directed to recommend to the Congress, on or before July 1, 1968, a model code to govern the administration of justice by courts of Indian offenses on Indian reservations.   Such code shall include provisions which will

(1)   assure that any individual being tried for an offense by a court of Indian offenses shall have the same rights, privileges, and immunities under the United States Constitution as would be guaranteed any citizen of the United States being tried in a Federal court for any similar offense.

(2)   assure that any individual being tried for an offense by a court of Indian offenses will be advised and made aware of his rights under the United States Constitution, and under any tribal constitution applicable to such individual,

(3)   establish proper qualifications for the office of judge of the court of Indian offenses, and

(4)   provide for the establishing of educational classes for the training of judges of courts of Indian offenses. In carrying out the provisions of this title, the Secretary of the Interior shall consult with the Indians, Indian tribes, and interested agencies of the United States.

Sec. 302.   There is hereby authorized to be appropriated such sum as may be necessary to carry out the provisions of this title.

TITLE IV — JURISDICTION OVER CRIMINAL AND CIVIL ACTIONS

Assumption by State

Sec. 401.   (a)   The consent of the United States is hereby given to any State not having jurisdiction over criminal offenses committed by or against Indians in the areas of Indian country situated within such State to assume, with the consent of the Indian tribe occupying the particular Indian country or part thereof which could be affected by such assumption, such measure of jurisdiction over any or all of such offenses committed within such Indian country or any part thereof as may be determined by such State to the same extent that such State has jurisdiction over any such offense committed elsewhere within the State, and the criminal laws of such State shall have the same force and effect within such Indian country or part thereof as they have elsewhere within that State.

(b)   Nothing in this section shall authorize the alienation, encumbrance, or taxation of any real or personal property, including water rights, belonging to any Indian or any Indian tribe, band, or community that is held in trust by the United States or is subject to a restriction against alienation imposed by the United States; or shall authorize regulation of the use of such property in a manner inconsistent with any Federal treaty, agreement, or statute or with any regulation made pursuant thereto; or shall deprive any Indian or any Indian tribe, band, or community of any right, privilege, or immunity afforded under Federal treaty, agreement, or statute with respect to hunting, trapping, or fishing or the control, licensing, or regulation thereof.

Assumption by State of Civil Jurisdiction

Sec. 402.   (a)   The consent of the United States is hereby given to any State not having jurisdiction over civil causes of action between Indians or to which Indians are parties which arise in the areas of Indian country situated within such State to assume, with the consent of the tribe occupying the particular Indian country or part thereof which would be affected by such assumption, such measure of jurisdiction over any or all such civil causes of action arising within such Indian country or any part thereof as may be determined by such State to the same extent that such State has jurisdiction over other civil causes of action, and those civil laws of such State that are of general application to private persons or private property shall have the same force and effect within such Indian country or part thereof as they have elsewhere within that State.

(b)   Nothing in this section shall authorize the alienation, encumbrance, or taxation of any real or person [sic] property, including water rights, belonging to any Indian or any Indian tribe, band, or community that is held in trust by the United States or is subject to a restriction against alienation imposed by the United States; or shall authorize regulation of the use of such property in a manner inconsistent with any Federal treaty, agreement, or statute, or with any regulation made pursuant thereto; or shall confer jurisdiction upon the State to adjudicate, in probate proceeding or otherwise, the ownership or right to possession of such property or any interest therein.

(c)   Any tribal ordinance or custom heretofore or hereafter adopted by an Indian tribe, band, or community in the exercise of any authority which it may possess shall, if not inconsistent with any applicable civil law of the State be given full force and effect in the determination of civil causes of action pursuant to this section.

Retrocession of Jurisdiction by State

Sec. 403. (a) The United States is authorized to accept a retrocession by any State of all or any measure of the criminal or civil jurisdiction or both, acquired by such State pursuant to the provisions of section 1162 of title 18 of the United States Code, section 1360 of title 28 of the United States Code, or section 7 of the Act of August 15, 1953 (67 Stat. 588), as it was in effect prior to its repeal by subsection (b) of this section.

(b) Section 7 of the Act of August 15, 1953 (67 Stat. 588), is hereby repealed but such repeal shall not affect any cession of jurisdiction made pursuant to such section prior to its repeal.

Consent to Amend State Laws

Sec. 404. Notwithstanding the provisions of any enabling Act for the admission of a State, the consent of the United States is hereby given to the people of any State to amend, where necessary, their State constitution or existing statutes, as the case may be, to remove any legal impediment to the assumption of civil or criminal jurisdiction in accordance with the provisions of this title. The provisions of this title shall not become effective with respect to such assumption of jurisdiction by any such State until the people thereof have appropriately amended their State constitution or statutes as the case may be.

Actions Not to Abate

Sec. 405. (a) No action or proceeding pending before any court or agency of the United States immediately prior to any cession of jurisdiction by the United States pursuant to this title shall abate by reason of that cession. For the purposes of any such action or proceeding, such cession shall take effect on the day following the date of final determination of such action or proceeding.

(b) No cession made by the United States under this title shall deprive any court of the United States of jurisdiction to hear, determine, render judgment, or impose sentence in any criminal action instituted against any person for any offense committed before the effective date of such cession, if the offense charged in such action was cognizable under any law of the United States at the time of the commission of such offense. For the purposes of any such criminal action, such cession shall take effect on the day following the date of final determination of such action.

Special Election

Sec. 406. State jurisdiction acquired pursuant to this title with respect to criminal offenses or civil causes of action or with respect to both, shall be applicable in Indian country only where the enrolled Indians within the affected area of such Indian country accept such jurisdiction by a majority vote of the adult Indians voting at a special election held for that purpose. The Secretary of the Interior shall call such special election under such rules and regulations as he may prescribe, when requested to do so by the tribal council or other governing body, or by 20 per centum of such enrolled adults.

Title V — Offenses Within Indian Country
Amendment

Sec. 501. Section 1153 of title 18 of the United States Code is amended by inserting immediately after "weapon," the following: "assault resulting in serious bodily injury,".

Title VI — Employment of Legal Counsel
Approval

Sec. 601. Notwithstanding any other provision of law, if any application made by an Indian, Indian Tribe, Indian council, or any band or group of Indians under any law requiring the approval of the Secretary of the Interior or the Commissioner of Indian Affairs of contracts or agreements relating to the employment of legal counsel (including the choice of counsel and the fixing of fees) by any such Indians, tribe, council, band, or group is neither granted nor denied within ninety days following the making of such application, such approval shall be deemed to have been granted.

Title VII — Materials Relating to Constitutional Rights of Indians
Secretary of Interior to Prepare

Sec. 701. (a) In order that the constitutional rights of Indians might be fully protected, the Secretary of the Interior is authorized and directed to —

141

(1)   have the document entitled "Indian Affairs, Laws, and Treaties" (Senate Document Numbered 319, volumes 1 and 2, Fifty-eighth Congress), revised and extended to include all treaties, laws, Executive orders, and regulations relating to Indian affairs in force on September 1, 1967, and to have such revised document printed at the Government Printing Office;

(2)   have revised and republished the treatise entitled "Federal Indian Law"; and

(3)   have prepared, to the extent determined by the Secretary of the Interior to be feasible, an accurate compilation of the official opinions, published and unpublished, of the Solicitor of the Department of the Interior relating to Indian affairs rendered by the Solicitor prior to September 1, 1967, and to have such compilation printed as a Government publication at the Government Printing Office.

(b)   With respect to the document entitled "Indian Affairs, Laws and Treaties" as revised and extended in accordance with paragraph (1) of subsection (a), and the compilation prepared in accordance with paragraph (3) of such subsection, the Secretary of the Interior shall take such action as may be necessary to keep such document and compilation current on an annual basis.

(c)   There is authorized to be appropriated for carrying out the provisions of this title, with respect to the preparation but not including printing, such sum as may be necessary.

IN DEFENSE OF TRIBAL SOVEREIGNTY: AN ANALYSIS OF JUDICIAL ERROR IN CONSTRUCTION OF THE INDIAN CIVIL RIGHTS ACT

By ALVIN J. ZIONTZ*

This article is one of two in this issue examining the Indian Civil Rights Act of 1968. The author contends that judicial interpretation of this Act has ignored the legislative history of the Act and has improperly assumed that the immunity of Indian tribes from suit has been waived.

INTRODUCTION

The field of American Indian law is complex and subtle. Its sources are numerous: statutes, treaties, decisions of the state and federal courts of the United States, decisions of the Solicitor for the Department of the Interior, decisions of the Secretary of the Interior, regulations of the Department of the Interior, opinions and decisions of the Indian Claims Commission, constitutions and corporate charters of Indian tribes, ordinances and resolutions of Indian tribes and the unwritten laws and codes of Indian tribes.

Under American law, Indian tribes are *sui generis*. They are quasi-sovereign, dependent nations within the borders of the United States, occupying territory over which they have the power of self-government, and having special rights derived from treaties, executive orders and judicial doctrines created in response to the special relationships between them and the United States Government. Furthermore, the relationship between the Indian and his tribe is quite different from the relationship between non-Indian citizens and their city or state government.

It was into this complex web of laws and relationships that the Senate Subcommittee on Constitutional Rights ventured when in 1961 it undertook a study of individual rights of Indians. Seven years later the Subcommittee offered, and Congress passed, what has come to be known as the Indian Civil Rights Act.[1] It resulted from Congressional concern that under the law, individual Indians appeared to have no constitutional rights vis-a-vis their tribal gov-

---

* Alvin J. Ziontz, J.D., University of Chicago, 1951. Member of the Bar of Washington State and the United States Supreme Court. The author's firm is General Counsel for the Colville Confederated Tribes, Lummi Tribe, Makah Tribe, and Suquamish, Washington; special counsel for the Metlakatla Indian Community, Alaska; Northern Cheyenne Tribe, Montana; and Quileute Tribe, Washington. The author and the firm of which he is a member have been counsel in several of the cases cited below. These cases are specifically identified in appropriate footnotes.
    1. 25 U.S.C. §§ 1301-41 (1970).

ernments. Individual Indians had been subjected to actions of tribal government which would be illegal if civil rights provisions in the United States Constitution were applicable.[2] Further, it appeared that federal courts had denied relief to individual Indian complainants, leaving them without any remedies.[3]

Starting with the simple premise that perhaps the time had come to extend the Bill of Rights to American Indian tribes, the Subcommittee on Constitutional Rights of the Senate Judiciary Committee ventured into the field of federal Indian law. The Subcommittee began its work in 1961. It sought to achieve a balance between individual rights of tribal members on the one hand and preservation of tribal autonomy, Indian customs, law and culture on the other. The Subcommittee felt it had found a way to accommodate these countervailing interests. It imposed upon Indian tribal governments certain specified restraints couched in language taken from the Bill of Rights, but altered to fit what it conceived to be special circumstances of Indian tribes. It scrapped proposals which would have involved the federal courts in a significant volume of Indian litigation and opted instead for the limited federal court remedy of habeas corpus for all persons detained by authority of tribal government. It strengthened tribal autonomy by providing for retrocession of state jurisdiction over Indian reservations and halted further state assumption of jurisdiction without Indian consent, and finally, it attempted to assist tribes in improving the quality of their judicial systems by directing preparation of a model code and proposals for improving the quality and training of Indian tribal judges.

On the whole, its intentions in attempting to reconcile the conflicting values before it were clear: reliance on the tribal governments and courts to carry out the mandates of the Act and federal court review limited to denial of constitutional rights in the context of actual detention of the person.

Although the intentions of the Subcommittee were beneficent, its efforts to avoid heavy-handed intrusion by the federal courts into the affairs of Indian tribes resulted in legislative ambiguity which has achieved exactly the opposite effect. Beginning in 1968 with the case of *Dodge v. Nakai*,[4] federal courts have entered into the thicket of Indian tribal disputes involving them in a species of legal problems, new to the federal courts, for which they are peculiarly ill-equipped.[5] Following *Dodge*, the federal courts have

---

2. *See, e.g.,* Talton v. Mayes, 163 U.S. 376 (1896) (tribal member not protected against tribe by fifth amendment guarantee of indictment by grand jury); Native American Church v. Navajo Tribal Council, 272 F.2d 131 (10th Cir. 1959) (tribal government not bound by first amendment freedom of religion clause).

3. *Id.*

4. 298 F. Supp. 17 & 26 (D. Ariz. 1968).

5. *See* Judd, *The Expanding Jurisdiction of the Federal Courts,* 60 A.B.A.J. 938 (1974).

gone on to misconstrue the Congressional intent as expressed in the Act and as a result, have expanded federal court jurisdiction on a wholly improper foundation. With the denial of certiorari on October 15, 1974, in the companion cases of *Thompson v. Tonasket* and *Laramie v. Nicholson*,[6] the United States Supreme Court left unanswered serious questions raised by the decisions interpreting the Act.

The purpose of this article is to point up some of those features of the legislative history which appear to establish the Congressional intent concerning the role of the federal courts in the enforcement of the Indian Civil Rights Act, and the methods Congress had in mind to implement the Act. The article will also take up the fundamental question of the jurisdiction of federal courts over Indian tribes in the absence of express Congressional waiver of tribal immunity from suit and the consequences of judicial failure to adhere to the governing principles of this rule of law. Finally, the article will deal with some of the consequences of the scope of federal jurisdiction as created by judicial interpretation of the Act, examining such questions as the danger of judicial ethnocentrism, the practical difficulties and unfairness inherent in attempts of federal courts to determine what are genuine cultural values, misuse of the Act for the purpose of obtaining a federal forum for money damage claims, and finally, pertinence of the Act to the establishment of tribal jurisdiction over non-Indians on reservations.

The Scope of Federal Intervention in Tribal Affairs Under Title II: Congressional Intent

An Indian Bill of Rights: Origins and Objectives

A. The Sources for the Idea of an Indian Bill of Rights

Concern for the civil rights of Indians seems to have become the focus of interest of three entirely separate and distinct groups: the Commission on the Rights, Liberties and Responsibilities of the American Indian,[7] an Interior Department Task Force and the Senate Constitutional Rights Subcommittee, chaired by Senator Sam

---

6. 487 F.2d 315 & 316 (9th Cir. 1973), *cert. denied*, 43 U.S.L.W. 3212 (Oct. 15, 1974).
   In both cases the plaintiffs sought enrollment in the Colville Confederated Tribes and brought suit under the Indian Civil Rights Act claiming denial of due process and equal protection. Plaintiffs sought court-ordered tribal enrollment and a money judgment for accumulated per capita shares of tribal funds, in one case extending back 18 years and in the other two years. The complaints also sought attorneys fees and interest. At issue was the question of whether the Indian Civil Rights Act vests jurisdiction in courts to award judgments for damages and attorneys fees against Indian tribes as well as the question of tribal immunity from suit and the sufficiency of the pleadings in the case. The writer's law firm represented the appellants, Colville Confederated Tribes, in both cases.
7. The final report of that Commission is contained in Commission on the Rights, Liberties and Responsibilities of The American Indian, The Indian: America's Unfinished Business (W. Brophy and S. Aberle eds. 1966) [hereinafter cited as W. Brophy & S. Aberle].

Ervin of North Carolina. The Commission published a preliminary report in 1961 which discussed the inapplicability of the Bill of Rights restraints to Indian governments. The Commission recommended:

> The authority of these bodies in local affairs should not be curtailed unilaterally by the United States except in one respect: federal law should require that tribal actions safeguard basic civil rights and provide for the appeal of civil rights cases to federal and state courts.[8]

The Commission's final report asserted that tribal immunity from civil rights suits violates the very assumptions on which our democratic society is established.[9] The Task Force, however, recommended that tribes be encouraged to protect civil liberties by their own ordinances.[10]

Almost concurrently with these reports a member of the staff of Senator Ervin's Subcommittee, an Indian herself, initiated a preliminary inquiry to determine whether immunity from constitutional restraint had resulted in actual deprivation of constitutional rights by Indian tribes. The investigation soon broadened into formal hearings by the Subcommittee.[11]

At the outset of its work the Subcommittee secured from the Attorney General a summary of the state of the law concerning the inapplicability of the Bill of Rights to Indian tribes in their relationships with their members.[12]

The legislative history of Title II of the Indian Civil Rights Act shows that Mr. Ervin's Subcommittee focused its attention in four general areas: protection of individual Indian rights, problems arising from assertion of state jurisdiction over Indian reservations, tribal court procedures and miscellaneous grievances.

The greatest volume of complaints voiced in the hearings concerned enforcement of state criminal laws by local authorities and communities near Indian reservations.[13] Another serious problem

---

8. *Id.* at 60.
9. *Id.* at 44.
10. TASK FORCE ON INDIAN AFFAIRS, REPORT TO THE SECRETARY OF THE INTERIOR 31-32 (1961).
11. For a more detailed discussion of the origin of the 1968 Civil Rights Act, see W. Brophy & S. Aberle, *supra* note 7, at vii; Burnett, *An Historical Analysis of the 1968 "Indian Civil Rights" Act,* 9 HARV. J. LEGIS. 557 (1972) [hereinafter cited as Burnett]; Lazarus, *Title II of the 1968 Civil Rights Act: An Indian Bill of Rights,* 45 N. DAK. L. REV. 337 (1969) [hereinafter cited as Lazarus].
12. Robert F. Kennedy, Attorney General, wrote a letter to the Subcommittee informing them that there were large areas in which constitutional restrictions were not applicable, citing Talton v. Mayes, 163 U.S. 376 (1896); Native American Church v. Navajo Tribal Council, 272 F.2d 131 (10th Cir. 1959); Barta v. Oglala Sioux Tribe, 259 F.2d 553 (8th Cir. 1958). *See Hearings Before the Subcommittee on Constitutional Rights of the Committee on the Judiciary, United States Senate: Constitutional Rights of the American Indian,* 87th Cong., 1st Sess., pt. 1, at 3 (1961) [hereinafter cited as *1961 Hearings*].
13. *1961 Hearings, supra* note 12, at 244.

involved procedural rights of those charged with offenses before tribal courts.[14] Finally, the Subcommittee heard a great deal of testimony from Indians complaining of violations of constitutional rights by the governing bodies of Indian tribes.[15]

B. *Tailoring the Objectives*

It appeared that the Subcommittee had no intention of using a bill of rights statute as an instrument for achieving assimilation of Indians into non-Indian communities. On the contrary, the Subcommittee appeared quite sensitive to the requirement that it avoid measures which would encroach on the functioning of Indian tribes as self-governing units.[16]

It was somewhat surprising then that S. 961, included in the first package of bills introduced by Senator Ervin in 1965, provided simply:

> That any Indian tribe in exercising its powers of local self-government shall be subject to the same limitations and restraints as those which are imposed on the government of the United States by the United States Constitution.[17]

In testifying at the hearing on this bill, Arthur Lazarus, Sr., a respected expert in Indian law, pointed out that such an approach would work serious economic and social injustice to Indian tribes. For instance, it would impose the requirement of a twelve man jury trial in all criminal cases and in all civil cases involving more than $20, and, further, if the equal protection clause were construed as imposing the doctrine of "one man, one vote," it would totally disrupt any Indian tribe still governed by a chief's council.[18] Mr. Frank Barry, Solicitor for the Interior Department, also testified in opposition to S. 961, pointing out the disruptions which would flow from imposition of the full panoply of United States constitutional guarantees.[19]

As a result, Senator Ervin redrafted S. 961 and the revised version was introduced as S. 1843. The bill undertook to enumerate the specific restraints on tribal government with particular revi-

---

14. *Id.* Pts. 1 & 2; *Hearings Before the Subcommittee on Constitutional Rights of the Senate Committee on the Judiciary, Constitutional Rights of the American Indian*, 87th Cong., 2d Sess., pt. 3 (1962); *Hearings Before the Subcommittee on Constitutional Rights of the Committee on the Judiciary. United States Senate: Constitutional Rights of the American Indian*, 88th Cong., 1st Sess., pt. 4 (1963).
15. Burnett, *supra* note 11, at 588.
16. Note, *The Indian Bill of Rights and the Constitutional Status of Tribal Governments*, 82 HARV. L. REV. 1343, 1359 (1969).
17. *Hearings on S. 961, S. 962, S. 963, S. 964, S. 966, S. 967, S. 968, S.J. Res. 40, to Protect the Constitutional Rights of American Indians, Before the Subcommittee on Constitutional Rights of the Senate Committee on the Judiciary*, 89th Cong., 1st Sess., at 5 (1965) [hereinafter cited as *1965 Hearings*].
18. *Id.* at 64-65.
19. *Id.* at 17-19.

sions tailored to Indian tribes. For instance, it deleted the "establishment of religion clause" from the language taken from the first amendment;[20] it omitted the language of the second and third amendments dealing with the right to bear arms and the quartering of soldiers; it omitted the fifth amendment requirement of federal grand jury indictment for felonies and provided that the right of counsel in criminal trials was at defendant's expense; it omitted the requirement of jury trial in suits involving more than $20; it added a limitation on imposition of penalties—six months or a $500 fine, or both; it prohibited bills of attainder and ex post facto laws; it included the fourteenth amendment prohibition against denial of due process and equal protection but omitted the provisions of the thirteenth amendment prohibiting slavery and involuntary servitude and the fifteenth amendment prohibiting abridgement of voting rights on account of race, color or previous condition of servitude. Finally, it imposed the obligation of extending the right of jury trial but authorized a minimum of six jurors.[21]

It is incorrect to say that Congress intended Indian tribes to be subject to the same constitutional restrictions as federal and state governments. Instead, the legislative history makes clear that Congress found it necessary to impose a specially designed set of restraints upon tribal governments.

Purpose of Section 202: A Uniform Bill of Rights Within the Structure of Tribal Government

The Congressional purpose in enacting an Indian Bill of Rights is obvious from a reading of the legislative background. Discovering that within the internal laws and constitutions of Indian tribes, individual rights were often not provided for at all, or if they were, the provisions were inadequate, Congress moved to enact what would amount to an Indian Bill of Rights, uniformly applicable to all tribes, and operating *within* the structure of tribal government.[22]

---

20. This clause was removed to accomodate various tribal societies based upon a theocratic form of government. For example, the New Mexico Pueblos are theocracies governed by religious leaders.

21. S. 1843, 90th Cong., 1st Sess. § 102 (1967).

22. One of the cases specifically considered by the Committee as representative of the problem was Native American Church v. Navajo Tribal Council, 272 F.2d 131 (10th Cir. 1959). Plaintiffs sought a federal order enjoining enforcement of a Navajo tribal ordinance prohibiting peyote and its use in Navajo country. Plaintiffs claimed the substance was used in connection with their religious ceremonies and charged that the ordinance violated their members' rights under the first, fourth and fifth amendments to the United States Constitution, and also sought damages for unlawful search and seizure. Additionally, plaintiffs claimed denial of the right to counsel and the right to jury trial. Dismissal of the action was sustained on the ground that no laws subjected the Navajo Tribe to the federal laws of the United States restricting internal police powers, nor was the tribe restricted by provisions of the Constitution which applied only to Congress. In 1962, the Tenth Circuit refused to interfere with the Secretary of Interior's approval of the Navajo adoption of the Interior Department Law and Order Code which included an ordinance banning use or sale of peyote.

A. *Legislative Record*

Testimony before the Subcommittee developed that of 247 organized tribes, 117 operated under constitutions protecting individual civil rights, while 130 did not. The civil rights provisions that existed in tribal constitutions were often incomplete. Additionally, 188 other tribes or bands were not organized under tribal constitutions.[23]

In its Summary Report on the hearings and investigations, the Subcommittee pointed out that many tribal witnesses objected to the proposed legislation because their tribes already had substantive guarantees of individual rights in their constitutions, but these witnesses had no objection to extension of such restraints to tribal governments not limited by their own organic instruments.[24]

In 1969, the Subcommittee submitted a report summarizing the purposes and effects of the 1968 Act. In describing the intention of Title II and the effect its enactment was deemed to have, the report said:

> Title II constitutes a Bill of Rights for American Indians.
> It provides that Indian tribes exercising powers of self-government shall be subject to many of the same limitations and restraints that are imposed on federal, state and local government by the Constitution of the United States.
> *It thus assures adequate protection of the basic rights of individual Indians who are members of tribes whose tribal constitutions now permit governmental action that would be unconstitutional if undertaken by federal, state, or local government.*[25]

Oliver v. Udall, 306 F.2d 819 (D.C. Cir. 1962), *cert. denied*, 372 U.S. 908 (1963).
 However, in 1967, the Navajo Tribal Council amended the peyote ordinance by adding the following proviso:
> Provided that it shall not be unlawful for any member of the Native American Church to transport peyote into Navajo country to buy, sell, possess or use peyote in any form in connection with the religious practices, sacraments or services of the Native American Church. NAVAJO TRIBAL CODE § 641.

The amendment was adopted in accordance with the tribal bill of rights ordinance. NAVAJO TRIBAL CODE § 1-A. The Navajo Bill of Rights incorporated the basic provisions of the first amendment (free speech, press, assembly, petition and religion); the second amendment (the right to bear arms); the third amendment (no government use of private houses without the consent of the owner except by specific prescription of Council resolution); the fourth amendment (search and seizure); the fifth amendment (double jeopardy, self-incrimination, and compensation for taking private property); the sixth amendment (criminal procedural rights, but excluding the right to counsel); the eighth amendment (prohibiting excessive bail and fines and cruel and unusual punishment) and the ninth amendment (preserving inherent rights of the people). Significantly, the Navajo Council chose not to adopt the due process and equal protection clauses of the fourteenth amendment, and of course, the prohibition against bills of attainder and ex post facto laws.
 23. Burnett, *supra* note 11, at 579.
 24. SUBCOMMITTEE ON CONSTITUTIONAL RIGHTS OF THE SENATE COMMITTEE ON THE JUDICIARY, SUMMARY REPORT OF HEARINGS AND INVESTIGATIONS: CONSTITUTIONAL RIGHTS OF THE AMERICAN INDIAN, 89th Cong., 2d Sess. 9 (1966) [hereinafter cited as 1966 SUMMARY REPORT].
 25. SENATE COMMITTEE ON THE JUDICIARY, PROTECTING THE RIGHTS OF THE

As the foregoing language makes clear, the view of the Judiciary Committee was that in enacting Title II, Congress imposed restraints on all American Indian tribes as a matter of federal law so that the rights of individual tribal members no longer depended on whether their particular tribes had written constitutions or whether those constitutions contained civil rights guarantees which corresponded with the body of individual guarantees in the United States Constitution. Individual rights of Indians were now uniformly defined throughout the United States.

B. *Legal Impact on Tribal Government*

It is well-established that Congress has plenary power over the tribal relations of Indians.[26] By the enactment of the Indian Civil Rights Act, Congress made its substantive provisions directly applicable to all Indian tribes exactly as if its provisions were a part of the tribes' own constitutions, ordinances and internal law.[27] In short, the Act became binding and enforceable within every tribal community and upon every tribal court. The Act is therefore self-executing and not a mere admonition to tribal government.[28]

C. *Legal Impact on the Federal Government*

Furthermore, the Act immediately affected the government in all its relationships with Indian tribes. The scope of such relationships is extremely broad, ranging from the Secretary of Interior's power to approve tribal constitutions and by-laws and their amendments and revisions,[29] to withdrawal of federal recognition of the governing body of a tribe.[30]

AMERICAN INDIAN, S. REP. No. 92-294, 91st Cong., 1st Sess. 2 (1969) (emphasis added).

26. Choate v. Trapp, 224 U.S. 665, 671 (1912); Lone Wolf v. Hitchcock, 187 U.S. 553 (1903); United States v. Kagama, 118 U.S. 375 (1885).

27. Many tribal constitutions contain the following provisions with reference to powers of government of the tribal council:
> The tribal council shall exercise the following powers, subject to any limitations imposed by the federal statutes, the Constitution of the United States, and subject further to all express restrictions upon all such laws provided by in this constitution and by-laws
> . . . .

See, e.g., CONSTITUTION AND BY-LAWS OF THE CONFEDERATED TRIBES OF THE COLVILLE RESERVATION, article V; CONSTITUTION AND BY-LAWS OF THE CONFEDERATED SALISH AND KOOTENAI TRIBES, article V; CONSTITUTION AND BY-LAWS OF THE MUCKLESHOOT INDIAN TRIBE, article VI; AMENDED CONSTITUTION AND BY-LAWS OF THE NORTHERN CHEYENNE TRIBE, article IV; CONSTITUTION AND BY-LAWS OF THE SQUAXIN ISLAND TRIBE, article III; CONSTITUTION AND BY-LAWS OF THE SUQUAMISH TRIBE, article III; CONSTITUTION AND BY-LAWS OF THE SWINOMISH INDIANS, article VI; CONSTITUTION AND BY-LAWS OF THE OGLALA SIOUX TRIBE, article IV; CONSTITUTION AND BY-LAWS OF THE ROSEBUD SIOUX TRIBE, article IV.

28. The report of the Ervin Committee describing Title I notes:
> The purpose of title 1 is to protect individual Indians from arbitrary and unjust actions of tribal governments. *This is accomplished by placing certain limitations on an Indian tribe in the exercise of its powers of self-government.* SENATE COMMITTEE ON THE JUDICIARY, PROTECTING THE RIGHTS OF THE AMERICAN INDIAN, S. REP. No. 841, 90th Cong., 1st Sess. 6 (1967) (emphasis added).

29. 25 U.S.C. § 476 (1970).

30. United States v. Pawnee Business Council, Civ. No. 73-C-11 (D.

The Act also immediately affected the entire administrative law system within the Interior Department. This body of law is applicable to adjudication of disputes involving actions or decisions of the Bureau of Indian Affairs. Federal regulations require that such administrative decisions shall be based on all applicable federal laws where there is a claim that administrative action violated the right or privilege of the appellant.[31] Thus, when there is any administrative review of tribal action by the Interior Department, Indian Civil Rights Act standards will control. Clearly, then, the Indian Civil Rights Act was binding on all agencies of the federal government, and certainly upon the administrative appeal system of the Bureau of Indian Affairs.

It was also immediately effective on all aspects of the decision-making processes of the Bureau of Indian Affairs. That agency obviously has numerous powers as part of its trusteeship functions which could be exercised to inhibit actions of tribal governments that might constitute violations of federal law. For instance, the Bureau of Indian Affairs has power of approval over many types of tribal ordinances. Additionally, legal opinions are given to the tribes and their judges by solicitors for the Department.[32]

Thus by enactment of a federal declaration of individual rights of Indians, Congress imposed a blanket system of restraints on the federal and tribal governments; it eliminated the differences of treatment of the subject among the various tribes and made the restraints uniform for all tribes. The substantive provisions of the Act became binding upon all tribal governments and enforceable within the framework of tribal institutions. The Act also imposed upon the agencies of the federal government, and particularly the Interior Department, the duty to implement the Act within the lawful authority of such agencies.[33] It would therefore be wholly in-

---

Okla. 1974). In that case a permanent injunction was issued on the application of the United States barring certain named defendants from acting or functioning as members of the tribal council following an administrative determination by the Secretary of the Interior that the defendants were not lawfully entitled to their posts on the tribal council.

31. 25 C.F.R. § 2.2 which provides in part:
This part provides appeals procedures for requesting correction of actions or decisions by officials of the Bureau of Indian Affairs where the action or decision is protested as a violation of the right or privilege of the appellant. Such rights or privileges must be based upon fundamental constitutional law, applicable Federal statutes, treaties or upon Departmental regulations . . . .
A major revision in these procedures has been adopted by the Interior Department. The new arrangement broadened the jurisdiction of the Board of Indian Appeals in the Interior Department's Office of Hearings and Appeals. *See* 38 Fed. Reg. 34812 (1973).

32. M. PRICE, LAW AND THE AMERICAN INDIAN, 717-30 (1973).

33. This is the present position of the Interior Department as expressed in a legal memorandum of the Solicitor, Mr. Kent Frizzell, to the Department of Justice, dated May 22, 1974, in which the Solicitor challenges the contention of some courts that judicial relief beyond habeas corpus must be given to avoid rendering the Act meaningless. In the memorandum the Solicitor says, at 10-11:
Nor would it, as some courts have suggested . . . render meaning-

correct to say that unless federal courts could grant all forms of judicial relief in private enforcement actions, the Act would be "meaningless" or merely an "admonition."[34]

Implementation of the Act: The Congressional Intent

At the outset, the Ervin Subcommittee was aware of the need for some measures which would implement the substantive guarantees of S. 961. It considered that such implementation would be achieved by three bills.

Senate Bill 962 authorized appeals of criminal convictions in tribal courts to federal district courts with the right of trial de novo. Senate Bill 963 placed responsibility on the Attorney General to investigate complaints of denial of constitutional rights of Indians and to bring appropriate criminal or civil actions. Senate Bill 964 called for the preparation of a model code governing the administration of justice by Courts of Indian Offenses.[35]

A. Senate Bill 962: The Genesis of the Habeas Corpus Remedy

As a result of its hearings and investigation, the Ervin Subcommittee concluded that the inability of an Indian to appeal his case from the tribal court system into the federal system was a key problem. The Subcommittee accordingly recommended that a means be provided for appeals from tribal courts to federal courts, saying:

> [W]here there has been a denial of some constitutional right [by a tribal court] the Subcommittee continues to believe that the best way to serve the interests of justice would be to provide for a trial *de novo* in the federal courts.[36]

Senate Bill 962 was drawn to accomplish this objective. It was strictly confined to *criminal* appeals. Nowhere in the legislative record is there any suggestion that the Subcommittee or Congress ever considered appeals in civil cases. Senate Bill 962 provided for an appeal to the federal district court from a criminal conviction by the tribal court if the defendant claimed a deprivation of constitutional rights. In such a case, notice of appeal could be filed and trial de novo would take place under the Federal Rules of Criminal Procedure. If the offense corresponded to one punishable under the federal criminal code, the prosecution would have to prove the same elements applicable under that code. If the offense were not covered by the federal criminal code, it would be punishable

---

less the substantive provisions of section 1302. Those provisions clearly bind tribal courts as well as all other tribal officers, and in addition bind the Secretary of the Interior in the exercise of his supervisory control over certain types of tribal action.

34. *See* Loncassion v. Leekity, 334 F. Supp. 370, 372-73 (D.N.M. 1971).
35. S. 961, 962, 963, 964, 89th Cong., 1st Sess. (1965).
36. 1966 SUMMARY REPORT, *supra* note 24, at 25-26.

under the Federal Assimilative Crimes Act.[37]

However, the Subcommittee in its final Summary Report concluded that S. 962 was defective since no sound reason required retrial of all such cases de novo and trial de novo should be limited to cases involving reasonable claims of denial of constitutional rights. The Subcommittee recommended therefore that S. 962 be amended to give the federal courts appeal authority to determine the probability of denial of constitutional rights through a preliminary hearing procedure.[38]

The Subcommittee said a system of appeals to the federal courts would be an important first step in according full due process of law and would improve the quality of justice rendered by tribal judges. It rejected the argument that this would overburden federal courts as outside its proper concerns. Therefore it recommended the passage of S. 962 with the suggested amendments.[39] The Summary Report received unanimous approval of the Subcommittee members and Senator Ervin began to prepare new bills for introduction early in the First Session of the 90th Congress.[40]

In May, 1967 Senator Ervin introductd S. 1843, which was to become Title II, "Appeals from Indian Courts," and which incorporated amendments to S. 962 recommended by the Subcommittee and which provided for a showing of "probable jurisdiction" prerequisite to trial de novo in federal courts. It was detailed and comprehensive. But despite the apparent completeness of this section, a new and separate section (section 103) was added: "The privilege of the writ of habeas corpus shall be available to any person, in a court of the United States, to test the legality of his detention by order of an Indian tribe."[41]

This marks the first appearance of the habeas corpus remedy in

---

37. 18 U.S.C. § 13 (1970).
38. 1966 SUMMARY REPORT, *supra* note 24, at 26.
39. *Id.*
40. STAFF OF SENATE COMMITTEE ON THE JUDICIARY, SUBCOMMITTEE ON CONSTITUTIONAL RIGHTS, 89TH CONG., 2D SESS., MONTHLY REPORT 1 (Nov. 1966).
41. S. 1843, 90th Cong., 1st Sess., § 103 (1967).
This section was apparently taken from the substitute bill proposed by the Interior Department, section 2(a) of which read:
> The privilege of the Writ of Habeas Corpus shall be available to an American Indian, in a court of the United States, to test the legality of his detention by order of a tribal court.
See 1965 Hearings, supra note 17, at 318; testimony of Solicitor Frank Barry in support of this bill. *Id.* at 24.
Mr. Lawrence Speiser, testifying on behalf of the American Civil Liberties Union urged inclusion of habeas corpus saying:
> This particular provision probably has been taken care of by the recent decision of the Ninth Circuit Court of Appeals in the Colliflower case which held that Indians could test their detention pursuant to a tribal court conviction by writ of habeas corpus. Although this court decision establishes this right, certainly it should be included if you are going to spell out a bill of rights for Indians. *Id.* at 22.

any of the proposed legislation. While there is little in the legislative history which directly explains the reason for insertion of this remedy, some of the background and related matters considered by the Subcommittee provide perspective.

In considering S. 962, the de novo review bill, the Subcommittee in 1965 took note of *Colliflower v. Garland*[42] and described it as holding that federal district courts had jurisdiction to issue writs of habeas corpus for determining the validity of tribal court decisions.[43]

In 1966, in its Summary Report, the Subcommittee commented that there had been considerable support for the idea of federal court review to determine questions of deprivation of constitutional rights in tribal courts. It was proposed in the event of a finding that there had been such constitutional deprivation, the case should be remanded by the federal district court with instructions for dismissal or retrial.[44] In that context, the report took note that under *Colliflower v. Garland*, habeas corpus might accomplish the same objective without *any* legislation.[45] The Subcommittee was quite aware of the problem of federal court overload. For instance, Frank J. Barry, Solicitor, Department of the Interior, testified as to S. 962:

> We believe that this would put a very great burden on the district courts and that that burden could be largely eliminated by permitting appeals within the Department, and after final determination in the Department, to the local district court.[46]

It appears that the Subcommittee determined initially to push forward with the idea of trials de novo even if it created problems of overload for federal district courts.[47] But it seems that Senator Ervin was later persuaded otherwise. Burnett writes that Senator Ervin was convinced by the arguments of many tribal attorneys and United States attorneys that trials de novo under S. 962 "would put an intolerable strain on the district courts, already suffering from a chronic overload of cases."[48] Another observer claims, how-

---

42. 342 F.2d 369 (9th Cir. 1965).
43. *1965 Hearings, supra* note 17, at 2.
44. 1966 SUMMARY REPORT, *supra* note 24, at 13.
45. Id. Testimony of Arthur Lazarus.
46. *1965 Hearings, supra* note 17, at 19.
47. In the Summary Report the Committee said:
Arguments that the federal district courts are overcrowded and could not handle the additional case load presented by S. 962 would not seem important enough to negate the very real need for providing the American Indian access to an appeal forum that is unbiased, already in operation, and staffed with trained personnel. The condition of the federal courts' docket is a matter for Congress to rectify, and should not concern this Subcommittee's recommendations on the administration of Indian justice . . . . 1966 SUMMARY REPORT, *supra* note 24, at 26.
However, though the appellate provisions of S. 961 were originally contained in S. 1843, the version which was reported out by the Senate Subcommittee deleted it entirely leaving in only the habeas corpus provision.
48. Burnett, *supra* note 11, at 602 n.240.

ever, that the Subcommittee itself deleted the appeals provisions before reporting the bill out, even though it was strongly endorsed by Senator Ervin, on the ground that trials de novo in federal court would cause too serious a disruption of tribal self-government.[49] These arguments appear to have been persuasive, for the trial de novo provisions as originally contained in S. 1843 were scrapped and as finally reported S. 1843 contained only one provision vesting jurisdiction in federal courts—the habeas corpus provision.

The habeas corpus remedy is the remnant of the original area of federal court jurisdiction envisaged in S. 962. In that respect, as Burnett notes, it did little more than confirm *Colliflower*.[50] Whether because of its concern with federal court overload or concern for inordinate disruption of tribal government, Congress clearly envisaged the role of the federal courts in the enforcement of the Indian Civil Rights Act as limited in scope.

We have thus seen how the Subcommittee's original proposal to provide for federal court review was transformed from full trial de novo, to limited trial de novo and finally, to review by way of habeas corpus. The habeas corpus provision stands out in glaring isolation as the only explicit provision for federal court intervention.

B. *Senate Bill 963: Federal Enforcement Actions in Support of Indian Rights*

Senate Bill 963 authorized the Attorney General to investigate and act on complaints of Indians alleging deprivation of constitutional rights. The bill ordered the Attorney General to bring criminal or civil actions to "vindicate or secure such rights to Indians." Prepared in response to complaints of deprivation of rights, including illegal detention by tribal officials and mistreatment by tribal law enforcement officers,[51] S. 963 was thus intended to be a second means of implementing the Indian Bill of Rights.

The Summary Report noted that while the bill did not elicit as much commentary as S. 962, it did arouse strong tribal opposition. The Summary Report quotes two comments as illustrative. One witness testified:

> This [bill] would in effect subject the tribal sovereignty of self-government to the federal government . . . . This bill by its broad terms, would allow the attorney general to bring any kind of action as he deems appropriate. By this bill, any time a member of a tribe would not be satisfied with an action by the council, it would allow them to file a complaint with the attorney general and subject

---

49. Lazarus, *supra* note 11.
50. Burnett, *supra* note 11, at 602 n.240.
51. *1965 Hearings, supra* note 17, at 2-3.

the tribe to a multitude of investigations and threat of court action.[52]

One tribe submitted the following statement:

> We are diametrically opposed to the provisions of Senate Bill 963 for the reason that we feel it would be used to undermine and harass existing tribal government.
> Every segment of society in the United States has a few perpetually dissatisfied members. If the perpetually dissatisfied individual Indian were to be armed with legislation such as proposed Senate Bill 963 he could disrupt the whole of a tribal government.
> Naturally, such legislation would be a potent weapon in hands of a political opponent, on an Indian Reservation.[53]

The Department of the Interior also expressed its opposition to S. 963 and proposed a substitute.[54] Senate Bill 963 was dropped by the Subcommittee, its final recommendations stating that "In view of the strong opposition to S. 963 expressed by interested witnesses and the Department of the Interior, the subcommittee recommends that this bill not be reported."[55]

The Subcommittee thus seems to have concluded that S. 963 would have presented too great a potential for intrusion by the federal government into disputes of tribal government.[56]

C. *Senate Bill 964: The Model Code*

Senate Bill 964 directed the Secretary of the Interior to recommend by July 1, 1965, a model code to govern the administration of justice by Courts of Indian Offenses on Indian reservations. From the legislative history, it appears that the Subcommittee was most impressed with the importance of the model code as the vehicle by which the objectives of the Indian Bill of Rights would be primarily achieved. It considered that inadequacies of proce-

---

52. 1966 SUMMARY REPORT, *supra* note 24, at 15 (testimony of Mr. Edison Real Bird).
53. *Id.* (statement of Mescalero Apache Tribal Council).
54. The substitute legislation would have channeled all complaints pertaining to the tribal council through the Secretary. Burnett, *supra* note 11, at 595.
55. 1966 SUMMARY REPORT, *supra* note 24, at 26.
56. Despite the Subcommittee's decision to delete S. 963 from the Act, 18 U.S.C. §§ 241-42 (1970) may have the effect now of authorizing criminal prosecution for violations of the Indian Civil Rights Act. The identical language was used by Senator Ervin on the Senate floor when the Indian Civil Rights Act was before the Senate for passage. 113 CONG. REC. 13473 (1967). It was also the point made by Congressman Ben Reifel (South Dakota) in debate on the legislation before the House. Mr. Reifel, who is himself an enrolled member of the Rosebud Sioux Tribe of South Dakota, and the only Indian in Congress at that time, told the House:
> Basically, these titles would accomplish two major objectives: First, they would create a bill of rights for the protection of Indians tried by tribal courts, and would improve the quality of justice administered by those courts; and second, they would provide for the assumption of civil and criminal jurisdiction by states over Indian country within their borders only with the consent of the tribes affected. 114 CONG. REC. 9552 (1968).

dures in the tribal courts were far and away the worst source of abuse of constitutional rights. In its Summary Report, the Subcommittee said:

> Though evidence of the denial of substantive and political rights has been brought to the Subcommittee's attention, it is apparent that an Indian citizen's rights are most seriously jeopardized by the tribal government's administration of justice. These denials occur, it is also apparent, not from malice or ill-will, or from a desire to do injustice, but from the tribal judges' inexperience, lack of training and unfamiliarity with the traditions and forms of the American legal system.[57]

Senate Bill 964 was therefore designed to provide a means of enforcing constitutional rights of all individuals facing criminal charges in Courts of Indian Offenses. The bill included measures to establish proper qualifications for tribal judges, and to achieve this by establishment of educational classes for judicial training. Senate Bill 964 clearly provided that the code would deal only with criminal procedure. There is here a direct parallel to S. 962, the de novo appeal bill, which limited review to criminal cases. Nevertheless, a number of witnesses suggested in testimony before the Subcommittee that the code might enumerate all of the rights guaranteed to the individual by S. 961.[58]

In general, the testimony of such witnesses tended to view S. 964 as "the proper vehicle by which the objectives of S. 961 and S. 962 could be realized."[59] As the Summary Report said, "A model code, it was suggested, could both enumerate Indian rights and specify and improve trial and appellate procedures to be instituted within the structure of tribal government."[60]

The Subcommittee recommended that the Bill of Rights and de novo review bills (S. 961 and S. 962) be combined into one bill, and concluded:

> In order to fully implement the recommended changes in S. 961 and S. 962 it is necessary to have a written tribal code for the federal judge to follow. These bills should be amended to set a time limit within which all tribes have to adopt a written tribal code or accept the one in 25 C.F.R. The effect of S. 961 and 962, as combined, should be postponed for one year after its enactment, thus affording Indian tribes a period in which to prepare themselves for a new concept of law and order.[61]

---

57. 1966 SUMMARY REPORT, *supra* note 24, at 24.
58. *See, e.g.,* 1966 SUMMARY REPORT, *supra* note 24, at 11 (testimony of Arthur Lazarus). Several witnesses before the Subcommittee proposed that before enacting S. 961 as a separate bill, its provisions should be incorporated into S. 964 to provide a comprehensive model code. *Id.* at 13.
59. 1966 SUMMARY REPORT, *supra* note 24, at 16.
60. *Id.*
61. *Id.* at 26.

It was here that the concept of the one-year moratorium was born. The concept appears to have been important to the Subcommittee's thinking. The year-long moratorium would enable tribes to adopt a written tribal code or accept the one in title 25 of the Code of Federal Regulations. Written tribal codes were considered essential for use by the federal judges in appeals by trial de novo. Further although the trial de novo provisions were soon transformed into the habeas corpus provision, the one-year moratorium was retained until much later in the legislative process, and eventually dropped in favor of a deadline for submission of the model code.[62]

While S. 964 and its latter version, S. 1844, provided only for the model code of criminal offenses, it must be remembered that the Subcommittee felt tribes should adopt tribal codes dealing with *all* the individual rights guaranteed in S. 961, including protection in areas not involving criminal offenses. It appears, therefore, that the intent of Congress in Title II of the Act as enacted was that tribes enact codes much more comprehensive in scope than merely dealing with criminal offenses. The reference in the Act to the model code in 25 Code of Federal Regulations supports this conclusion since that model code contains both criminal and civil jurisdictional provisions.[63]

As of this writing, a draft of a Model Criminal Procedure Code and Commentary has been prepared and circulated for comment by the Indian Civil Rights Task Force, an Interior Department agency created to comply with the requirements of title 25 United States Code, sections 1311 and 1341. The concept of the model code is central to Congressional intent, since the Subcommittee made

---

62. Section 104 of S. 1843 made the entire bill effective one year after enactment and it directed the Secretary of Interior to recommend a model code to Congress on or before July 3, 1968. There is some suggestion that section 104 was lost in the legislative shuffle when S. 1843 was incorporated into Pub. L. 90-284 and that there was concern about the Civil Rights Act becoming effective immediately. The report of the staff of the Senate Subcommittee dealt with the matter as follows:

> Provisions of S. 1843 were incorporated into Pub. L. 90-284 as Titles II through VII. Title II became effective upon enactment of the law on April 19, 1968. This provision as defined in S. 1843, was scheduled to become effective one year after the date of enactment. Senator Ervin, various tribal leaders, individual Indians and prominent attorneys for the Indian tribes expressed their views that the immediate effective date of Title II will not work an undo [sic] hardship on individual Indians and tribes.
> Senator Ervin stated: "The Subcommittee on Constitutional Rights has been in constant consultation with the Bureau of Indian Affairs concerning implementation of the Indian rights measures and the subcommittee hopes to conduct field investigations in the near future, possibly in the early fall, to monitor the process and determine whether assistance can be given to Indian tribes in applying the new provisions."

STAFF OF SENATE COMMITTEE ON THE JUDICIARY, SUBCOMMITTEE ON CONSTITUTIONAL RIGHTS, 89th Cong., 2d Sess., MONTHLY REPORT (Nov. 1966).
63. 25 C.F.R. §§ 11.5(b), 11.23(a)-(c). In general these sections contain elementary procedural provisions and also require the court to apply all applicable laws of the United States to any civil actions before it.

clear that it was for the purpose of allowing tribes time to adopt new tribal codes that it recommended a one-year moratorium on the effectiveness of the substantive rights section of the bills. The Subcommitte contemplated that the entire substantive rights section of the bills be held in abeyance pending preparation and adoption of written tribal codes by which federal district courts hearing de novo criminal appeals could be guided.

Summary of Congressional Intent: Senator Ervin Speaks

From this review of the implementing provisions of the Act, it can now be seen that Congress' principal focus was on the protection of Indian rights in the context of criminal proceedings. Two of the principal cases which were before the Subcommittee and which were repeatedly referred to in the hearings, *Native American Church v. Navajo Tribal Council*[64] and *Colliflower v. Garland*[55] involved criminal sanctions, one through a criminal ordinance prohibiting certain practices, and the other through a criminal punishment for violating a trespass order of the tribal judge. The only measure ever considered by the Subcommittee regarding civil matters was S. 963, authorizing the Attorney General to file civil actions. This bill was dropped, largely because tribal leaders urged that it would lead to substantial federal intrusion in tribal politics and internal conflicts. The Model Code was intended to provide a framework for protection of constitutional rights in tribal courts, at least in the criminal context, and the habeas corpus provision was intended to guarantee federal court intervention only in those cases in which individual liberty was threatened and constitutional questions were presented.

This is in fact what Senator Ervin himself said in explaining the impact of the bill one year later in Subcommittee hearings on proposed amendments. The Senator engaged in a dialogue with Mr. Domingo Montoya, chairman of the Pueblo Council, who delivered a message of protest as to the effect of the bill on the traditional customs and practices of the Pueblos. The following exchange occurred:

> SENATOR ERVIN: When people are tried in one of the Pueblos, are they allowed to have any friends to represent them or speak for them?

> MR. MONTOYA: Yes. The Council itself sits in there and argues. Some of the Council argue for the defendant, some argue for the state and for the Pueblo. *If its a claim for damage,* everything is taken into consideration. I can't see where representation is lacking from either side.

---

64. 272 F.2d 131 (10th Cir. 1959).
65. 342 F.2d 639 (9th Cir. 1965).

> SENATOR ERVIN: This bill does not provide for the
> federal courts to review all the decisions of the Indian
> courts. In fact, provision for federal review was in
> there originally, and at the request of a number of
> tribes we eliminated that entirely. *The only provision
> in this bill that provides for federal court interference
> is writ of habeas corpus,* and that probably exists as
> law now, although I am not quite certain. If the man
> was convicted in violation of a law, the federal court
> would have the jurisdiction to issue a writ of habeas
> corpus. I don't imagine that there would be too many
> of those.[66]

Senator Ervin's comments were made in the context of a general discussion of Indian trials and must be taken to include both civil and criminal cases. His declaration was to the effect that federal courts only interfere by issuance of writs of habeas corpus, that is, when there is incarceration or the threat of it.

This review of the legislative history would appear to demonstrate that Congress intended to take a first and limited step in imposing what are essentially Anglo-Saxon constitutional standards on Indian tribes. By providing federal court review of detention of persons and uniform principles of individual rights applicable to all tribal governments and their constitutions, Congress made a major and unusual incursion into the internal affairs of Indian tribes. Further, Congress was well aware that should it appear that tribal governments ignored the commandments of the Act so that additional remedies were needed, it could take such steps as were necessary and vest federal courts with additional jurisdiction.

This "first step" doctrine was specifically expressed by the Subcommittee itself. Noting some drawbacks of the trial de novo measure, the Subcommittee stated that it felt that the right to appeal would be "an important first step in according the Indian full due process of law . . . ."[67]

---

66. *Hearing Before the Subcommittee on Constitutional Rights of the Senate Committee on the Judiciary, Amendments to the Indian Bill of Rights,* 91st Cong., 1st Sess. 15 (1969) (emphasis added).

Senator Ervin was presiding at hearings on S. 2173, a bill which would amend the 1968 Act in order to meet the objections of the Pueblos and other Southwest tribes who felt the 1968 Act would destroy their theocratic form of government. Title II of S. 2173 was identical to the language of Title II of the 1968 Act. S. 2173 was passed by the Senate on July 11, 1969, but was later killed by the Indian Affairs Subcommittee in the House of Representatives. 115 CONG. REC. 19239 (1969).

67. 1966 SUMMARY REPORT, *supra* note 24, at 26. Senator Ervin himself made this clear in his speech to the Senate introducing the legislation, when he said:

> In introducing these proposals, I wish to emphasize that these bills
> should not be considered as the final solution to the many serious
> constitutional problems confronting the American Indian. A system
> tem of law and order for the Indian tribes of America which is
> in keeping with the rights and privileges other Americans enjoy,
> will take years to develop. The substance of these bills, however,
> is an exceedingly important and necessary part of this goal. 113
> CONG. REC. 13473 (1967).

Finally, in its conclusions and recommendations, the Subcommittee said that its position was essentially that of the House Committee on Indian Affairs reporting to the 23rd Congress in 1834, saying in part that "what is now proposed is only an approximation to a perfect system. Much is necessarily left out for the present to executive discretion, and still more to future legislation."[68]

The Congressional Intent as Reflected by the Overall Legislation

In its final form, the Indian Civil Rights Act contained six titles: "Rights of Indians," "Model Code Governing Court of Indian Offenses," "Jurisdiction Over Civil and Criminal Actions," "Offenses Within Indian Country," "Employment of Legal Counsel," and "Materials Relating to Constitutional Rights of Indians." The overall pattern disclosed the following judgments of the Ervin Subcommittte and Congress. Individual Indian rights should no longer be a matter of choice for tribes, but should be imposed uniformly on all tribes as a matter of federal law, with rights specifically defined in language taken largely from the United States Constitution. The quality of justice in tribal courts should be improved and procedures should be prepared either by the tribe or by the Secretary of Interior to insure that these rights were protected in the tribal courts. Persons threatened with arrest or incarceration by tribal courts should have the right to bring constitutional questions before the federal courts for review. The vitality of the concept of tribal sovereignty should be recognized by the courts. Law enforcement deficiencies should be cured by restoring Indian or federal jurisdiction in states which failed to act or wished to relieve themselves of responsibility. Extension of state jurisdiction should be halted absent tribal approval. The full protection of legal rights of Indian tribes should be improved by requiring the Bureau of Indian Affairs to act promptly in approving tribal attorneys' contracts and by requiring the Interior Department to update and publish legal materials vitally affecting the rights of Indian tribes.

This review of the legislative history has led the writer to conclude that Congress considered the role of the federal courts in the enforcement of rights under this Act to be narrowly circumscribed. It deliberately scrapped the bill which would have given the Attorney General the power and duty to bring civil or criminal actions in the federal courts to enforce the substantive rights provisions of the Act. It did this largely because of the protest of tribal witnesses that this would result in substantial intrusion of the federal courts into tribal internal affairs. For this reason and also because it was concerned about the additional burden in the case load of the federal district courts, it scrapped an entire section authorizing

---

68. *Id.* at 25.

trial de novo, even where there was a means of determining that the case presented constitutional questions. It very deliberately left the federal courts with the duty to respond only to habeas corpus petitions. The model code provisions and the accompanying moratorium revealed the intention that the heart of enforcement of the substantive rights was to be the tribes' own justice system. Further it had complete confidence that by the enactment of the substantive bill of rights, it was achieving its desired object: the extension of constitutional rights to American Indians. There are no words in the entire legislative record to suggest any Congressional awareness that title 28 United States Code section 1331 or section 1343(4) would be available for use in private actions by Indians against their tribes. Nor is there anything in the legislative history to suggest that Congress ever intended that any federal court would exercise jurisdiction other than that of habeas corpus.[69]

FEDERAL REMEDIES: A JUDICIAL SUPPLEMENT TO THE INDIAN CIVIL RIGHTS ACT

The Question of Jurisdiction, Remedies and Sovereign Immunity of Indian Tribes From Suit

Following enactment of the Indian Civil Rights Act, both Indians and non-Indians began suits in federal courts against Indian tribes, their councils, their courts and their judges claiming denial of constitutional protections and asking for every form of relief: injunction, mandamus, declaratory judgment, money damages, and in a few cases, writs of habeas corpus. Almost every conceivable type of tribal dispute has been brought to the federal courts: election procedures,[70] legislative apportionment,[71] propriety of conduct of tribal government,[72] criminal procedures and penal facilities,[73]

---

69. It is significant that none of the statements on the proposed legislation submitted to the Subcommittee by Indian tribes, Indian organizations and tribal attorneys (including the writer) indicated any awareness of the possibility that federal courts would go beyond the habeas corpus provisions in the Act, and no comments were directed to such a contingency. *See* 1965 Hearings, *supra* note 17.

70. Means v. Wilson, Civ. No. 74-5010 (D.S.D. Sept. 20, 1974); United States v. San Carlos Apache, Civ. No. 74-52TUC (D. Ariz. April 12, 1974); Pawnee Business Council, Civ. No. 73-C-11 (D. Okla. 1974); Barrackman v. Artichoker, Civ. No. 71-366 (D. Ariz. Jan. 16, 1973); McCurdy v. Steele, 353 F. Supp. 629 (D. Utah 1973); Joshua v. Goodhouse, Civ. No. 4469 (D.N.D. April 7, 1971); Solomon v. LaRose, 335 F. Supp. 715 (D. Neb. 1971). *Cf.* Groundhog v. Keeler, 442 F.2d 674 (10th Cir. 1974).

71. Brown v. United States, 486 F.2d 658 (8th Cir. 1973); Daly v. Crow Creek Sioux Tribe, 483 F.2d 700 (8th Cir. 1973); White Eagle v. One Feather, 478 F.2d 1311 (8th Cir. 1973); St. Marks v. Canan, Civ. No. 2928 (D. Mont. Jan. 20, 1971).

72. Seneca Const. Rts. Org. v. George, 348 F. Supp. 48, 51 (W.D.N.Y. 1972); Loncassion v. Leekity, 334 F. Supp. 370 (D.N.M. 1971); Lefthand v. Crow Tribal Council, 329 F. Supp. 728 (D. Mont. 1971); Cornelius v. Moxon, 301 F. Supp. 783 (D.N.D. 1969).

73. Oliphant v. Schlie, Civ. No. 511-73C2 (W.D. Wash. April 5, 1974); *In re* Pablo, Civ. No. 72-99 (D. Ariz. July 21, 1972); Richards v. Pine Ridge Tribal Court, Civ. No. 70-74W (D.S.D. 1971); Richards v. Pine Ridge Tribal

enrollment questions,[74] the legality of tribal qualifications for office,[75] for membership and for voting,[76] property disputes,[77] propriety of tribal court decisions in civil matters,[78] job discrimination,[79] and exclusion.[80] Although some decisions question the jurisdiction of federal courts to entertain such claims and grant such relief, the general trend now appears to be established: federal courts will take jurisdiction of these claims and will in appropriate cases grant all forms of relief against tribes, tribal governing bodies, tribal court judges and other tribal officials. All of these courts find they have jurisdiction to hear these cases and authority to grant relief because of their view of the effect of the Indian Civil Rights Act.

However, before such conclusions can be accepted, three basic questions must be answered in the affirmative: (1) Does a statute vest federal jurisdiction over such claims in the United States district courts? (2) Apart from jurisdiction, is there a statutory or common law right sufficient to support a court remedy for its invasion? (3) Has the sovereign immunity from suit of Indian tribes been expressly waived? As we examine the decided cases, we shall find that these questions are closely related, and in fact their answers are interdependent.

To begin with, the Indian Civil Rights Act itself vests no jurisdiction in federal courts over any claim arising under the Act except habeas corpus jurisdiction. Nor does the Act itself make mention of any private cause of action for securing relief against claimed invasions of rights thereunder. In fact, it may be asked whether

---

Court, Civ. No. 70-74W (D.S.D. 1970); Low Dog v. Cheyenne River Sioux, Civ. No. 69-21C (D.S.D. Mar. 14, 1969); Spotted Eagle v. Blackfeet Tribe, 301 F. Supp. 85 (D. Mont. 1969).

74. Thompson v. Tonasket, 487 F.2d 316 (9th Cir. 1973), *cert. denied*, 95 S. Ct. 132 (1974); Laramie v. Nicholson, 487 F.2d 315 (9th Cir. 1973); Hein v. Nicholson, Civ. No. 3459 (E.D. Wash. Nov. 30, 1971); Pinnow v. Shoshone Tribal Council, 314 F. Supp. 1157 (D. Wyo. 1970), *aff'd sub nom.* Slattery v. Arapahoe Tribal Council, 453 F.2d 278 (10th Cir. 1971).

75. Groundhog v. Keeler, 442 F.2d 674 (10th Cir. 1971); Yellowbird v. Oglala Sioux Tribe, Civ. No. 74-5009 (D.S.D. Aug. 8, 1974); Luxon v. Rosebud Sioux Tribe, 337 F. Supp. 243 (D.S.D. 1971), *rev'd* 455 F.2d 698 (8th Cir. 1972).

76. Armstrong v. Howard, Civ. No. 6-72-CIV-315 (D.C. Minn. Jan. 22, 1974); Wounded Head v. Tribal Council of Oglala Sioux, Civ. No. 73-5096 (D.S.D. 1974).

77. Johnson v. Lower Elwha Tribal Community, 484 F.2d 200 (9th Cir. 1973); O'Neal v. Cheyenne River Sioux Tribe, 482 F.2d 1140 (8th Cir. 1973); Brendale v. United States, Civ. No. C-74-21 (E.D. Wash. April 16, 1974); Hickey v. Crow Creek Housing Authority, Civ. No. 73-3002 (D.S.D. July 8, 1974); Clark v. Land & Forestry Committee, Civ. No. 74-3021 (D.S.D. Aug. 9, 1974); Crowe v. Eastern Band of Cherokees, Civ. No. 3412 (W.D.N.C. Dec. 11, 1973).

78. O'Neal v. Cheyenne River Sioux Tribe, 482 F.2d 1140 (8th Cir. 1973); Pickner v. Aikins, Civ. No. 73-3012 (D.S.D. Aug. 13, 1974); Towersap v. Ft. Hall Indian Tribal Court, Civ. No. 4-70-37 (D. Idaho, 1971); Claw v. Armstrong, Civ. No. C-2307 (D. Colo. Aug. 7, 1970); Regan v. Blackfeet Tribal Court, Civ. No. 2850 (D. Mont. July 7, 1969).

79. Cudmore v. Executive Comm'n of the Cheyenne River Sioux Tribal Court, Civ. No. 70-360 (D.S.D. 1970).

80. Dodge v. Nakai, 298 F. Supp. 17 & 26 (D. Ariz. 1968).

the Act does not preclude the creation of individual rights by expressly declaring that it is a set of restraints on tribal government.[81] Most important, the Act contains no mention of waiver of sovereign immunity from suit, nor does it grant the right to bring suit against Indian tribes or their officers. The habeas corpus provision of the Indian Civil Rights Act merely vests federal courts with jurisdiction to examine the constitutionality of detention pursuant to tribal authority and at most requires only those persons detaining tribal prisoners to appear to justify the detention orders.

But as we shall see, the federal courts have borrowed jurisdictional authority from other statutes predating the Indian Civil Rights Act and have borrowed a legal doctrine from civil rights cases to authorize an unlimited and wholly inappropriate scope of relief. Some of the federal courts have recognized the problem of sovereign immunity of Indian tribes from suit but have overcome this obstacle by concluding that the Indian Civil Rights Act, by implication, abrogated tribal sovereign immunity from suit and constituted authority by Congress to bring such actions.[82]

Most of the cases have considered these questions on motions to dismiss brought by defendant tribes. Many federal courts have limited their inquiry solely to the question of jurisdiction and have concluded that general jurisdiction statutes and non-Indian civil rights case doctrines authorize maintenance of broad-ranging suits against tribes. A few courts have recognized the problem of lack of waiver of sovereign immunity from suit and some have even concluded the doctrine to be an absolute bar. But on the whole, few courts have seriously analyzed the rationale and legal foundation of the doctrine of sovereign immunity of Indian tribes from suit, and their failure to do so has led them to improper application of jurisdictional statutes and civil rights cases. These courts have rejected the idea that the Congress intended to limit relief to the express remedy of habeas corpus and have reasoned that without additional judicial relief, the Act would be meaningless and unenforceable. This reasoning which is the basis of the very first case under the Act, *Dodge v. Nakai*,[83] and the later case of *Spotted Eagle v. Blackfeet Tribe*[84] is faulty. The direction set by these cases has not yet been altered.

---

81. "[N]o Indian tribe in exercising powers of self-government shall . . . ." 25 U.S.C. § 1302 (1970).

82. A number of commentators have considered the serious jurisdiction and sovereign immunity problems raised by the Indian Civil Rights Act. *See* Lazarus, *supra* note 11, wherein he says that suits to enforce the Act under 28 U.S.C. § 1331 (1970) federal question jurisdiction will have to overcome the "formidable sovereign immunity hurdle" and that since the Act does not authorize the filing of any civil action, 28 U.S.C. § 1343(4) (1970) would not sustain such a claim. *See also*, Rieblich, *Indian Rights Under the Civil Rights Act of 1968*, 10 ARIZ. L. REV. 617 (1968); Note, *Indian Bill of Rights*, 5 S.W.L. REV. 139 (1973); Note, *Indians—Criminal Procedure, Habeas Corpus as an Enforcement Procedure Under the Indian Civil Rights Act of 1968*, 46 WASH. L. REV. 541 (1971).

83. 298 F. Supp. 17 & 26 (D. Ariz. 1968).

84. 301 F. Supp. 85 (D. Mont. 1969).

The Courts' Refusal to Accept Limitation of Remedies

A. *Dodge and Spotted Eagle: Jurisdiction Creates a Remedy*

The first two reported cases in which there was an analysis of the scope of the remedies under Title II of the Indian Civil Rights Act were *Dodge v. Nakai* and *Spotted Eagle v. Blackfeet Tribe.* In *Dodge,* Theodore Mitchell, the principal plaintiff, was a white lawyer who directed the Navajo Legal Services program and sued to challenge the constitutionality of the action of the tribal council in excluding him from the Reservation. He sought an injunction and money damages against the chairman of the Navajo Tribal Council, the superintendent of the Navajo Police Department and the area director of the Bureau of Indian Affairs. The district court denied a motion to dismiss and found that it had jurisdiction.

In *Spotted Eagle,* a group of Blackfeet Indians brought a class action against the tribe, the chief of the tribal police force and the judges of the tribal courts. The plaintiffs sought to enjoin the use of the tribal jail, to require tribal judges to grant all state and federal rights including the right for alcoholics to be treated rather than jailed, to nullify the law and order code of the tribe and to obtain damages. Here again, the district court denied a motion to dismiss for want of jurisdiction.

Though the decision in *Dodge* on the motion to dismiss was made December 20, 1968, it was not referred to in the *Spotted Eagle* decision which was made in July, 1969. It may be assumed, therefore, that the two federal district courts proceeded quite independently in their analyses of remedies available under the Act. In each case, the court was considering a motion to dismiss, and each court looked first to its jurisdictional authority. Each was satisfied of its jurisdiction under title 28 United States Code section 1331[85] (federal question jurisdiction) and title 28 United States Code section 1343(4)[86] (actions authorized by law to secure relief under any act of Congress providing for the protection of civil rights). Finally each court relied on *Jones v. Mayer*[87] as authority for its jurisdiction under section 1343(4) and simply applied what they conceived to be the *Jones* rule, *i.e.,* whenever a federal law declares a civil right, persons protected by the law are authorized to bring actions

---

85. 28 U.S.C. § 1331(a) provides in part:
  (a) The district courts shall have original jurisdiction of all civil actions wherein the matter in controversy exceeds the sum or value of $10,000, exclusive of interest and costs, and arises under the Constitution, laws, or treaties of the United States.
86. 28 U.S.C. § 1343(4) provides in part:
  The district courts shall have original jurisdiction of any civil action authorized by law to be commenced by any person:
  . . . .
  (4) To recover damages or to secure equitable or other relief under any Act of Congress providing for the protection of civil rights, including the right to vote.
87. 392 U.S. 409 (1968).

to enforce the right and federal district courts are vested with jurisdiction of such actions.

Both courts reasoned that by the creation of a federal statutory civil right, remedies were available under the *Jones* rule or under the doctrine of pendent jurisdiction over claims arising under substantive principles of state law. *Spotted Eagle* alone took note of the limited remedy provided in the Act itself—the habeas corpus remedy—but it did so only in passing and promptly went on to reason that *Jones* provided a sufficient foundation for equitable and other remedies even though the Act establishing the right mentioned no such remedies.

B. *Rationales for Overcoming the Limited Jurisdiction in the Act*

The first cases to deal with the significance of the remedy limitation in the Act were the district court cases of *Loncassion v. Leekity*[88] and *Solomon v. LaRose*.[89] In *Loncassion* the court considered whether by providing only the habeas corpus remedy, Congress had indicated any intent to limit the jurisdiction of federal courts under the Act. The *Loncassion* court answered negatively, saying:

> Violations of constitutional rights, however, do not always take the form of incarceration and if enforcement of the act were limited to habeas corpus proceedings, some provisions of the Act would be unenforceable and thus meaningless. Because it cannot be presumed that Congress would pass an act containing provisions which could not be enforced, the existence of the habeas corpus provision of the Act cannot be said to limit federal court jurisdiction to those proceedings.[90]

In *Solomon* the court was unable to accept the idea of jurisdiction being limited to habeas corpus, saying this would "render nugatory" many of the rights secured by section 1302.[91]

But the court apparently felt it necessary to deal with the question of why Congress chose to provide only the specific habeas corpus remedy—a question which should surely excite some judicial curiosity.

Searching for a reason for the enactment of the habeas corpus provision, the court concluded it must be found in the wording of the existing federal habeas corpus statute,[92] which, said the court, "palpably indicates" that it would not provide jurisdiction over tribal courts or councils.[93]   Therefore, the court concluded, "Con-

---

88. 334 F. Supp. 370 (D.N.M. 1971).
89. 335 F. Supp. 715 (D. Neb. 1971).
90. 334 F. Supp. at 372-73.
91. 335 F. Supp. at 721.
92. 28 U.S.C. § 2241(c)(1)-(5) (1970).
93. 335 F. Supp. at 721.

gress felt compelled to enact a special jurisdictional statute for habeas corpus relief in the federal court."[94]   Having thus disposed of the troublesome issue of limited statutory jurisdiction, the court felt free to consider the applicability of other jurisdictional statutes to the type of relief sought by the plaintiff.

As we have seen from an examination of the legislative history, the court's assertion that Congress "felt compelled" to provide a special jurisdictional statute for habeas corpus is wholly unsupportable.   It is in fact contradicted by the legislative history, which explains how it came about that habeas corpus was specifically left standing alone as the only remedial provision in the statute.   It is, of course, the successor to the trial de novo of S. 962.

Moreover, not only is the court wrong as a matter of fact as to the reason why the habeas corpus remedy is found in the Indian Civil Rights Act, it is also wrong in its analysis of the law.   Title 28 United States Code section 2241(c) provides:

> The writ of habeas corpus shall not extend to a prisoner unless . . . .
>
> . . . .
>
> (3) He is in custody in violation of the Constitution or laws and treaties of the United States . . . .

Prior to the enactment of the Indian Civil Rights Act, the only claim which could be made by one confined under authority of a tribal court would be that his confinement in some way violated the United States Constitution.   This precise section was, in fact, held to be applicable and jurisdiction was taken under it by the court in *Colliflower v. Garland*,[95] a case which is even cited by the court in *Solomon*.   It was also the jurisdictional statute employed to consider the habeas corpus petition from a tribal court in *Settler v. Yakima Tribal Court*.[96]   Both of those cases predated the Indian Civil Rights Act, and under strained reasoning, the courts there were considering the applicability of provisions of the United States Constitution.   After the passage of the Indian Civil Rights Act, there could be little question that detention in violation of some substantive right under the Act would confer jurisdiction on the federal court for habeas corpus relief.   In fact, the habeas corpus remedy is probably surplusage, since the federal courts would have such jurisdiction without it.   As we have seen, the Ervin Subcommittee was aware of *Colliflower v. Garland*, but may well have felt that any questions as to the availability of habeas corpus could be laid to rest by a specific statutory enactment.   This is supported by the comment of Senator Ervin referred to, which bears repeating:

---

94. *Id.*
95. 342 F.2d 369 (9th Cir. 1965).
96. 419 F.2d 486 (9th Cir. 1969).

The only provision in this bill which provides for federal court interference is writ of habeas corpus, *and that probably exists as law now, although I am not quite certain . . . .*[97]

The decisions in *Loncassion, Solomon* and *Luxon v. Rosebud Sioux Tribe*[98] would seem to have laid to rest the question of whether Congress had intended to limit jurisdiction by its specific and isolated enactment of habeas corpus as the only remedy expressly incorporated in the Act. But the question was raised again in 1973 in *McCurdy v. Steele.*[99] The *McCurdy* court disposed of the question in the same manner as *Solomon* and *Luxon* but not without some uneasiness. The court acknowledged in a footnote that *Colliflower v. Garland* was inconsistent with the argument that it was necessary to enact habeas corpus in order to provide jurisdiction which would not otherwise be available under title 28 United States Code section 2241.

It appears as though courts which have examined the question of remedies and jurisdiction have been completely convinced that unless additional remedies were afforded individual litigants by the federal courts, the Act would be "meaningless." The courts therefore gave only passing attention to the rather curious phenomenon of a single jurisdictional and remedial clause: the habeas corpus clause. Courts which did consider it, as noted above, contented themselves with the answer that it must have been out of concern for the inapplicability of the federal habeas corpus statute. The inquiry ended there.

Nevertheless, the striking isolation of the habeas corpus provision of the Indian Civil Rights Act has troubled every court which has examined the Act. In two cases, district courts dismissed lawsuits brought against Indian tribes under the Act on the ground that the habeas corpus provision was the only express provision for federal jurisdiction under the Act and the court was without jurisdiction to entertain the claim. These cases were *Pinnow v. Shoshone Tribal Council*[100] and *Luxon v. Rosebud Sioux Tribe of South Dakota.*[101] However, this reasoning was not sustained on appeal. In *Luxon,* the Eighth Circuit utilized the familiar argument that to hold that there was no jurisdiction beyond habeas corpus "would, in effect destroy the efficacy of the Indian Bill of Rights."[102]

This reaction to the statute presents a rather interesting study in statutory construction. If the statute had not contained any re-

---

97. *Hearings Before the Subcommittee on Constitutional Rights of the Committee on the Judiciary, Amendments to the Indian Bill of Rights,* 91st Cong., 1st Sess. 15 (1969) (emphasis added).
98. 337 F. Supp. 243 (D.S.D. 1971), *rev'd* 455 F.2d 698 (8th Cir. 1972).
99. 353 F. Supp. 629 (D. Utah 1973).
100. 314 F. Supp. 1157 (D. Wyo. 1970), *aff'd sub nom.* Slattery v. Arapahoe Tribal Council, 453 F.2d 278 (10th Cir. 1971).
101. 337 F. Supp. 243 (D.S.D. 1971), *rev'd* 455 F.2d 698 (8th Cir. 1972).
102. *Id.* at 700.

medial provisions whatever, it might be understandable that the courts would feel compelled to make their own presumptions about the Congressional intent. However, the inclusion of the single and isolated jurisdictional section would be expected to provoke rather thorough exploration of legislative history before concluding that the statute could not mean what it said. It could certainly not be expected that Congress would include language in the habeas corpus section declaring that it was the intention of Congress that *only* habeas corpus jurisdiction was vested in the federal courts and no other jurisdiction should apply. Such legislative language would be surprising indeed.

Furthermore, the courts should appreciate that the Indian Civil Rights Act is very much like the fourteenth amendment in that its provisions operate to restrain and limit the power and authority of quasi-sovereign governments, whose autonomy Congress was careful to protect. The limitation of remedies to habeas corpus is precisely what Congress intended. Failure to understand this has led the courts into serious error.

Jurisdiction Under the Indian Civil Rights Act—An Exception to 100 Years of Congressional Procedure?

The absence of any jurisdictional provision in the Act other than the habeas corpus provision is of very great significance in light of the fact that every other major civil rights act passed by Congress, including those passed after the enactment of title 28 United States Code section 1343(4),[103] contains a jurisdictional provision enabling federal courts to hear cases brought under it.[104]

In each of these acts, uniform structure is found: (1) a right is established, (2) a remedy for that right is specified and (3) the federal courts are vested with the necessary jurisdiction to hear the claim and grant appropriate relief. The Indian Civil Rights Act follows the pattern by its provision for habeas corpus review. If the habeas corpus section were not treated as the jurisdictional provision of the Act, then the Act would be left without any specific

---

103. This section was relied upon as a jurisdictional basis under the Indian Civil Rights Act in Thompson v. Tonasket, 487 F.2d 316 (9th Cir. 1973), *cert. denied*, 95 S. Ct. 132 (1974); Johnson v. Lower Elwha Tribal Community, 484 F.2d 200 (9th Cir. 1973); McCurdy v. Steele, 353 F. Supp. 629 (D. Utah 1973); Seneca Const. Rts. Org. v. George, 348 F. Supp. 48 (W.D.N.Y. 1972); Solomon v. LaRose, 335 F. Supp. 715 (D. Neb. 1971); Spotted Eagle v. Blackfeet Tribe, 301 F. Supp. 85 (D. Mont. 1969); Dodge v. Nakai, 298 F. Supp. 17 & 26 (D. Ariz. 1968).

104. Act of April 11, 1968, Pub. L. No. 90-284 § 101(a), 82 Stat. 73 (codified at 18 U.S.C. § 245 (1970)); Act of August 6, 1965, Pub. L. No. 89-110 § 10, 79 Stat. 437 (codified at 42 U.S.C. § 1973 (1970)); Act of July 2, 1964, Pub. L. No. 88-352 § 207, 78 Stat. 241 (codified at 42 U.S.C. § 1971 (1970)); Act of May 6, 1960, Pub. L. No. 86-449 § 101, 74 Stat. 86 (codified at 18 U.S.C. § 1509 (1970)); Act of September 9, 1957, Pub. L. No. 85-315, 71 Stat. 634 (codified at 42 U.S.C. § 1975 (1970)); Act of April 20, 1871, c. 22, § 1, 17 Stat. 13 (codified at 42 U.S.C. § 1983 (1970)); Act of May 31, 1870, c. 114, § 16, 16 Stat. 144 (codified at 42 U.S.C. § 1981 (1970)); Act of April 9, 1866, c. 31, § 1, 14 Stat. 27 (codified at 42 U.S.C. § 1982 (1970)).

jurisdictional provision whatever, thereby standing in stark contrast to all of the other civil rights acts enacted over the last 100 years. The very same act which includes the Indian Civil Rights Act follows the identical pattern in the fair housing portion, Title VIII, which contains a specific jurisdictional provision.[105]

All of the civil rights acts reflect scrupulous attention to the jurisdiction of the courts and the powers they may exercise in the enforcement of the rights established by the acts. There is no reason to assume that Congress was any less careful in drafting the Indian Civil Rights Act. In fact, since the Act originated in the Senate Judiciary Committee, with the chairman of the Subcommittee devoting his personal attention to the Act, one would have to assume the contrary. Nowhere in the legislative history of the Act can there be found any suggestion that the Subcommittee or Congress considered that any other jurisdictional act, such as title 25 United States Code section 1343(4), would provide a jurisdictional base for enforcement of this Act. The conclusion that Congress intended quite clearly that the habeas corpus section be the only jurisdictional section seems obvious.[106]

INDIAN SOVEREIGN IMMUNITY: AN OBSTACLE TO JURISDICTION

Distinction Between General Principle of Indian Sovereignty and Sovereign Immunity from Suit

The principle that an Indian tribe may not be subject to suit without the express consent of Congress is one deeply rooted in our law and based on the fundamental and broader principle of Indian tribal sovereignty. The Ervin Subcommittee was well aware of the concept of Indian sovereignty. However, its concerns focused mainly on two aspects of tribal sovereignty: internal autonomy and the inapplicability per se of federal civil rights guarantees.[107]

---

105. Section 812(a) provides in part:
> The rights granted by §§ 803, 804, 805 and 806 may be enforced by civil action in appropriate United States District Court without regard to the amount in controversy and in appropriate state or local courts of general jurisdiction . . . .

. . . .

> (c) the court may grant as relief, as it deems appropriate, any permanent or temporary injunction, temporary restraining order, or other order, and may award to the plaintiff actual damages and not more than $1,000 punitive damages, together with court costs and reasonable attorneys fees in the case of a prevailing plaintiff: provided, that the said plaintiff in the opinion of the court is not financially able to assume said attorney's fee.

106. The analysis of the basic significance of patterns of jurisdiction in civil rights legislation is based upon the Memorandum of Law prepared by the Indian Civil Rights Task Force, U.S. Department of Interior and the Memorandum of Law dated May 22, 1974 sent by the Office of the Solicitor, U.S. Department of the Interior to the Justice Department in reference to the pending question of the position to be taken by the United States in Thompson v. Tonasket, 487 F.2d 316 (9th Cir. 1973), cert. denied, 95 S. Ct. 132 (1974), in the United States Supreme Court.

107. *See* Solomon v. LaRose, 335 F. Supp. 715, 718 (D. Neb. 1971); 1966 SUMMARY REPORT, *supra* note 24, at 1-2; *1961 Hearings, supra* note 12, at 2-3.

The Subcommittee was always aware that tribal sovereignty is subject to limitation by act of Congress.

The Indian Civil Rights Act can only be properly understood if one keeps in mind the two distinct aspects of traditional Indian tribal sovereignty. On the one hand, tribal sovereignty has by its very existence precluded the application of federal civil rights guarantees to tribal governmental actions;[108] on the other hand, tribal sovereign immunity *from suit* precluded any jurisdiction in federal courts to entertain actions of any kind against Indian tribes, absent express Congressional consent.[109]

Sovereign immunity from suit is an attribute of Indian tribal sovereignty, but it is surrounded by special rules. It appears that failure to appreciate the distinction between sovereign tribal immunity from applicability of general laws and tribal sovereign immunity from suit explains in part the serious error into which the courts have fallen in dealing with jurisdictional questions under the Indian Civil Rights Act.

Sovereign Immunity From Suit and Jurisdiction: The Requirement of Express Congressional Consent

Where a government has sovereign immunity from suit, a court cannot acquire jurisdiction over an action brought against that government.[110] An Indian tribe is a quasi-sovereign governmental body possessing some of the characteristics of the totally immune sovereign. The principles underlying the sovereign status of Indian tribes has been classically stated by Cohen:

> The whole course of judicial decision on the nature of Indian tribal powers is marked by adherence to three fundamental principles: (1) An Indian tribe possesses, in the first instance, all the powers of any sovereign state. (2) Conquest renders the tribe subject to the legislative powers of the United States and, in substance, terminates the external powers of sovereignty of the tribe, e.g., its power to enter into treaties with foreign nations, but does not by itself affect the internal sovereignty of the tribe, i.e., its powers of local self-government. (3) These powers are subject to qualification by treaties and by express legislation of Congress, but, save as thus expressly qualified, full powers of internal sovereignty are vested in the Indian tribes and in their duly constituted organs of government.[111]

A principal attribute of an Indian tribe's status, therefore, is immunity from suit in the absence of express Congressional consent.

---

108. Talton v. Mayes, 163 U.S. 376 (1896); Native American Church v. Navajo Tribal Council, 272 F.2d 131 (10th Cir. 1959).
109. Thebo v. Choctaw Tribe, 66 F. 372 (8th Cir. 1895).
110. United States v. King, 395 U.S. 1 (1969); United States v. Sherwood, 312 U.S. 584 (1941).
111. F. COHEN, HANDBOOK OF FEDERAL INDIAN LAW 123 (1942).

General jurisdictional statutes will not overcome the requirement of express consent. The leading case is *Thebo v. Choctaw Tribe*.[112]

This was an action brought in the United States Court in Indian Territory by an attorney seeking to recover his fee from the Choctaw Tribe. He relied on two jurisdictional statutes. The first was the Act establishing the United States Court in Indian Territory and defining its jurisdiction as follows:

> That the court hereby established shall have jurisdiction in all civil cases between citizens of the United States who are residents of the Indian Territory, or between citizens of the United States or of any state or territory therein, and any citizens of or persons residing or found in the Indian Territory, and when the value or money claimed shall amount to $100 or more.[113]

The second was an Act of Congress a year later which expanded the jurisdiction of the territorial court:

> That the court established by said act [Act of March 1, 1889] *shall* in addition to the jurisdiction conferred thereon by said Act, *have and exercise within the limits of the Indian Territory, jurisdiction* in all civil cases in the Indian Territory, except cases over which the tribal courts have exclusive jurisdiction; and *in all cases on contracts entered into by citizens of any tribe or nations with citizens of the United States* in good faith and for valuable consideration, and in accordance of the laws of such tribe or nation, and such contract shall be deemed valid and enforced by such courts.[114]

The Eighth Circuit Court of Appeals ruled that the Choctaw Tribe had sovereign immunity from suit and that the plaintiff's claim must fail. The court found that although the jurisdictional statute spoke in terms of "all civil cases" and "all cases on contracts entered into, etc.," the statute nowhere expressly granted authority to bring suits against the tribe. While the latter act appeared to give both the federal courts and tribal courts jurisdiction over contract claims, the court made a clear distinction between acts granting jurisdiction and acts waiving sovereign immunity. The foundation of the ruling was the status of the tribe as a domestic dependent nation which, as a sovereign, may not be sued without its consent. Indian tribes occupy a position on the same plane occupied by the states under the eleventh amendment to the Constitution,[115]

---

112. 66 F. 372 (8th Cir. 1895).
113. Act of March 1, 1889, ch. 333, § 6, 25 Stat. 783.
114. Act of May 2, 1890, ch. 182, § 28, 26 Stat. 81 (emphasis added).
115. *Cf.* Edelman v. Jordan, 94 S. Ct. 1347, 1361 (1974), where the court said:

> In deciding whether a State has waived its constitutional protection under the Eleventh Amendment, we will find waiver only where stated "by the most express language or by such overwhelming implications from the test as will leave no room for any other reasonable construction" (footnote omitted).

the court said. However, because a tribe is a domestic dependent state, the United States might authorize suits to be brought against it. The court noted, however, that such authorization had been "sparingly exercised" and said:

> As rich as the Choctaw Nation is said to be in lands and money, it would soon be impoverished if it was subject to the jurisdiction of the courts, and required to respond to all the demands which private parties chose to prefer against it. The intention of Congress to confer such a jurisdiction upon any court would have to be expressed in plain and unambiguous terms.[116]

In *Turner v. United States*,[117] the plaintiff sued the Creek Nation and the United States as trustee of Creek funds for damages to his property which resulted from the failure of the tribe and its officers to keep the peace. The plaintiff, apparently a man of great determination, secured a special act of Congress specifically authorizing the Court of Claims to consider, adjudicate and render judgment upon his claim. The Act provided:

> That the Court of Claims is hereby authorized to consider and adjudicate and render judgment as law and equity may require in the matter of the claim of Clarence W. Turner of Muskogee, Oklahoma against the Creek Nation, for the destruction of personal property and the value of the loss of the pasture of said Turner or his assigns, by the action of any of the responsible Creek authorities or with their cognizance and acquiesence, either party in said cause had the right to appeal to the Supreme Court of the United States.[118]

The United States Supreme Court affirmed a judgment of dismissal by the Court of Claims because (1) there was no substantive right to recover damages for such a claim in the absence of any specific legislation creating such a cause of action and (2) an act granting authority to sue for such a claim does not expressly waive sovereign immunity of an Indian tribe, and without such authorization from Congress no suit could be maintained.[119]

In *Adams v. Murphy*[120] the Court of Appeals refused to find any waiver of Indian tribal immunity by reason of the Curtis Act which provided:

> When in the progress of any civil suit pending in the United States Court in any district, in said territory, it shall appear to the court that the property of any tribe is in any way affected by the issues being heard, said court is hereby authorized and required to make said tribe a party to said suit.[121]

---

116. 66 F. at 376.
117. 248 U.S. 354 (1919).
118. Act of May 29, 1908, ch. 216, 35 Stat. 444, 457.
119. 248 U.S. 354 (1919).
120. 165 F. 304 (8th Cir. 1908).
121. 30 Stat. 495.

The principle that any waiver of sovereign immunity must be founded upon express language and cannot be based upon implication has been forcefully stated in numerous cases involving the federal government. For instance, in *United States v. King*,[122] the Supreme Court held that the jurisdiction of the Court of Claims to grant relief against the United States depends wholly on the extent to which the United States has waived its immunity to suit, a waiver which cannot be implied but must be unequivocally expressed. The rule has found similar expression in numerous other cases.[123]

The same rule and the same clear language has been repeatedly expressed in connection with the claim of waiver of sovereign immunity of Indian tribes.[124] The rule has been stated with classic simplicity by the Supreme Court in *United States v. United States Fidelity and Guaranty Co.*[125] where the Court said:

> These Indian Nations are exempt from suit without Congressional authorization. It is as though the immunity which was theirs as sovereigns passed to the United States for their benefit, as their tribal properties did.[126]

The Court held that public policy forbade suits against an Indian tribe without express consent.

The principle was recently restated in *Hamilton v. Nakai*,[127] where an action was brought by the Hopi Indian Tribe against the Navajo Tribe and the Attorney General of the United States to quiet title to certain lands within the Navajo Reservation. The court said that under the rule of *United States v. United States*

---

122. 395 U.S. 1 (1969).
123. Soriano v. United States, 352 U.S. 270 (1957); Ford Motor Co. v. Dept. of Treasury of Indiana, 323 U.S. 459 (1945); United States v. Sherwood, 312 U.S. 584 (1941); United States v. Michel, 282 U.S. 656 (1931); Price v. United States, 174 U.S. 373 (1899); Schillinger v. United States, 155 U.S. 163 (1894); Stanton v. United States, 434 F.2d 1273 (5th Cir. 1970); Leyerly v. United States, 162 F.2d 79 (10th Cir. 1947); Barnes v. United States, 205 F. Supp. 97 (D. Mont. 1962); General Mutual Ins. Co. v. United States, 119 F. Supp. 352 (N.D.N.Y. 1953).
124. United States v. United States Fidelity & Guaranty Co., 309 U.S. 506 (1940); Turner v. United States, 248 U.S. 354 (1919); Cherokee Nation v. State, 461 F.2d 674 (10th Cir. 1972); Twin Cities Chippewa Tribal Council v. Minnesota Chippewa Tribe, 370 F.2d 529 (8th Cir. 1967); Maryland Casualty Company v. National Bank, 361 F.2d 517 (5th Cir. 1966); Greene v. Wilson, 331 F.2d 769 (9th Cir. 1964); Dicke v. Cheyenne-Arapahoe Tribe, Inc., 304 F.2d 113 (10th Cir. 1962); Whitefoot v. United States, 293 F.2d 658 (Ct. Cl. 1961), *cert. denied*, 369 U.S. 818 (1962); Native American Church v. Navajo Tribal Council, 272 F.2d 131 (10th Cir. 1959); Haile v. Saunooke, 246 F.2d 293 (4th Cir. 1957), *cert. denied*, 355 U.S. 893 (1957); Iron Crow v. Oglala Sioux Tribe, 231 F.2d 89 (8th Cir. 1956); Adams v. Murphy, 165 F. 304 (8th Cir. 1908); Thebo v. Choctaw Tribe, 66 F. 372 (8th Cir. 1895); City of Salamanca v. Seneca Nation, 47 F. Supp. 939 (W.D.N.Y. 1942); Yazzie v. Morton, 59 F.R.D. 377 (D. Ariz. 1973); White Mountain Apache Tribe v. Shelley, 107 Ariz. 4, 480 P.2d 654 (1971); Morgan v. Colorado River Tribe, 103 Ariz. 425, 443 P.2d 421 (1968); Employment Security Department v. Cheyenne River Sioux Tribe, 80 S.D. 79, 119 N.W.2d 285 (1963).
125. 309 U.S. 506 (1940).
126. *Id.* at 512.
127. 453 F.2d 152 (9th Cir. 1971).

Fidelity & Guaranty Co.,[128] the sovereign immunity of Indian tribes is co-extensive with that of the United States and went on to say that even express consent of Congress to suit is subject to such conditions and limitations as Congress sees fit to impose and "exceptions thereto are not to be implied."[129]

The basic principle that suit may not be maintained against Indian tribes in the absence of express Congressional authority to sue and express waiver of immunity has been uniformly followed.[130]

Indian Tribal Immunity From Suit—Underlying Public Policy

The doctrine of sovereign immunity of Indian tribes from suit is grounded both on political theory and federal policy. Indian tribes have been and remain today in a state of dependency in their relationships with the federal government.[131]

The tribes are composed of the poorest minority group in America. As Brophy and Aberle report "In most Indian communities the pattern is one of bare subsistence . . . ."[132] According to the 1971 figures of the Bureau of Indian Affairs 57% of the total Indian labor force was unemployed or in temporary employment.[133] Although the educational level of Indians is rising, it remains generally low. Most tribal governments have difficulty in finding qualified people to staff tribal governmental positions. The governing bodies of most tribes are made up of men and women of relatively low educational level, and little or no experience in non-Indian government, finance or commerce.

While total tribal income may in some cases appear to be substantial, it must be remembered that it is an aggregate and wholly inadequate to alleviate tribal poverty when distributed and applied to tribal needs. Tribal funds are fully programmed under Congressional approval and require specific budget approval by the Bureau of Indian Affairs.

Tribal income is generally committed to payrolls and projects designed to uplift the economic level of the people wherever possible and to sustain at least minimal levels of employment and governmental services on the reservations. Many tribal services de-

---

128. 309 U.S. 506 (1940).
129. 453 F.2d at 159 *citing* Soriano v. United States, 352 U.S. 270, 276 (1957).
130. *See* text and cases cited note 124 *supra*.
131. Hallowell v. United States, 221 U.S. 317, 324 (1911); Tiger v. Western Investment Company, 221 U.S. 286 (1911); United States v. Kagama, 118 U.S. 375 (1886); United States v. Holliday, 70 U.S. 407, 418 (1866); Cherokee Nation v. Georgia, 30 U.S. 1, 9 (1831); United States v. Clapox, 35 F. 575, 577 (D. Ore. 1888); T. TAYLOR, THE STATES AND THEIR INDIAN CITIZENS 115 (1972).
132. W. Brophy & S. Aberle, *supra* note 7, at 62.
133. STATISTICS DIVISION, BUREAU OF INDIAN AFFAIRS, U.S. DEP'T OF INTERIOR, INDIAN POPULATION, LABOR FORCE, UNEMPLOYMENT AND UNDEREMPLOYMENT; BY AREA (1971).

pend on funds received directly from agencies of the federal government under programs designed to assist Indians as an economically depressed group.

Most tribal income is derived from the sale of tribal natural resources such as timber and minerals, leasing of land, and sale of permits. Unlike state and federal governments, Indian tribes cannot simply determine a level of spending and then legislate taxes to generate the necessary income. Most of the occupants of the reservations are without ability to pay any kind of personal property or excise tax, and tribal and individual trust land is exempt from taxation.

The principle of immunity from suit, therefore, is of tremendous importance to Indian tribes and is so viewed by them and by the United States government.[134]

Judicial Treatment of the Sovereign Immunity Question Under Title II of the Indian Civil Rights Act

Several of the early decisions under the Act examined only the question of federal court jurisdiction and scope of relief but ignored altogether the thorny problem of the need for express waiver of tribal sovereign immunity from suit.[135] The district court opinion in *Pinnow v. Shoshone Tribal Council*[136] was the first published opinion which recognized the problem of sovereign immunity and found that it defeated jurisdiction in that action. But on appeal, the Tenth Circuit Court of Appeals[137] cast serious doubt on the district court's ruling by suggesting that jurisdiction might well exist had there been a properly pleaded complaint. The court made no mention of the question of nonwaiver of sovereign immunity from suit.

However, in *Loncassion v. Leekity*[138] the district court met the sovereign immunity question head on. The plaintiff sued a tribal policeman and his employer, the Pueblo of Zuni, alleging the tribal policeman violated the plaintiff's rights under the Indian Civil Rights Act in shooting him. The complaint also alleged the Pueblo was negligent in hiring and training the officer.

Rejecting the argument that jurisdiction was limited to habeas corpus, the court went on to conclude that Congress had, in effect,

---

134. *See* text and material at note 172 *infra.*
135. Dodge v. Nakai, 298 F. Supp. 17 & 26 (D. Ariz. 1968); Spotted Eagle v. Blackfeet Tribe, 301 F. Supp. 85 (D. Mont. 1969). Where there is no waiver of sovereign immunity, jurisdiction may not be upheld even where the parties do not question the jurisdiction of the court. Cherokee Nation v. State, 461 F.2d 674 (10th Cir. 1972).
136. 314 F. Supp. 1157 (D. Wyo. 1970), *aff'd sub nom.* Slattery v. Arapahoe Tribal Council, 453 F.2d 278 (10th Cir. 1971).
137. Slattery v. Arapahoe Tribal Council, 453 F.2d 278 (10th Cir. 1971).
138. 334 F. Supp. 370 (D.N.M. 1971).

nullified the tribe's sovereign immunity from suit by mere enactment of the Indian Civil Rights Act:

> The Act does not, in so many words, provide that a tribe may be sued under its provisions nor does it explicitly waive sovereign immunity as a defense. However, since enforcement of the provisions of the Act could only occur through suits in courts of law, the Act must be held to imply that suits may be brought under its provisions. To hold otherwise would render the Act an unenforceable admonition.[139]

The court also found that the Pueblo had waived sovereign immunity by an agreement with the Bureau of Indian Affairs whereby the Pueblo set up a law enforcement organization and the Bureau provided three-fifths of the funding. The Pueblo agreed to be responsible for all damages or injuries to any person, to pay attorneys fees and to provide liability insurance to protect the Pueblo from suit brought because of wrongful conduct of tribal police officers. The contract was held to have waived sovereign immunity, and the court struck the defense of sovereign immunity from the Pueblo's answer to the complaint.

Loncassion thus involves two rather sweeping and novel rulings concerning tribal sovereign immunity: first, sovereign immunity from suit is waived by implication (since otherwise the court could not see how the federal statute would be meaningful); second, the court finds sovereign immunity from suit was waived by the contract of the Pueblo. Each of these holdings flies in the face of an established principle of law concerning tribal sovereign immunity from suit. First, sovereign immunity cannot be waived except by act of Congress, and the waiver must be express and not implied; second, sovereign immunity may not be waived by officials of the sovereign.[140] Hence, the contract between the Zuni Pueblo and the Bureau of Indian Affairs furnished no foundation for a finding of waiver.[141]

---

139. *Id.* at 373.

140. United States v. United States Fidelity & Guaranty Co., 309 U.S. 506 (1940).

141. S. 1343, 93d Cong., 1st Sess. (1973) was an effort to deal properly with some of the questions of public protection raised when tribes undertake to perform federal functions by contract with the Bureau of Indian Affairs. Section 2(a) of the bill provided for transfer of control or operation of programs to Indian tribes but prohibited such transfers:

> [U]nless the Secretary has determined that the tribe or communities involved have obtained general public liability insurance, motor vehicle insurance, and other appropriate insurance, which shall provide coverage to the tribes or communities in amounts which shall be comparable to the minimum insurance carried by other persons or organizations in the same general area performing similar activities as determined by the Secretary. *Such immunity to suit as a tribe or community which assumes control of a program pursuant to this section may have shall be waived with respect to suits arising out of its operation of that program but only to the extent of the coverage required by the Secretary . . . .* (emphasis supplied).

If the bill had been passed, tribal immunity would have been waived in such circumstances.

The rationale of *implied* waiver of sovereign immunity has been subsequently adopted by numerous courts in dealing with claims against tribes and tribal officials under the Indian Civil Rights Act.[142] A number of other courts have, as in *Dodge v. Nakai*, upheld the claims under the Act on strict jurisdictional grounds without any mention of sovereign immunity.[143]

Given the strict principle that sovereign immunity may not be deemed waived by implication, these decisions cannot be justified. For if, in fact, there has been no express waiver and none may be implied, the federal courts may not entertain claims against Indian tribes, no matter what jurisdictional statutes may be found to cover similar claims in other contexts.[144]

Inapplicability of Bell, Jones and Bivens

The cases upholding the federal jurisdiction and entertaining claims for damages against Indian tribes have relied on the applicability of two jurisdictional statutes: title 28 United States Code section 1331 and title 28 United States Code section 1343. Section 1331, the federal question provision, requires establishing the requisite damages of $10,000. In *Spotted Eagle*[145] the court found federal jurisdiction under title 28 United States Code section 1331 as construed in *Bell v. Hood*[146] and title 28 United States Code section 1343(4), which provides:

> The district court shall have original jurisdiction of any civil action *authorized by law* to be commenced by any per-

---

142. Johnson v. Lower Elwha Tribal Community, 484 F.2d 200 (8th Cir. 1973); Daly v. Crow Creek Sioux Tribe, 483 F.2d 700 (8th Cir. 1973); Mc-Curdy v. Steele, 353 F. Supp. 629 (D. Utah 1973); Seneca Const. Rts. Org. v. George, 348 F. Supp. 48 (W.D.N.Y. 1972).

143. Thompson v. Tonasket, 487 F.2d 316 (9th Cir. 1973), *cert. denied* 95 S. Ct. 132 (1974); Brown v. United States, 486 F.2d 658 (8th Cir. 1973); Daly v. Crow Creek Sioux Tribe, 483 F.2d 700 (8th Cir. 1973); O'Neal v. Cheyenne River Sioux Tribe, 482 F.2d 1140 (8th Cir. 1973); White Eagle v. One Feather, 478 F.2d 1311 (8th Cir. 1973); Solomon v. LaRose, 335 F. Supp. 715 (D. Neb. 1971).

144. The grant of habeas corpus jurisdiction in the Indian Civil Rights Act may not be inconsistent with tribal immunity from suit. The respondent to such a writ will be some individual responsible for the detention or threat of detention of petitioner. *But see* Settler v. Yakima Tribal Court, 419 F.2d 486 (9th Cir. 1969) which held that the court was not precluded from adjudicating petitioner's constitutional claim even though there was no person who was his actual physical custodian. The court remanded the case to the district court to name the specific individual who was in the position to act for the tribal court. *Settler* took no notice, however, of the sovereign immunity question.

145. 301 F. Supp. 85 (D. Mont. 1969).

146. 71 F. Supp. 813 (S.D. Cal. 1947), *on remand from Supreme Court*, 327 U.S. 678 (1946). *Bell* held that the fourth and fifth amendments only protect rights from invasion by the federal government and not from individuals. By analogy, the court in *Spotted Eagle*, 301 F. Supp. 85 (D. Mont. 1969) concluded that the Indian Civil Rights Act did not create any rights as against individuals, but that a federal question was presented as to whether the Civil Rights Act gave rights against those individuals and where requisite jurisdictional amounts are pleaded, the court will take jurisdiction under § 1331(a).

son . . . to recover damages or to secure equitable or other relief under any act of Congress providing for the protection of civil rights, including the right to vote   (emphasis supplied).

The court recognized that there was no statute authorizing commencement of actions for deprivation of rights under the Indian Civil Rights Act but concluded from the decision in *Jones v. Mayer*[147] that it was empowered under section 1343(4) to fashion an appropriate remedy.

On the strength of *Jones*, the court in *Spotted Eagle* concluded, as did the court in *Dodge*, that it was vested with jurisdiction of actions against the tribe and its officers in their official capacity but not as individuals. Both *Bell* and *Jones* are false analogues to cases involving Indian tribes since neither deals with the question of soveregin immunity from suit or the question of the circumstances under which government officials lose the cloak of such immunity.

Jones has thus been the funnel for vesting the federal courts with jurisdiction under title 28 United States Code section 1343(4). While section 1343(4) requires that a civil action be authorized by law, *Jones* is cited for authority that actions are implicitly authorized under section 1343(4) once rights are established by federal statute, i.e., that the creation of rights and section 1343(4) act in concert to vest the federal courts with jurisdiction.

It is curious that *Jones* should be cited by the *Spotted Eagle* court and that the court should attempt to transfer such a rule to a case involving an Indian tribe where there is a serious barrier to federal court jurisdiction of sovereign immunity from suit. This is especially so since the jurisdictional question was mentioned by the United States Supreme Court in *Jones* only in a footnote which gave no hint that the lower court considered jurisdiction to be a problem. The Supreme Court merely noted that failure of a statute creating rights in individuals to provide an explicit method of enforcement did not prevent the federal court from fashioning an equitable remedy. The principal question involved in *Jones* was the constitutional power of the federal government to reach discriminatory action by individuals, not the jurisdictional reach of section 1343(4). Furthermore, the action in *Jones* was against a private person and sovereign immunity from suit posed no obstacle.

Bivens v. Six Unknown Named Agents of the Federal Bureau of Narcotics[148] is also frequently cited to support the conclusion that damage claims are allowable under the Indian Civil Rights Act even though not expressly provided therein.[149]   In *Bivens*, the

---

147. 392 U.S. 409 (1968).
148. 403 U.S. 388 (1971).
149. *See, e.g.,* Loncassion v. Leekity, 334 F. Supp. 370, 374 (D.N.M. 1971).

United States Supreme Court held that violation of fourth amendment rights against unreasonable searches and seizures by federal agents acting under color of authority gives rise to a cause of action for damages, but only as against the individual officers, not as against the United States. *Bivens*, then, is a case which does not even invoke the doctrine of sovereign immunity from suit, let alone the question of waiver. In fact, the court in *Bivens* carefully reviewed cases imposing liability on federal employees acting in violation of constitutional prohibitions and concluded that the case involved "no special factors counselling hesitation [of the courts to act] in the absence of affirmative action by Congress."[150]

However, in Indian Civil Rights Act cases, one is immediately met by extremely important factors counselling hesitation of the courts in creating rights of action when none are authorized by Congress. Paramount is the fundamental policy of upholding the law of Indian tribal sovereign immunity from suit in the absence of express Congressional waiver. Indian tribes are not in a position comparable to municipalities or state and federal governments. Federal policy is involved in any decision affecting the welfare of Indian tribes. Changes in that status must clearly emanate from Congress. Furthermore, given their endemic poverty, the question of opening tribal treasuries to the effects of costly litigation and possible damage awards, dictates extreme caution in considering fundamental changes in this area.

This writer believes the sovereign immunity of Indian tribes from suit has not been destroyed by implication, *Loncassion* to the contrary notwithstanding. Jurisdictional statutes do not overcome such immunity and title 28 United States Code section 1331 and section 1343(4) are wholly insufficient to sustain jurisdiction against Indian tribes under the Indian Civil Rights Act. *Jones, Bell* and *Bivens* are of no assistance for the same reasons.

Sovereign Immunity and the Liability of Tribal Officers Under the Indian Civil Rights Act

In a large number of the reported cases under the Indian Civil Rights Act, injunctive relief or damages were sought against officers and employees of tribal government.[151] A tribe which has escaped inclusion as a named defendant in a civil rights action by

---

150. 403 U.S. at 396.
151. Groundhog v. Keeler, 442 F.2d 674 (10th Cir. 1971); Daly v. Crow Creek Sioux Tribe, 483 F.2d 700 (8th Cir. 1973); O'Neal v. Cheyenne River Sioux Tribe, 482 F.2d 1140 (8th Cir. 1973); White Eagle v. One Feather, 478 F.2d 1311 (8th Cir. 1973); McCurdy v. Steele, 353 F. Supp. 629 (D. Utah 1973); Seneca Const. Rts. Org. v. George, 348 F. Supp. 48 (W.D.N.Y. 1972); Solomon v. LaRose, 335 F. Supp. 715 (D. Neb. 1971); Loncassion v. Leekity, 334 F. Supp. 370 (D.N.M. 1971); Spotted Eagle v. Blackfeet Tribe, 301 F. Supp. 85 (D. Mont. 1969); Cornelius v. Moxon, 301 F. Supp. 783 (D.N.D. 1969); Dodge v. Nakai, 298 F. Supp. 17 & 26 (D. Ariz. 1968).

invoking its sovereign immunity will have won a somewhat hollow victory if the benefits achieved can be negated by injunctions and awards of money damages against tribal officials and employees, thus disrupting tribal operations and depleting tribal assets. But the use of civil rights actions against such individual defendants to circumvent sovereign immunity is a very real threat.

It is hornbook law that litigants cannot emasculate the law of sovereign immunity by bringing suits for injunctive and monetary relief against individuals acting on behalf of the sovereign. Agents of the sovereign who are engaged in the business of government share the government's immunity.[152] A dilemma is raised, however, when government agents acting within the scope of their authority deprive individuals of their federally protected rights. The sovereign's need to operate freely, without undue interference by the courts, is balanced against the needs of individuals who claim to have been deprived of their rights and against society's need to prohibit unconstitutional conduct. Where injunctive and monetary relief are available against government officials under certain of the civil rights acts, the courts have allowed relief only under very narrow exceptions to the doctrine. Two recent court cases, *Scheuer v. Rhodes*[153] and *Edelman v. Jordan*,[154] define the nature and extent of these exceptions.

In *Edelman* the plaintiffs sought an order requiring the defendant Director of the Illinois Department of Public Aid to make retroactive payments of benefits improperly withheld. The defendants contended that the eleventh amendment[155] barred any such relief.[156] Noting the general rule "that a suit by private parties seeking to impose a liability which must be paid from public funds in the state treasury is barred by the eleventh amendment,"[157] the Supreme Court denied the monetary relief sought.

In *Scheuer* the personal representative of students killed in the "Kent State Massacre" sued the Governor of Ohio, the Adjutant General of the Ohio National Guard, various Guard officers and enlisted men and the President of the University, claiming money damages under title 42 United States Code section 1983 for deprivation of civil rights. The defendants contended that the action was barred by the eleventh amendment. Certiorari was granted to determine whether the district court had properly dismissed the actions on the ground that they were barred as a matter of law by the eleventh amendment. The Supreme Court reversed and re-

---

152. Scheuer v. Rhodes, 94 S. Ct. 1683 (1974); Edelman v. Jordan, 94 S. Ct. 1347 (1974). *See* Thebo v. Choctaw Tribe, 66 F. 372 (8th Cir. 1895).
153. 94 S. Ct. 1683 (1974).
154. 94 S. Ct. 1347 (1974).
155. Immunity of states under the eleventh amendment and tribal sovereign immunity under the common law doctrine are analogous. *See* Thebo v. Choctaw Tribe, 66 F. 372 (8th Cir. 1895).
156. 94 S. Ct. at 1353.
157. *Id.* at 1356.

manded. Chief Justice Burger's opinion, in attempting to strike a balance between official immunity and individual rights, defined the extent of the immunity available:

> These considerations suggest that, in varying scope, qualified immunity is available to officers of the executive branch of Government, the variation dependent upon the scope of discretion and responsibilities of the office and all the circumstances as they reasonably appeared at the time of the action on which liability is sought to be based. It is the existence of reasonable grounds for the belief formed at the time and in light of all the circumstances, coupled with good faith belief, that affords basis for qualified immunity of executive officers for acts performed in the course of official conduct.[158]

It is apparent that actions against tribal officials or employees are barred by the doctrine of official immunity in the same way that actions against tribes are barred by the doctrine of sovereign immunity. If the Indian Civil Rights Act did somehow provide an enforceable claim for individuals, actions against the tribe would still be barred, as would actions against tribal officials and employees. At most, a narrow exception would be made in those extreme cases where an individual defendant acts in bad faith without a reasonable belief that his conduct is justified.

But this will not be the usual case under the Indian Civil Rights Act. More often, actions under the Act will involve disputes of a political nature within the tribal community. Indiscriminate use of civil rights actions, instead of performing the lofty function of protecting the individual from the great impersonal state, will merely transfer a local dispute out of the tribal community into a remote and politically uninformed courtroom.

Use of the Indian Civil Rights Act in Actions for Money Damages

One consequence of the failure to properly analyze the law of tribal immunity from suit is the new availability of the federal district court forum to plaintiffs seeking money damages against Indian tribes. If a complainant has his choice of forums, he will naturally seek that forum in which he feels he will secure the highest amount of damages. This rationale may explain *Loncassion v. Leekity.*[159] Although the opinion does not clarify the point, the defendant tribal policeman, Leekity, may have been a tribal member. If so, he would have been subject to a claim for damages in the tribal court. But, since the plaintiff's injuries consisted of bullet wounds, his attorney may well have concluded that he could obtain far greater damages in federal court than he could in tribal court.

---

158. 94 S. Ct. at 1692.
159. 334 F. Supp. 370 (D.N.M. 1971).

The plaintiff's lawyer would almost certainly have considered whether the evaluation of a claim for money damages by a federal judge accustomed to awarding large judgments would likely be greater than that of an Indian judge who was not. This may be pure speculation, of course, but attorneys handling claims with a potential for a large recovery can surely be expected to cast complaints for damages in the language of civil rights deprivation in order to insure entry into the federal courts. In *Loncassion,* the court does not mention any requirement of exhaustion of remedies; thus the tribal court system is ignored altogether.

Similarly, an overriding desire to bring a money damage claim before a federal court may have been the motivating reason for the complaint in *Lohnes v. Cloud.*[160] This action for damages resulted from an automobile accident within the boundaries of the Fort Totten Indian Reservation. Both plaintiff and defendant were members of the Devil's Lake Sioux Tribe on that reservation. The plaintiff brought his action in federal court, and, to establish federal jurisdiction, alleged a federal question under title 28 United States Code section 1331, namely, that the tribal court system was unconstitutional and violative of the due process and equal protection provisions of title 25 United States Code section 1302(8). In addition, plaintiff complained that the tribal code improperly denied him a jury trial in a civil case. The court, after a long and sensitive analysis of Congress' policy of supporting Indian self-determination, and out of concern that courts not impose legal concepts without due regard for the integrity of tribal structures and values, denied the plaintiff's claim and granted the motion to dismiss.

Lohnes represents an interesting and unique application of the Indian Bill of Rights. The tribe itself was not a party to the suit but well could have been affected by an adjudication that its tribal court system was unconstitutional. Fortunately, the court ruled that jurisdiction in the case was vested in the tribal court, despite the fact that the plaintiff sought to raise constitutional issues upon which to predicate his right to proceed in a federal forum.

The plaintiff may well have had serious injuries and his case may have had a large potential for money damages in a state court. But since the state of North Dakota had not assumed jurisdiction over the reservation pursuant to Public Law 83-280, its courts had no jurisdiction. The plaintiff was probably unwilling to submit his claim to the adjudication of the tribal court because he felt he could not expect to receive a large enough damage award. The forum of choice, therefore, was the federal district court.

It is not unrealistic to expect that in the future plaintiffs seeking a way to recover money damages from Indian tribes will try to make use of the Indian Civil Rights Act by allegations charging

---

160. 366 F. Supp. 619 (D.N.D. 1973).

denial of constitutional rights. If the complaints are carefully drawn, they may be able to keep the matters in federal court.[161] Even if they pursue a tribal court remedy first, it will often be possible to make allegations of denial of due process in the tribal court system. The quest for money damages against Indian tribes will take on new interest for claimants whose attorneys try to find a constitutional issue which will get them into the federal courthouse. Such is the unfortunate consequence of the holding that the Indian Civil Rights Act has waived tribal sovereign immunity by implication.

SOME CONSEQUENCES OF THE JUDICIAL CONSTRUCTION
OF THE ACT

Critical Views

It may be useful here to take note of specific criticisms directed at the Act and its interpretaton by those intimately affected by, or having legal responsibilities under, the Indian Civil Rights Act.

A. *The Southwest Tribes*

The Indian tribes of the Southwest, the Navajos, the Pueblos, the Zuni, and the Hopi, are among the most traditional Indian societies in the United States today. These tribes have been most deeply disturbed by the Act and the most outspoken against it.

As a result, the Senate Subcommittee prepared an amendatory bill, S. 2173,[162] and held hearings on it in April of 1969 in Albuquerque, New Mexico.[163] The Indians expressed their position at the hearings: (1) Their societies are intimate, democratic and theocratic and concepts embodied in the United States Bill of Rights are wholly foreign to their way of life; such a law is therefore irrelevent and unnecessary. (2) They felt deeply offended that Congress would impose upon them requirements which superseded their tribal autonomy and eroded their treaty rights. (3) They feared that one man-one vote systems would destroy traditional Pueblo methods of choosing their leaders. (4) They feared the admission into tribal courts of professional attorneys ignorant of Indian language and customs. (5) They feared they would be prevented from evicting non-Indians from their reservations. (6) They feared that imposition of American legal standards on their traditional govern-

---

161. In Hickey v. Crow Creek Housing Authority, Civ. No. 73-3002 (D.S.D. July 8, 1974) a non-Indian business establishment sued a tribal housing authority under 25 U.S.C. § 1302 and 28 U.S.C. § 1331. The district court dismissed the action for failure to properly allege denial of constitutional rights. The court also indicated the plaintiff would have to exhaust his tribal remedies.
162. S. 2173, 91st Cong., 1st Sess. (1969).
163. *Hearings Before the Subcommittee on Constitutional Rights of the Senate Committee on the Judiciary, Constitutional Rights of the American Indian,* 91st Cong., 1st Sess. (1969).

ments would erode their tribal identity and sovereignty. A number of witnesses specifically objected to the ruling in *Dodge*. Senate Bill 2173, which would have exempted some traditional tribal customs and practices from the Act passed the Senate on July 11, 1969 but was not acted on by the House and died.[164]

B. *Indian Civil Rights Act Conference*

In May, 1973, a conference was called by the American Indian Lawyers Association in Denver, Colorado and was attended by approximately 75 persons representing a cross-section of Indian lawyers, tribal council members and tribal court judges. A transcript of the proceeding was published in 1974 under the title: *The Indian Civil Rights Act, Five Years Later.*

Most of those present decried the negative effect the Indian Civil Rights Act litigation was having on tribes and tribal practices. Participants agreed that no one really knows that the Act means in practice and that uncertainties abound. Governor Robert Lewis of the Zuni Pueblo said:

> [T]he Indian Civil Rights Act was imposed upon Indian tribes without any measures taken to prepare them to assume the additional burdens required. On top of that, some reservations were faced with Legal Services attorneys ready to represent individuals to force tribal authorities to conform to the Act and most tribes were not prepared to set up procedures to adequately carry out tribal government functions while at the same time following requirements of the act . . . .[165]

Governor Lewis indicated that problems arise because many of the tribes have never documented their customs. He described the difficulty of trying to explain new laws and procedures to tribal members accustomed to traditional ways that had been part of Indian life for generations. He emphasized the central tenet of the Pueblo culture as protection of group rights rather than individual rights.[166] Finally he enumerated eleven cases against the Zuni Pueblo under the Civil Rights Act and their estimated cost to the Pueblo of $10,000 each.[167]

Mr. Paul Tafoya, Governor of the Santa Clara Pueblo, New Mexico outlined the subtle but crucial differences between community customs of the various Pueblos, all of which are unwritten. He protested the unfairness of imposition of alien standards on his people by those ignorant of Pueblo culture.[168]   Attorney John

---

164. 115 CONG. REC. 19239 (1969).
165. AMERICAN INDIAN LAWYERS ASSOCIATION, THE INDIAN CIVIL RIGHTS ACT, FIVE YEARS LATER 49 (1974).
166. *Id.* at 50-51.
167. *Id.* at 55.
168. *Id.* at 64.

Kennedy said:

> On one hand, in many cases you have a publicly funded
> organization opposing the tribe which has a limited amount
> of resources. The impetus on the grievance in that case
> is usually pretty small because it doesn't cost them any-
> thing to litigate. He just tells his lawyer to go ahead and
> litigate the case and the lawyer who is being funded by
> Ford, OEO or some other outfit. On the other hand, the
> tribes scrape together whatever they have to pay for this,
> and we lawyers, of course, stand to benefit because we
> charge the tribes. . . .[169]

Clyde Sanchez, a Pueblo governor said: "white men preach to us,
love thy neighbor, but you can sue him . . . ."[170]

C. National Tribal Chairmen's Association

Other critical views were expressed in a resolution of the National Tribal Chairmen's Association at a meeting in December, 1973.
The resolution charged that judicial construction of title 25 United
States Code section 1302(8) as purportedly vesting the federal
courts with jurisdiction over such matters as tribal membership,
tribal elections, selection of tribal officers, land assignments and
conduct of tribal business, was an affront to the principle of self-
government. The resolution declared that since federal courts had
construed the Act to subject Indian tribes to the panoply of federal
constitutional law, and to constitute a complete waiver of tribal
sovereign immunity from suit besides, the Act should be amended
to make it wholly subject to acceptance by an affirmative vote of
each tribe.

D. Position of the Department of Interior

While *Thompson v. Tonasket*[171] was pending before the United
States Supreme Court on Petition for Certiorari, the Court requested a memorandum from the United States. Accordingly, the
Solicitor for the Interior Department prepared a memorandum of
law for the guidance of the Justice Department.[172] In its memorandum the Interior Department stated that a writ of certiorari should
be granted since the Ninth Circuit Court of Appeals failed to give
sufficient consideration to the principle of Indian sovereignty and
decided the case in conflict with that principle and other important
federal policies regarding Indians. The memorandum attacked the
Johnson v. Lower Elwha Tribal Community[173] decision for its hold-

---

169. *Id.* at 72.
170. *Id.* at 89.
171. 487 F.2d 316 (9th Cir. 1973), *cert. denied,* 95 S. Ct. 132 (1974).
172. Memorandum of Law and Accompanying Letter from Kent Frizzell,
Solicitor, U.S. Dep't of Interior, to Lawrence G. Wallace, Deputy Solicitor
General, U.S. Dep't of Justice May 22, 1974 [hereinafter cited as Solicitor's
Memorandum].
173. 484 F.2d 200 (9th Cir. 1973).

ing that tribal immunity from suit had been waived by implication as a result of the Indian Civil Rights Act. The Solicitor viewed the decision as violative of the fundamental doctrine requiring express waiver of sovereign immunity, citing *Edelman v. Jordan*,[174] *Thebo*,[175] and *Adams v. Murphy*.[176]

The memorandum argued that by analogy to the eleventh amendment and in accordance with the principles in *Scheuer v. Rhodes*, if federal courts have any jurisdiction over section 1302 cases, "suits may be brought against tribal officials on the basis of alleged violations of the act, but that the tribes themselves are immune from suit."[177]

The memorandum also urged that judicial construction of the Act presents a serious conflict with federal Indian policy:

> The practical dangers posed by the holding below are, in the Department's view, substantial. Incursions clearly will be made on the federal policy of encouraging tribal self-government—a policy reflected in fact, in the Civil Rights Act itself—as tribes are brought before federal courts on frivolous as well as more plausible ground, with the possibility always in the background that the provisions of §1302 may be interpreted and applied by non-Indian judges and juries in ways that ignore important and accepted aspects of a tribe's heritage. Even more importantly, perhaps, the parallel federal aim of aiding tribes to achieve economic independence will be undermined, and the limited resources possessed by most tribes depleted, as the tribes are forced not only to pay money judgments in various instances but also, in a much broader range of instances, to expend substantial funds to employ or retain tribal counsel. Such frustration of federal policy would have unfortunate consequences not only for the tribes, but for the United States and its treasury as well.[178]

The memorandum went on to state that there were serious jurisdictional questions in view of the fact that the only jurisdictional section was section 1303 and that this was particularly significant in light of the general history of civil rights legislation.[179] The Solicitor's memorandum also concluded that the legislative history strongly suggested that section 1303 had been deliberately adopted as the only provision vesting the federal courts with remedies. It reiterated the view that the Act would not be meaningless if judicial interference were limited to habeas corpus, by reason of the binding effect of the Act on tribal officials and the Secretary of the Interior. The memorandum closed with the observation that

---

174. 94 S. Ct. 1347 (1974).
175. 66 F. 372 (8th Cir. 1895).
176. 165 F. 304 (5th Cir. 1908).
177. Solicitor's Memorandum, *supra* note 172.
178. *Id.* at 6-7.
179. *See* discussion of Civil Rights Task Force Memorandum, *supra*, note 106, and accompanying text.

the decision below had "far-reaching implications for federal policy toward American Indians."[180]

E. *Position of the Justice Department*

Pursuant to the Solicitor's memorandum, the Justice Department filed a memorandum in the Supreme Court for the United States as amicus curiae in *Thompson v. Tonasket*.[181] The government urged the court to grant review. The memorandum incorporated some of the positions urged by the Interior Department but differed on others. For example:

> The act contains no specific provisions for enforcement of rights that might be infringed without detention, nor does it contain any provision explicitly waiving tribal immunity from suit. This has left to the courts the duty of interpreting the act in such a way to make it effective, while still protecting Indian self-government. Both of these objectives are within the Congressional intent.[182]

While the Justice Department wrongly conceded that federal review under the Act is not limited to writs of habeas corpus and that under title 28 United States Code section 1343(4) the courts have jurisdiction to hear cases for recovery of damages or to secure equitable or other relief,[183] it did urge that the court recognize that neither section 1343(4) nor the Indian Civil Rights Act had the effect of waiving the sovereign immunity of Indian tribes from suit and that the tribes are protected just as the eleventh amendment protects the states, and just as the principle of sovereign immunity protects the United States.[184] The memorandum argued that just as state and federal officers must have qualified personal immunity from suit in order to perform their duties without fear of harassment, so tribal officers must be similarly protected.

The United States challenged the correctness of the Ninth Circuit decision insofar as it would permit suits and money judgments against an Indian tribe itself, noting that under the decision, no doctrine of sovereign immunity remains to preclude a money judgment against tribal officers. The government memorandum concluded by saying that the United States felt that the decision gives too little effect to Congress' intent to protect tribal sovereignty and self-government as well as the rights of tribal members. Acknowledging that jurisdiction might exist to grant injunctive relief and

---

180. Solicitor's Memorandum, *supra* note 172, at 13.
181. Memorandum for the United States as Amicus Curiae, Thompson v. Tonasket, 487 F.2d 316 (9th Cir. 1973), *cert. denied*, 95 S. Ct. 132 (1974.
182. *Id.* at 6.
183. *Id.*
184. *Id.* at 6-7.

in some instances monetary damages against tribal officers, the government argued that grants of monetary damages against tribes themselves are inconsistent with the basic principles of tribal sovereign immunity from suit under *United States v. United States Fidelity and Guaranty Co.*[185] and *Edelman v. Jordan.*[186]

A Plea for Judicial Understanding

So long as the courts continue to operate on the belief that they have jurisdiction to review all facets of Indian tribal government under the Indian Civil Rights Act, it will be necessary for federal judges to develop an understanding of the unique factors which characterize the life of Indian political communities. In the observation of this writer, the most important issues in the mind of Indian people today are tribal autonomy and Indian separatism. The two are intertwined. Often the issue is phrased in terms of "tribal sovereignty;" other times, one hears of "the right to be Indian." But there appears to be a broad agreement among all members of the American Indian community that Indian government must be restored to a position of power and respect. American judges who find themselves facing the need to apply civil rights principles to Indian communities face the difficult task of cultivating sensitivity to the right to maintain a separate and distinct social community. It is always difficult for judges to avoid unconscious ethnocentrism, and this leads, perhaps, to the indignity which Indians find most offensive: that is, having to submit to the judgments of non-Indians as to matters involving the life of their tribe. In a broad way, some basic principles can be outlined which should serve as guidelines to federal courts dealing with Indian civil rights questions. Courts should be cognizant of:

(1) The necessity of Indian tribes to function as governments, with sovereign powers over their territory and people;

(2) The need of Indian tribes to operate tribal governments, including courts, utilizing persons without law degrees;

(3) The need for Indian communities to maintain their own values and concepts of fairness and justice to the fullest extent. This would necessarily imply an extremely narrow application of the Indian Civil Rights Act where there is a showing of countervailing customary tribal values, beliefs or standards;

(4) Recognition that informality in the operation of tribal governments is often the rule. To insist on formalism, legalism and documentation may result in asking the impossible. Most Indians have not yet begun to develop a "bureaucratic mentality;" many

---

185.   309 U.S. 506 (1940).
186.   94 S. Ct. 1347 (1974).

tribes do not have the resources or techniques to maintain a bureaucracy;

(5) Full recognition of the tribes' own institutions of government, their constitutions, ordinances and regulations, should be extended by the courts. Only in this way will respect for tribal self-government be maintained. This obviously implies a stringent application of the doctrine of exhaustion of remedies in compliance with tribal procedures;

(6) Serious recognition must be given to the right of the tribes to protect their community character by maintaining a tribal society which is closed or limited to outsiders, if it chooses, and to reject cultural pluralism;

(7) The tribes' inherent right to determine their own membership must be understood as vital to the survival of these people, and the broadest recognition must be given to the tribes' determination;

(8) Questions relating to the propriety of tribal elections must be treated as basically internal to the tribes except where a clear showing of gross violation of individual rights is made and proper standing is shown;

(9) Remedies must be attuned to the concept of the tribes as extended families;

(10) Courts must be sensitive to the fact that most Indian tribes are impoverished. Litigation is costly for tribes. Opening the door to money judgments means that lawyers will seek and find ways to claim denial of constitutional rights in many circumstances in order to obtain money judgments.

Above all, courts must avoid the unconscious tendency to bring missionary zeal to the task of extending the blessings of our philosophy of individual liberties to Indian tribes and tribal members. Many courts do recognize the importance of avoiding action which would "undermine the authority of the tribal courts over reservation affairs . . . which would infringe on the rights of the Indians to govern themselves."[187]

Ethnocentrism: A Serious Handicap for Federal Courts

Federal judges charged with the duty of responding to Indian litigants who bring civil rights cases before them are often handicapped by ignorance of, or insensitivity to, the operative standards of Indian political and personal relationships, by ethnocentrism, or by simple prejudice against the idea of Indian separatism. Even with the best of intentions, judges have the difficult and often impossible task of preventing their own personal beliefs concerning individual rights from influencing their judgments. Anglo-Saxon

---

187. Williams v. Lee, 358 U.S. 217 (1959).

standards of fairness in group life are derived from a wholly different historical and social context.

The great triumph of Western democracy is the establishment of the primacy of individual liberty against the power of the state. This is an enormous achievement and deserves the high place we accord it in our scale of values. However, we may fail to recognize that the principles developed to protect individual rights have their greatest relevance in mass societies where the state is a great and impersonal force. They may have less relevance, and in some cases be absolutely irrelevant, for tribal communities in which there is a closer parallel to an extended family. As one observer has put it:

> One constant within the Indian world is the importance placed on the extended family as the basic social unit. In this, it contrasts strikingly with the "typical American" nuclear family which consists of independent couples and their offspring. The extended family is a major and persistent cultural difference between Indians and non-Indians. As the economic level of the Indian people rises, the extended family is strengthened despite the loss of some members through relocation. It has withstood countless small and large scale attempts to destroy it. Furthermore, the extended family constitutes the basic building block of tribal organization and its strength is directly related to tribal viability. Today family and tribal reorganization reinforce each other as they have in the past.[188]

It is extremely difficult for a non-Indian, or even an Indian who is an outsider to a particular tribal community, to understand the reasons and the importance of some Indian actions. Some examples taken from the case law may illustrate this.

In *Dodge v. Nakai*,[189] the federal court was dealing with the Navajo tribe's exclusion of a white lawyer, Mr. Theodore Mitchell, who was director of the Navajo Legal Services Program. For almost a year he had been embroiled in a dispute with the tribal council over his insistence that the lawyers in the program be totally independent from and free to oppose the tribal council and its policies. The council sought to have him removed, and when attorneys from the program became involved in a dispute concerning operation of a tribal school system, the council voted to demand his resignation. When this demand was rejected, the council asked the tribal attorney for legal advice and was told that its only recourse was to exclude Mitchell from the reservation.

Several days later, the council met with an attorney from the office of the Solicitor in Washington, D. C. to discuss the Civil

---

188. Witt, *Nationalistic Trends Among American Indians*, in THE AMERICAN INDIAN TODAY 123 (S. Levine & N. Lurie eds. 1968).
189. 298 F. Supp. 17 & 26 (D. Ariz. 1968).

Rights Act of 1968. A council member, Mrs. Annie Wauneka, asked whether the Act would prevent the tribe from evicting someone from the reservation. When the government official asked whether she had anyone in particular in mind, there was laughter from several individuals, including two members of the council. But the laughter of Mr. Mitchell was the loudest and the most noticeable. Mrs. Wauneka rebuked him for laughing in the council chambers and the meeting went on.

The next day during a reconvened session of the council, committee member Wauneka, seeing Mitchell seated in the council chamber, got up from her seat, walked over to him and asked whether he intended to laugh again. When he attempted to apologize for his laughter of the previous day, Mrs. Wauneka told him she was not interested in an apology and then struck him several times and ordered him to leave the council chambers. He left.

The following day the council passed a resolution directing the chairman to cause immediate removal of Mitchell from the reservation and to serve notice upon him that he could re-enter the reservation on the following day in the company of a Navajo policeman for the purpose of presenting himself before the advisory committee to show cause why he should not be permanently excluded.

Mitchell appeared at the show cause hearing at the appointed time and was permitted to testify in his own behalf. The committee rejected his request to be allowed to continue the hearing past noon in order to present witnesses and voted 12-3 to permanently exclude him from the reservation.

The district court, after trial, struck down the order of exclusion and enjoined tribal officials from enforcing it. There were a number of critical factors influencing the court. One factor was that the subject of the exclusion was a lawyer whose exclusion might deprive Navajo tribal members of his needed legal services. A second concern of the court was that his exclusion was not based on grounds stated in the tribal code. The court expressed its apprehension that if the tribe could deal with Mr. Mitchell in a manner which the court considered arbitrary, many other white persons living on the reservations would also be subject to such action.

But the aspect of the case which appears to be most significant in terms of ethnocentric judgments is the decision of the court that exclusion of Mitchell because of his laughter was unreasonable. The court rejected the contention of the defendants that Mitchell's laughter was opprobrious because it was an expression of ridicule and scorn for members of the council. The court insisted upon treating the matter simply as a question of disorderly conduct at a meeting. Unfortunately, the court gave no consideration to the significance such an act may have had to Indians. For a white man

192

who had previously placed himself in defiance of tribal government to enter into the seat of government of that tribe, on their reservation and to laugh scornfully in the face of tribal government, may, within the culture of the Navajo tribe, constitute a grave transgression.

If Anglo-Saxon standards, and the contemporary mores of parliamentary life are applied, such conduct may be considered trivial —something which could be ignored. But in the context of Indian life, given the sensitivity of Indians to the idea that when they are on their reservation, they are on their land, it is the writer's opinion, based on his experiences representing Indian tribes, that the conduct of Mr. Mitchell constituted a deep and unforgiveable offense. Certainly the action of council-woman Wauneka in rising from her seat at the council, walking to the chamber entrance where Mitchell was seated and striking him several times and ordering him to leave, is some evidence of the strength of emotion involved. The action of the federal court in deciding that the banishment was "unreasonable" may reflect either mere ignorance of tribal values or a decision to reject those values in favor of Anglo-Saxon standards of acceptable conduct.

Another example of what may be an unwarranted and unjustified imposition of Anglo-Saxon standards of equal protection is *Luxon v. Rosebud Sioux Tribe.*[190] The tribal constitution disqualified employees of the Bureau of Indian Affairs and of the United States Public Health Service from holding tribal office. The plaintiff, an employee of the Public Health Service, sought a seat on the tribal council. When she was barred by the tribal constitutional provision she brought suit in federal court under the Act.

The Eighth Circuit determined that the court had jurisdiction under the equal protection provision of the Indian Civil Rights Act and remanded the case for trial. The trial court ruled that the constitutional provision was violative of the plaintiff's rights and declared it illegal.

Such a decision is questionable at best. The tribal constitutional restriction involved here might well be reasonable and necessary in the context of an Indian community, though wholly improper for a white political community.

Given the extensive services and relationships between Bureau of Indian Affairs personnel and Public Health Service personnel with Indians on reservations, such persons may be in a very strong position to grant or withhold favors. There may be other reasons, unknown to outsiders, why the tribe feels it is unhealthy or unfair for such persons to be allowed to run for office. This exclusion,

---

190. 337 F. Supp. 243 (D.S.D. 1971), *rev'd,* 455 F.2d 698 (8th Cir. 1972).

which was contained in the constitution of the Rosebud Sioux Tribe, is not uncommon.

The Problem of Exclusion

One of the most difficult and delicate problems arising out of the Act is the problem of exclusion. The very first case decided under the Act, *Dodge v. Nakai*, considered the question and its decision to overrule a tribal decision on exclusion has had long-lasting repercussions throughout Indian country. As one Indian leader commented:

> Before the Civil Rights Act of 1968 we had the ability to exclude anyone from our Pueblo who was a troublemaker, or who we believed would upset the serenity of our village. The Act has already been interpreted to prevent tribal leaders from evicting from the reservation non-Indians who they deemed undesirable.[191]

In *Dodge v. Nakai*, the court overruled the tribe's exclusion on a number of grounds. The action was taken after a hearing by the tribal council rather than by a court, and so was said to constitute a bill of attainder because there was no general rule covering the offense. Further, the first amendment guaranty of free speech extended to Indians who were entitled to an Indian spokesman on the reservation and also to their non-Indian spokesman.[192] Third, the court concluded that the action was a violation of due process requirements because in fact the plaintiff had been barred as a result of political disapproval of his actions by the council.

These rulings raise some profound issues for Indian tribes. It must be remembered that for many tribes, the reservation is their ancestral homeland. For many others, the reservation was bought at the price of the blood of their forefathers. It is a homeland, the land of a people. The treaties and executive orders establishing these reservations declare that these lands are set apart for "exclusive use and occupancy" of their Indian inhabitants. In *Dodge v. Nakai*, the court held that the Indian Civil Rights Act overruled this language in the treaty to the extent that the tribe's exclusion of non-members was subject to approval by the white man's courts under principles developed by the white man for open societies.

The Navajo Tribal Code enumerated specific grounds for exclusion. The decision raised serious doubts as to whether it would be possible for a tribe to specify any grounds similar to the grounds of the Navajo Council. For example, could a tribe exclude an outsider who comes onto the reservation to preach a political or religious doctrine which is offensive to the tribe? Would this be sus-

---

191. Statement of Benny Atencio in *Hearing Before the Subcommittee on Constitutional Rights of the Senate Committee on the Judiciary, Amendments to the Indian Bill of Rights*, 91st Cong., 1st Sess. 29 (1969).
192. *See also* State v. Fox, 82 Wash. 2d 289, 510 P.2d 230 (1973).

tained under any circumstances; for example, would it be sustained where missionaries attempt to preach a hostile religious doctrine on a reservation which is a theocracy? How can such questions be decided by the tribe in a manner which is constitutionally sustainable? Can a tribe determine that a ground for exclusion shall be the demonstration of open disrespect, hostility, scorn or derision to the tribe, its members or its government? Can the tribe declare that a ground for exclusion shall be intermeddling or interfering in internal tribal affairs? None of these grounds would, of course, be defensible as complying with constitutional standards in the general society. The problem may present a serious threat to Indian cultural preservation for some Indian tribes. Furthermore, it must be recognized that the exclusion power may well be the only way a tribe can deal with a non-Indian whose conduct is offensive, particularly if it has no jurisdiction over non-Indians in tribal courts.

Exclusion is rarely resorted to by tribes, except in serious cases. Tribes should have the right to exclude outsiders under appropriate ordinances with standards bearing a reasonable relationship to the preservation of the peace and harmony of the community.

The Proposal for Limitation of the Act Under the Principle of Wisconsin v. Yoder

In an accompanying article, Mr. deRaismes sets forth his conviction that the full body of American constitutional law should be applicable to Indian tribes except where they are able to prove to a court that such application would greatly endanger, if not destroy, a "central cultural value." The analogy is based on the decision in *Wisconsin v. Yoder*.[193] There the Supreme Court upheld the right of the Amish people to be exempt from the Wisconsin compulsory education law upon first amendment "free exercise of religion" rationale. Mr. deRaismes argues that the courts could apply the same test in interpreting and applying the Indian Civil Rights Act which would require treating cultural values as analogous to religious values.

As can be seen in the language quoted from the opinion by Mr. deRaismes,[194] the exemption from the compulsory education laws was grudgingly granted, upon the narrowest grounds and upon a stern set of proof restrictions. The Amish had to satisfy several requirements. First, they had to show that the law in question would gravely endanger, if not destroy, the free exercise of the Amish religious beliefs. Second, they had to show that they had a long (in their case, three centuries) history as an identifiable religious sect. Third, they had to prove that they had long history as a successful and self-sufficient segment of American society.

---

193. 406 U.S. 205 (1972).
194. DeRaismes, *The Indian Civil Rights Act of 1968 and the Pursuit of Responsible Tribal Self-Government*, 20 S.D.L. Rev. 59, 83 (1975) [hereinafter cited as deRaismes].

Fourth, they had to make a convincing demonstration of the *sincerity* of their religious beliefs. Fifth, they were required to demonstrate the interrelationship of their belief with their mode of life. Sixth, they had to make a *persuasive* showing of the vital role which belief in daily conduct plays in the survival of their community. Seventh, they had to demonstrate the hazards presented by enforcement of the statute in question. Eighth, they had to demonstrate the adequacy of their alternate mode of education. Finally they had to make a convincing showing that few other groups could qualify for the exemption.

To argue that this ought to be the rule of law applicable to Indian tribes under the Indian Civil Rights Act seems to be a remarkably narrow and insensitive view of the integrity of tribal government and tribal life. The idea of a core exemption only in cases where a tribe was able to prove to the satisfaction of a non-Indian judge that it should be exempt from the strict requirements of constitutional law principles because they would endanger some "central cultural value" is wholly inappropriate to political entities occupying distinct territorial areas. It would require courts to respect only "cultural" values. The court would be able to ignore all other aspects of the tribe's political and social structure in determining the extent to which constitutional law should be applied to that tribal government. Furthermore, the burden of proof would be on the tribe to satisfy the judge.

How many of us would be willing to submit the preservation of our most precious values to the judgment of one from a foreign culture? Furthermore, how can a judge decide what is a "cultural value" and what is a value which is unique to Indian life but arises from the special circumstances of the Indian community, and which may have little or no demonstrable relationship to aboriginal Indian customs or practices?

Under such a standard, it would appear that only where the Indian tribe can show that a practice is aboriginal, or authentically native, could it qualify for any consideration from a federal judge. It would presumably follow, that to the extent that the dominant culture succeeds in destroying Indian "culture," it will also succeed in destroying Indian autonomy.

Mr. deRaismes' article seems to be based on a rather low opinion of Indian tribal government. Mr. deRaismes echoes the views of some in militant Indian movements today, challenging the legitimacy of tribal governments on the ground that their organizational form was "imposed on most tribes"[195] by the federal government in 1934. Mr. deRaismes therefore concludes that "there is no reason to defer to the judgments of nontraditional Indian governments ex-

195. DeRaismes, *supra* note 194, at 69.

ercising municipal powers under the charter and guardianship of the federal government."[196]

While this may make good political rhetoric, this writer cannot accept its validity. It is somewhat misleading to speak of the elected tribal council form of government as one "imposed" by the federal government. Section 18 of the Indian Reorganization Act left the decision of whether to organize under the Act a matter for each tribe to decide by majority vote.[197] According to an official report of the Bureau of Indian Affairs submitted to a special subcommittee of the House Committee on Interior and Insular Affairs, as of 1950, 99 Indian tribal groups had voted to organize under the Indian Reorganization Act, while 95 had chosen not to do so. Four other tribes had adopted constitutions outside the provisions of the Act.[198]

Mr. deRaismes claims that the new system of elected councils "has been so alien to large numbers of Indians on many reservations," that "majorities . . . on many reservations have consistently refused to vote in tribal elections."[199] This is demonstrated, he claims, by the fact that it is not infrequent to find the precentage voting in a tribal election varying between 10% and 25% of the qualified electorate. Since this claim is not documented it is difficult to know how frequently this in fact occurs. However, Brophy and Aberle report that data from elections in 46 tribes in 1958-1960 show eligible voter participation ranging from a low of 37% to a high of 60%, with a three year average of 50%.[200]

While it is true that there are in specific cases high degrees of voter apathy in tribal elections, there is also a high degree of intense political involvement in tribal elections by those who are interested. I note that the majority of the cases coming before the federal courts under the Indian Civil Rights Act are cases which involve in some fashion questions relating to the propriety of elections. I see no general sentiment in the American Indian community for the abolishment of elected tribal councils.

I hesitate to suggest what future course Indian government can or will take. Mr. deRaismes and I are not Indians, and it is not for us to say. However, I suggest that there are few Indian tribes left today which retain such traditional societies that alternate systems of government and leadership could be reconstructed. This writer's opinion is, in fact, that the portion of the Indian Reorganization Act authorizing tribes to organize for self-government is

---

196. DeRaismes, *supra* note 194, at 104.
197. 25 U.S.C. § 478 (1970).
198. REPORT WITH RESPECT TO THE HOUSE RESOLUTION AUTHORIZING THE COMMITTEE ON INTERIOR AND INSULAR AFFAIRS TO CONDUCT AN INVESTIGATION OF THE BUREAU OF INDIAN AFFAIRS, 82nd Cong., 2nd Sess. 1040-42 (1952).
199. DeRaimes, *supra* note 194, at 70.
200. W. Brophy & S. Aberle, *supra* note 7, at 33.

the most successful single example of Indian legislation in the entire field.

This writer is disturbed that characterizations of tribal governments as "corrupt little tyrannies"[201] may be taken to have general validity. Obviously, my views are biased by my experiences but I caution readers against the unquestioning acceptance of such descriptions of American Indian tribal life. Certainly, cases of corruption, nepotism, exploitation, tyranny and oppression do exist, but to expand such examples into generalizations as to all Indian tribal governments is unjustifiable. This misinformation can only serve to undermine the integrity and status of Indian tribes as governmental entitles—a status which they are struggling to maintain and improve.

What seems to be missing from Mr. deRaismes' analysis is appreciation of the desperate struggle of Indians to survive as a *people*. Furthermore, there is the special social relationship which we call "tribal." In many cases, these tribal relationships reach back beyond recorded history. While the Congress of the United States has the power to disrupt and destroy these relationships, it has not demonstrated any inclination to do so. In fact, the contrary is the case.

In summary, the thesis which is urged by Mr. deRaismes seems to be wholly at odds with the Congressional intent underlying the Indian Civil Rights Act, with the entire body of American law recognizing Indian tribal sovereignty and with the direction in which Indian people themselves seem to be moving, i.e., greater tribal sovereignty, not less.

THE ACT'S CONTRIBUTION TO INDIAN SOVEREIGNTY: JURISDICTION OVER NON-INDIANS

One of the most urgent problems for Indian tribes is the issue of the ability of the tribe to exercise effective governmental authority over the entire reservation and all persons within its boundaries, be they Indians or not. There has been a great deal of discussion and debate about the matter and it is not without difficulty as a matter of law. However, some tribes are resorting to an "implied consent" ordinance to obtain jurisdiction over those who enter reservation lands. Others are asserting inherent tribal authority upon the ground that it has never been expressly withdrawn by Congressional acts.

In *Oliphant v. Schlie*,[202] the district court upheld the criminal jurisdiction of an Indian tribe over a non-Indian. This was a habeas

---

201. DeRaismes, *supra* note 194, at 70.
202. Civ. No. 511-73C2 (W.D. Wash. April 5, 1974) *app. pending*. The author's partner, Mr. Barry Ernstoff, represented the respondent on behalf of the Suquamish Indian Tribe in this case.

corpus petition brought under the Indian Civil Rights Act by a non-Indian. He had been arrested by a tribal police officer whom he had assaulted. Subsequently, he resisted arrest and was charged in tribal court with both assault and resisting arrest. He was brought before the tribal judge, duly arraigned and then taken to jail. Subsequently, he was released on his own recognizance. He thereafter petitioned the federal court for a writ of habeas corpus.

After examining the record of the proceeding in the tribal court, the federal district judge ruled that the petitioner's rights had been fully protected under title 25 United States Code section 1302. He also found that the Suquamish Tribal Court had jurisdiction over the subject matter and person of the petitioner and had provided the petitioner with all appropriate protections under the Indian Civil Rights Act in accordance with concepts of due process and equal protection of the laws. Ruling that the tribe's inherent sovereign jurisdiction over non-Indians had not been taken away or limited by Congress except as to major crimes, the tribal court was found to have jurisdiction. The petition for habeas corpus was denied.

In the *Oliphant* case the Act functioned precisely as the author is contending Congress intended. A federal court was available for determination of only the most extreme consequence of tribal action, incarceration of a person.

Perhaps, as Mr. deRaismes argues, courts will be reluctant to recognize the authority of Indian tribes over non-Indians within their boundaries unless they are assured that Indian tribes will afford all persons the Bill of Rights protections and that they, the federal courts, will be accessible to review such governmental actions. Perhaps some tribes would be willing to accede to full authority for federal court review of all tribal governmental actions if that were the price that had to be paid to firmly establish jurisdiction over non-Indians. This may be a matter for Congress. If the Act is to give courts broad jurisdiction over Indian tribes, it should be amended to specifically provide this, and further to provide that in such cases, Indian tribes shall have full jurisdiction over all non-Indians within the reservation to the same extent as the state has jurisdiction outside the boundaries of the reservation.

CONCLUSION

The thesis of this article has been that the courts have badly misconstrued and misapplied the Indian Civil Rights Act. The fault is perhaps not all theirs. Inadequate exposition of the legislative history may have left the courts to grope for explanations for the existence of the exclusive statutory remedy of habeas corpus. Failure to appreciate the significance of such legislation for the internal processes of tribal government and the federal government may have contributed to false directions—to an interpretation which would provide the federal courts with power over all aspects of tribal life.

However, there is little excuse for the casual treatment accorded sovereign immunity from suit. The notion of waiver of immunity by implication has never before been indulged in American law. It has led to serious consequences for Indian tribes—consequences never contemplated or intended by Congress in enacting this legislation. These are the views not merely of tribal governments and their attorneys, but also of the Solicitor General, speaking to the United States Supreme Court on behalf of the United States, and of the Interior Department, speaking as trustee for both tribal and individual Indian interests.

It is not too late to remedy the error. If Congress should in the future feel it necessary to broaden federal court jurisdiction, it can go further in a considered and principled way. But until Congress takes such action, the courts should not permit the impulse to find a way to right individual wrongs to override the fundamental and rightful position of American Indian tribes in the American legal system.

INDIANS AND EQUAL PROTECTION

Ralph W. Johnson* and E. Susan Crystal**

I. INTRODUCTION

Equal protection challenges to federal, state, and tribal laws and administrative actions have become increasingly popular in recent years. Since 1974 the Supreme Court has decided five equal protection cases concerning Indians, covering challenges to federal Indian hiring preferences,[1] a criminal conviction of an Indian in federal court,[2] the distribution of an Indian claims award,[3] the preemption of state jurisdiction in an Indian adoption proceeding,[4] and a state criminal and civil jurisdiction scheme on reservation land.[5] All of these equal protection challenges were rejected.

Additional challenges have been made in the lower federal and state courts resulting in decisions that have not reached the Supreme Court. These include a challenge to a New Mexico policy allowing only enrolled Indians to sell crafts on the veranda of a state museum,[6] a state law exempting the Leech Lake Band of Indians from a fishing license fee in Minnesota,[7] and a federal court treaty interpretation awarding a specific percentage of salmon to treaty Indian tribes in Washington.[8] The first two of these equal protection challenges were rejected. The third, concerning the allocation of salmon fishing rights,

---

* Professor of Law, University of Washington; B.S. in Law, 1947, LL.B., 1949, University of Oregon.

** Staff Counsel, Senate Appropriations Committee, Washington, D.C.; B.A., 1974, Washington University; J.D., 1978, University of Washington.

This article was supported by a grant from the National Oceanographic and Atmospheric Administration under Sea Grant No. 04-7-158-44021.

1. Morton v. Mancari, 417 U.S. 535 (1974). *See* Part V–*A infra.*
2. United States v. Antelope, 430 U.S. 641 (1977). *See* Part V–*B–3 infra.*
3. Delaware Tribal Business Comm. v. Weeks, 430 U.S. 73 (1977). *See* Part V–B–2 infra.
4. Fisher v. District Court, 424 U.S. 382 (1976) (per curiam). *See* Part V–B–1 infra.
5. Washington v. Confederated Bands & Tribes of the Yakima Indian Nation, 99 S. Ct. 740 (1979). *See* notes 124 & 125 and accompanying text *infra.*
6. Livingston v. Ewing, 455 F. Supp. 825 (D.N.M. 1978).
7. State v. Forge, 262 N.W.2d 341 (Minn. 1977), *appeal dismissed*, 435 U.S. 919 (1978).
8. United States v. Washington, 384 F. Supp. 312 (W.D. Wash. 1974), *aff'd*, 520 F.2d 676 (9th Cir. 1975), *cert. denied*, 423 U.S. 1086 (1976), *cert. granted*, 99 S. Ct. 277 (1978).

587

was sustained by the Washington Supreme Court but on highly tenuous grounds.

Under the Indian Civil Rights Act of 1968[9] numerous equal protection challenges to tribal government laws and actions have been heard in federal courts, including challenges to enrollment requirements,[10] voting procedures,[11] residency requirements for tribal office,[12] conduct of tribal government business,[13] and procedures for terminating a lease of a tribal member.[14] The only equal protection challenge to succeed was subsequently reversed by the Supreme Court on different grounds.[15]

Two important observations emerge from an analysis of these cases: (1) equal protection analysis in Indian-related cases, whether brought under the United States Constitution or the Indian Civil Rights Act, differs from the analysis in other equal protection cases, and (2) at least the federal courts have been hesitant to impose equal protection limitations on laws affecting Indians.

This article analyzes the recent Indian equal protection cases in an attempt to formulate the equal protection doctrine as applied to Indians, to examine the theoretical foundation for that doctrine, and to indicate how that doctrine will likely be applied in situations not yet addressed by the courts.

II. THE FEDERAL GOVERNMENT'S TRUST RELATIONSHIP WITH INDIAN TRIBES

The uniqueness of the equal protection doctrine as applied to Indians is attributable, in large part, to the fiduciary relationship existing between the federal government and Indian tribes.[16] This relationship was first articulated by the United States Supreme Court in *Cherokee*

---

9.   25 U.S.C. §§ 1301–1303 (1976).

10.   Santa Clara Pueblo v. Martinez, 436 U.S. 49 (1978).

11.   McCurdy v. Steele, 506 F.2d 653 (10th Cir. 1974); Daly v. United States, 483 F.2d 700 (8th Cir. 1973); White Eagle v. One Feather, 478 F.2d 1311 (8th Cir. 1973).

12.   Howlett v. Salish & Kootenai Tribes, 529 F.2d 233 (9th Cir. 1976).

13.   Groundhog v. Keeler, 442 F.2d 674 (10th Cir. 1971).

14.   Johnson v. Lower Elwah Tribal Community, 484 F.2d 200 (9th Cir. 1973).

15.   Santa Clara Pueblo v. Martinez, 540 F.2d 1039 (10th Cir. 1976), *rev'd on other grounds,* 436 U.S. 49 (1978) (reversed on grounds that the federal courts lacked jurisdiction over the subject matter).

16.   The relationship is between the tribes as political entities and not between individuals and the United States. Delaware Tribal Business Comm. v. Weeks, 430 U.S. 73 (1977); Morton v. Mancari, 417 U.S. 535 (1974); In re Heff, 197 U.S. 488 (1905). This proves to be significant in equal protection analysis. *See* notes 57 & 75–77 and accompanying text *infra.*

Nation v. Georgia,[17] and is founded on both the special status accorded Indians in the United States Constitution[18] and the Indian tribes' subordinating their inherent sovereignty to that of the United States in exchange for the protection and supervision of the government.[19]

Thus, a federal trusteeship of Indians exists accompanied by a need for the federal government to enact laws concerning trust property and tribal government powers.[20] Because these laws treat an identifiable class of citizens (tribal Indians) differently than the rest of society, three potential equal protection problems arise: (1) a non-Indian

---

17. 30 U.S. (5 Pet.) 1 (1831). The case involved the question of whether the Supreme Court had original jurisdiction to enjoin Georgia from enforcing its laws on the Cherokee reservation. The Indians argued that this was a controversy between a "state" and a "foreign state" and thus fell under article III, section 2 of the Constitution granting jurisdiction to the Supreme Court. The Court rejected the argument that Indian tribes were sovereign nations. *See also* Worcester v. Georgia, 31 U.S. (6 Pet.) 515 (1832). For a study of the Cherokee cases, see Burke, *The Cherokee Cases: A Study in Law, Politics, and Morality,* 21 STAN. L. REV. 500 (1969).

18. "Congress shall have Power . . . [t]o regulate Commerce with foreign Nations, and among the several States, and with the Indian Tribes . . . ." U.S. CONST. art. 4, § 8, cl. 3. *See also id.* art. 1, § 8, cls. 1 & 10; art. II, § 2; art. III, § 3, cl. 2.

19. United States v. Kagama, 118 U.S. 375 (1886); Worcester v. Georgia, 31 U.S. (6 Pet.) 515 (1832). It is interesting to speculate on the difference in legal relationships between the federal government and Blacks and Indians. In addition to the judicial articulation of the guardian-ward relationship between the government and Indian tribes, Congress and the executive branch have created a special department, the Bureau of Indian Affairs, to administer federal programs for Indians, and developed volumes of laws and dozens of programs designed to benefit Indians and Indian tribes. This special relationship was developed because the United States had conquered the Indian tribes, taken away most of their land, destroyed their cultural and religious heritage, and caused fundamental changes in life style so that Indians were dependent for survival on the federal government. Many of the same factors apply to Blacks. They were taken away from their lands in Africa, their cultural and religious heritage was destroyed, and their life style was fundamentally changed. They were not, however, conquered by the U.S. government as such, but were captured individually or in small groups by private entrepreneurs, brought to the United States, and made slaves. They were dependent for survival on their owners rather than the United States. Although Blacks were legally freed by the Civil War and the fourteenth amendment, they were in fact subjected to continued racial discrimination and denied equal educational and employment opportunities well past the middle of the 20th century. But no guardian-ward relationship was ever evolved between the federal government and Blacks similar to that between the federal government and Indians. One is reminded of the moral of the play *The Mouse That Roared, i.e.,* the best way to get "aid" from the United States is to fight a war with the United States and lose.

20. Congress' power to enact laws affecting Indians has been said to be "plenary." Morton v. Mancari, 417 U.S. 535, 551–52 (1974); United States v. Kagama, 118 U.S. 375 (1886). Whatever plenary may mean in this context, it does not mean absolute. Delaware Tribal Business Comm. v. Weeks, 430 U.S. 73, 84 (1977). *See* Part V–B-2 *infra.* Federal treaties must be separately considered and are examined at Part VII *infra.*

589

may either claim the same benefits accorded Indians or claim to be prejudiced by the special Indian benefits;[21] (2) an individual Indian or a particular tribe may complain that a law that benefits Indians in general prejudices that individual or tribe in particular;[22] and (3) Indians may claim that a law passed ostensibly for their benefit in fact prejudices them.[23] The outcome may vary in each case, depending upon whether federal, state, or tribal action is involved.[24]

Before a cognizable Indian equal protection can be formulated, it is first necessary to outline briefly the doctrine of equal protection applied in cases that do not involve Indians.

III. TRADITIONAL EQUAL PROTECTION ANALYSIS

The principal tenet of the equal protection doctrine is that persons similarly situated should be treated alike under the law.[25] The central inquiry in equal protection cases is whether there is an appropriate governmental interest suitably furthered by the differential treatment.[26] In traditional equal protection analysis, the validity of the relationship between the means (the classification) and the ends (the government interest) is analyzed by applying a two-tier level of scrutiny.[27] On the first tier, courts will subject most statutory classifications to only a minimal scrutiny.[28] This standard, sometimes termed "the rational relationship test," permits governments broad discretion in enacting laws which affect some groups of citizens differently than

---

21. *See* Morton v. Mancari, 417 U.S. 535 (1974); United States v. Washington, 384 F. Supp. 312 (W.D. Wash. 1974), *aff'd*, 520 F.2d 676 (9th Cir. 1975), *cert. denied*, 423 U.S. 1086 (1976), *cert. granted*, 99 S. Ct. 277 (1978).

22. United States v. Antelope 430 U.S. 641 (1977); Delaware Tribal Business Comm. v. Weeks, 430 U.S. 73 (1977).

23. This would arguably breach Congress' fiduciary duty toward Indians and thus be actionable without the necessity of an equal protection analysis. To date such a theory has never succeeded. *See* Delaware Tribal Business Comm. v. Weeks, 430 U.S. 73 (1977). In general, the courts avoid invalidating federal legislation by applying a rule of construction that all doubts are to be construed in favor of Indians. *See, e.g.,* Bryan v. Itasca County, 426 U.S. 373, 392 (1976).

24. *See* Part IX *infra.*

25. Royster Guano Co. v. Virginia, 253 U.S. 412, 415 (1920). *See also* Tussman & tenBroek, *The Equal Protection of the Laws,* 37 CAL. L. REV. 341, 344 (1949).

26. Chicago Police Dept. v. Mosley, 408 U.S. 92 (1972).

27. Gunther, *The Supreme Court 1971 Term, Forward: In Search of Evolving Doctrine on a Changing Court: A Model for a Newer Equal Protection,* 86 HARV. L. REV. 1 (1972).

28. *Id.* at 19.

590

others.[29] Legislatures are presumed to have acted within their constitutional power despite the fact that, in practice, their laws result in some inequality. The constitutional safeguard is offended only if the classification is wholly irrelevant to the achievement of any valid governmental objective. Statutory classifications will not be set aside if facts can be found that reasonably justify the unequal treatment.[30]

Strict scrutiny, the second tier, is applied when a statute either infringes on a fundamental right[31] or is based on a "suspect classification."[32] Under this often fatal test,[33] the classification must be *necessary* to achieve a *compelling* state interest.[34]

In recent years the two-tiered analysis has been augmented with a middle-level analysis in which courts scrutinize the relationship between the means and the ends more rigorously than under the minimal level scrutiny, and require the legislation to satisfy an important rather than a compelling government interest.[35] This standard has been applied most notably to classifications based on gender[36] and illegitimacy.[37] This "middle-tier" scrutiny examines the means

---

29. *See, e.g.,* McGowan v. Maryland, 366 U.S. 420 (1961); Royster Guano Co. v. Virginia, 253 U.S. 412 (1920).

30. McGowan v. Maryland, 366 U.S. 420, 425–26 (1961).

31. *See, e.g.,* Shapiro v. Thompson, 394 U.S. 618 (1969) (right to travel); Harper v. Virginia Bd. of Elections, 383 U.S. 663 (1966) (voting).

32. The Court has defined a suspect class as one "saddled with such disabilities, . . . subjected to such a history of purposeful unequal treatment, [or] relegated to such a position of political powerlessness as to command extraordinary protection from the majoritarian political process." San Antonio Indep. School Dist. v. Rodriguez, 411 U.S. 1, 28 (1973). To date suspect classifications have been limited to those based on race, Korematsu v. United States, 323 U.S. 214, 216 (1944); alienage, Sugarman v. Dougall, 413 U.S. 634 (1973); and national origin, Hernandez v. Texas, 347 U.S. 475 (1954). This reflects the view of Justice Stone that there is an important judicial function in protecting certain "discrete and insular minorities" who, because of prejudice, are denied access to the "political processes ordinarily to be relied upon to protect minorities." United States v. Carolene Products Co., 304 U.S. 144, 152 n.4 (1938). Legislation which tends to affect such minorities should be "subjected to more exacting judicial scrutiny under the general prohibition of the 14th Amendment than are most other types of legislation." *Id.*

33. Strict scrutiny has been called "strict in theory and fatal in fact." Gunther, *supra* note 27, at 8. *But see In re* Griffiths, 413 U.S. 717, 722 (1973) (permissible and substantial interest in determining the fitness of a candidate for admission to the bar); Roe v. Wade, 410 U.S. 113, 162–64 (1973) (compelling state interest in regulating abortions during some stages of pregnancy); Korematsu v. United States, 323 U.S. 214 (1944) (national security during wartime justified incarceration of Japanese-Americans during World War II).

34. Dunn v. Blumstein, 405 U.S. 330, 342–43 (1972).

35. Trimble v. Gordon, 430 U.S. 762 (1977); Craig v. Boren, 429 U.S. 190 (1976).

36. Reed v. Reed, 404 U.S. 71 (1971).

37. *See, e.g.,* Trimble v. Gordon, 430 U.S. 762 (1977); Weber v. Aetna Casualty & Surety Co., 406 U.S. 164 (1972); Levy v. Louisiana, 391 U.S. 68 (1968).

591

and the ends in some detail, closing "the wide gap between the strict scrutiny of the new equal protection and the minimal scrutiny of the old not by abandoning the strict but by raising the level of the minimal from virtual abdication to genuine judicial inquiry."[38]

IV. EARLY EQUAL PROTECTION CASES AND INDIANS

Most federal Indian law developed prior to the modern activist doctrine of equal protection.[39] The leading Indian equal protection cases, however, have all occurred since 1954, when modern equal protection doctrine received its impetus with the decision in *Brown v. Board of Education*.[40] Consequently, many early laws and administrative practices concerning Indians would be unconstitutional if challenged under modern equal protection principles. Felix Cohen, in his 1942 treatise, *Handbook of Federal Indian Law,* documented numerous state laws and state constitutions that deprived Indians of their right to vote, serve on a jury, testify in a lawsuit, or attend public schools with whites.[41] Federal laws, in turn, sometimes prohibited Indians from riding on railroads, "hampered freedom of speech, em-

---

38. Gunther, *supra* note 27, at 24.

39. The modern activist stance of the Supreme Court in equal protection cases dates essentially from the 1954 decision in Brown v. Board of Education, 347 U.S. 483 (1954), in which the Court rejected the separate but equal philosophy that had prevailed since its 1896 decision in Plessy v. Ferguson, 163 U.S. 537 (1896), and ruled that racial segregation constituted an impermissible means of accomplishing even legitimate governmental goals. *Brown* heralded a new judicial approach to equal protection. Since the early 1960's, the Court has consistently invalidated explicit governmental discrimination against minorities.

On the same day the Court decided *Brown,* it decided Bolling v. Sharpe, 347 U.S. 497 (1954), ruling that the equal protection concept of the fourteenth amendment, which constrains state government actions, is part of what is meant by due process in the fifth amendment, which constrains federal government actions. *See* Buckley v. Valeo, 424 U.S. 1 (1976); Weinberger v. Wiesenfeld, 420 U.S. 636, 638 n.2 (1975); Schlesinger v. Ballard, 419 U.S. 498 (1975); Jiminez v. Weinberger, 417 U.S. 628 (1974); Frontiero v. Richardson, 411 U.S. 677 (1973). In *Bolling* the Court articulated the relationship of the equal protection analysis under the fourteenth amendment to the fifth amendment. It stated:

> [T]he concepts of equal protection and due process, both stemming from our American ideal of fairness, are not mutually exclusive. The "equal protection of the laws" is a more explicit safeguard of prohibited unfairness than "due process of law," and, therefore, we do not imply that the two are always interchangeable phrases.

Id. at 499. *See* J. NOWAK, R. ROTUNDA, & J. YOUNG, CONSTITUTIONAL LAW ch. 16 (1978).

40. 347 U.S. 483 (1954). *See* note 39 *supra.*

41. F. COHEN, HANDBOOK OF FEDERAL INDIAN LAW 174 (University N.M. ed. 1971).

powered the Commissioner of Indian Affairs to remove from an Indian reservation 'detrimental' persons, and sanctioned various measures of military control within the boundaries of the reservations."[42] Federal administrative action often infringed on the civil liberties of the Indians, primarily through the near-despotic power held by the superintendent of the reservation, who could act as judge, jury, prosecuting attorney, police officer, and jailer in arresting, trying, and imprisoning Indians.[43] Administrative actions also denied Indians religious freedom.[44]

There are few cases challenging these early laws and administrative practices.[45] Among the early cases that did reach the courts were those challenging legislation prohibiting the sale of liquor to Indians.[46] In *Perrin v. United States,*[47] the United States Supreme Court held that it "does not admit of any doubt" that Congress can prohibit the sale of liquor to "tribal" Indians, wherever they might be, under the commerce clause and the guardian-ward relationship.[48] In *In re*

---

42. *Id.*

43. *Id.* at 175.

44. One purpose of the oppressive administrative practices was to make life on the reservation so intolerable for the Indians that they would choose to leave the reservation and assimilate into the non-Indian society. The more intolerable the oppression, the more Indians left the reservations, and the more successful was the Bureau of Indian Affairs in achieving its objective of assimilation. F. COHEN, *supra* note 41, at 174-75.

45. *See* cases cited in F. COHEN, *supra* note 41, at 177-79. The one remedy that was available to an Indian was to leave the reservation, renounce his political connection with the tribe, and assimilate into the non-Indian culture. By thus changing his status he was relieved of the burdens of discriminatory legislation and administrative practices. Standing Bear v. Crook, 25 F. Cas. 695 (C.C.D. Neb. 1879) (No. 14,891); F. COHEN, *supra* note 41, at 177.

46. An 1834 act prohibited the sale of liquor to Indians in Indian country. Laws enacted in 1862 and 1897 broadened this prohibition to include all Indians under federal trust, even outside Indian country. Act of June 30, 1834, ch. 161, § 20, 4 Stat. 729 (1834), *as amended by* Act of Feb. 13, 1862, ch. 24, 12 Stat. 338 (1862) & Act of Jan. 30, 1897, ch. 109, 29 Stat. 405 (1897). In Perrin v. United States, 232 U.S. 478, 486-87 (1914), the Court said these restrictions might be of questionable constitutionality if not repealed at some future date. All these prohibitions on sale of liquor on ceded lands were repealed in 1934. Act of June 27, 1934, Ch. 846, Pub. L. 73-478, 48 Stat. 1245 (1934). The sale of liquor to Indians is still prohibited in limited circumstances. 18 U.S.C. § 1154 (1976).

47. 232 U.S. 478 (1914). The Court held that Congress could prohibit the sale of liquor to anyone, Indian or non-Indian on all ceded land for a period of years after the reservation was created. *Id.* at 482-83.

48. *Id.* at 482. The Court in *Perrin* cites United States v. Kagama, 118 U.S. 375 (1886), for the guardian-ward relationship. *Id.* This same language was used in United States v. Mazurie, 419 U.S. 544 (1975). "This Court has repeatedly held that [the commerce] clause affords Congress the power to prohibit or regulate the sale of alcoholic beverages to tribal Indians, wherever situated . . . ." *Id.* at 554. *But see* Craig v. Boren,

593

Heff,[49] the Court held that an 1897 act[50] applied only to Indians who were neither citizens nor emancipated. Once citizenship was granted, an Indian was no longer *personally* the ward of the government, even though she still might hold equitable title to property held in trust by the United States. As a citizen living off the reservation, she was subject to state and federal laws in the same manner as other citizens.

These early cases provided the foundation for the principle that legislation concerning Indians was constitutional provided it was based not on race, but rather on the political or ancestral affiliation of the individual to a tribe.[51] If that affiliation were severed, the individual would no longer be considered an Indian within the meaning of the legislation.

V.   EQUAL PROTECTION CASES INVOLVING FEDERAL LAW

Although most statutes prohibiting the sale of liquor to Indians have been repealed,[52] there is still an entire title of the United States Code[53] devoted to Indians, as well as a substantial body of law consisting of treaties[54] and administrative regulations.[55] If the modern doctrine of strict scrutiny were to be applied to all classifications based on "Indian-ness," the entire structure of Indian law would crumble.[56] This result has been avoided, first, by characterizing clas-

---

429 U.S. 190, 208 n.22 (1976) (Indian liquor laws would now be of "questionable constitutionality").

49.   197 U.S. 488 (1905).

50.   *See* note 46 *supra.*

51.   Some early cases, for example, Montoya v. United States, 180 U.S. 261 (1901), and United States v. Rogers, 45 U.S. (4 How.) 572 (1846), referred to Indians as a "race." More contemporary cases do not do so. The explanation of these early cases probably lies in the different meanings of the word race.

The contemporary concept of the race of Indians includes Indians from the Carribean, Latin America, and Canada, none of whom enjoy a special status under United States law. In addition, there are United States citizens who, although racially Indian, do not share the special status. Reasons for that lack of status include: (1) the tribe is one toward which the United States has never assumed a trust relationship; (2) the tribe has been terminated by Congress, *see, e.g.,* 25 U.S.C. § 564 (1976); and (3) the individual has severed his or her tribal ties, *see* Standing Bear v. Crook, 25 F. Cas. 695 (C.C.D. Neb. 1879) (No. 14,891).

52.   *See* note 46 *supra.*

53.   25 U.S.C. (1976).

54.   *See* note 147 *infra.*

55.   *See* 25 C.F.R. (1978).

56.   Morton v. Mancari, 417 U.S. 535 (1974). The Court stated:

Literally every piece of legislation dealing with Indian tribes and reservations, and certainly all legislation dealing with the BIA, single out for special treatment a constituency of tribal Indians living on or near reservations. If these laws, derived

594

sifications between Indians and non-Indians as political rather than racial[57] and, second, by according the federal government special deference in the area of Indian legislation because of the *sui generis* status of Indians both constitutionally and historically.

A. *The* Mancari *Test*

The cornerstone of modern Indian equal protection doctrine is *Morton v. Mancari.*[58] In *Mancari* a federal statute provided for an employment preference for qualified Indians in the Bureau of Indian Affairs (BIA).[59] Non-Indian employees of the BIA challenged the preference on grounds that it was impliedly repealed by the 1972 Equal Employment Opportunity Act[60] and that it constituted invidious racial discrimination in violation of the due process clause of the fifth amendment.[61] The lower courts found that the preference had been repealed by the 1972 Act which proscribed discrimination in federal employment on the basis of race.[62] The Supreme Court reversed.

The Court began its analysis by noting the long history of Indian preference statutes.[63] The purpose of these statutes, according to the

---

from historical relationships and explicitly designed to help only Indians, were deemed invidious racial discrimination, an entire Title of the United States Code (25 U.S.C.) would be effectively erased and the solemn commitment of the Government toward the Indians would be jeopardized.
Id. at 552–53.

57. The Court generally uses the term Indian in the restricted sense meaning those persons who are members of federally recognized tribes. This definition excludes many persons whose racial makeup would be classified as Indian. *See id.* at 553 n.24; notes 48, 49 & 51 and accompanying text *supra.* There is authority for the proposition that technical "membership" in a tribal entity is not essential, so long as there is an ancestral relationship to the tribe; this is especially true where there is a close, continuing cultural, religious, and domicile relationship. *See* Morton v. Ruiz, 415 U.S. 199 (1973).

58. 417 U.S. 535 (1974).

59. Indian Reorganization Act of 1934, ch. 576, 48 Stat. 984 (1934) (codified in scattered sections of 25 U.S.C. §§ 461–479 (1976)). The statute also provides that the Secretary of the Interior shall establish standards "for Indians who may be appointed, without regard to civil-service laws, to the various positions [of the BIA] .... Such qualified Indians shall hereafter have the preference to appointment to vacancies in any such positions." *Id.* § 472. The Bureau adopted a policy in 1972 to accord a preference not only at the initial hiring stage but also in granting a promotion when both an Indian and a non-Indian were in competition. *Mancari,* 417 U.S. at 538.

60. *Mancari,* 417 U.S. at 551. *See* 1972 Equal Employment Opportunity Act, 42 U.S.C. §§ 2000e to 2000e–17 (1976).

61. 417 U.S. at 551.

62. Morton v. Mancari, 359 F. Supp. 585 (D.N.M. 1973).

63. *See, e.g.,* Act of June 24, 1910, ch. 431, § 23, 36 Stat. 861 (1910) (codified at 25 U.S.C. § 47 (1976)) (preferences for Indian labor); Act of June 7, 1897, ch. 3, § 1, 30

595

Court, "has been to give Indians a greater participation in their own self-government; to further the Government's trust obligation toward the Indian tribes; and to reduce the negative effect of having non-Indians administer matters that affect Indian tribal life."[64] The Indian Reorganization Act,[65] which contained the employment preference, was designed to foster self-government by giving tribal Indians an increased role in BIA operations.[66] The preference was necessary because no adequate training program existed to qualify Indians to compete on civil service examinations.[67] Displacement of non-Indians was both unavoidable and desirable.[68] The Court also concluded that the Equal Employment Opportunity Act did not impliedly repeal the Indian preference.[69]

1. The Indians' unique legal status

Turning to the due process issue, the Court rejected a traditional equal protection analysis, because of the unique legal status of Indian tribes under federal law.[70] Congress derives broad power to deal with Indian tribes from two sources. The first source is express constitutional authority to deal with Indians. The commerce clause provides that Congress shall have the power "[t]o regulate commerce . . . with the Indian Tribes."[71] The Constitution also provides the President with the power to make treaties with Indian tribes with the consent of two-thirds of the Senate.[72] The second source is the guardian-ward re-

---

Stat. 83 (1897) (codified at 25 U.S.C. § 274 (1976)) (employment in Indian schools); Act of July 4, 1884; ch. 180, § 6, 23 Stat. 97 (1884) (codified at 25 U.S.C. § 46 (1976)) (employment on reservations).

64. 417 U.S. at 541–42 (citations omitted).

65. The Act is codified in scattered sections of 25 U.S.C. §§ 461–479 (1976). See note 59 supra.

66. 417 U.S. at 542 (quoting Hearings on S. 2755 Before the Senate Committee on Indian Affairs, 73d Cong., 2d Sess. pt. 1, 26 (1934) (remarks of John Collier, Commissioner of Indian Affairs)).

67. 417 U.S. at 543–44 (quoting 78 CONG. REC. 11,729 (1934) (remarks of Rep. Howard)).

68. 417 U.S. at 544.

69. The Court looked to previous statutes and executive orders that treated Indian preference as exceptions. Id. at 545–46. See, e.g., Title VII of the Civil Rights Act of 1964, 42 U.S.C. §§ 2000e(b), 2000e-2(i) (1976) (preferential employment of Indians by Indian tribes on Indian reservations exempted from coverage). See Exec. Order No. 7423, 3 C.F.R. 189 (1935). The Court looked also to new Indian preference laws enacted after the 1972 Act. 417 U.S. at 548–49. See, e.g., 20 U.S.C. §§ 887c(a), (d), 1119a (1976) (giving Indians preference in teacher training programs for Indian children).

70. 417 U.S. at 551–52.

71. U.S. CONST. art. I, § 8, cl. 3.

72. Id. art. II, § 2, cl. 2. In 1871 Congress passed a bill notifying the President that it would no longer consent to any treaties with the several Indian tribes. Act of Mar. 3,

596

lationship[73] between the federal government and the Indian tribes that came about as a result of the "conquest" of the Indians which left them "an uneducated, helpless and dependent people, needing protection against the selfishness of others and their own improvidence. Of necessity, the United States assumed the duty of furnishing that protection, and with it the authority to do all that was required to perform that obligation."[74]

2. Tribal Indians as a political rather than a racial group

The Court characterized the preference not as a racial classification but as an employment criterion to allow Indians to participate in their own governance. "The preference . . . is granted to Indians not as a discrete racial group, but, rather, as members of quasi-sovereign tribal entities whose lives and activites are governed by the BIA in a unique fashion."[75] The Court continually referred to "tribal" Indians—it noted that the preference "is not directed towards a 'racial' group consisting of 'Indians'; instead it applies only to members of 'federally recognized' tribes. This operates to exclude many individuals who are racially to be classified as 'Indians.' In this sense, the preference is political rather than racial in nature."[76] The Court's analysis, then, is based on the political status of the Indian tribes and on the federal government's unique responsibility to the tribes.[77]

The political classification is useful only in describing the group to

---

1871, ch. 120, § 1, 16 Stat. 566 (1871) (codified at 25 U.S.C. § 71 (1976)). *See generally* Antoine v. Washington, 420 U.S. 194, 201–02 (1975).

73. *See* notes 16–19 and accompanying text *supra*.

74. *Mancari,* 417 U.S. at 552 (quoting Board of County Comm'rs v. Seber, 318 U.S. 705, 715 (1943)).

75. 417 U.S. at 554. The Court stressed the "sui generis" status of the BIA which made it unnecessary to deal with Indian preference statutes which did not relate to the Indian agency. *Id.* The rationale of *Mancari* has been applied, however, in other contexts. *See, e.g.,* Fisher v. District Court, 424 U.S. 382 (1976); notes 83–85 and accompanying text *infra*.

76. *Mancari,* 417 U.S. at 553 n.24. The eligibility criteria required that the individual be one-fourth or more degree Indian blood and a member of a federally recognized tribe. *Id. See also* 25 C.F.R. pt. 259 (1978).

77. *See* notes 16–19 and accompanying text *supra*. *Cf.* Regents of the Univ. of Cal. v. Bakke, 438 U.S. 265 (1978), in which the Court indicates that the analysis used for Indian preference legislation will not be transferred to cases involving preferences for other minorities:

We observed in [*Mancari*], however, that the legal status of BIA is *sui generis*. Indeed, we found that the preference was not racial at all, but "an employment criterion reasonably designed to further the cause of Indian self-government and to

597

whom the government owes a unique trust relationship.[78] This relationship exists toward tribal Indians and those with ancestral ties to tribes,[79] but not toward all Indians as a racial group.[80]

make the BIA more responsive to groups . . . whose lives are governed by the BIA in a unique fashion.

Id. at 304 n.42 (quoting from *Mancari,* 417 U.S. at 554) (citations omitted).

78.   The Court's characterizing the classification as political, however, is not useful in determining what level of scrutiny to apply to federal Indian legislation in equal protection cases. A law may be suspect and subject to the strict scrutiny-compelling governmental interest test without discriminating against all members of a race. For example, if the state of Washington enacted a law that all tribal Indians in the state must ride in the rear of buses, or that all black members of the Democratic Party must use separate rest rooms, such a law, although depending in part on a political classification, would nonetheless be racially discriminatory. It would discriminate against many, although not all, Indians or blacks in the state and would be subject to strict scrutiny.

79.   United States v. John, 98 S. Ct. 2541 (1978); Morton v. Ruiz, 415 U.S. 199 (1973). Various federal regulations, particularly in 25 C.F.R., providing benefits to Indians include more than just members of politically operating tribes in the benefited class.

In part 16 of the regulations in 25 C.F.R., dealing with estates of the Five Civilized Tribes, "[t]he Term 'Indian of the Five Civilized Tribes' means an individual who is either an enrolled member of the Cherokee, Chickasaw, Choctaw, Creek or Seminole Tribes of Oklahoma, or a descendant of an enrolled member thereof." 25 C.F.R. § 16.1(d) (1978). Part 20, concerning financial assistance and social services programs defines "Indian" as meaning "any person who is a member or a one-fourth degree or more blood quantum descendant of a member of any Indian tribe." *Id.* § 20.1(n).

Part 31 deals with federal schools for Indians:

Enrollment in Bureau-operated schools is available to children of one-fourth or more degree of Indian blood reside [*sic*] within the exterior boundaries of Indian reservations under the jurisdiction of the Bureau of Indian Affairs except when there are other appropriate school facilities available to them as hereinafter provided in paragraph (c) of this section.

(b) Enrollment in Bureau–operated boarding schools may also be available to children of one-fourth or more degree of Indian blood who reside near the reservation when a denial of such enrollment would have a direct effect upon Bureau programs within the reservation.

Id. § 31.1(a).

Part 32 governs the administration of educational loans, grants and other assistance for higher education:

Funds appropriated by Congress for the education of Indians may be used for making educational loans and grants to aid students of one-fourth or more degree of Indian blood attending accredited institutions of higher education or other accredited schools offering vocational and technical training who reside within the exterior boundaries of Indian reservations under the jurisdiction of the Bureau of Indian Affairs. Such educational loans and grants may be made also to students of one-fourth or more degree of Indian blood who reside near the reservation when a denial of such loans or grants would have a direct effect upon Bureau programs within the reservation. After students meeting these eligibility requirements are taken care of, Indian students who do not meet the residency requirements but are otherwise eligible may be considered.

Id. § 32.1.

80.   The United States clearly does not accept such a trust relationship toward Canadian, Mexican, or Guatemalean Indians.

598

It is important to note the test the Court applied in *Mancari:*

> As long as the special treatment can be tied rationally to the fulfill-
> ment of Congress' unique obligation toward the Indians, such legisla-
> tive judgments will not be disturbed. Here, where the preference is
> reasonable and rationally designed to further Indian self-government,
> we cannot say that Congress' classification violates due process.[81]

Although it is clear that the Court has eschewed strict scrutiny,[82] it
has nevertheless employed something more rigorous than minimal
scrutiny. The permissible legislative purposes have been limited to
those which fulfill Congress' unique obligation toward the Indians. In
addition, although the Court requires that the special treatment be
tied only "rationally" to the permissible purpose, the approach that
the Court in fact undertook in *Mancari* suggests something more than
minimum rationality.

Several questions remained unanswered after *Mancari.* Would the
Mancari test be applied if the legislation, although designed to fulfill
Congress' obligation to Indians, prejudiced an individual Indian?
Must the legislation be limited to tribal members? To what extent
would a court defer to a declaration by Congress that a particular act
was enacted for the benefit of Indians?

B. Subsequent Cases

Three subsequent cases have provided some of the answers to (and
left some confusion regarding) these questions.

1. Fisher v. District Court

In *Fisher v. District Court,*[83] all the parties to an adoption proceeding were members of the Northern Cheyenne Tribe. The plaintiffs
were denied access to state courts on the grounds that the tribal court
had exclusive jurisdiction. They contended that this denial of access
constituted invidious discrimination in violation of the equal protection clause of the Montana Constitution.[84]

---

81.   417 U.S. at 555.

82.   Although the "unique obligation toward the Indians" may be a compelling governmental interest, the classification need be tied only rationally to that end. *Id.* at 555.
See notes 31–34 and accompanying text *supra.*

83.   424 U.S. 382 (1976) (per curiam).

84.   The Montana Supreme Court held that the denial of access to the state court violated the equal protection provision of the Montana Constitution. Firecrow v. District

599

The Supreme Court rejected this claim and characterized the issue as a jurisdictional question between state and tribal courts. The solution depended on " 'whether the state action infringed on the right of reservation Indians to make their own laws and be ruled by them,' "[85] a test first enunciated in the landmark case of *Williams v. Lee*.[86] Because state court jurisdiction over this adoption proceeding would clearly interfere with the tribe's powers of self-government, it was impermissible.[87]

In summarily rejecting the equal protection challenge, the Court noted that the "exclusive jurisdiction of the Tribal Court does not derive from the race of the plaintiff but rather from the quasi-sovereign status of the Northern Cheyenne Tribe under federal law."[88] The Court further noted that even in a situation in which an Indian plaintiff is denied access to a judicial forum which is available to a non-Indian, the different treatment is justified "because it is intended to benefit the class of which he is a member by furthering the congressional policy of Indian self-government."[89]

2. Delaware Tribal Business Committee v. Weeks

In *Delaware Tribal Business Committee v. Weeks*,[90] a federal

---

Court, 167 Mont. 149, 536 P.2d 190 (1975). Federal recognition of Indian tribes and the creation of the reservation preempt state authority from interfering with tribal self-government in matters affecting Indians within Indian country. Bryan v. Itasca County, 426 U.S. 373 (1976); Fisher v. District Court, 424 U.S. 382 (1976); McClanahan v. Arizona State Tax Comm'n, 411 U.S. 164 (1973); Williams v. Lee, 358 U.S. 217 (1959); The Kansas Indians, 72 U.S. (5 Wall.) 737 (1867); Worcester v. Georgia, 31 U.S. (6 Pet.) 515 (1832). The state constitution would, therefore, not be applicable to a situation involving Indians on the reservation.

85.   424 U.S. at 386 (quoting Williams v. Lee, 358 U.S. 217, 220 (1959)).

86.   358 U.S. 217 (1959). The test has been relied upon by the Court in many cases since *Williams. See, e.g.,* McClanahan v. Arizona State Tax Comm'n, 411 U.S. 164, 168-73 (1973); Mescalero Apache Tribe v. Jones, 411 U.S. 145, 148 (1973); Kennerly v. District Court, 400 U.S. 423, 426-27 (1971).

87.   *Fisher*, 424 U.S. at 387-89. Plaintiffs sought to invoke the jurisdiction of the state court in an effort to circumvent an order of the tribal court of the Northern Cheyenne Tribe that they allow the mother of their foster son to have temporary custody for six weeks during the summer. Plaintiffs wanted to adopt the boy in state court. *Id.* at 383.

88.   *Id.* at 390. The quasi-sovereign status of Indian tribes was articulated by Chief Justice Marshall in Cherokee Nation v. Georgia, 30 U.S. (5 Pet.) 1 (1831). *See* note 17 *supra*.

89.   424 U.S. at 391.

90.   430 U.S. 73 (1977).

600

statute[91] providing for the disbursement of funds to certain Delaware Indians while excluding other Delawares was challenged as a violation of equal protection under the fifth amendment. The Supreme Court rejected an argument that the constitutionality of Congress' action presented a nonjusticiable political question because of Congress' pervasive authority to control tribal property provided for by the Constitution.[92] Regardless of the political nature of Congress' power, the Court may still examine Indian legislation in light of equal protection guarantees. " 'The power of Congress over Indian affairs may be of a plenary nature; but is not absolute.' "[93]

The Court applied the *Mancari* test to determine the validity of the distribution statute and found that it was "tied rationally" to Congress' obligation toward the Indians.[94] In so doing, the Court noted that Congress has traditionally been thought to have extensive constitutional power in the control and disbursement of tribal property.[95] Nevertheless, the Court analyzed the statute in some detail before concluding that it is rationally related to the trust purpose set out in *Mancari*.[96]

Weeks is significant in that it demonstrates that the Court will not summarily dismiss equal protection challenges to federal Indian legislation even when the legislation is in an area in which Congress' constitutional power with respect to Indians is greatest. Also, despite the fact that no Indian/non-Indian[97] classification was involved in *Weeks*,

---

91. 25 U.S.C. §§ 1291–1297 (1976).

92. 430 U.S. at 83–84.

93. *Id*. at 84 (quoting United States v. Alcea Band of Tillamooks, 329 U.S. 40, 54 (1946)).

94. 430 U.S. at 85.

95. *Id*. at 84. The Court noted that Congress may "differentiate among groups of Indians in the same tribe in making a distribution, . . . or on the other hand to expand a class of tribal beneficiaries entitled to share in royalties from tribal lands, United States v. Jim." *Id*. at 84–85 (citations omitted). The Court also quotes Felix Cohen for the proposition that the "authority of Congress to control tribal assets has been termed 'one of the most fundamental expressions, if not the major expression, of the constitutional power of Congress over Indian affairs . . . .' Cohen, Handbook of Federal Indian Law 94, 97 (1942)." 430 U.S. at 86.

96. Justice Stevens, in his dissent, argues that the statute lacks any reasonable explanation and does not "represent any rational attempt at 'fulfillment of Congress' unique obligation toward the Indians.' " 430 U.S. at 93 (quoting *Mancari*, 417 U.S. at 555). He notes that Congress' obligation toward Indians "surely includes a special responsibility to deal fairly with similarly situated Indians." 430 U.S. at 97 n.8.

97. Indian/non-Indian is used here in a racial sense because the plaintiffs in *Weeks*, although racial Indians, were not affiliated with any tribe. *Id*. at 77–78.

601

the Court applied the *Mancari* standard of review—whether the challenged classification has a rational relation to fulfillment of Congress' obligation toward Indians.[98]

3. United States v. Antelope

In *United States v. Antelope*,[99] decided two months after *Weeks,* the Supreme Court upheld the convictions of three Indian defendants for the murder of a non-Indian woman in the course of a burglary. Under the Major Crimes Act, federal law defined the murder as first-degree felony murder.[100] If the defendants had been non-Indian, they would have been subject to Idaho law which contained no felony-murder provisions and required proof of premeditation and deliberation for a conviction of first-degree murder.

The Indians, on appeal, contended that they were victims of dis-

---

98. "The standard of review most recently expressed is that the legislative judgment should not be disturbed '[a]s long as the special treatment can be tied rationally to the fulfillment of Congress' unique obligation toward the Indians . . . .' " *Id.* at 85 (quoting *Mancari,* 417 U.S. at 555).

99. 430 U.S. 641 (1977).

100. 18 U.S.C. § 1111 provides that "every murder . . . committed in the perpetration of, or attempt to perpetrate, any arson, rape, burglary, or robbery . . . is murder in the first degree." 18 U.S.C. § 1111 (1976).

Criminal jurisdiction on Indian reservations, because of the complexity inherent in a division of jurisdiction between state, federal, and tribal governments, presents a host of potential equal protection problems. Treatment of these complexities is beyond the scope of this article. *See* F. COHEN, *supra* note 41, at 358; Clinton, *Criminal Jurisdiction Over Indian Lands: A Journey Through a Jurisdictional Maze,* 18 ARIZ. L. REV. 503 (1976); Goldberg, *Public Law 280: The Limits of State Jurisdiction Over Reservation Indians,* 22 U.C.L.A. L. REV. 535 (1975). Which court has jurisdiction and what law is applied are both dependent upon the nature of the crime, whether the victim is Indian or non-Indian, whether the defendant is Indian or non-Indian, and in which state (and even which reservation within the state) the crime occurs.

Of importance for the inquiry here, however, is a line of cases out of the courts of appeals decided since *Mancari* that have overturned convictions of Indian defendants because Indians were subject to harsher penalties than were non-Indians. *See* United States v. Big Crow, 523 F.2d 955 (8th Cir. 1975), *cert. denied,* 424 U.S. 920 (1976); United States v. Cleveland, 503 F.2d 1067 (9th Cir. 1974). *See also* Gray v. United States, 394 F.2d 96 (9th Cir. 1967). *But see* United States v. Analla, 490 F.2d 1204 (10th Cir.), *vacated and remanded on other grounds,* 419 U.S. 813 (1974).

In *Big Crow,* for example, the court held the statute unconstitutional on the ground that a non-Indian committing an assault on an Indian on a reservation would be subject to six months imprisonment under state law while an Indian would be subject to five years imprisonment under federal law. 523 F.2d at 957. The court found that, while special legislation had been upheld by the Supreme Court in *Mancari* when tied to the "fulfillment of Congress' unique obligation toward the Indians," it was difficult for the court "to understand how the subjection of Indians to a sentence ten times greater than

602

crimination "because of the racially based disparity of governmental burdens of proof" under federal and state law.[101] The Ninth Circuit Court of Appeals reversed the convictions.[102] The court thought that the federal guardianship of Indians could not justify a criminal statute that worked to the disadvantage of the Indian defendant.[103] Having placed the case outside the *Mancari* rule, the court strictly scrutinized the law and found that the defendant had been subject to invidious racial discrimination.[104]

In reversing the court of appeals, the Supreme Court rejected the claim that the statute put Indians at a racially based disadvantage. The essential question was whether legislation which may operate to disadvantage Indians can be tied to the fulfillment of the federal government's unique obligation to Indian tribes.[105]

The Court began by rejecting the claim that legislation which singles out Indian tribes for different treatment is based on racial classifications.[106] The Court relied on *Mancari* and *Fisher,* in which such legislation had been sustained against claims of racial discrimination on the ground of the important governmental purpose to further Indian self-government.[107] The situation in *Antelope* did not involve self-government; the issue was one of federal regulation of criminal

---

that of non-Indians is reasonably related to their protection." *Id.* at 959. The court suggested that strict scrutiny should be used when racial classifications "are used to impose burdens on a minority group rather than, as in *Mancari,* to help the group overcome traditional legal and economic obstacles." *Id.* at 959–60. The government would then have to demonstrate a compelling interest to justify the racial classification. In this situation, the government had "failed to offer any justification for this disparate treatment of Indians." *Id.* at 960. The court implied that a dual standard of review exists. If the legislation helped further the guardian-ward relationship, a rational basis test would be applied. Where a greater burden was placed on Indians than on non-Indians, strict scrutiny would be the proper standard of review. *Id.* at 959–60.

101.   United States v. Antelope, 523 F.2d 400, 403 (9th Cir. 1975), *rev'd,* 430 U.S. 641 (1977).

102.   *Id.* at 407.

103.   *Id.* at 406. The court also rejected the argument that sufficient governmental justification can be found in the need for uniform federal law:

> [W]e view a possible legal fortuity based on location to be much less onerous than one based on the inherently suspect classification of race. Consistency in federal criminal law is ordinarily a highly laudable legislative objective, but not when it operates to deprive citizens of their right to equal treatment.

Id.

104.   *Id.* at 403–05.

105.   *See Mancari,* 417 U.S. at 555.

106.   430 U.S. at 641.

107.   *See* Parts V–*A* & V–*B–1 supra.*

603

activity in Indian country.[108] The Court noted, however, that "principles reaffirmed in *Mancari* and *Fisher* point more broadly to the conclusion that federal regulation of Indian affairs is not based upon impermissible classifications. Rather, such regulation is rooted in the unique status of Indians as 'a separate people' with their own political institutions."[109]

Antelope may provide authority for expanding the holding of *Mancari* to permit special federal Indian legislation applicable to individual Indians, regardless of affiliation with a tribe. First, it should be noted that the foundation of both *Mancari* and *Fisher* was the relationship of the federal government with Indian tribes. The Court attempted to include the situation of the defendants in *Antelope* within this framework by stating that they were enrolled members of the tribe. Enrollment in a tribe, however, is not a requirement for the exercise of jurisdiction under the Major Crimes Act.[110] The Court declined to hold that the term "any Indian" in the statute means an enrolled tribal member.[111] The statute, then, appears to apply to Indians on the basis of race or ancestry.[112] Second, the Court stated that federal regulation of Indian "affairs" was not based on an impermissible classification.[113] The use of the term "affairs" rather than "tribes" also indicates potential validity of legislation directed at individual Indians.[114]

The Court's position regarding the deference granted Congress' extensive power to legislate regarding Indians is uncertain. Unlike

---

108. 430 U.S. at 646.

109. *Id.*

110. 18 U.S.C. § 1111 (1976).

111. 430 U.S. at 647 n.7.

112. The Court notes that there are situations in which the statute would not apply to an individual racially classified as an Indian, for example, members of terminated tribes, citing the Klamath Indians as elucidated in United States v. Heath, 509 F.2d 16 (9th Cir. 1974), as one example. 430 U.S. at 647 n.7. The Major Crimes Act was held not to apply to the Klamaths. It is significant that the Klamath Termination Act specifically provided that "statutes of the United States which affect Indians because of their status as Indians shall no longer be applicable to the members of the tribe." 25 U.S.C. § 564(q) (1976). In the absence of such a statute, it is not at all clear that the Major Crimes Act would not be applicable to members of terminated tribes.

113. 430 U.S. at 646. However, the Court in discussing Public Law 280, 18 U.S.C. § 1162 (1976), states that "Congress' selective approach in § 1162 reinforces, rather than undermines the conclusion that legislation directed toward Indian tribes is a necessary and appropriate consequence of federal guardianship under the Constitution." 430 U.S. at 647 n.8. This statement stresses the federal guardianship relation to Indian tribes rather than the broad scope of "affairs."

114. See also United States v. John, 98 S. Ct. 2541 (1978), in which the Court upheld a racial-ancestral definition of Indian in 25 U.S.C. § 479 (1976). This statute was intended to provide benefits to, rather than to disadvantage, the Indians involved.

604

Weeks, the Court in *Antelope* presents no analysis of the rationale behind the Major Crimes Act to determine whether it bears, in reality, a rational relationship to the furtherance of the trust relationship. The Court thus apparently increases its deference to congressional judgment. In essence, the Court in *Antelope* seems to imply that Congress always acts in good faith, and any legislation enacted which singles out Indians for special treatment is presumptively valid—regardless of detriment or benefit to Indians.

The Court avoids the problem of the increased vulnerability of Indian defendants to a first-degree murder conviction by declaring that the Indians were subjected to the same body of law as "any other individual, Indian or non-Indian, charged with first-degree murder committed in a federal enclave."[115] This statement is misleading. A non-Indian who murders a non-Indian on the reservation is subject to state, not federal law.[116] As to him, the reservation is not a federal enclave, at least not for jurisdictional purposes. The race of the perpetrator and the victim determine whether state or federal law is applicable.[117]

In summary, the opinion may be said to expand the *Mancari* rule in three respects. First, the *Antelope* Court skirts the issue of a tribal relationship as a requirement for the application of the Major Crimes Act.[118] The guardian-ward relationship is premised on viewing Indian tribes as entities to which the federal government owes a unique responsibility. The Court finds that, since the defendants are tribal members, it need not address the question of whether the Act could constitutionally be applied to nontribal members, thus leaving a gap in its analysis.[119] Second, the Court does not engage in the means-end

---

115. 430 U.S. at 648. Federal enclaves also include national parks, military installations, and U.S. vessels on the high seas.

116. This is the result of the Court's holding in United States v. McBratney, 104 U.S. 621 (1882).

117. The Court reserved judgment on the issue of whether an Indian defendant could be subject to a different penalty than a non-Indian when tried in the same court for the same offense. 430 U.S. at 649 n.11. Such a situation was possible under the Major Crimes Act prior to its 1976 amendments. 18 U.S.C. § 1153 (1970) (amended 1976). Lower court decisions holding that a differing penalty is a denial of equal protection thus retain their precedential value. Of particular importance is United States v. Big Crow, 523 F.2d 955 (8th Cir. 1975), *cert. denied,* 424 U.S. 920 (1976), in which the Eighth Circuit Court of Appeals held that a statute that disadvantages Indians does not fulfill the federal guardianship purpose and is therefore outside the *Mancari* rule. The court in that case applied a strict scrutiny analysis. *Id.* at 959–60.

118. *See* notes 110–11 and accompanying text *supra.*

119. If a tribal relationship is required, then the Act would fit more squarely into the *Mancari* rationale. If not, the court is expanding *Mancari* to cover individual racial

605

analysis by which it decided *Mancari* and later *Fisher.* Finally, the *Mancari* rule is applied to a situation where Indians are clearly prejudiced. In *Fisher,* although the plaintiffs were denied access to the state courts, they were not denied a forum.[120] Furthermore, any detriment suffered by the plaintiffs in *Fisher* was balanced by the benefit realized by the tribe through the enhancement of the integrity of the tribal court. The counterbalancing benefits in *Antelope* are much more speculative and are left unexamined by the Court.

The purpose of legislation which singles out Indians should be viewed in the context of the trust relationship which was designed to protect Indians. The logic of *Mancari,* based on the federal guardianship of Indian tribes,[121] is weakened when utilized to uphold prejudicial rather than beneficial treatment of Indians. At some point the prejudice to Indians must be great enough to raise the issue whether the challenged federal action indeed furthers Congress' fiduciary obligation to Indians.[122] Legislation which operates to the disadvantage of Indians should be examined to determine if it is closely related to furthering this obligation. The Court in *Antelope* did not so examine the Major Crimes Act, choosing instead the use of broad generalizations which indicate that any legislation directed toward Indians is not based upon impermissible racial classification and is therefore presumptively valid. This is scrutiny at its most minimal. Indians were accorded the status of wards of the federal government because Congress, not local government, was thought better able to protect them.[123] This justifies the quasi-racial classification. If such is the case, only statutes which benefit and protect Indians ought to be sustained. Laws which place an individual at a disadvantage because he is an Indian are antithetical to the trust relationship.

Before discussing the equal protection analysis that should be applied to state laws concerning Indians, it will be useful to summarize the doctrine that has emerged from *Mancari, Fisher, Weeks,* and *Antelope.* Read together, *Mancari, Fisher,* and *Weeks* may be said to

---

Indians. This raises the spectre of racial classification, which was disavowed in *Mancari* on the logic that the legislation was directed toward tribal members.

120. The tribal court had jurisdiction to handle child custody matters. 424 U.S. at 384 n.5.

121. *See* Part V–*A supra.*

122. *See* United States v. Big Crow, 523 F.2d 955 (8th Cir. 1975), *cert. denied,* 424 U.S. 920 (1976); United States v. Cleveland, 503 F.2d 1067 (9th Cir. 1974). *See* note 100 *supra.*

123. United States v. Kagama, 118 U.S. 375, 383–84 (1886). *See also* Note, *Indian Civil Rights Task Force, Development of Tripartite Jurisdiction in Indian Country,* 22 KAN. L. REV. 351, 353–55 (1974).

606

express a unique equal protection analysis applicable to Indians. First, the legislation is not characterized as a racial classification but is instead intended to further the federal government's trust responsibility toward Indians who are presently members of tribes subject to the United States' trust relationship or who have ancestral ties to such members. Second, legislation is to be tested with a standard of review requiring it to be tied "rationally" to the fulfillment of Congress' "unique" obligation toward the Indians. The examination of the means chosen to achieve this purpose is somewhat greater than that under minimal scrutiny. The standard, however, appears to be one closer to the rational basis test than to strict scrutiny, especially in light of the results—*i.e.*, the statutes generally withstand constitutional challenge.

The *Antelope* decision is troublesome because of the minimal level of scrutiny employed and because of the questions left unanswered, although the principles of *Mancari* and *Fisher* were reaffirmed.

VI. STATE ACTION, INDIANS, AND EQUAL PROTECTION

The federal trust responsibility toward Indian tribes is the dominant factor that shapes equal protection analysis of federal laws about Indians. Although states do not share this same relationship toward Indians,[124] state laws that are enacted under the explicit authority of federal legislation, such as Public Law 280,[125] are deemed to be expressions of the federal trust responsibility and are judged by the same equal protection standards used in determining the validity of federal laws.[126]

---

124. "It is settled that 'the unique legal status of Indian tribes under federal law' permits the Federal Government to enact legislation singling out tribal Indians, legislation that might otherwise be constitutionally offensive. . . . States do not enjoy this same unique relationship to Indians . . . ." Washington v. Confederated Bands & Tribes of Yakima Indian Nation, 99 S. Ct. 740, 761 (1979).

125. 18 U.S.C. § 1162 (1976); 28 U.S.C. § 1360 (1976).

126. Washington v. Confederated Bands & Tribes of Yakima Indian Nation, 99 S. Ct. 740 (1979). The Court said that a Washington state law enacted pursuant to Public Law 280 was authorized under a federal law enacted in the exercise of Congress' plenary power over Indians. *Id.* at 746. The state law imposed state jurisdiction over (1) non-Indians on all lands of Indian reservations within the state, (2) Indians on fee patent lands on reservations, and (3) Indians on trust lands on reservations for eight subject-matter areas. The Ninth Circuit Court of Appeals had struck down this law as a violation of the fourteenth amendment equal protection clause. Confederated Bands & Tribes of the Yakima Indian Nation v. Washington, 552 F.2d 1332 (1977). It had found that the statutory classification was not on its face racially discriminatory and was not

607

The federal government has, through statutes and treaties, preempted most of the field of Indian affairs. It is not surprising, therefore, to find very few cases raising Indian equal protection issues in connection with state laws or administrative actions that are not derivative from federal laws.[127]

It is clear that states can enact legislation and take administrative action to implement Indian treaty rights and that such action does not violate the fourteenth amendment equal protection clause.[128] Going one step further, the Minnesota Supreme Court held that a settlement between an Indian tribe and the state did not violate the equal protection clause.[129] The settlement, which was ratified by state law, resolved an issue in litigation between the tribe and the state and gave to the Indians fishing rights not shared by non-Indians. The court used the standard rational basis test to determine the validity of the state law. Because the settlement agreement and ratifying law were designed to preserve the fishery resource for the people of the state and

---

adopted to mask racial discrimination. *Id.* at 1334. However, the court found that the title-based assumption of state jurisdiction could not meet even the rational basis test. The Washington Attorney General had identified the purpose of the legislation as providing criminal jursidiction over areas where the state "has the most fundamental concern for the welfare of those least able to care for themselves." *Id.* at 1334. The Ninth Circuit, however, could not detect any rational connection between this or any other valid purpose, and the imposition of state jurisdiction based on land title within the reservation. The court said the state's interest in enforcing criminal law was no less "fundamental" or "overriding" on nonfee lands than on fee lands, and held that this checkerboarding of jurisdiction on reservations was "the very kind of arbitrary legislative choice forbidden by the Equal Protection Clause." *Id.* at 1336. The Supreme Court rejected this reasoning and ruled that a rational basis existed for the state law and that it did not violate fourteenth amendment equal protection principles. 99 S. Ct. at 762.

127.   Only two such cases have been found. Livingston v. Ewing, 455 F. Supp. 825 (D.N.M. 1978); State v. Forge, 262 N.W.2d 341 (Minn. 1977). In Washington State Commercial Passenger Fishing Vessel Ass'n v. Tollefson, 89 Wash. 2d 276, 51 P.2d 1373 (1977), *cert. granted*, 99 S. Ct. 276 (1978), the Washington court erroneously characterized the issue as one involving state action involving the fourteenth amendment, when, in fact, it involved federal action and raised a fifth amendment question. *See* notes 150–51 and accompanying text *infra.*

128.   Puyallup Tribe v. Department of Game, 433 U.S. 165 (1977).

129.   State v. Forge, 262 N.W.2d 341 (Minn. 1977). The court upheld a Minnesota law requiring non-Indians to pay a special license fee and secure a reservation stamp on their fishing licenses to fish on the reservation. The State Commissioner of Natural Resources collects the fee. Treaty Indians are exempt from payment of the fee. The statute was the result of a settlement agreement between the Indians and the state following lengthy litigation to determine the Indians' right to fish on the reservation. *See* Leech Lake Citizens Comm. v. Leech Lake Band of Chippewa Indians, 355 F. Supp. 697 (D. Minn. 1973). Non-Indian fishermen claimed the statute denied them equal protection under both the fourteenth amendment and the Minnesota Constitution because it exempted tribal members from paying the fee.

608

to compensate the Indians for their treaty rights, the court found that the classification was "reasonably related" to the resolution of the competing claims of the parties.[130] Upholding Indian treaty rights was held to be a valid state purpose for enactment of such legislation.[131]

States do not have the same trust relationship toward Indians as the federal government, and thus the equal protection analysis applied to state action would ordinarily differ from that applied to federal legislation. One court has held, however, that under the right circumstances the special federal relationship toward Indians also enables a state to single out tribal Indians for preferential treatment.[132] This presents some analytical problems. While it is not invalid for the state to adopt a protective attitude toward the tribes, a trust relationship between states and Indians has never been recognized by Congress or the Supreme Court. It is not clear, therefore, that because Indian preferential treatment is constitutional for the federal government, it is valid for a state.[133] The Court in *Mancari* stresses the unique status of

---

130. State v. Forge, 262 N.W.2d 341, 348 (Minn. 1977).

131. *Id.*

132. Livingston v. Ewing, 455 F. Supp. 825 (D.N.M. 1978). Plaintiffs challenged the constitutionality of state administrative action involving Indians. The Museum of New Mexico, a state owned and operated facility, had a policy of allowing only Indians to sell their crafts under its veranda. Two non-Indians challenged this policy as a violation of the equal protection clause of the fourteenth amendment. The court rejected this challenge. The court said the museum was established to preserve New Mexico's "multicultural traditions." Although the policy favoring Indian vendors was not limited to New Mexico Indians, it was limited to members of federally recognized tribes. Looking to the importance to the tribal Indians of the income derived from the sales, the court found a link between the museum's program and the national policy of encouraging Indian self-determination. The Indians were "the only remaining, relatively unchanged craftsmen of the original group who sold their wares under the portal," thus satisfying the purpose of the museum's policy which was to advance native art, "give impetus to the communities from which these arts arise, educate the public, and protect a unique tradition from assimilation so as to maintain, as best they can, its purity." *Id.* at 829.

The court rejected the argument that this preference was racial in nature, concluding instead that it was political and cultural, and saying that the state, as well as the federal government, had an obligation to insure the political, economic, and cultural survival of Indian tribes. *Id.* at 831.

133. There is nothing in the history of tribal-state relations to suggest any consistent altruistic attitude of most states toward Indians. Indeed, the opposite has often been the case. *See* United States v. Kagama, 118 U.S. 375 (1886). *See generally* W. BROPHY & S. ABERLE, THE INDIAN: AMERICA'S UNFINISHED BUSINESS—REPORT OF THE COMMISSION ON THE RIGHTS, LIBERTIES, AND RESPONSIBILITIES OF THE AMERICAN INDIAN (1966).

The historic attitude of some states toward Indians is perhaps adequately demonstrated by the following quote:

The premise of Indian sovereignty we reject. The treaty is not to be interpeted in that light. At no time did our ancestors in getting title to this continent ever regard the aborigines as other than mere occupants, and incompetent occupants, of the soil. . . . Only that title was esteemed which came from white men, and the rights of

609

Indians in the context of federal action. Preferential state policy should ordinarily be sustained, if at all, on the basis of its relationship to other valid state interests, without putting the state in the same relationship to Indians as the federal government.[134]

VII. EQUAL PROTECTION AND TREATY RIGHTS

In addition to federal law, treaties are a source of many rights guaranteed to Indians. Treaties are analogous to contracts, inasmuch as the treaty is an exchange of promises that then operates as the law by which the parties agree to be bound.[135] Rights established in treaties are, by definition, not guaranteed to those who are not parties.

Members of treaty-signing Indian tribes are guaranteed rights and benefits not shared by nonmembers. The existence of special Indian treaty rights, especially rights to limited resources such as water or fish, has at times had a significant impact on non-Indians wishing to use the same resource.[136] Several recent cases have questioned

---

these have always been ascribed by the highest authority to lawful discovery of lands, occupied, to be sure, but not owned by anyone before. . . .

The Indian was a child, and a dangerous child, of nature, to be both protected and restrained. In his nomadic life he was to be left, so long as civilization did not demand his region. When it did demand that region, he was to be allotted a more confined area with permanent subsistence. . . .

These arrangements [for treaties and reservations] were but the announcement of our benevolence which, notwithstanding our frequent frailties, has been continuously displayed. Neither Rome nor sagacious Britain ever dealt more liberally with their subject races than we with these savage tribes, whom it was generally tempting and always easy to destroy and whom we have so often permitted to squander vast areas of fertile land before our eyes.

State v. Towessnute, 89 Wash. 478, 481–82, 154 P. 805, 807 (1916). A recent example of a state court's hostility toward Indian sovereignty can be found in Brough v. Appawora, 553 P.2d 934 (Utah 1976), *vacated and remanded, mem.*, 431 U.S. 901 (1977).

134. It should be noted that, even if insuring the survival of Indian culture may be articulated as a valid state interest, the state action cannot conflict with federal law which would preempt state law. *See generally* McClanahan v. Arizona State Tax Comm'n, 411 U.S. 164 (1973).

135. *See* D. GETCHES, D. ROSENFELT, & C. WILKINSON, CASES AND MATERIALS ON FEDERAL INDIAN LAW 30–32 (1972); Wilkinson & Volkman, *Judicial Review of Indian Treaty Abrogation: "As Long as Water Flows or Grass Grows Upon the Earth"—How Long a Time is That?*, 63 CALIF. L. REV. 601, 608–19 (1975). At the risk of over-extending the analogy, it might be noted that contracts between a government and its citizens or corporations have never been thought to raise equal protection issues with respect to contracting and noncontracting citizens.

136. *See, e.g.*, Winters v. United States, 207 U.S. 564 (1908) (water); United States v. Washington, 384 F. Supp. 312 (W.D. Wash. 1974), *aff'd*, 520 F.2d 676 (9th Cir. 1975), *cert. denied*, 423 U.S. 1086 (1976), *cert. granted*, 99 S. Ct. 277 (1978) (fishing).

610

whether either the treaties themselves,[137] or state classifications required by the treaties,[138] are a denial of equal protection to non-Indians.

No treaty of any sort has ever been invalidated because it violated equal protection principles.[139] Treaties are normally made with foreign nations, thus, equal protection of the laws is inapposite. Treaties with Indian tribes, however, do involve the federal government and groups of its own citizens.[140] Nevertheless, there is little or no theoretical basis for equal protection challenges to Indian treaties themselves. The Constitution provides for treaty-making power,[141] and the Supreme Court has repeatedly enforced Indian treaties as a valid exercise of that constitutional power. Indeed, treaty rights are part of "Congress' unique obligation toward the Indians" that justifies special federal legislation favoring Indians.[142]

In order to fulfill Indian treaty rights, many statutes and regulations necessarily treat Indians and non-Indians differently.[143] When

---

137. *See* Washington State Commercial Passenger Fishing Vessel Ass'n v. Tollefson, 89 Wn. 2d 276, 571 P.2d 1373 (1977), *cert. granted,* 99 S. Ct. 276 (1978).

138. *See* State v. Forge, 262 N.W.2d 341 (Minn. 1977), *appeal dismissed,* 435 U.S. 919 (1978); Department of Game v. Puyallup Tribe, Inc., 86 Wn. 2d 664, 548 P.2d 1058 (1976), *vacated and remanded,* 433 U.S. 165 (1977).

139. *But see* Washington State Commercial Passenger Fishing Vessel Ass'n v. Tollefson, 89 Wn. 2d 276, 571 P.2d 1373 (1977), *cert. granted,* 99 S. Ct. 276 (1978).

Because treaties are federal law, any equal protection analysis of them would be under the fifth amendment rather than the fourteenth amendment. *See* note 39 *supra.* Challenges to treaties may be nonjusticiable issues. *Cf.* Delaware Tribal Business Council v. Weeks, 430 U.S. 73 (1977) (challenge to congressional settlement of an Indian claim arising out of treaty rights held to be a justiciable issue).

140. All Indians are now United States citizens. 8 U.S.C. § 1401(a)(2) (1976).

There have been no new treaties with Indian tribes since 1871, when Congress proscribed any additional treaties. Act of Mar. 3, 1871, ch. 120, § 3, 16 Stat. 566 (1871) (codified at 25 U.S.C. § 21 (1976)).

141. U.S. Const. art. VI, §2.

142. *Mancari,* 417 U.S. at 555. *See* notes 70–74 and accompanying text *supra.*

Some equal protection challenges to treaties are based on a false premise that the treaty granted a special benefit to tribal Indians. The Supreme Court has held that many treaty rights, rather than being grants from Congress, are reserved rights that tribes have always possessed. United States v. Winans, 198 U.S. 371 (1905). The Court has held that the reserved rights of Indian tribes are valid against all but the federal government. Oneida Indian Nation v. County of Oneida, 414 U.S. 661 (1974); Worcester v. Georgia, 31 U.S. (6 Pet.) 515 (1832); Johnson v. McIntosh, 21 U.S. (8 Wheat.) 543 (1823). Even those treaty rights which might be said to be a grant of a benefit to Indians constitute consideration to Indians for the cancellation of Indian claims to vast areas of land. *See* United States v. Washington, 384 F. Supp. 312, 333 (W.D. Wash. 1974), *aff'd,* 520 F.2d 676 (9th Cir. 1975), *cert. denied,* 423 U.S. 1086 (1976), *cert. granted,* 99 S. Ct. 277 (1978); F. Prucha, American Indian Policy in the Formative Years: Indian Trade and Intercourse Acts, 1790–1834, at 43–50 (1962).

143. *See* cases cited in notes 136–39 *supra,* and notes 166–68 and accompanying text *infra.*

611

federal laws are involved, the *Mancari* analysis is clearly appropriate.[144] In light of the holding in *Washington v. Yakima Tribes,*[145] the *Mancari* rule appears to be appropriate in cases involving state laws as well. If state laws permitted by federal enabling legislation are tested in light of a rational relation to the fulfillment of the government's obligation toward Indians, then state laws required by federal treaties should be entitled to no less deference. An examination of a series of state and federal cases involving Indian fishing rights in the state of Washington[146] perhaps best illustrates the present state of law in this area.

In 1974, a federal district court held that certain 1855 treaties[147] guaranteed signatory Indian tribes the opportunity to take up to 50% of the harvestable salmon and steelhead in treaty waters instead of about 4% which they had taken in the past under state law.[148] Subse-

---

144.   *See* Part V *supra.*

145.   99 S. Ct. 740 (1979). *See* notes 124–26 and accompanying text *supra.* .

146.   For general treatment of this controversy, see AMERICAN FRIENDS SERVICE COMMITTEE, AN UNCOMMON CONTROVERSY (1967); Johnson, *The States Versus Indian Off-Reservation Fishing: A United States Supreme Court Error,* 47 WASH. L. REV. 207 (1972); Comment, *Indian Treaty Analysis and Off-Reservation Rights: A Case Study,* 51 WASH. L. REV. 61 (1975).

147.   The treaties were all negotiated by Territorial Governor Isaac Stevens with different Indian tribes and bands in the Pacific Northwest in 1854 and 1855. The treaties are: Treaty with the Nisqually and Other Indian Tribes, Dec. 26, 1854, 10 Stat. 1132 (Treaty of Medicine Creek); Treaty with the Duwamish and Other Indian Tribes, Jan. 22, 1855, 12 Stat. 927 (Treaty of Point Elliott); Treaty with the S'kallam and Other Indian Tribes, Jan. 28, 1855, 12 Stat. 933 (Treaty of Point No Point); Treaty with the Makah Tribe, Jan. 31, 1855, 12 Stat. 939 (Treaty of Neah Bay); Treaty with the Yakima and Other Indian Tribes, June 9, 1855, 12 Stat. 951 (Treaty of Camp Stevens); Treaty with the Quinaielt and Other Indian Tribes, July 1, 1855, 12 Stat. 971 (Treaty of Quinaielt River). The Treaty of Medicine Creek provides that "The right of taking fish, at all usual and accustomed grounds and stations, is further secured to said Indians, in common with all citizens of the territory." 10 Stat. 1132, 1133. Each of the other treaties contains a virtually identical provision. These provisions were intended to preserve Indian fishing rights at traditional off-reservation sites. United States v. Washington, 384 F. Supp. 312, 350 (W.D. Wash. 1974), *aff'd,* 520 F.2d 676 (9th Cir. 1975), *cert. denied,* 423 U.S. 1086 (1976), *cert. granted,* 99 S. Ct. 277 (1978).

148.   United States v. Washington, 384 F. Supp. 312 (W.D. Wash. 1974), *aff'd,* 520 F.2d 676 (9th Cir. 1975), *cert. denied,* 423 U.S. 1086 (1976), *cert. granted,* 99 S. Ct. 277 (1978). The court also interpreted the treaty as entitling the treaty tribes to take fish for subsistence and ceremonial purposes. *Id.* at 343. The off-reservation treaty fishing right was construed as meaning the treaty Indians were entitled to the *opportunity* to harvest up to 50%. *Id.* In fact, to date they have only increased their take of the total Washington landing from about 4% in 1971 to about 18% in 1978. Brief of Respondents, United States v. Washington, 99 S. Ct. 277 (1978). The off-reservation entitlement is in addition to the on-reservation catch of fish which generally cannot be regulated at all by the state. *But see* Puyallup Tribe v. Washington Dep't of Game, 433 U.S. 165 (1977).

Because this article concerns the equal protection issue, it will not analyze the ques-

612

quently, several non-Indian fishermen's organizations brought suit in Washington courts to prevent the State Directors of the Department of Fisheries from implementing the federal district court decision.[149] In the most recent of these cases to reach the Washington Supreme Court, *Washington State Commercial Passenger Fishing Vessel Association v. Tollefson*,[150] the court held that the allocation of a proportionally unequal percentage of harvestable fish to treaty Indians was a denial of equal protection to non-Indians under the fourteenth amendment to the U.S. Constitution.[151] This is a position that the

---

tion whether the treaties were intended to guarantee to the Indians 50% or some other specific portion of the salmon and steelhead runs in treaty waters. The treaty interpretation issue has been examined exhaustively by the federal courts. *See* Puget Sound Gillnetters Ass'n v. United States District Court, 573 F.2d 1123 (9th Cir.), *cert. granted,* 99 S. Ct. 277 (1978); Sohappy v. Smith, 529 F.2d 570 (9th Cir. 1976); United States v. Washington, 384 F. Supp. 312 (W.D. Wash. 1974), *aff'd* 520 F.2d 676 (9th Cir. 1975), *cert. denied,* 423 U.S. 1086 (1976), *cert. granted,* 99 S. Ct. 277 (1978). The Washington State Supreme Court has also examined the issue. Department of Game v. Puyallup Tribe, Inc., 86 Wn. 2d 664, 548 P.2d 1058 (1976), *vacated and remanded,* 433 U.S. 165 (1977).

The background of the Indian fishing rights cases is explored in depth in Comment, *Accommodation of Indian Treaty Rights in an International Fishery: An International Problem Begging for an International Solution,* 54 WASH. L. REV. 403 (1979).

149.   Washington State Commercial Passenger Fishing Vessel Ass'n v. Tollefson, 89 Wn. 2d 276, 571 P.2d 1373 (1977), *cert. granted,* 99 S. Ct. 276 (1977); Purse Seine Vessel Owners Ass'n v. Moos, 88 Wn. 2d 799, 567 P.2d 205 (1977); Puget Sound Gillnetters Ass'n v. Moos, 88 Wn. 2d 677, 565 P.2d 1151 (1977), *cert. granted,* 99 S. Ct. 276 (1978).

Reacting to the anger of the non-Indian fishing organizations at the decision in United States v. Washington, 384 F. Supp. 312 (W.D. Wash. 1974), *aff'd,* 520 F.2d 676 (9th Cir. 1975), *cert. denied,* 423 U.S. 1086 (1976), *cert. granted,* 99 S. Ct. 277 (1978), agencies of the state of Washington took administrative action designed to thwart the Indians' rights. This prompted the Ninth Circuit Court of Appeals to comment, "[e]xcept for some desegregation cases [citations omitted], the district court [that decided *United States v. Washington*] has faced the most concerted official and private efforts to frustrate the decree of a federal court witnessed in this century." Puget Sound Gillnetters Ass'n v. United States District Court, 573 F.2d 1123, 1126 (9th Cir.), *cert. granted,* 99 S. Ct. 277 (1978).

150.   89 Wn. 2d 276, 571 P.2d 1373 (1977), *cert. granted,* 99 S. Ct. 276 (1978). For an analysis of other issues in the case see Note, *The Interaction of Federal Equitable Remedies with State Sovereignty,* 53 WASH. L. REV. 787 (1978).

151.   The Washington court has voiced this opinion with increasing conviction over the past ten years. *See* Puget Sound Gillnetters Ass'n v. Moos, 88 Wn. 2d 677, 684, 565 P.2d 1151, 1154 (1977), *cert. granted,* 99 S. Ct. 276 (1978); Department of Game v. Puyallup Tribe, Inc., 86 Wn. 2d 664, 680-81, 548 P.2d 1058, 1070 (1976), *vacated and remanded,* 433 U.S. 165 (1977); Department of Game v. Puyallup Tribe, Inc., 70 Wn. 2d 245, 252, 422 P.2d 754, 759 (1967). In Puyallup Tribe v. Department of Game, 391 U.S. 392 (1968), Justice Douglas, for the majority, said that "any ultimate finding" on the validity of fish conservation laws "must also cover the issue of equal protection implicit in the [treaty] phrase 'in common with.' " *Id.* at 403.

The Washington court misconceived the nature of the equal protection issue. An In-

613

Washington court had previously taken in *Department of Game v. Puyallup Tribe, Inc.*[152] That decision was vacated about the time *Tollefson* was decided.[153] Although the soundness of *Tollefson* is questionable in light of the U.S. Supreme Court decision in *Puyallup Tribe, Inc. v. Department of Game*[154] *(Puyallup III)*, it may provide some limited authority for the proposition that Indian treaties are subject to equal protection limitations.[155]

Three cases brought by the Washington State Department of Game

---

dian treaty cannot violate the fourteenth amendment to the federal Constitution. That amendment applies only to state action. The treaty is federal action. Nor can there be an issue in this case of state laws or administrative actions violating the fourteenth amendment. Under the supremacy clause, federal law, including treaties, preempts state law, even state constitutional law. U.S. CONST. art. VI, § 2. Thus, the real question is whether the treaties, which constitute federal action, violate the fifth amendment to the federal Constitution. The fifth amendment analysis, however, is virtually identical to that under the fourteenth. *See* note 39 *supra*.

152. 86 Wn. 2d 664, 680-81, 548 P.2d 1058, 1070 (1976), *vacated and remanded*, 433 U.S. 165 (1977).

153. 433 U.S. 165 (1977).

154. *Id*.

155. The limited authority for this proposition represented by *Tollefson* is further eroded by the weakness of the Washington court's analysis. The court begins by defining the issue as whether "Congress and the executive department, by treaty, or . . . a court of law, in interpreting a treaty, [may] ignore and supersede provisions of the federal constitution." 89 Wn. 2d at 279, 571 P.2d at 1375. The question as phrased clearly begs the issue and requires a "no" answer. Certainly no treaty or act of Congress can "ignore and supersede" provisions of the Constitution. Reid v. Covert, 354 U.S. 1 (1957); The Cherokee Tobacco, 78 U.S. (11 Wall.) 616 (1871); L. TRIBE, AMERICAN CONSTITUTIONAL LAW 169-70 (1978).

The *Tollefson* court proceeds to argue that the treaty itself violates the fourteenth amendment by use of the following analogy:

> We think there can be no doubt that were the executive department to enter into a treaty with a foreign nation or were the Congress to pass a law which allocated a portion of the states' natural resources to a group of its citizens, based on their race or ancestry, that provision would be struck down as a denial of equal protection.

89 Wn. 2d at 281, 571 P.2d at 1376. The analogy clearly misses the mark on several accounts. First, the treaty did not allocate resources to citizens of a state, both because Washington was not a state in 1855 when the treaty was signed, *see* note 147 *supra*, and, more importantly, because Indians were not citizens, but rather members of sovereign entities. Second, the basis of the allocation is not race or ancestry but membership in the political entity of the tribe. *See Mancari*, 417 U.S. at 553 n.24, 554; *Tollefson*, 89 Wn. 2d at 299-300, 571 P.2d at 1385-86 (Utter J., dissenting). Finally, instead of being struck down as a denial of equal protection, Indian treaty rights have repeatedly been upheld and enforced by the U.S. Supreme Court. *See, e.g.*, Puyallup Tribe Inc. v. Department of Game, 433 U.S. 165 (1977); United States v. Winans, 198 U.S. 371 (1905).

The *Tollefson* court also concludes, in rather novel fashion, that the federal court's interpretation of the treaty violates the fourteenth amendment. 89 Wn. 2d at 285-86, 571 P.2d at 1378. It is not clear how a judicial interpretation itself, as distinguished from the statute or treaty as interpreted, violates equal protection principles. But if true, it would imply that when a court makes an incorrect ruling on an equal protection issue, it has

614

against the Puyallup Tribe, commonly referred to as *Puyallup I*,[156] *Puyallup II*,[157] and *Puyallup III*,[158] seem to have established, however, that the Supreme Court will not entertain equal protection challenges to Indian treaties.

In *Puyallup I* the Supreme Court held that the off-reservation fishing rights of treaty Indians could be regulated when necessary for conservation.[159] In the last sentence of the opinion Justice Douglas, for the majority, said that "any ultimate findings on the conservation issue must also cover the issue of equal protection implicit in the [treaty] phrase 'in common with.' "[160]

When this case again reached the Washington Supreme Court, the majority ruled that treaty Indians do have special off-reservation fishing rights not shared by non-Indians.[161] The court approved state fisheries department regulations allowing treaty Indians to fish for salmon in the Puyallup River at different times and with different equipment than non-Indians.[162] The court banned entirely, however, Indian net fishing for steelhead in the river.[163] The two dissenting justices explicitly raised the equal protection issue, arguing that the majority's decision recognizing special rights in treaty Indians "not only deprives citizens of the equal protection of the laws, but grants to some Indians as a class immunities and privileges not enjoyed by all citizens, including most Indians—all in violation of the Fourteenth Amendment."[164]

On appeal the United States Supreme Court reversed that part of

---

not merely committed reversible error, but may also have violated either the fifth or fourteenth amendments.

Finally, although retaining its precedential value at least in Washington, the *Tollefson* decision received the following criticism from the Ninth Circuit Court of Appeals:

We reject [the Washington Supreme Court's equal protection arguments] for the reasons given [herein] and in Justices Horowitz' and Utter's dissents: We assume that the Washington court has unwittingly misconstrued the basic concepts of Indian law and failed to understand a long line of Supreme Court decisions beginning with *United States v. Winans*.

Puget Sound Gillnetters Ass'n v. United States District Court, 573 F.2d 1123, 1128–29 n.5, *cert. granted*, 99 S. Ct. 277 (1978) (citations omitted).

156   Puyallup Tribe v. Department of Game, 391 U.S. 392 (1968).

157.   Department of Game v. Puyallup Tribe, 414 U.S. 44 (1973).

158.   Puyallup Tribe, Inc. v. Department of Game, 433 U.S. 165 (1977).

159.   391 U.S. at 398.

160.   *Id.* at 403.

161.   Department of Game v. Puyallup Tribe, Inc., 80 Wn. 2d 561, 571, 497 P.2d 171, 178 (1972), *rev'd and remanded*, 414 U.S. 44 (1973).

162.   *Id.* at 570, 497 P.2d at 177.

163.   *Id.* at 576, 497 P.2d at 180.

164.   *Id.* at 579, 497 P.2d at 182 (Hale, J., dissenting).

615

the state court decision approving the total ban on net fishing, saying that the state had failed to show that a complete ban on treaty Indian steelhead net fishing was necessary for conservation.[165] The Court remanded the case to allow the state to come up with a formula that "fairly apportioned" steelhead between Indian net fishing and non-Indian sports fishing.[166] The Court did not discuss the state court dissenters' equal protection argument. To the contrary, the Court held that the total ban on Indian net fishing was discrimination under the treaty "because all Indian net fishing is barred and only hook-and-line fishing entirely preempted by non-Indians is allowed."[167] Thus, in light of Indian treaty rights, the state could avoid discriminating against Indians only by making special provisions for them.

Subsequent regulations allocated 45% of the natural steelhead run to the Puyallup Indian Tribe for their off-reservation fishing sites. The Washington Supreme Court in reviewing this allocation ruled that both the fourteenth amendment equal protection clause and the treaty language prohibited treating Indians and non-Indians differently, but that if the United States Supreme Court rejected this reasoning then an allocation of 45% to the Indians met the *Puyallup I* and *Puyallup II* criteria.[168] The United States Supreme Court approved the 45% allocation, but again failed to discuss the equal protection issue.[169]

That the Supreme Court in the three *Puyallup* cases ignored the equal protection arguments made by the Washington court argues with considerable force that the Court believes equal protection principles are not a basis for challenging Indian treaty rights. At the very least, the Court has upheld a preferential right to catch fish for members of a treaty tribe and required state action to implement that right.

VIII. THE INDIAN CIVIL RIGHTS ACT OF 1968

The Indian Civil Rights Act[170] (ICRA) was enacted in 1968 and contains an equal protection clause.[171] This clause, copied substan-

---

165.   *Puyallup II,* 414 U.S. 44 (1973).

166.   *Id.* at 48–49.

167.   *Id.* at 48.

168.   Department of Game v. Puyallup Tribe, Inc., 86 Wn. 2d 664, 681, 687–88, 548 P.2d 1058, 1070, 1074 (1976), *vacated and remanded,* 433 U.S. 165 (1977).

169.   *Puyallup III,* 433 U.S. 165 (1977).

170.   25 U.S.C. §§ 1301–1341 (1976).

171.   *Id.* at § 1302(8).

616

tially from the fourteenth amendment to the federal Constitution,[172] constrains all three branches of tribal governments—legislative, executive, and judicial—and protects non-Indians as well as Indians.[173] Not surprisingly, the federal courts' interpretation of the ICRA equal protection clause has drawn upon both traditional equal protection doctrine and the analysis developed by the courts in fifth amendment equal protection cases involving Indians.

Long before the ICRA, the case of *Talton v. Mayes*[174] held that the grand jury requirement of the federal Bill of Rights did not apply to Indian tribal governments. The rationale was that because Indian tribes derive their governing authority from inherent sovereignty rather than from the Constitution, the Bill of Rights does not apply to them.[175] As a result of alleged abuses of civil liberties by some Indian

---

172. The fourteenth amendment provides that no state shall "deny to any person within its jurisdiction the equal protection of the laws." U.S. CONST. amend. XIV, § 1.

The constitutional provision differs from the ICRA provision in that the latter guarantees "the equal protection of its [the tribes] laws," rather than "the laws." This difference was noted by the Supreme Court in Santa Clara Pueblo v. Martinez, 436 U.S. 49, 57, 62 n.14 (1978). No court, however, has yet relied on this difference to produce a different result.

173. Dry Creek Lodge, Inc. v. United States, 515 F.2d 926 (10th Cir. 1975); Dodge v. Nakai, 298 F. Supp. 26 (D. Ariz. 1969).

174. 163 U.S. 376 (1896).

175. *Id.* at 989–90. *See* Santa Clara Pueblo v. Martinez, 436 U.S. 49 (1978). There the Court said:

As separate sovereigns pre-existing the Constitution, tribes have historically been regarded as unconstrained by those constitutional provisions framed specifically as limitations on federal or state authority. Thus, in *Talton v. Mayes* . . . this Court held that the Fifth Amendment did not "operat[e] upon" "the powers of local self-government enjoyed by the tribes." . . . In ensuing years the lower federal courts have extended the holding of *Talton* to other provisions of the Bill of Rights, as well as to the Fourteenth Amendment.

Id. at 56. The court cited, *inter alia,* Twin Cities Chippewa Tribal Council v. Minnesota Chippewa Tribe, 370 F.2d 529, 533 (8th Cir. 1967) (due process clause of the fourteenth amendment); Native American Church v. Navajo Tribal Council, 272 F.2d 131 (10th Cir. 1959) (freedom of religion under first and fourteenth amendments); Barta v. Oglala Sioux Tribe, 259 F.2d 553 (8th Cir. 1959), *cert. denied,* 358 U.S. 932 (1959) (fourteenth amendment). *But see* Settler v. Yakima Tribal Court, 419 F.2d 486 (9th Cir. 1969), *cert. denied,* 398 U.S. 903 (1970); Colliflower v. Garland, 342 F.2d 369 (9th Cir. 1965). Both cases held that when a tribal court was so pervasively regulated by a federal agency that it was, in effect, a federal instrumentality, a writ of habeas corpus would lie to a person detained by that court in violation of the Constitution. The Court in *Martinez* also noted that "[t]he line of authority growing out of *Talton,* while exempting Indian tribes from constitutional provisions addressed specifically to State or Federal Governments, of course does not relieve State and Federal Governments of the obligations to individual Indians under these provisions." 436 U.S. at 56 n.7. *See also* United States v. Wheeler, 435 U.S. 313 (1978); Oliphant v. Suquamish Indian Tribe, 435 U.S. 191, 194 n.3 (1978).

617

governments, Congress enacted the Indian Civil Rights Act in 1968, thus statutorily applying selected constitutional limitations to Indian tribes.[176]

A.   Access to Federal Courts

Prior to *Santa Clara Pueblo v. Martinez*,[177] the federal courts had held that the ICRA waived tribal sovereign immunity and that a tribe could be enjoined in federal court from violating the provisions of the ICRA.[178] The Supreme Court in *Martinez*, however, held that habeas corpus was the exclusive basis for federal court jurisdiction to test tribal violations of the ICRA.[179] This remedy is traditionally available only when the plaintiff is in custody.[180] Thus, while the ICRA limits tribal government action,[181] a person complaining of a violation of the ICRA will generally have recourse only to the tribal court or the tribal government, unless habeas corpus is available.[182] Access to fed-

---

176.   25 U.S.C. §§ 1301–1303 (1976). The Supreme Court has observed:

The provisions of § 1302 [of the Act] differ in language and in substance in many other respects from those contained in the constitutional provisions on which they were modeled. The provisions of the Second and Third Amendments, in addition to those of the Seventh Amendment, were omitted entirely. The provision here at issue, § 1302(8), differs from the constitutional Equal Protection Clause in that it guarantees "the equal protection of *its* [the tribe's] laws," rather than of "the laws". Moreover, § 1302(7), which prohibits cruel and unusual punishments and excessive bails, sets an absolute limit of six months' imprisonment and a $500 fine on penalties which a tribe may impose. Finally, while most of the guarantees of the Fifth Amendment were extended to tribal actions, it is interesting to note that § 1302 does not require tribal criminal prosecutions to be initiated by grand jury indictment, which was the requirement of the Fifth Amendment specifically at issue and found inapplicable to tribes in *Talton v. Mayes*.

Santa Clara Pueblo v. Martinez, 436 U.S. 49, 63 n.14 (1978). In addition, the ICRA provides that a defendant in tribal court is entitled "at his own expense to have the assistance of counsel for his defense." 25 U.S.C. § 1302(6) (1976). Under the right to counsel provision found in the sixth amendment, as construed by the Supreme Court, an indigent defendant charged with a crime in a state or federal court where imprisonment is a possible punishment must be provided counsel at the expense of the government. Argersinger v. Hamlin, 407 U.S. 25 (1972).

177.   436 U.S. 49 (1978).

178.   Johnson v. Lower Elwha Tribal Community, 484 F.2d 200 (9th Cir. 1973); Daly v. Crow Creek Sioux Tribe, 483 F.2d 700 (8th Cir. 1973); McCurdy v. Steele, 353 F. Supp. 629 (W.D. Wash. 1973); Seneca Constitutional Rights Organization v. George, 348 F. Supp. 48 (W.D. N.Y. 1972).

179.   436 U.S. 66–70.

180.   *See, e.g.,* Parker v. Ellis, 362 U.S. 574 (1959).

181.   *Martinez*, 436 U.S. at 57.

182.   When the plaintiff is in custody the court often applies stricter standards of due process and equal protection than it does in nonhabeas corpus cases. *See* Oliphant v. Suquamish Indian Tribe, 435 U.S. 191 (1978).

618

eral courts generally cannot be obtained, for example, for issues involving denial of enrollment in the tribe, voting rights, election apportionment, taxation, or zoning.[183]

The ten years of lower federal court decisions applying the ICRA to nonhabeas corpus issues nevertheless merit attention. These opinions are likely to provide the standards of due process and equal protection that federal courts will apply in ICRA habeas corpus cases, and to indicate the extent to which these standards differ from the traditional standards. The standards developed in the pre-*Martinez* decisions will also provide helpful, although not binding, authority for Indian courts interpreting the ICRA. Finally, the principles developed in these cases can provide a basis for future evaluation of the ICRA to determine whether it has achieved a proper balance between the rights of the individual and the interests of the tribe in preserving tribal customs and traditions.[184]

B. Standard of Equal Protection: Balancing Tribal Culture Against Individual Rights

The ICRA does not include all of the civil rights guarantees of the U.S. Constitution, nor is the language of those that are included identical to the wording in the Constitution.[185] The intent of Congress in enacting the ICRA was to guarantee individual rights with a mini-

---

183. *See Martinez,* 436 U.S. at 71.

184. Sooner or later Congress is likely to review tribal court experience under the ICRA to determine whether the present scope of federal court review should be broadened or whether substantive changes in the ICRA are needed. As Justice Marshall wrote for the majority in *Martinez,* "Congress retains authority expressly to authorize civil actions for injunctive or other relief to redress violations of § 1302, in the event that the tribes themselves prove deficient in applying and enforcing its substantive provisions." *Id.* at 72.

Most Indian courts are not yet courts of record. NATIONAL AMERICAN INDIAN COURT JUDGES ASSOCIATION, INDIAN COURTS OF THE FUTURE (1978). Even fewer have appellate courts that regularly publish opinions. Thus their decisions on ICRA or on other questions are not readily available in printed form. A trend is now apparent to make more Indian courts courts of record and to publish Indian appellate court decisions. Any congressional review of the ICRA should, of course, examine these sources. Such a review will also have to rely on testimony of participants and observers in the Indian court process regarding application of ICRA principles, as Congress did when considering the ICRA itself. SUBCOMM. ON CONSTITUTIONAL RIGHTS, SENATE COMM. ON THE JUDICIARY, SUMMARY REPORT OF HEARINGS AND INVESTIGATIONS ON CONSTITUTIONAL RIGHTS OF AMERICAN INDIANS, 88th Cong., 2d Sess. (1964). *See* Burnett, *An Historical Analysis of the 1968 "Indian Civil Rights" Act,* 9 HARV. J. LEGIS. 557 (1972).

185. *See* note 176 *supra.*

619

mum infringement on tribal self-determination.[186] Courts interpreting the ICRA equal protection clause are faced with the problem of developing a standard of review that properly balances tribal and individual interests. The Supreme Court has not provided any definitive answer to this question. Its most substantial comment appears in *Martinez* when the court said, "Given the often vast gulf between tribal traditions and those with which federal courts are more intimately familiar, the judiciary should not rush to create causes of action that would intrude on these delicate matters," referring to the right of a tribe to define its own membership.[187] The Court was reluctant to "substantially interfere with a tribe's ability to maintain itself as a culturally and politically distinct entity."[188]

In the absence of a conclusive answer, the lower federal court decisions have varied considerably.[189] However, they have generally accorded considerable weight to Indian cultural autonomy and traditional values and have given considerable deference to the judgment of tribal governments.[190] A careful and complete treatment of

---

186. Three court of appeals opinions have cited with approval a statement contained in a report by a Senate subcommittee:

The Department of Interior's bill would, in effect, impose upon the Indian governments the same restrictions applicable presently to the Federal and State governments with several notable exceptions, viz., the 15th amendment, certain of the procedural requirements of the 5th, 6th, and 7th amendments, and, in some respects, the equal protection requirement of the 14th amendment.

SUBCOMM. ON CONSTITUTIONAL RIGHTS, SENATE COMM. ON THE JUDICIARY, 89TH CONG., 2D SESS., CONSTITUTIONAL RIGHTS OF THE AMERICAN INDIAN: SUMMARY REPORT OF HEARINGS AND INVESTIGATIONS, PURSUANT TO S. RES. 194, 25 (Comm. Print 1966). *See* Wounded Head v. Tribal Council of Oglala Sioux Tribe, 507 F.2d 1079, 1082 (8th Cir. 1975); White Eagle v. One Feather, 478 F.2d 1311, 1313 (8th Cir. 1973); Groundhog v. Keeler, 442 F.2d 674, 682 (10th Cir. 1971).

Reliance on this language is misplaced. The subcommittee was discussing a different version of the equal protection clause that was not enacted into law. This earlier version prohibited denial of equal protection to "members of the tribe." This explains why the subcommittee said the fourteenth amendment equal protection requirement applies only "in some respects." The enacted law prohibits denial of equal protection to any "person." *See* Burnett, *supra* note 184, at 602 n.239.

187. 436 U.S. at 72 n.32 (dictum).

188. *Id.* at 71–72 (dictum).

189. For examples of different approaches used by federal courts, see Ziontz, *In Defense of Tribal Sovereignty: An Analysis of Judicial Error in Construction of the Indian Civil Rights Act*, 20 S. DAK. L. REV. 1 (1975). *See also* de Raismes, *The Indian Civil Rights Act of 1968 and the Pursuit of Responsible Tribal Self-Government*, 20 S. DAK. L. REV. 59 (1975). *Cf.* Crowe v. Eastern Band of Cherokee Indians, 506 F.2d 1231 (1974) (court has power to set aside tribal action but could not substitute its judgment on merits for that of the tribe).

190. *See, e.g.,* Martinez v. Santa Clara Pueblo, 540 F.2d 1039 (10th Cir. 1975), *rev'd on other grounds*, 436 U.S. 49 (1978); Howlett v. Salish & Kootenai Tribes, 529

620

this issue is contained in the opinion of the Court of Appeals for the Tenth Circuit in *Martinez v. Santa Clara Pueblo*.[191] Although this decision was reversed by the Supreme Court on other grounds, the Court nonetheless confirmed the ICRA equal protection analysis of the lower federal courts.[192]

1. Tribal enrollments

In *Martinez,* Mrs. Martinez, a member of the Santa Clara Pueblo, asserted that a tribal ordinance denying tribal enrollment of her children violated the equal protection clause of the ICRA. Her husband was a non-Santa Claran. The ordinance permitted enrollment of the children of male, but not the children of female, Santa Clarans who married outside the tribe. Holding that the ordinance did not violate the ICRA equal protection section, the district court ruled for the tribe.[193] That court's rationale was that restriction of the Pueblo's ability to determine tribal membership would threaten its culture because the male-female distinction was rooted in the Pueblo's patrilineal and patrilocal tradition.[194]

The circuit court of appeals reversed.[195] The court extensively reviewed the legislative history of the ICRA and concluded that Congress intended to temper the normal application of equal protection principles where the cultural autonomy and integrity of the tribe would be unduly impacted.[196] The court then adopted a "comparative weighing," or balancing, approach, saying:

> [T]he scope, extent and importance of the tribal interest is to be taken into account. The individual right to fair treatment under the law is likewise to be weighed against the tribal interest by considering the clearness of the guarantee together with the magnitude of the interest. . . .
>
> . . . . .
>
> . . . The concern of Congress was to protect against serious deprivations of constitutional rights while giving as much effect as the facts would allow to tribal autonomy.

F.2d 233 (9th Cir. 1976); McCurdy v. Steele, 506 F.2d 653 (10th Cir. 1974); Daly v. Crow Creek Sioux Tribe, 483 F.2d 400 (8th Cir. 1973); Groundhog v. Keeler, 442 F.2d 674 (10th Cir. 1971).

191.   540 F.2d 1039 (10th Cir. 1976), *rev'd on other grounds,* 436 U.S. 49 (1978).
192.   436 U.S. at 71–72.
193.   Martinez v. Santa Clara Pueblo, 402 F. Supp. 5 (D.N.M. 1975).
194.   *Id.* at 16.
195.   540 F.2d 1039 (1976), *rev'd on other grounds,* 436 U.S. 49 (1978).
196.   *Id.* at 1042–45.

621

. . . .

. . . [W]here the tribal tradition is deep-seated and the individual injury is relatively insignificant, courts should be and have been reluctant to order the tribal authority to give way.[197]

Applying this test the court nevertheless held that the denial of enrollment to Mrs. Martinez' children on the basis of gender effectively denied female members of the tribe "fundamental rights" that were extended to men, including rights of inheritance, residency, voting, and the right to pass tribal membership to their offspring.[198] The court said that under normal constitutional standards such a classification would be subject to strict scrutiny and would violate equal protection principles.[199] Although recognizing the special weight to be given to tribal culture and autonomy, the court nevertheless held that the evidence failed to establish a compelling tribal interest justifying such discrimination.

The tribal ordinance in question was enacted in 1939 to deal with an unprecedented number of mixed marriages arising out of boarding school contacts between Santa Claran young people and other Indians. Prior to that time enrollment rights had not been determined on the basis of sex. The ordinance was therefore not the product of any ancient or venerable Santa Claran patrilineal or patrilocal custom, but rather of "economics and pragmatics."[200]

The *Martinez* court clearly believed that a heightened level of scrutiny is appropriate in ICRA equal protection cases involving fundamental rights. Thus, an ordinance such as the one in question can survive judicial examination only if it is supported by a compelling tribal

---

197. *Id*. at 1045–46. This characterization of the test was first pronounced in Daly v. United States, 483 F.2d 700 (8th Cir. 1973), and was adopted in Howlett v. Salish & Kootenai Tribes, 529 F.2d 233, 238 (9th Cir. 1976).

198. 540 F.2d at 1045.

199. The court cited Frontiero v. Richardson, 411 U.S. 677 (1973), which applied strict scrutiny to a gender discrimination issue, but which was only a plurality opinion. It also cited the earlier case of Reed v. Reed, 404 U.S. 71 (1971), which in a majority opinion applied the midlevel scrutiny test to a gender discrimination case. 540 F.2d at 1046–47.

200. *Id*. at 1047. The "economics and pragmatics" referred to involved the tribes' fear that the offspring of mixed marriages would "swell the population of the Pueblo" and diminish individual shares of the property. *Id*. The court noted that the Martinez children were 100% Indian and 50% Santa Claran. They spoke Tewa, the language of the Santa Clara Pueblo. They practiced the customs of the tribe and were accepted into the tribe's religion. They were persons "within the cultural group who have been allowed to develop a substantial stake in the life of the Tribe," and to allow this arbitrary discrimination "would be tantamount to saying that the Indian Bill of Rights is merely an abstract statement of principle." *Id*. at 1048.

622

interest.[201] This approach differs significantly from the test applied to federal statutes in *Mancari* and in subsequent cases where the Supreme Court has explicitly rejected a strict scrutiny standard when examining federal action toward Indians.[202]

Although the *Martinez* standard more closely resembles the standard used in traditional equal protection analyses than the one used in *Mancari* and its progeny, it possesses some distinct features. As already noted, the circuit court implied that ancient customs and traditions, contrasted with mere "economics and pragmatics,"[203] are to be given special deference. It also noted that once a compelling tribal interest is found, the deference granted tribal autonomy might compel the court to require something less than a necessary relationship of the classification to that interest.[204]

2. *Right to hold tribal office*

Cases involving voting rights and the right to hold tribal office illustrate the balancing test that the court adopted in *Martinez*.[205] For

---

201. Other cases also apply the same standard as that applied under the Constitution. For example, the Ninth Circuit Court of Appeals applied the compelling governmental interest test to determine the validity of a residency requirement for tribal council candidacy, and held that the ordinance met this test. Howlett v. Salish & Kootenai Tribes, 529 F.2d 233, 243–44 (1976). In Means v. Wilson, 522 F.2d 833 (8th Cir. 1975), the court characterized the right to vote in the Oglala Sioux tribal election as a right of citizenship "protected by the Constitution." *Id.* at 839. It should be noted that the fundamental nature of a right seems to be determined by reference to traditional equal protection analysis and not by reference to the internal values of the tribe.

202. *See* Part V *supra*.

203. *See* note 200 *supra*.

204. *Cf.* Howlett v. Salish & Kootenai Tribes, 529 F.2d 233 (9th Cir. 1976). The equal protection clause in the ICRA may be implemented differently than "its constitutional counterpart" when a tribal practice or custom might be significantly altered and when the individual injury is likely to be comparatively small. *Id.* at 238.

205. In Groundhog v. Keeler, 442 F.2d 674 (10th Cir. 1971), a federal court refused to enjoin on equal protection grounds officials of the Cherokee Tribe who were allegedly not operating the government in the best interests of the tribe because the defendants' actions violated neither fourteenth amendment nor ICRA equal protection principles. In the course of its discussion the court noted that section 1302(8) of the ICRA "was not as broad" as the fourteenth amendment. *Id.* at 682 (dictum).

In McCurdy v. Steele, 506 F.2d 653 (10th Cir. 1974), the court held that neither the equal protection principles of the Bill of Rights nor those of section 1302(8) required candidates for tribal council to file for office in order to be elected by write-in ballots or prohibited the use of write-in ballots. Again the court noted that, even though the language of the fourteenth amendment and that of the ICRA were essentially the same, "this does not necessarily mean . . . [that the ICRA clause carries] full constitutional impact." *Id.* at 655 (dictum). The court added that the ICRA was directed primarily at "the administration of justice by tribal authority" rather than at "tribal governmental structure, office holding, or elections." *Id.*

623

example, *Howlett v. Salish & Kootenai Tribes*[206] concerned a residency requirement for members of the tribal council. The tribal con-

Other courts of appeals' opinions concerning the distinction between ICRA and constitutional equal protection principles have announced the same general rule as *Martinez*, although the precise formulation has varied from case to case. *See, e.g.,* Howlett v. Salish & Kootenai Tribes, 529 F.2d 233 (9th Cir. 1976); Means v. Wilson, 522 F.2d 833 (8th Cir. 1975); Wounded Head v. Tribal Council of Oglala Sioux Tribe, 507 F.2d 1079 (8th Cir. 1975); Daly v. United States, 483 F.2d 700 (8th Cir. 1973); White Eagle v. One Feather, 478 F.2d 1311 (8th Cir. 1973). *See also* Johnson v. Lower Elwha, 484 F.2d 200 (9th Cir. 1973) (due process issue).

No decision from these circuits, or from the Fourth Circuit, the only other court of appeals to have considered the question, has given the issue the careful and extensive treatment accorded it by the Tenth Circuit in *Martinez*. The Eighth Circuit has considered the unique aspects of section 1302(8) on four occasions. In White Eagle v. One Feather, 478 F.2d 1311 (8th Cir. 1973), the court held that the one-person-one-vote principle was applicable via the equal protection clause of the ICRA to tribal elections where the tribe had established voting procedures precisely parallel to Anglo-American procedures. The court acknowledged that section 1302(8) does not "embrace in entirety all of its content in our applicable constitutional law," and noted, as examples of tribal practices "at variance with Anglo-American tradition," ethnic restrictions on tribal membership and blood percentage requirements for inheritance rights and for voting in tribal elections. *Id.* at 1313-14. But the court concluded that under the facts of this case, "we have no problem of forcing an alien culture, with strange procedures, on this tribe." *Id.* at 1314.

In Wounded Head v. Tribal Council of Oglala Sioux Tribe, 507 F.2d 1079 (8th Cir. 1975), the court held that section 1302(8) did not limit the power of the tribe to fix 21 years old instead of 18 or 19 as the age for allowing tribal members to vote in tribal elections. The court said it was "questionable" whether the result would be any different under constitutional principles in light of the recent United States Supreme Court decision in Oregon v. Mitchell, 400 U.S. 112 (1970). 507 F.2d at 1083.

In Means v. Wilson, 522 F.2d 833 (8th Cir. 1975), the court ruled that allegations of a conspiracy to confuse the voting in a tribal election so that a certain candidate would be elected were sufficient, if proven, to establish an interference with plaintiff's voting rights and thus a denial of equal protection guarantees under either section 1302(8) or the Constitution. The court noted in passing that no tribal custom or governmental purpose was involved. *Id.* at 842. The right to vote is "fundamental" and its denial can only be sustained on a showing of a compelling governmental interest. *Id.* at 838-39.

Finally, in Daly v. United States, 483 F.2d 400 (8th Cir. 1973), the court decided that a classification that arguably violated the fourteenth amendment standards did not violate the equal protection clause of the ICRA. In *Daly* the district court ordered reapportionment of election districts for tribal elections in accordance with the one-person-one-vote principle. The court also ordered eliminated from the tribe's remedial plan a requirement based on a provision of the tribe's constitution that specified that at least one-half of the councilmen from each district had to be of at least one-half Indian blood. The court of appeals said this constitutional provision did not violate the ICRA equal protection clause because "this is one of those 'respects' [in which] the equal protection requirement of the 14th amendment should not be embraced in the Indian Bill of Rights." *Id.* at 705 (quoting Groundhog v. Keeler, 442 F.2d 674, 682 (10th Cir. 1971)). This is dictum, however, because the court of appeals declined to overturn the lower court's elimination of the classification from the election plan. The court of appeals explained that the blood quantum requirement did not fit the tribe's remedial plan, which included two single-member districts. 483 F.2d at 706.

206.   529 F.2d 233 (9th Cir. 1976).

624

stitution required that all candidates for the tribal council reside on the reservation for a period of one year preceding the election. The two plaintiffs, aspirants for office, had been physically absent from the reservation for five and one-half and six months respectively during the year preceding the election. The constitution also provided that the tribal council was the "sole judge of the qualifications of its members."[207] The council, which included plaintiffs' opponents, had ruled that "reside" meant physically present rather than domiciled. Plaintiffs claimed this gave the tribal council exclusive power to determine whether aspiring candidates met the necessary qualifications for council office and thus violated section 1302(8) of the ICRA.

The Ninth Circuit Court of Appeals held that while the non-Indian society did not generally give the legislative branch of government the power to interpret the law, such a governmental structure does not necessarily constitute a deprivation of equal protection.[208] The court then held that although the right to hold office was fundamental, the one-year residency requirement served a compelling governmental interest in allowing tribal voters to know personally the candidates for office. The court relied on federal constitutional cases to support this holding,[209] adding that because of the extremely local nature of tribal concerns, such as promoting Indian cultural identity and administering tribal government, the case for a compelling governmental interest was stronger than in the federal cases cited.[210]

IX. FUTURE APPLICATION OF THE INDIAN EQUAL PROTECTION DOCTRINE

In summary, the equal protection doctrine applicable to Indians derives from federal law, state law, and tribal law governed by the ICRA. The future application of the doctrine with respect to each of these sources bears discussion.

---

207. CONFEDERATED SALISH AND KOOTENAI TRIBES CONST. art. 3, § 7, *quoted in Howlett,* 529 F.2d at 240.

208.   529 F.2d at 240.

209.   Chimento v. Stark, 353 F. Supp. 1211 (D.N.H. 1973), *aff'd,* 414 U.S. 802 (1973); Draper v. Phelps, 351 F. Supp. 677 (W.D. Okla. 1972); Hadnott v. Amos, 320 F. Supp. 107 (M.D. Ala. 1970), *aff'd,* 401 U.S. 968 (1971); *aff'd,* 405 U.S. 1035 (1972). These cases were cited in *Howlett,* 529 F.2d at 243.

210.   "The case presently before us, even more so than the previously cited cases, presents a situation where compelling interests justify the imposition of a one-year durational residency requirement upon candidates." 529 F.2d at 244.

625

A. Federal Law

The better rule regarding federal law and derivative state law would require the courts to provide more rigorous scrutiny to laws concerning Indians in order to assure that they bear a rational relationship to the nation's trust responsibility toward Indians.

The United States' fiduciary responsibility toward Indians covers lands, minerals, waters, forests, and fisheries, as well as rights to self-government.[211] Important deposits of coal, oil, and natural gas, as well as timber, water, land, and fisheries are included in this trust. In recent years, as available non-Indian supplies of these resources have dwindled, the non-Indian community has begun to view Indian resources with increasing covetousness. Pressure to develop these trust-protected resources is certain to increase in the future as alternative sources of supply are depleted.

Recent non-Indian/Indian conflicts over natural resources and government powers have already resulted in several important court decisions favoring Indians,[212] and these have produced fright and anger among politically powerful groups in the affected areas of the country. Because they constitute less than one-half percent of the national population and are scattered widely across the nation, Indians are especially vulnerable to these political forces. Their political powerlessness has both permitted and encouraged the current anti-Indian "backlash," a phenomenon which poses a threat to the federal government's capacity to carry out its trust responsibility toward Indians. Congress is now being importuned to enact laws that would have the effect of dismantling some Indian reservations, imposing state laws on

---

211. *See* F. COHEN, *supra* note 41, at chs. 7 & 15.

212. The decisions concerning the Maine land claims, Joint Tribal Council of Passamaquoddy v. Morton, 528 F.2d 370 (1st Cir. 1975), and the Pacific Northwest fishing rights controversy, United States v. Washington, 520 F.2d 676 (9th Cir. 1975), *cert. denied,* 423 U.S. 1086 (1976), *cert. granted,* 99 S. Ct. 277 (1978), have received the widest publicity, although numerous other Indian claims to land, minerals, water, and timber, and to governmental powers such as zoning and taxation have recently been decided or are still in the courts and have contributed to the growth of non-Indian political pressure to legislatively reduce Indian rights to their powers and resources. *See, e.g.,* Bryan v. Itasca County, 426 U.S. 373 (1976); Moe v. Confederated Salish & Kootenai Tribe of the Flathead Indian Reservation, 425 U.S. 463 (1976); Arizona v. California, 373 U.S. 546 (1963); Santa Rosa Band of Indians v. Kings County, 532 F.2d 655 (9th Cir. 1975); Confederated Tribes of Colville Indian Reservation v. Washington, 446 F. Supp. 1339 (E.D. Wash. 1978) (3 judge panel), *cert. granted,* 99 S. Ct. 740 (1979).

626

others, eliminating tribal courts, limiting the powers of tribal governments, and making tribal resources available to non-Indians.[213]

In the light of the imbalance of political power, Indian rights may be seriously imperiled if courts too readily presume that legislation affecting Indians has been enacted for the benefit of Indians. With adroit draftsmanship such legislation can be couched in language ostensibly benign toward Indians.[214] While it is true that at least since the 1930's, Indian tribal property can no longer be taken without payment of compensation,[215] this protection is in no sense coincident with the scope of the United States' trust responsibility toward Indians. There is, therefore, an important role for the courts in assuring that the nation's trust responsibility toward Indians is not abused.

To assure that both federal and derivative state legislation concerning Indians in fact furthers the government's trust responsibility toward Indians, the courts should subject such legislation to substantial, rather than minimal, judicial review.[216] To the degree that a law disadvantages Indians the scrutiny should become increasingly strict. Indeed, a law that disadvantages Indians should ordinarily be considered outside the scope of the government's trust responsibility toward Indians, and therefore subject to standard equal protection analysis. Because it would be dealing with a racial group,[217] such a law should ordinarily receive strict scrutiny.[218]

---

213. Norgren & Shattuck, *Still Fighting the Indians: America's Old-Fashioned Response to Native Legal Victories,* JURIS DOCTOR, Oct./Nov. 1978, at 30. *See* S. BRAKEL, AMERICAN INDIAN TRIBAL COURTS: THE COSTS OF SEPARATE JUSTICE (1978) (study commissioned by The American Bar Foundation); H. WILLIAMS & W. NEUBRECH, INDIAN TREATIES: AMERICAN NIGHTMARE (1976).
There exist organizations whose primary purpose is to seek the abrogation of Indian treaty rights such as the Interstate Congress for Equal Rights and Responsibilities, Inc., 422 Main Street, Winner, S. Dak. 57580. The political pressure to abrogate Indian treaties has resulted in the introduction before Congress of legislation to achieve that end. H.R. 9054, 95th Cong., 1st Sess. (1977) (Native American Equal Opportunity Act).

214. *See* H.R. 9054, 95th Cong., 1st Sess. (1977) (Native American Equal Opportunity Act which proposes to abrogate all Indian treaties).

215. *See, e.g.,* United States v. Creek Nation, 295 U.S. 103 (1935).

216. The justification for the *Mancari* rule allowing a low-level scrutiny of federal Indian legislation is the federal trust relationship toward Indians. If a law does not further that trust relationship, the rationale for the *Mancari* rule is absent. The courts should therefore insist on an adequate guarantee that the condition precedent to the *Mancari* rule has been met.

217. *See* notes 76–80 and accompanying text *supra.*

218. An additional or alternative guarantee could be provided by a rule of construction analogous to the rule that, as between a constitutional and an unconstitutional construction of a statute, Congress is presumed to have intended the constitutional construction. Whenever more than one interpretation is possible, the courts will choose the

627

B.   State Law

The dangers faced by Indians due to their lack of political power are accentuated at the state level as compared to the federal level because of the immediate impact that Indian rights have on the surrounding non-Indian population. Therefore, state legislation should be subject to strict scrutiny, rather than the *Mancari* standard, unless the state law is derivative legislation.

C.   Indian Civil Rights Act

Cases involving the ICRA equal protection clause have used standard constitutional equal protection language for determining the validity of tribal action challenged under that act. The difference between these cases and cases involving the equal protection clause of the Constitution lies in the application of the guarantee: the courts give special deference to long established tribal customs and tradition in the ICRA cases. Whether the courts will give more than lip service to the deference accorded custom and tradition in Indian equal protection cases remains to be seen.

Tribal treatment of nonmembers is one of the potentially most volatile areas for application of the equal protection clause of the ICRA.[219] The nonmember population of many reservations far exceeds the member population.[220] The equal protection problems in this context are particularly troublesome because nonmembers, lacking a right to vote in tribal elections, are not represented in tribal governments.[221] A tribal government's authority extends to all inhabitants of the reservation in many subject matters,[222] and tribal courts appar-

---

one that is consistent with the government's trust responsibility toward Indians. Such a legal principle would be consistent with the rule of construction that a statute shall not be construed as abrogating treaty or statutory rights of Indians unless the court finds a clear congressional intent to do so. *See* McClanahan v. Arizona State Tax Comm'n, 411 U.S. 164, 174 (1973); United States v. Kagama, 118 U.S. 375, 383–84 (1886).

219.   Section 1302(8) proscribes denial of equal protection of a tribe's laws to "any person." *See* notes 176 & 186 *supra.*

220.   *See* Washington v. Yakima Tribe, 99 S. Ct. 740 (1979).

221.   In addition to lacking representation in tribal government, nonmembers will have only a limited right to obtain review of tribal decisions affecting them. After the Supreme Court decision in *Martinez,* nonmembers, as well as members, will be able to test tribal ICRA equal protection issues in federal court only when a habeas corpus action can be brought. *See* notes 177–82 and accompanying text *supra.*

222.   *See* Gonzalez, *Indian Sovereignty and the Tribal Right to Charter a Municipality for Non-Indians: A New Perspective for Jurisdiction on Indian Land,* 7 N.M.L. REV. 153 (1976); Comment, *Jurisdiction to Zone Indian Reservations,* 53 WASH. L. REV. 677 (1978).

628

ently have concurrent jurisdiction with state courts to try civil cases involving non-Indians.[223] Two areas of particular concern are taxation and zoning.

1. Taxing

Indian tribes have long been held to have the power to tax non-Indians owning property or doing business on the reservation.[224] A few cases have upheld such taxes, suggesting that the tax is imposed on the privilege of doing business or carrying on some other activity on the reservation and is thus akin to a license.[225] In the past, when few non-Indians did business on Indian reservations and when they were not competing with Indian businesses, such taxes probably would not have raised equal protection questions. Today, however, cities and towns exist on some reservations that are largely inhabited by non-Indian populations. A court might now question whether a tribal tax burdening a non-Indian grocery more heavily than an Indian grocery one block away can withstand an equal protection challenge.[226] One commentator, after analyzing the equal protection tax topic, concluded:

> Separate treatment of outsiders for purposes of matters such as voting, jury service, issuance of grazing permits, and perhaps even freedom of speech, may be justifiable to maintain tribal identity and distinctiveness. The problem is that special taxation of outsiders has no connection with these values, except perhaps as a means of regulating entry by outsiders, or protecting the income and property of Indians whose traditional pursuits do not leave them with sufficient funds to pay taxes.[227]

---

223. *See* Williams v. Lee, 358 U.S. 217 (1959). In *Martinez*, the Court stated: "Tribal courts have repeatedly been recognized as appropriate forums for the exclusive adjudication of disputes affecting important personal and property interests of both Indians and non-Indians." 436 U.S. at 65.

224. *See, e.g.,* Buster v. Wright, 135 F. 947 (8th Cir. 1905); Confederated Tribes of Colville v. Washington, 446 F. Supp. 1339, 1361 (E.D. Wash. 1978) (the power to tax both Indians and non-Indians is "vested" in the Indian tribe by existing law).

225. *See* Fort Mojave Tribe v. County of San Bernardino, 543 F.2d 1253 (9th Cir. 1976); Eastern Band of Cherokee v. North Carolina Dept. of Natural & Economic Resources, No. BC–C–76–65 (D.N.C. Aug. 27, 1976) (appeal pending); Red Lake Band of Chippewa Indians v. State, 248 N.W.2d 722 (Minn. 1976).

226. Such a differential effect can in fact occur when a non-Indian enterprise, such as a smoke shop, is subject to state taxation while a tribal smoke shop is exempt. *See* Confederated Tribe of Colville v. Washington, 446 F. Supp. 1339 (E.D. Wash. 1978). This result, however, raises a jurisdictional, rather than an equal protection question.

227. Goldberg, *A Dynamic View of Tribal Jurisdiction to Tax Non-Indians*, 40 L. & CONTEMP. PROB. 166, 178 (1976).

629

Courts might possibly uphold a tribal tax that burdened nonmembers more heavily than members under either the fifth amendment or the ICRA if they were to treat nonmembers analogously to aliens; a reasonable relationship between the discriminatory treatment and the objective of the tax might then be sufficient.[228] Thus, such a tax might be upheld if it were based on certain rationales as, for example, that nonmembers deplete tribal resources, that it is more difficult to collect taxes from nonmembers than members, or possibly that there is a need to compensate Indians for long-suffered disadvantages.[229]

2. Zoning

Tribal zoning of privately owned lands on an Indian reservation also raises potential equal protection questions.[230] More restrictive zoning of non-Indian land than Indian land would be difficult to justify under an equal protection challenge. As applied to non-Indian held land which has meaning to the tribe as an historic meeting ground or as a religious site, such restrictive zoning might be justified, but the classification would be based on the historic or religious significance of the land, rather than on its non-Indian ownership. In theory it is arguable that the greater political influence and legal control that the tribe has over its members,[231] plus the likelihood that members of the tribe share cultural values, justify more restrictive zoning of non-Indian or nonmember land than Indian member land. It is not clear, however, how land use is related to either the landowner's cultural values or political control over the landowner.

The standard of review to apply in ICRA equal protection cases involving nontribal members is an area of the law completely devoid of authority. Because the tribe bears no relationship to nonmembers an-

---

228. *See generally* Albrecht, *The Taxation of Aliens Under International Law,* [1952] 29 Brit. Y.B. Int'l L. 145, 169–71 (1953); Choate, Huroh, & Klein, *Federal Tax Policy for Foreign Income and Foreign Taxpayers—History, Analysis and Prospects,* 44 Temp. L.Q. 441 (1971).

229. *See* Goldberg, *supra* note 227, at 177. *Cf.* Kahn v. Shevin, 416 U.S. 351 (1974) (state property tax exemption for widows upheld because it bore a reasonable relation to public policy).

230. The question of tribal power to zone non-Indian lands on a reservation has not been explicitly resolved by the United States Supreme Court and is not addressed in this article. *See* note 222 *supra. See generally* Bryan v. Itasca County, 426 U.S. 373 (1976); Santa Rosa Band of Indians v. Kings County, 532 F.2d 655 (9th Cir. 1975).

231. Tribal legal control may extend to all Indians on the reservation, members and nonmembers. *See* Oliphant v. Suquamish Tribe, 435 U.S. 191 (1978); note 223 *supra.*

630

alogous to the trust relationship between the federal government and Indian tribes, the *Mancari* test appears inapposite.[232] The equal protection analysis applied in state cases,[233] with some changes where appropriate, appears more viable. Thus, the *Mancari* rule would be applied to tribal law that was expressly authorized by Congress or that was an exercise of a guaranteed treaty right. Other tribal classifications between members and nonmembers or between Indians and non-Indians would be tested at some middle level of scrutiny. Even in these cases, however, special deference should be accorded tribal laws designed to further tribal self-determination or to preserve ancient customs and traditional values.

---

232. *See* Part V *supra.*
233. *See* Part VI *supra.*

631

POLITICAL RIGHTS UNDER THE
INDIAN CIVIL RIGHTS ACT

*Prior to the passage of the Indian Civil Rights Act of
1968, no federal constitutional or legislative provision restricted tribal governments from denying many of the basic
political rights afforded by the United States Constitution.
After the Act was implemented, federal courts allowed numerous plaintiffs declaratory and injunctive relief from alleged tribal deprivations of rights protected under the Act.
The political rights once thought protected by the Act may
again go unguarded in light of the United States Supreme
Court decision of Santa Clara Pueblo v. Martinez, which
eliminated declaratory and injunctive relief under the Act.*

INTRODUCTION

The framers of the American Constitution considered the protection of a citizen's political rights essential to the establishment
and operation of a democratic government.[1] They established the
Bill of Rights, guaranteeing freedom of religion, freedom of speech,
freedom of press, the right to peaceably assemble, the right to petition for redress of grievances and the right to due process of law.[2]
Many of these rights have also been protected from infringement
by state governments through the due process and equal protection clauses of the fourteenth amendment.[3] These precedents
notwithstanding, no such restrictions were placed on the governmental bodies of American Indian tribes until the passage of the
Indian Civil Rights Act of 1968.[4]

---

1. Sweezy v. New Hampshire, 354 U.S. 234, 250 (1957).
2. U.S. CONST. amends. I & V.
3. Cantwell v. Connecticut, 310 U.S. 296, 303 (1940).
4. The Indian Civil Rights Act of 1968, Pub. L. No. 90-284, 82 Stat. 77 (codified at 25 U.S.C. §§ 1301-1303 (Supp. 1978)), reads as follows:
§ 1301. Definitions
For purposes of this subchapter, the term—
(1) "Indian tribe" means any tribe, band, or other group of Indians subject to the jurisdiction of the United States and recognized as
possessing powers of self-government;
(2) "powers of self-government" means and includes all governmental powers possessed by an Indian tribe, executive, legislative,
and judicial, and all offices, bodies, and tribunals by and through
which they are executed, including courts of Indian offenses; and
(3) "Indian court" means any Indian tribal court or court of Indian offense.
§ 1302. Constitutional rights
No Indian tribe in exercising powers of self-government shall—
(1) make or enforce any law prohibiting the free exercise of religion, or abridging the freedom of speech, or of the press, or the right of
the people peaceably to assemble and to petition for a redress of grievances;
(2) violate the right of the people to be secure in their persons,
houses, papers, and effects against unreasonable search and seizures,
nor issue warrants, but upon probable cause, supported by oath or affirmation, and particularly describing the place to be searched and the
person or thing to be seized;

The Act was used by numerous plaintiffs who brought suit in federal court alleging denial of political rights. Although the Act did not expressly so provide, numerous federal courts allowed actions seeking declaratory and injunctive relief to be brought under the Act. This expansion of remedies seemed necessary in order to give full protection to the rights enumerated in the Act. This was especially true in the area of political rights, because the listed remedy of habeas corpus would offer little or no protection to one deprived of such rights.

When the federal courts applied the Act to such situations, they were cautious to respect tribal culture and custom. The courts required plaintiffs to exhaust tribal remedies before a federal action could be brought. Then, on the merits of the case, the courts would balance the possible harm to the tribe's cultural interests against the individual's possible loss of political rights. Despite this cautious approach, the United States Supreme Court recently held in *Santa Clara Pueblo v. Martinez*[5] that the doctrine of tribal sovereign immunity bars actions for declaratory and injunctive relief for alleged violations of rights protected by the Indian Civil Rights Act.

The purpose of this article is to examine the political rights cases brought under the Indian Civil Rights Act in an effort to determine the effect of the *Santa Clara* decision. This analysis will begin with a short look at the *Santa Clara* holding, then move to a discussion of the doctrine of sovereign immunity. Then it will explore the development of the Act and the judicial interpretations of the political rights given by it and conclude with an analysis of the opinion in *Santa Clara* and possible justifications for the holding.

---

(3) subject any person for the same offense to be twice put in jeopardy;

(4) compel any person in any criminal case to be a witness against himself;

(5) take any private property for a public use without just compensation;

(6) deny to any person in a criminal proceeding the right to a speedy and public trial, to be informed of the nature and cause of the accusation, to be confronted with the witnesses against him, to have compulsory process for obtaining witnesses in his favor, and at his own expense to have the assistance of counsel for his defense;

(7) require excessive bail, impose excessive fines, inflict cruel and unusual punishments, and in no event impose for conviction of any one offense any penalty or punishment greater than imprisonment for a term of six months or a fine of $500, or both;

(8) deny to any person within its jurisdiction the equal protection of its laws or deprive any person of liberty or property without due process of law;

(9) pass any bill of attainder or ex post facto law; or

(10) deny to any person accused of an offense punishable by imprisonment the right, upon request, to a trial by jury of not less than six persons.

§ 1303. Habeas corpus

The privilege of the writ of habeas corpus shall be available to any person, in a court of the United States, to test the legality of his detention by order of an Indian tribe.

5. 436 U.S. 49 (1978).

SANTA CLARA PUEBLO V. MARTINEZ, THE REASONING

For almost ten years the federal courts have granted jurisdiction to plaintiffs seeking declaratory and injunctive relief under the Indian Civil Rights Act. Then, in the spring of 1978, the United States Supreme Court made a startling announcement in *Santa Clara Pueblo v. Martinez*[6] in holding that suits seeking declaratory and injunctive relief against the tribes were barred by the tribes' sovereign immunity and that similar suits against tribal officials were barred because no such remedy could be implied from the statute. The Court's holding was based on the principle that tribes retain the internal governmental powers of a sovereign except to the extent that those powers had been modified by treaty or expressed congressional declaration.[7] In turning to possible remedies against tribal officers, the Court found that "Congress' failure to provide remedies other than habeas corpus was a deliberate one."[8] The Court concluded that Congress' objectives in protecting these constitutional rights could be achieved in tribal courts without federal interference.[9]

TRIBAL SOVEREIGNTY

The principle of tribal sovereignty was recognized early in the development of American Indian Law. In 1831, the United States Supreme Court held that the Indian tribes should properly be viewed as "domestic dependent nations," and that "[t]heir relation to the United States resembles that of a ward to his guardian."[10] Only one year later, the Court held "[t]he treaties and laws of the United States contemplate the Indian territory as completely separated from that of the States; . . . ."[11] The tribes were considered a "distinct community" where the laws of the various states could have no force.[12] By these decisions the Court established the tribes as "domestic dependent nations," sovereign to the extent of being free from state control.

Federal power over the tribes was established through constitutional provisions giving Congress the power to regulate commerce among the Indian tribes,[13] and through the "guardian/ward" relationship established by the courts. Through this plenary power, exclusive federal jurisdiction was extended over crimes committed by one Indian against another on an Indian reservation.[14] Despite broad federal control over the tribes, however,

---

6. *Id.*
7. *Id.* at 59.
8. *Id.* at 61.
9. *Id.* at 71.
10. Cherokee Nation v. Georgia, 30 U.S. (5 Pet.) 1, 17 (1831).
11. Worcester v. Georgia, 31 U.S. (6 Pet.) 515, 516 (1832).
12. *Id.* at 561.
13. U.S. CONST. art. I, § 8, cl. 3.
14. United States v. Kagama, 118 U.S. 375 (1886), upholding the application of the Major Crimes Act which is now found, as amended, at 18 U.S.C. § 1153 (Supp. 1978).

the courts still recognized the tribes as sovereigns who retained all the internal governmental powers of a sovereign state, unless such power was qualified by treaty or express legislation of Congress.[15] Therefore, general acts of Congress are said not to apply to the Indian tribes unless the act expressly indicates such an application.[16] Also, the powers of a tribe are to be viewed as inherent powers lawfully vested in the tribe, and not as powers delegated to it by the federal government.[17]

Although tribal powers may not be considered federal powers, the question of the applicability of the United States Constitution to tribal governments was not met squarely until *Talton v. Mayes*[18] in 1896. The United States Supreme Court held that because the local governmental powers of a tribe were not federal powers as such, the United States Constitution did not limit the exercise of those powers.[19] The Court did not address the question whether the Constitution could be applied to the tribes through the fourteenth amendment in a manner similar to its application to state governments. Nonetheless, it became generally understood that tribes were not to be included in the definition of "state" contemplated by the fourteenth amendment. The tribes were said to have a higher status than the states by means of their sovereign powers and the fact that no provision of the Constitution or act of Congress had made the Constitution applicable to tribal governments.[20]

As a result, local governmental activities of the tribes went unchecked by federal constitutional restrictions. Because the tribes were considered sovereigns, they were also found immune from suit.[21] This rule was clearly expressed by the United States Supreme Court in *United States v. United States Fidelity & Guaranty Co.*,[22] where the Court said, "The public policy which exempted the dependent as well as dominant sovereignties from suit

---

15.   The whole course of judicial decision on the nature of Indian tribal powers is marked by adherence to three fundamental principles:
(1) An Indian tribe possesses, in the first instance, all the powers of a sovereign state. (2) Conquest renders the tribe subject to the legislative power of the United States and, in substance, terminates the external powers of sovereignty of the tribe, *e.g.*, its power to enter into treaties with foreign nations, but does not by itself affect the internal sovereignty of the tribe, *i.e.*, its powers of local self-government. (3) These powers are subject to qualification by treaties and by the expressed legislation of Congress, but, save as thus expressly qualified, full powers of internal sovereignty are vested in the Indian tribes and in their duly constituted organs of government.
F. COHEN, FEDERAL INDIAN LAW 123.
16.   *Id.*
17.   *Id.* at 122.
18.   163 U.S. 376 (1896).
19.   *Id.* at 384.
20.   Native American Church v. Navajo Tribal Council, 272 F.2d 131, 134 (10th Cir. 1959). *See also* Berta v. Oglala Sioux Tribe, 259 F.2d 553 (8th Cir. 1958).
21.   Thebo v. Choctaw Tribe of Indians, 66 F. 372 (8th Cir. 1895).
22.   309 U.S. 506 (1940).

without consent continues this immunity even after dissolution of the tribal government. These Indian Nations are exempt from suit without congressional authorization."[23] This authorization to waive immunity must, like any other waiver of sovereign immunity, "be expressed in plain and unambiguous terms."[24]

The doctrine of tribal immunity was abrogated somewhat by the recent case of *Puyallup Tribe v. Washington Dep't of Game.*[25] In that case the Supreme Court stated that an action to enjoin individual tribal members as not barred by sovereign immunity.[26] This finding seems to allow tribal immunity to be circumvented by bringing suit directly against tribal members or officials. The validity of the doctrine of tribal immunity was seriously questioned in Justice Blackmun's concurring opinion, where he said, "I entertain doubts, however, about the continuing vitality in this day of the doctrine of tribal immunity . . . . I am of the view that the doctrine may well merit re-examination in an appropriate case."[27]

Even before this pronouncement in *Puyallup Tribe* the doctrine of tribal sovereignty had been eroded. In *Colliflower v. Garland,*[28] the Ninth Circuit Court of Appeals partially abrogated the established rule of nonapplicability of the United States Constitution to local tribal governments. In this case, the court examined the tribal court in the Fort Belknap Indian community and discovered an overriding federal presence in the establishment, funding and supervision of this tribal court. Under these circumstances the court of appeals declared:

> In spite of the theory that for some purposes an Indian tribe is an independent sovereignty, we think that, in the light of their history, it is pure fiction to say that the Indian courts functioning in the Fort Belknap Indian community are not in part, at least, arms of the federal government. Originally they were created by the federal executive and imposed upon the Indian community, and to this day the federal government still maintains a partial control over them.[29]

Because of this federal control, the court of appeals found that the federal district court had jurisdiction to determine the validity of plaintiff's detention by the tribal court.[30] The court carefully confined the decision to the facts existing on the Fort Belknap reservation and the habeas corpus remedy.

---

23. *Id.* at 512.
24. Thebo v. Choctaw Tribe of Indians, 66 F. 372, 376 (8th Cir. 1895).
25. 433 U.S. 165 (1977).
26. *Id.* at 173. The Court held that suits to enjoin individual tribal members from violating state fishing laws were not barred by the tribe's sovereign immunity.
27. *Id.* at 178-79.
28. 342 F.2d 369 (9th Cir. 1965).
29. *Id.* at 378-79.
30. *Id.* at 379. Jurisdiction was obtained under 28 U.S.C. § 2241(c)(1) & (3) (1971).

THE INDIAN CIVIL RIGHTS ACT: LEGISLATIVE HISTORY

Even prior to *Colliflower*, decided in 1965, work had started on the Indian Civil Rights Act. In 1961, Senator Sam Erwin's Subcommittee on Constitutional Rights made preliminary inquiry into the area of Indian constitutional rights. The project of drafting federal legislation guaranteeing basic constitutional protections to Native Americans soon developed into a personal project for Senator Ervin.[31] Official hearings, conducted from 1961 to 1965, disclosed that some tribes extended constitutional protections to persons under their jurisdiction by means of established tribal constitutions and laws. Many tribes, which had not previously done so, drafted tribal constitutions and established tribal courts under the 1934 Indian Reorganization Act.[32] Most of these constitutions were drafted by the Bureau of Indian Affairs and were very similar in nature,[33] many containing some sort of bill of rights protection.[34]

Despite these protections, it was apparent that tribal governments often exceeded the constitutional limitations that restrict state and federal governments.[35] For example, in many instances the right of a individual to trial by jury was at least partially abridged by tribal governments.[36] Tribes occasionally refused to allow professional attorneys as counsel, unfairly restricted tribal membership, infringed on religious freedom, and ejected non-Indians from reservations without proper hearings.[37] Under the structure of many tribal governments, the tribal court either consisted of the tribal council or was directly appointed by the tribal council. With no separation of powers, the tribal council held firm control over the tribal courts and no checks and balances existed to correct abuses.[38] Often, these abuses occurred because the tribes had limited funds available to spend on tribal courts, rather than deliberate attempts to deny individual rights.[39] The hearings disclosed that some form of federal legislation was necessary to insure that persons under the jurisdiction of tribal governments would receive the same protections afforded citizens by federal and state constitutions. The hearings also made it clear that the tribes could not be subjected to full constitutional restrictions because of their obvious financial limitations and their interest in preserving tribal culture.[40]

In 1965, Senator Ervin tested the legislative waters by intro-

---

31. Burnett, *An Historical Analysis of the 1968 'Indian Civil Rights' Act*, 9 HARV. J. LEGIS. 557, 576 (1972).
32. Note, *The Constitutional Rights of the American Tribal Indian*, 51 VA. L. REV. 121, 135 (1965).
33. *Id.* at 135.
34. Burnett, *supra* note 31, at 579.
35. Note, *The Indian Bill of Rights and the Constitutional Status of Tribal Governments*, 82 HARV. L. REV. 1343, 1344 (1969).
36. Burnett, *supra* note 31, at 580.
37. Note, *supra* note 35, at 1344.
38. Burnett, *supra* note 31, at 580, 581.
39. *Id.* at 581.
40. *Id.* at 589.

ducing several bills that would have, among other things, placed constitutional limitations on the tribes similar to those limitations already placed on state and local governments, with the exception of equal protection standards.[41] In 1967, modified bills were drafted and introduced. In its report to the Senate on these bills, the subcommittee stated, "The purpose of S 1843, (The Indian Civil Rights Act) as amended, is to insure that the American Indian is afforded the broad constitutional rights secured to other Americans."[42] Senator Ervin said of the bill, "It is designed to make the Indian a first class citizen."[43]

Originally, the Act provided for appeal of criminal convictions in tribal court by a *de novo* review in federal district court.[44] This was subsequently revised to allow appeals by writ of habeas corpus,[45] thus recognizing the situation that already existed in light of the *Colliflower*[46] decision. The bills, as modified, were subsequently passed as a rider to the Civil Rights Act of 1968 and became Title II of that Act.[47]

The provisions of the Act that are relevant to the area of political rights are:

No Indian tribe in exercising powers of self-government shall—

    (1)   make or enforce any law prohibiting the free exercise of religion, or abridging the freedom of speech, or of the press, or the right of the people peaceably to assemble and to petition for a redress of grievances;

. . . .

    (8)   deny to any person within its jurisdiction the equal protection of its laws or deprive any person of liberty or property without due process of law;

    (9)   pass any bill of attainder or ex post facto law;[48]

These enumerated rights established guarantees of political expression and action. Denial of these rights, however, would seldom create a situation in which the habeas corpus remedy provided in section 1303[49] would be effective. Absent some other jurisdictional basis, these rights could not be protected by the federal courts.

JUDICIAL INTERPRETATION OF THE ACT

The federal courts found this additional jurisdictional basis for plaintiffs seeking declaratory and injunctive relief under 28 U.S.C.

---

41. *Id.* at 588-601.
42. S. REP. NO. 841, 90th Cong., 1st Sess. (1968).
43. 113 CONG. REC. 35472 (1967).
44. Burnett, *supra* note 31, at 592.
45. *Id.* at 602. It should be noted that this modification only concerned criminal appeals. No mention was made of any other forms of federal review.
46. Colliflower v. Garland, 342 F.2d 369 (9th Cir. 1965). *See* text accompanying notes 28-30 *supra*.
47. Pub. L. No. 90-284, 82 Stat. 73 (1968). The Indian Civil Rights Act is codified at 25 U.S.C. §§ 1301-1303 (Supp. 1978). *See* note 4 *supra*.
48. *Id.* § 1302.
49. 25 U.S.C. § 1303 (Supp. 1978). *See* note 4 *supra*.

§ 1343(4).[50] This statute gives the federal district courts jurisdiction to grant damages and other equitable relief in any civil action authorized by an act of Congress providing for the protection of civil rights.[51] The courts established other principles in order to interpret the Act in a manner that would protect tribal interests. Tribal cultural interests were to be protected whenever possible.[52] Whenever these tribal interests conflicted with personal rights, courts balanced the injury of the individual against the importance of the tribal interest involved.[53] In the due process and equal protection areas the standards required of the tribe were not the same as those required of state and federal governments.[54] These and other principles established by the courts allowed federal protection of political rights guaranteed by the Act with only a minimal interference with tribal autonomy and self government.

Before accepting jurisdiction over an Indian Civil Rights case the federal courts also required that two jurisdictional requirements be met. A plaintiff was required not only to show that he had exhausted all available tribal remedies, but he also was required to present a complaint alleging sufficient facts indicating that rights protected by the Act had been violated. The courts created these two requirements to promote settlement of disputes within the tribal framework whenever possible. The following sections will explore the various political rights cases brought under the Act in an effort to determine the need for federal protection and examine the approach taken by the courts in applying these restrictions to tribal governments. It will conclude with a discussion of the jurisdictional requirements established by the federal courts.

Reapportionment of Voting Districts

In 1962, the United States Supreme Court announced in *Baker v. Carr*[55] that the equal protection clause of the fourteenth amendment required a standard of "one-man-one-vote" for organization of election districts. After the passage of the Indian Civil Rights Act several cases were presented to the federal courts claiming that the right to equal protection of the laws stated in section 1302(8)[56] extended the "one-man-one-vote" principle of *Baker* to apportionment of tribal election districts. The plaintiffs in these actions generally claimed that tribal election districts had substan-

---

50. 28 U.S.C. § 1343 (1976), provides, "The district courts shall have original jurisdiction of any civil action authorized by law to be commenced by any person: . . . (4) To recover damages or to secure equitable or other relief under any Act of Congress providing for the protection of civil rights, including the right to vote."
51. *See* the text accompanying notes 151-57 *supra* for a discussion of the section 1343(4) jurisdictional basis.
52. Dodge v. Nakai, 298 F. Supp. 26 (D. Ariz. 1969).
53. Martinez v. Santa Clara Pueblo, 540 F.2d 1039 (10th Cir. 1976).
54. Groundhog v. Keeler, 442 F.2d 674 (10th Cir. 1971).
55. 369 U.S. 186 (1962).
56. *See* note 4 *supra*.

tial population variations not relative to the population distribution of the reservation.

In the three apportionment cases brought before it, the Eighth Circuit Court of Appeals required tribal governments to meet the standards established in *Baker*.[57] The court made it clear that it was not discounting the portions of the Indian Civil Rights Act's history expressing concern about the imposition of full constitutional guarantees on tribal culture,[58] but found that were the tribes had adopted election procedures "precisely paralleling those commonly found in our culture, if not taken verbatim therefrom,"[59] the imposition of the *Baker* rule would not be forcing an "alien culture" on the tribes.[60]

In each of these three cases problems arose in formulating a permissible apportionment plan. The court of appeals rejected district court plans based on votes cast in the previous election,[61] and plans based on the number of eligible voters in each district.[62] Stating that the *sine qua non* in apportionment decisions was population, the court required the plans to be based solely on population.[63] Later, however, the court stated that apportionment on the basis of "qualified voters" was permissible if the tribal constitution so provided.[64] Other deviations from population equality in the apportionment would have to be justified by "legitimate tribal considerations."[65]

In addition to these standards, the apportionment cases of the Eighth Circuit Court of Appeals raised several other noteworthy points. The court in *White Eagle v. One Feather*,[66] indicated that in situations involving first amendment rights it may not be proper to issue a temporary restraining order *ex parte*. The court also stated that the *Baker* standard could be adjusted because of the difficulty in achieving a perfect balance of population in voting districts where the numbers of tribal voters were so small.[67] In addition, the United States Government was required in one case to aid the tribe in establishing an acceptable plan.[68]

At first glance, the interference of the federal court in these

---

57. Brown v. United States, 486 F.2d 658 (8th Cir. 1973); Daly v. United States, 483 F.2d 700 (8th Cir. 1973); White Eagle v. One Feather, 478 F.2d 1311 (8th Cir. 1973).
58. White Eagle v. One Feather, 478 F.2d 1311, 1313 (8th Cir. 1973).
59. *Id.* at 1314. *Accord*, Brown v. United States, 486 F.2d 658, 661 (8th Cir. 1973); Daly v. United States, 483 F.2d 700, 705 (8th Cir. 1973).
60. White Eagle v. One Feather, 478 F.2d 1311, 1314 (8th Cir. 1973).
61. *Id.* at 1315.
62. Daly v. United States, 483 F.2d 700, 706 (8th Cir. 1973).
63. White Eagle v. One Feather, 478 F.2d 1311, 1315 (8th Cir. 1973).
64. Brown v. United States, 486 F.2d 658, 662 (8th Cir. 1973), stating that Burns v. Richardson, 384 U.S. 73, 91 (1966), indicated that apportionment could be based on: (1) total population (2) citizen population or (3) voter population. The Court in *Brown* stated that it would approve a plan based on any of these measurements if the tribal constitution so authorized.
65. Daly v. United States, 483 F.2d 700, 707 (8th Cir. 1973).
66. 478 F.2d 1311 (8th Cir. 1973).
67. Daly v. United States, 483 F.2d 700, 707 (8th Cir. 1973).
68. *Id.*

matters may seem an improper intrusion into the internal political affairs of the tribes. Similar objections were expressed in reference to state governments when the *Baker* decision was announced.[69] Nonetheless, this situation would seem to exemplify the need for the Indian Civil Rights Act. In these cases, the various tribal councils had the means to reapportion their voting districts but failed to do so, and the tribal courts also refused to order reapportionment. The court did not mention if any of the tribes had apportioned their voting districts on the basis of historical power structures within the tribe. A situation in which representation was based on a certain number of representatives for certain groups or bands within the tribe may have caused the court to reconsider the *Baker* standard in light of the tribe's cultural interests. Where the tribes had adopted "Anglo-American" voting procedures, however, and displayed no significant tribal cultural interest to justify the unbalanced apportionment, the court intervention merely compelled the tribes to comply with their own voting procedures.[70]

Tribal Membership and Voter Eligibility

Tribal membership is the foundation for most tribal political rights. Unless the individual is a member, he is incapable of voting in tribal elections or running for tribal office. Discriminations in tribal enrollment created claims under the equal protection clause of the Indian Civil Rights Act.[71] Tribal membership, however, was one area in which the legislative record of the Act indicated a desire on Congress' behalf to allow the tribes to maintain their governmental and cultural identity by allowing a "racial definition of membership rights."[72] The right of a tribe to determine its own membership had been declared "vital to the survival of these people."[73] With these important considerations at stake, the tribes fiercely fought to protect their enrollment practices from attacks under the Act. The tribes' interest in maintaining their cultural and racial identity was not ignored by the federal courts. In interpreting the scope of application of the equal protection clause of the Indian Civil Rights Act, a balancing test of tribal interest against the rights of the individual was applied.

Such was the situation in *Martinez v. Santa Clara Pueblo*.[74] The membership ordinance of the Santa Clara Pueblo was attacked on equal protection grounds because its provisions granted membership to all children born to male members married to non-

---

69. Baker v. Carr, 369 U.S. 186, 266 (1962) (Frankfurter, J., dissenting).
70. White Eagle v. Lone Feather, 478 F.2d 1311, 1314 (8th Cir. 1973).
71. 25 U.S.C. § 1302(8) (1970). *See* note 4 *supra*.
72. Note, *supra* note 35, at 1362.
73. Ziontz, *In Defense of Tribal Sovereignty: An Analysis of Judicial Error in Construction of the Indian Civil Rights Act*, 20 S.D.L. REV. 1, 48 (1975).
74. 540 F.2d 1039 (9th Cir. 1976). As discussed in the text accompanying note 6 *supra*, this case was later reversed by the United States Supreme Court on jurisdictional grounds. Santa Clara Pueblo v. Martinez, 436 U.S. 49 (1978).

members, but not to children born to marriages of female members and non-members. The district court held this ordinance was proper because the male-female distinction was "rooted in certain traditional values."[75] The Tenth Circuit Court of Appeals established the balancing test in determining the case:

> About the only way to resolve this conflict is to recognize the necessity to evaluate and weigh both of these interests. Thus the scope, extent and importance of the tribal interest is to be taken into account. The individual right to fair treatment under the law is likewise to be weighed against the tribal interest by considering the clearness of the guarantee together with the magnitude of the interest generally and as applied to the particular facts.[76]

The court suggested that individual guarantees be given more weight in this balancing test because the legislative history manifested "a congressional intent to recognize the specific guarantee unless the tribal custom or principle outweighs the specific guarantee."[77] *Howlett v. Salish and Kootenai Tribes*[78] was cited for the principle that tribal tradition must be deep-seated and the individual injury relatively insignificant before tribal authority should stand. After indicating that had the ordinance been measured by the fourteenth amendment alone it would have violated equal protection, the court held that the tribe's interest was not significant enough to outweigh this violation. Unlike the district court, the court of appeals could not find that the ordinance was rooted in tribal values. Instead, it found that evidence indicated the ordinance to be "the product of economics and pragmatics," and not based on a "venerable tradition."[79] This fact, coupled with the understanding that children who were offspring of either type of marriage were raised in the Pueblo and "for all practical purposes, Santa Clara,"[80] convinced the court that little harm would come to the tribe's cultural identity by eliminating the membership distinction.

Courts have looked with more approval on membership requirements based on percentage of Indian blood. In *Slattery v. Arapahoe Tribal Council*,[81] the Tenth Circuit Court of Appeals discussed Arapahoe and Shoshone Tribal ordinances requiring at least a one-quarter degree of Indian blood before one could be enrolled as a member of the tribe. Plaintiffs in this case alleged that applications for tribal enrollment were rejected "arbitrarily and without just cause."[82] This did not place the ordinances themselves before the court as violating the Indian Civil Rights Act, but

---

75. Martinez v. Santa Clara Pueblo, 402 F. Supp. 5, 16 (D.N.M. 1975).
76. Martinez v. Santa Clara Pueblo, 540 F.2d 1039, 1045 (9th Cir. 1976).
77. *Id.*
78. 529 F.2d 233 (9th Cir. 1976).
79. Martinez v. Santa Clara Pueblo, 540 F.2d 1039, 1047, 1048 (10th Cir. 1976).
80. *Id.* at 1048.
81. 453 F.2d 278 (10th Cir. 1971).
82. *Id.* at 280.

only the acts of the Tribal Council in rejecting such applications. The Tenth Circuit held that the pleadings indicated on their face that the applications were properly refused because all of the applicants failed to meet the blood quantum requirement. This being the case, there was no denial of due process or equal protection and the trial court was not presented with sufficient facts to invoke jurisdiction under the Act.[83]

The question of blood quantum requirements for tribal membership and concomitant violation of equal protection under the Indian Civil Rights Act was indirectly answered in *Daly v. United States*.[84] Not only did the court in that case approve the application of the *Baker* rule to tribal apportionment, but also approved a provision of the tribe's constitution designed to assure that at least one-half of the tribe's Councilmen would be of one-half, or more, Indian blood. The Crow Creek Sioux Tribe had a membership requirement of one-quarter Indian blood. The court stated the tribe had a sufficient cultural interest in setting a higher blood requirement for office holders and indicated that this was one area where the full scope of equal protection should not apply.[85] This would imply that the membership blood quantum requirement was also within the tribe's cultural interest.

Blood quantum standards for membership should be upheld as long as they are reasonable, for they certainly play an important role in maintaining a tribe's cultural identity. This cultural interest would seem to merit more protection than the weighted balancing test established in *Martinez*. The test would better meet the purpose of the Act if it was balanced in favor of the tribe's cultural interests. Some infringement of personal rights may often be necessary in order to maintain the tribe's cultural independence. In all cases, it is very important that the courts be presented with adequate information in the tribe's heritage, customs, traditions, and other significant cultural aspects.

An issue closely related to tribal membership is voter eligibility. Two cases considered the question of whether the Indian Civil Rights Act extends the provisions of the twenty-sixth amendment[86] (18 year old vote) to tribal elections. In *Jacobson v. Forest County Potwatomi Community*,[87] the court ruled that a complaint challenging provisions of the tribal constitution and bylaws that prohibited females from holding office and precluded tribal members under twenty-one years of age from voting in tribal elections failed to state a cause of action under the Indian Civil Rights Act.[88]

---

83. *Id.* at 282.
84. 483 F.2d 700 (8th Cir. 1973).
85. *Id.* at 705, citing Groundhog v. Keeler, 442 F.2d 674 (10th Cir. 1972).
86. U.S. CONST. amend. XXVI.
87. 389 F. Supp. 994 (E.D. Wis. 1974).
88. *Id.* at 996. The court noted that the Act only enumerated some of the governmental restraints that are included in the United States Constitution and stated that the old doctrine of internal controversies still operated to de-

In *Wounded Head v. Tribal Council of the Oglala Sioux Tribe*,[89] the Eighth Circuit Court of Appeals held that a similar tribal constitutional provision establishing a twenty-one year old voting age for tribal elections denied no rights protected by the Act. The court based its holding on the previously established judicial rule that the equal protection provision of the Act is not coextensive with the equal protection clause of the fourteenth amendment.[90] In distinguishing this case from *Daly*[91] and *White Eagle*[92] the court stated that requiring the tribe to enfranchise a "new class of tribal population" would force an alien culture on the tribe.[93] The court was reluctant to interfere with the internal affairs of the tribe absent explicit federal legislation directing it to do so. Thus, in these cases the courts found the tribal cultural interest to outweigh the possible individual harm.

Candidacy for Tribal Office

Several individuals utilized the Indian Civil Rights Act to challenge tribal election laws that precluded their candidacy for tribal office. In these cases the balancing of tribal interests was once again found significant. The case of *Luxon v. Rosebud Sioux Tribe*[94] was one of the first to recognize that tribal candidacy was protected under the Act. The plaintiff-appellant claimed that a tribal constitutional provision disqualifying from candidacy for tribal office any person employed by the Department of Interior or the Public Health Service denied her equal protection. The Eighth Circuit Court of Appeals held that the district court had jurisdiction under the Act to hear such a case.[95]

In *Daly v. United States*,[96] the Eighth Circuit Court of Appeals held that a tribe had a sufficient cultural interest to require a higher blood quantum requirement for office holders than for mere membership. In dealing with the requirement that assured at least one-half of the Tribal Council would be of one-half or more

---

prive federal courts or jurisdiction, except where the Act specifically provided otherwise.

89. 507 F.2d 1079 (8th Cir. 1975).

90. *Id.* at 1082. The courts have held that the legislative history of the Act made it clear that certain provisions of the equal protection requirement of the fourteenth amendment "should not be embraced by the Indian Bill of Rights." Groundhog v. Keeler, 442 F.2d 674, 682 (10th Cir. 1971). *See also* White Eagle v. One Feather, 478 F.2d 1311 (8th Cir. 1973); Note, *supra* note 35, at 1360.

91. Daly v. United States, 483 F.2d 700 (8th Cir. 1973). *See* the text accompanying notes 57-60 *supra.*

92. White Eagle v. One Feather, 478 F.2d 1311 (8th Cir. 1973). *See* text accompanying notes 57-60 *supra.*

93. Wounded Head v. Tribal Council of the Oglala Sioux Tribe, 507 F.2d 1079, 1083 (8th Cir. 1975).

94. 455 F.2d 698 (8th Cir. 1972).

95. *Id.* at 700. The district court had originally held that it lacked jurisdiction "to hear intratribal controversies." *Id.* at 699. Although the opinion was not reported, at least one authority has indicated that the plaintiff, on remand, was granted the declaratory and injunctive relief she requested. Ziontz, *supra* note 73, at 51.

96. 483 F.2d 700 (8th Cir. 1973).

Indian blood, the court stated that if applied uniformly, the requirement would not conflict with the Indian Civil Rights Act guarantee of equal protection of the laws.

The cultural interest test, however, was not used in the case of *Howlett v. Salish and Kootenai Tribes.*[97] The case involved two plaintiffs who were denied the right to run as candidates for the Tribal Council because they failed to meet the tribe's one year residency requirement. The court first held that plaintiffs had not shown that the Tribal Council had in any manner denied them equal protection or due process in the review of their qualifications. In reaching this conclusion, the court, in a significant pronouncement, found that "[s]o long as the Tribes do not violate the Indian Civil Rights Act, they may structure their government in any manner they please."[98] Then, in turning to the residency requirement itself, the court found that here, as in the apportionment cases, the tribe had established procedures that closely paralleled "Anglo-American" procedures. Because this situation existed, the court subjected the residency requirement to the compelling state interest test that had been announced for state residency requirements in *Dunn v. Blumstein.*[99] The court found the tribe to have met this test because the "extremely localized problems" of the tribe necessitated a situation where a candidate would have extended exposure to such problems.[100] Even here, where the federal court applied the state rule to the tribe, the court recognized the unique characteristics of tribal government.

As previously discussed,[101] the challenge of a tribal constitutional provision excluding women from holding office on the Tribal Council was found to be an internal controversy not cognizable under the Indian Civil Rights Act in *Jacobson v. Forest County Potawatomi Community.*[102] That opinion makes no mention of any tribal heritage or custom that would justify the exclusion of women in this situation. The court seemed to side-step this equal protection argument by pointing out that the plaintiff had not challenged sections of the tribal constitution establishing ethnic restrictions on tribal membership and voting. The fact that other portions of the constitution were not challenged would appear unimportant to the question of whether the alleged facts constituted a denial of equal protection. Without any examination of tribal

---

97. 529 F.2d 233 (9th Cir. 1976).
98. *Id.* at 240.
99. 405 U.S. 330 (1972). In *Dunn*, the United States Supreme Court concluded that the right to travel was a constitutionally protected right and any classification that would "penalize the exercise of that right" was unconstitutional, unless shown "to be necessary to promote a compelling governmental interest." *Id.* at 339.
100. Howlett v. Salish & Kootenai Tribes, 529 F.2d 233, 244 (9th Cir. 1976).
101. *See* text accompanying note 88 *supra.*
102. 389 F. Supp. 994 (E.D. Wis. 1974). The internal controversies doctrine was established prior to the passage of the Act. This doctrine allowed tribes to settle internal disputes within the tribal framework when it was best suited to do so and where Congress had expressed no intention to interfere. Cohen, *supra* note 15, at 117.

culture or heritage in explaining this exclusion this dismissal would not appear to be justified.[103]

Another candidacy case produced some points of interests for future plaintiffs using the Act. The plaintiff in *Two Hawk v. Rosebud Sioux Tribe*[104] challenged a Tribal Election Board decision that excluded him from the primary. ballot. The Eighth Circuit Court of Appeals ruled the issue was moot because the plaintiff had allowed the primary election to proceed without his name on the ballot. The plaintiff failed to seek a stay of judgment pending appeal and did not request that the appeals court hear and resolve the suit on an "expedited basis."[105]

These candidacy cases again show that where the courts found a significant tribal interest, the balancing test was applied. Where, however, the tribe had established "Anglo-American" procedures, it was held to the same standards applicable to the states under the equal protection clause of the fourteenth amendment. Even in those situations, the courts considered the tribal interests and allowed the tribes to structure their own requirements so long as the Act was not violated.

Election Irregularities

Alleged irregularities in the application or administration of tribal election laws were the subject of numerous suits under the Indian Civil Rights Act. The federal courts clearly indicated that they would not allow a tribe to ignore, either purposely or by informality, election laws and rules that the tribe itself had established, when such disregard violated due process or equal protection. This doctrine was established despite an announced reluctance to involve the federal courts in tribal elections.

The first reported case in this area was *Solomon v. LaRose*.[106] Plaintiffs had brought an action seeking a restraining order enjoining the Tribal Council from seating certain members after a disputed election. The Tribal Council had made a ruling in the dispute, but the district court found no express provision in the tribe's constitution giving the Council the power to do so. Absent such authorization, the court held that the Tribal Council had exceeded its authority, thereby denying the plaintiffs due process.

In *Williams v. Sisseton-Wahpeton Sioux Tribal Council*[107] two claims concerning election disputes were brought under the Indian Civil Rights Act. The court found jurisdiction to hear these claims even though it recognized "the dangers of succumbing to

---

103. Jacobson v. Forest County Potawatomi Community, 389 F. Supp. 994, 996 (E.D. Wis. 1974). The court also found that the plaintiffs failed to exhaust all available tribal remedies. *Id.* On this ground the dismissal would seem proper.
104. 534 F.2d 101 (8th Cir. 1976).
105. *Id.* at 103.
106. 335 F. Supp. 715 (D. Neb. 1971).
107. 387 F. Supp. 1194 (D.S.D. 1975).

ethnocentrism" in applying the Act.[108] It stated the belief that:

> [A]t the very core of due process is the proposition that a governing body must abide by and be governed by its own constitution and ordinances adopted pursuant to that constitution. . . . To say that enforcement of the above proposition would somehow impose elements of an alien culture upon the Indians is, in this court's opinion, incorrect.[109]

With this proposition in mind, the court went on to explore the tribe's election ordinances, found no authority for the second election that the Tribal Council had authorized, and held that the second election was violative of due process. Concerning the other claim, the court found that a recount of the ballots was within the power of the Tribal Election Board and stated that the court would refuse to examine the ballots themselves "absent allegations of criminality."[110]

Perhaps the most publicized election dispute case under the Indian Civil Rights Act was *Means v. Wilson*.[111] Russell Means, one of the leaders of the American Indian Movement, sought election to the office of Tribal Chairman of the Oglala Sioux Tribe and opposed the incumbant Richard Wilson. After the election, Means brought suit alleging that numerous election errors and irregularities had affected the election results. In discussing the claims under the Indian Civil Rights Act the court stated that in other situations the federal courts had "refused to decide election contests based on equal protection arguments in the absence of allegations of intentional deprivation of the right to vote."[112] Agreeing with the district court that the standard for setting aside a tribal election must be at least as restrictive, the court found no allegations sufficiently showing that the tribe or the Tribal Council had acted in such a manner. The court of appeals did find, however, that a claim was properly stated against the Tribal Election Board. This claim was established by the allegation that the board failed to properly instruct election judges and clerks in an attempt to deliberately achieve illegal results together with the allegation of other irregularities. The court stated that the determination of this claim would not interfere with tribal culture because the alleged interference with voting rights was not founded on tribal custom.

In *Rosebud Sioux Tribe v. Driving Hawk*,[113] the Indian Civil Rights Act was used as the basis for a counterclaim alleging election irregularities. Because of the numerous allegations and counter-allegations involved, the district court appointed a special master to review the election results. The Eighth Circuit Court of Appeals reluctantly accepted jurisdiction, and hinted that it might

---

108. *Id.* at 1199.
109. *Id.* (citation omitted).
110. *Id.* at 1201.
111. 522 F.2d 833 (8th Cir. 1975), *cert. denied*, 424 U.S. 958 (1976).
112. *Id.* at 841, citing Snowden v. Hughes, 321 U.S. 1 (1944); Smith v. Cherry, 489 F.2d 1098 (7th Cir. 1974); Cameron v. Brock, 473 F.2d 608 (6th Cir. 1973).
113. 534 F.2d 98 (8th Cir. 1976).

not have done so had the tribe itself provided a system by which election contests could have been fairly tried within the guidelines of equal protection and due process. The court of appeals then reviewed the findings of the master and the trial record and concluded that the election dispute had been fairly resolved.

Selection of a tribal leader by means other than election was challenged under the Indian Civil Rights Act in *Groundhog v. Keeler*.[114] A federal statute provided that the Secretary of the Interior would appoint the Chief of the Cherokee Nation. The Tenth Circuit Court of Appeals found the Act only imposed "restrictions on Indian tribes in the exercise of the power of self-government,"[115] but imposed no restrictions on Congress or the Secretary of the Interior, and therefore the court had no power to review this action. The court also noted that nothing in the Act even requires a tribe select its leaders by election.

An overview of these cases indicates that the courts would interpret the Act to allow tribes to structure their government in any manner, as long as the Act's due process and equal protection provisions were not violated. The tribes were required to establish procedures to fairly hear election disputes. The courts preferred settlement of these questions within the tribal governmental framework, but where these procedures did not assure the protections enumerated in the Act, the federal courts intervened despite this expressed reluctance.

Freedom of Speech

Freedom of speech has always been one of the most cherished and protected rights in American society. Without this guarantee, political activity would turn into a meaningless, secretive exercise. Freedom of speech was protected from infringement by tribal governments through section 1302(1)[116] of the Indian Civil Rights Act.

The case of *Dodge v. Nakai*[117] was one of the first cases decided under the Act and served as a guide in subsequent interpretations of various provisions of the Act. For several months the Director of a legal services program on the Navajo Reservation had experienced difficulty with the Navajo Tribal Council. This culminated in a tribal committee requesting that the program's Board of Directors remove the Director. The Board of Directors refused to dismiss its Director. Later, at a tribal committee meeting, the Director allegedly laughed rudely at a comment by one of the committee's members. After this incident, the committee passed a resolution excluding the Director from the reservation for his "obnoxious conduct."[118] The Director of the program was neither an Indian nor a member of the tribe, therefore it is signifi-

---

114. 442 F.2d 674 (10th Cir. 1971).
115. *Id.* at 678.
116. *See* note 4 *supra*.
117. 298 F. Supp. 26 (D. Ariz. 1969).
118. *Id.* at 31.

cant that the court interpreted the words "any person" in the Act
to mean all persons, and not just American Indians. The court
found the tribe's action lacked due process and constituted a denial of free speech. The action was also found to be a bill of attainder, which is also prohibited under the Act.

A denial of free speech and due process was claimed in *Janis v.
Wilson.*[119] The plaintiffs were former employees of the Tribe's
Community Health Program who alleged that the Tribal Council
had terminated their employment because they had protested
against tribal policies. The Eighth Circuit Court of Appeals did not
reach the merits of the case because it found that the plaintiffs had
failed to exhaust all available tribal administrative and judicial
remedies, but the court revealed that it had "serious reservations
about the correctness of the summary judgment"[120] granted by the
district court to the defendants.

The courts thus recognized free speech protections of the Act.
By recognizing this cornerstone of political rights, the courts made
certain that the other rights enumerated in the Act would not become meaningless.

Jurisdictional Requirements

Just as the various courts had interpreted the substantive
rights provisions of the Act with an eye towards protecting tribal
cultural interests, the courts established jurisdictional requirements to protect the integrity of tribal courts. The two significant
doctrines created by the courts were: (1) plaintiff had to show that
all available tribal remedies had been exhausted; and (2) plaintiff
had to allege sufficient facts indicating a violation of his rights protected by the Act.

The question of exhaustion arose shortly after the Act was
passed. The court in *Dodge v. Nakai*[121] recognized the question
and noted that the plaintiffs admitted never having presented their
claims to the tribal court. In discussing the exhaustion requirement the court said:

> Several factors support the implication of such a condition
> into Title II. First, this interpretation would reconcile the
> statute with "a strong Congressional policy to vest Navajo
> Tribal Government with the responsibility for their own
> affairs." . . . Second, this interpretation would place pri-
> mary responsibility for the vindication of rights violated
> by Indian governmental agencies upon the tribal courts.
> Such responsibility may well enhance the development of
> an independent Indian judiciary, thus reconciling the stat-
> ute with recognized federal policy. . . . Third, this inter-
> pretation would insure that this Court would intervene
> only in those instances in which local conflicts cannot be

119. 521 F.2d 724 (8th Cir. 1975).
120. *Id.* at 729.
121. 298 F. Supp. 17 (D. Ariz. 1969).

resolved locally.[122]

The court held, however, that exhaustion would not be required of the plaintiffs because several defendants were not under tribal court jurisdiction and, therefore, exhaustion would cause delay and multiple lawsuits.

Exhaustion was later fully discussed in *O'Neal v. Cheyenne River Sioux Tribe*.[123] Here the court found the plaintiffs had not availed themselves of remedies available to them in the tribal courts, and that until they did so, no federal court had jurisdiction to hear their case. The court fully supported the exhaustion requirement recognized prior to the passage of the Act stating, "We conclude that the adoption of the Indian Bill of Rights was not meant to detract from the generally recognized policy, . . ., of preserving the 'authority of the tribal courts.' "[124]

This rule was not without exception. No exhaustion of remedies was required when a plaintiff proved that no tribal remedies were available.[125] Also, a plaintiff was not required to exhaust tribal remedies when it would have been futile to do so.[126] "The exhaustion requirement is not an inflexible one. 'Certainly plaintiffs bringing suit under the Indian Bill of Rights are not required to first exhaust futile or inadequate tribal remedies.' "[127]

In the apportionment cases, where a timely remedy was often necessary, exhaustion was not required.[128] In those cases the plaintiff often requested a temporary restraining order, and a delay caused by waiting for the tribal court to act may have allowed the issue to become moot.[129] When these circumstances were not present, the federal courts required plaintiffs to exhaust all available tribal administrative and/or judicial remedies.[130] In one case the court went so far as to require the plaintiff to attempt to amend the tribal constitution when such action would have provided her relief.[131]

The goal of the exhaustion rule was certainly a proper one considering the federal courts reluctance to intervene in tribal affairs which were capable of being resolved within the tribal framework. The flexibility recognized by the courts was also necessary to allow the courts to give the plaintiff a timely and effective remedy. These considerations should always come into play. In some circumstances, forcing the plaintiff to attempt the process of amend-

---

122. *Id*. at 25 (citations omitted).
123. 482 F.2d 1140 (8th Cir. 1973).
124. *Id*. at 1146.
125. Daly v. United States, 483 F.2d 700, 705 (8th Cir. 1973).
126. Howlett v. Salish & Kootenai Tribes, 529 F.2d 233, 240 (9th Cir. 1976).
127. *Id*.
128. *E.g.*, Brown v. United States, 486 F.2d 658 (8th Cir. 1973).
129. Two Hawk v. Rosebud Sioux Tribe, 534 F.2d 101 (8th Cir. 1976). *See* text accompanying notes 104-05 *supra*.
130. Janis v. Wilson, 521 F.2d 724, 726 (8th Cir. 1975); Brown v. United States, 486 F.2d 658, 661 (8th Cir. 1973); Luxon v. Rosebud Sioux Tribe, 455 F.2d 698, 699 (8th Cir. 1972).
131. Jacobson v. Forest County Potawatomi Community, 389 F. Supp. 994, 996 (E.D. Wis. 1974).

ing the tribal constitution may be reasonable, considering the injury and the time frame involved, but usually such a requirement would deny the plaintiff a timely remedy.

As an additional jurisdictional safeguard against frivolous appeals, the federal courts required a plaintiff to allege sufficient facts indicating that the provisions of the Act had been violated. In *Luxon v. Rosebud Sioux Tribe*[132] the Eighth Circuit Court of Appeals made this statement concerning jurisdiction under the Act: "In our opinion, 28 U.S.C. § 1343(4) gives the district court jurisdiction to determine, *in a proper case*, whether an Indian tribe has denied to one of its members any of the rights given to the members under the Indian Bill of Rights."[133] At least one court interpreted this statement to mean that a court may look into the scope of the Act's protections by interpreting past decisions to determine if the facts alleged fall within those parameters and dismiss the action if they do not.[134]

This rule is clarified by a review of the jurisdictional portions of *Groundhog v. Keeler*.[135] The court held that jurisdiction "must be determined from the allegations of fact in the complaint, without regard to mere conclusionary allegations of jurisdiction."[136] This same jurisdictional rule was stated in *Slattery v. Arapahoe Tribal Council*.[137]

DECLARATORY AND INJUNCTIVE RELIEF UNDER THE ACT

As previously stated,[138] the United States Supreme Court held in *Santa Clara Pueblo v. Martinez*[139] that actions for declaratory and injunctive relief alleging violations of the Indian Civil Rights Act are barred by sovereign immunity of the tribes. The Supreme Court could find no expressed congressional intention to modify this immunity in the language of the Act and therefore held that no suit could be brought under the Act against a tribe. It also held that actions for such relief could not be brought against tribal officials because of the interference with tribal self-government that such a remedy would create. Prior to this holding, numerous federal courts had held that actions for declaratory and injunctive relief could be brought under the Act. This section will explore how those courts established jurisdiction for these remedies and examine the *Santa Clara* decision in light of the approach adopted by the federal courts.

---

132. 455 F.2d 698 (8th Cir. 1972).
133. *Id.* at 700 (emphasis added).
134. Yellow Bird v. Oglala Sioux Tribe, 380 F. Supp. 438, 439 (D.S.D. 1974).
135. 442 F.2d 674 (10th Cir. 1971).
136. *Id.* at 677.
137. 453 F.2d 278, 279 (10th Cir. 1971).
138. *See* text accompanying notes 6-9 *supra*.
139. 436 U.S. 49 (1978).

Differing Views on Available Remedies

The Act itself only makes mention of one form of remedy, a writ of habeas corpus, which is set forth in section 1303 of the Act.[140] This writ may be used by a person in federal court "to test the legality of his detention by order of an Indian tribe."[141] At least one authority indicates that examination of the Act's legislative record reveals that Congress considered other remedies, but settled on the habeas corpus provision and intended it to be the sole federal court jurisdictional basis for suits under the Act.[142] Any extention of remedies would have difficulty overcoming the problem of the tribes' sovereign immunity from suit, and the lack of an expressed congressional waiver of such immunity.[143]

Others who comment on the Act differ from this view, stating that Senator Ervin's committee expressed no intention to limit remedies under the Act to habeas corpus and that section 1303 specifically enumerated the habeas corpus writ because of the committee's special concern with criminal procedural rights.[144] This view is supported by the fact that the committee spent a great deal of its time considering alleged tribal deprivations of procedural rights of criminal defendants.[145] The original bills introduced by Senator Ervin contained provisions establishing an appeal of criminal cases from tribal courts with *de novo* review in the federal district court.[146] The modification of this provision to establish the writ did nothing to change the protections given by the Act, but established habeas corpus as a *right* and not just another of the remedies listed in the Committee's report.[147] Also, to so limit the Act's remedies would have done little but recognize the realities that already existed in light of the *Colliflower v. Garland*[148] decision.

Perhaps the most compelling argument for the extension of remedies beyond the stated habeas corpus writ is a consideration of the number of protections given in the Act that are rendered meaningless by limiting the federal remedies under the Act to habeas corpus. The habeas corpus remedy is available only to those persons "detained" by order of a tribe.[149] Few, if any, of the political rights discussed in this article would be protected by such habeas corpus review. Unless some extension of a political conflict would cause a person to be "detained" for his actions, plaintiffs claiming defective apportionment of election districts, wrongful denial of tribal membership or candidacy, election irregularities,

---

140. 25 U.S.C. § 1303 (Supp. 1978), *see* note 4 *supra*.
141. *Id.*
142. Ziontz, *supra* note 73, at 18.
143. *Id.* at 21.
144. Note, *supra* note 35, at 1371-73.
145. *Id.* at 1356.
146. Burnett, *supra* note 31, at 592-94.
147. Note, *supra* note 35, at 1371.
148. 342 F.2d 369 (9th Cir. 1965); *see* text accompanying notes 28-30 *supra*.
149. 28 U.S.C. § 1303 (Supp. 1978); *see* note 4 *supra*.

dismissal from employment for political reasons, or exclusion from the reservation will all be turned away be the federal courts. "Any person" can be denied equal protection or due process by a tribal government and have no means to defend those rights except through the tribal courts. Furthermore, in these tribal courts the person seeking declaratory and injunctive relief will often have to face the same individuals, or groups controlled by those individuals, he was seeking to enjoin.[150] The information presented at the Senate hearings raised serious questions about the ability of tribal courts to give a fair hearing to this or any other person before it. Congress certainly could not have intended to limit individuals with claims outside the scope of habeas corpus to these so-called remedies. To do so would have rendered meaningless many of the protections set forth in the Act.

Federal Courts Find Jurisdiction

The federal courts wasted little time in adopting an expansive interpretation of remedies available under the Act. In the first Indian Civil Rights case, *Dodge v. Nakai*,[151] the Court held that it has jurisdiction over the action under 28 U.S.C. §§ 1331(a) & 1343(4).[152] The court granted the plaintiffs a prohibitory injunction and denied any recovery of money damages.[153] Shortly thereafter the question of jurisdiction was discussed fully in *Solomon v. LaRose*.[154] The court stated:

> It does not follow that Congress intended § 1303 to be the exclusive jurisdictional basis for enforcement. Such a finding would render nugatory the rights secured by provisions (1), (5) and (8) of § 1302. The reason for Congress' enacting a habeas corpus remedial statute lies in the explicit wording of 28 U.S.C. § 2241(c)(1)(5), which palpably indicates that tribal courts or councils would not be subject to jurisdiction. Therefore, Congress felt compelled to enact a special jurisdictional statute for habeas corpus relief in the federal courts.
>
> In contrast, there existed no need to provide a special jurisdictional statute to enforce provisions (1), (5) and (8)

---

150. Burnett, *supra* note 31, at 580.
151. 298 F. Supp. 17 (D. Ariz. 1968).
152. *Id.* at 25. 28 U.S.C. § 1331(a) (Supp. 1978) reads:
   (a) The district courts shall have original jurisdiction of all civil actions wherein the matter in controversy exceeds the sum or value of $10,000, exclusive of interest and costs, and arises under the Constitution, laws, or treaties of the United States except that no such sum or value shall be required in any such action brought against the United States, any agency thereof, or any officer or employee thereof in his official capacity.
28 U.S.C. § 1343(4) (1976) reads:
   The district courts shall have original jurisdiction of any civil action authorized by law to be commenced by any person: . . .
   (4) To recover damages or to secure equitable or other relief under any Act of Congress providing for the protection of civil rights, including the right to vote.
153. Dodge v. Nakai, 298 F. Supp. 26, 34 (D. Ariz. 1969).
154. 335 F. Supp. 715 (D. Neb. 1971).

of § 1302, since a basis of jurisdiction was already present—28 U.S.C. § 1343(4).[155]

Of course few plaintiffs claiming denial of political rights would fall within the scope of section 1331 because seldom would such a plaintiff be able to show damages in an amount sufficient to satisfy the $10,000 jurisdictional requirement.[156] The majority of plaintiffs chose to bring the action under 28 U.S.C. § 1343(4), which prior to 1968 had only been used sparingly. Nonetheless, the statutory language of section 1343(4) would certainly seem broad enough to include actions under the Indian Civil Rights Act because tribal governments violating the Act are denying civil rights that are protected by Congress. Numerous courts found jurisdiction under section 1343(4) for civil rights cases brought before them.[157] In two early cases, suits were dismissed because plaintiffs sought remedies other than habeas corpus, however, these rulings at the district court level were reversed on appeal.[158]

Once the question of a statutory basis for remedies other than habeas corpus was solved, the next hurdle to be cleared was that of tribal sovereign immunity. As previously discussed, the tribes retain all the internal powers of a sovereign government except where those powers are modified by treaty or express congressional action.

The federal courts had little difficulty in overcoming this barrier of sovereign immunity. They generally held that the passage of the Act waived tribal immunity. In *Dodge v. Nakai*,[159] the court stated that the Act's legislative history indicated a clear congressional intent "to make substantial changes in the manner in which Indian tribes could exercise their quasi-sovereign powers."[160] Other cases held that the Act does not abrogate the sovereign immunity of Indian tribes by specific language, but does so by *implication*.[161] This "abrogation by implication" suggestion certainly clashes with the established doctrine that the tribes are vested with full powers of internal sovereignty unless *expressly* qualified.[162] Whether the courts were unaware of this principle or simply misstated their ruling is unknown, but the statement did raise serious questions about the Act's removal of tribal sovereignty.

The courts had clearly interpreted the goals of the Act as being

---

155. *Id.* at 721.
156. *But see* Halderman v. Pittenger, 391 F. Supp. 872 (E.D. Pa. 1975); C. WRIGHT, A. MILLER & E. COOPER, FEDERAL PRACTICE AND PROCEDURE § 3709 (1976 & Supp. 1978) and cases cited therein.
157. *See* previously discussed political rights cases, in text accompanying notes 50-120 *supra*. All found jurisdiction under 28 U.S.C. § 1343(4) (1976).
158. Luxon v. Rosebud Sioux Tribe, 455 F.2d 698 (8th Cir. 1972); Slattery v. Arapahoe Tribal Council 453 F.2d 278 (10th Cir. 1971).
159. Dodge v. Nakai, 298 F. Supp. 17, 24 (D. Ariz. 1968).
160. *Id.* at 24.
161. *E.g.*, Daly v. United States, 483 F.2d 700, 705 (8th Cir. 1973).
162. Thebo v. Choctaw Tribe of Indians, 66 F. 372 (8th Cir. 1895), *see* text accompanying notes 21-24 *supra*.

broader than could be achieved through the habeas corpus remedy. The justification for this expansion was the need to give full effect to the rights conferred by the Act. This was the status of the case law under the Act when the United States Supreme Court rendered its decision in *Santa Clara Pueblo v. Martinez*.[163]

Santa Clara Pueblo: Declaratory and Injunctive Relief Removed

In *Martinez v. Santa Clara Pueblo*,[164] the Tenth Circuit Court of Appeals had, like so many other courts, found jurisdiction under 28 U.S.C. § 1343(4)[165] for a Indian Civil Rights Act claim seeking declaratory and injunctive relief. As discussed earlier in this article,[166] the case involved a claim that a Santa Clara Pueblo ordinance, which denied tribal membership to children of female tribal members who married outside the tribe but allowed membership to children of male tribal members who married outside the tribe, denied equal protection. The Tenth Circuit reversed the district court's holding that the ordinance was valid.

The Supreme Court never reached the merits of the case because it held that the Indian Civil Rights Act did not authorize civil actions for declaratory and injunctive relief against the tribe or its officers. The Court stated the threshold issue of the case to be "whether the Act may be interpreted to impliedly authorize such actions, against a tribe or its officers, in the federal courts."[167]

In discussing the history of the case, the Court stopped to note the statement made by the Tenth Circuit Court of Appeals when it explained its finding of jurisdiction under 28 U.S.C. § 1343(4): "It found that 'since [the Indian Civil Rights Act] was designed to provide protection against tribal authority, the intention of Congress to allow suits against the tribe was an essential aspect [of the Act]. Otherwise, it would constitute a mere unenforceable declaration of principles.' "[168]

The Court then approached the question of possible suit against the tribe. After examining the principle of sovereign tribal governmental powers and the related doctrine of tribal immunity from suit, the Court recognized the fact that tribal sovereign powers and tribal immunity could be removed by Congress through its "superior and plenary control" over the tribes.[169] It then set forth the established rule that, "a waiver of sovereign immunity 'cannot be implied but must be unequivocally expressed.' "[170] The Court stated that it could find nothing on the face of the Act subjecting

---

163. 436 U.S. 49 (1978).
164. 540 F.2d 1039 (10th Cir. 1976).
165. *See* note 152 *supra*.
166. *See* text accompanying notes 74-80 *supra*.
167. Santa Clara Pueblo v. Martinez, 436 U.S. 49, 52 (1978).
168. *Id*. at 55, citing Martinez v. Santa Clara Pueblo, 540 F.2d 1039, 1042 (10th Cir. 1976).
169. Santa Clara Pueblo v. Martinez, 436 U.S. 49, 58 (1978).
170. *Id*. at 58-59, quoting United States v. Testan, 424 U.S. 392 (1976), which quoted United States v. King, 395 U.S. 1 (1969).

the tribes to suit under the Act. It noted that the Act made no mention of declaratory and injunctive relief, and even the expressed habeas corpus remedy must be brought against "the individual custodian of the prisoner."[171] Therefore it found that the Act contained no expressed waiver of tribal sovereign immunity. In light of these observations, the Court held: "In absence here of any unequivocal expression of contrary legislative intent, we conclude that suits against the tribe under the ICRA are barred by its sovereign immunity from suit."[172]

The Court's holding that the tribe's sovereign immunity barred the suit is certainly in line with the established principles of tribal sovereignty. The Act obviously makes no expressed waiver of immunity and, without such a waiver, a barrier exists against any suit. The holding contradicts prior lower court cases which held that the Act could abrogate the tribe's immunity by mere implication.[173] It is interesting to note that Justice Rehnquist did not join in this part of the opinion,[174] which appears to be the crux of the case; whereas the only dissenter, Justice White, did.[175]

The Court then proceeded to the question of whether an officer of the Pueblo, also a petitioner-defendant in this case, was subject to claims for declaratory and injunctive relief. Allowing such an action would have provided plaintiffs with the remedy they sought, namely, placement on the tribal membership rolls. The Court did say that the officer could not seek the protection of the tribe's immunity.[176] The Court then framed the issue as whether the relief sought by the respondent was implied in the terms of the Act.

In addressing this contention, the Court indicated that one must bear in mind that providing a federal forum for the issues arising under section 1302 interferes with tribal government. This statement overlooks the safeguards that the federal courts established to promote settlement of disputes within the tribal framework. The doctrine of exhaustion promotes this goal by requiring a plaintiff to pursue all opportunities available within tribal government before proceeding to federal court.[177] In addition, the courts were reluctant to determine matters such as election disputes, which were more properly decided on the tribal level, except where the tribes refused to adopt proper methods for settlement of such disputes.[178] The requirement that the plaintiff allege sufficient facts to indicate a violation of rights under the Act

---

171. Santa Clara Pueblo v. Martinez 436 U.S. 49, 59 (1978).
172. *Id.*
173. *E.g.*, Daly v. United States, 483 F.2d 700 (8th Cir. 1973).
174. Santa Clara Pueblo v. Martinez, 436 U.S. 49, 51 n.4 (1978).
175. *Id.* at 73 n.2.
176. *Id.* at 59. The Court cited Payallup Tribe v. Washington Game Dep't, 433 U.S. 165 (1977); *see* text accompanying notes 25-27 *supra*, and *Ex Parte Young*, 209 U.S. 123 (1908), where it held that a federal court could enjoin state officials from enforcing state statutes which violated the federal constitution.
177. *See* text accompanying notes 121-31 *supra*.
178. *See* text accompanying notes 106-16 *supra*.

also kept cases more properly decided at the tribal level out of the federal courts.[179] The Supreme Court did not take note of the fact that the Act itself is a major intrusion into tribal affairs whether enforced by tribal or federal courts. The statement also fails to recognize the guidance that the federal courts could provide for tribal courts in these matters, in addition to serving as a safety valve in assuring that rights would not be ignored.

Continuing with its opinion, the Court set forth the factors that were to be used in determining whether a private action was implicit in the statute.[180] In discussing these factors, the majority opinion acknowledged the rule that a federal cause of action will be inferred to enforce federal rights, even when Congress spoke only in declarative terms. The Court discounted this rule's applicability to the Act, however, by viewing the legislative history of the Act as displaying a deliberate intent on the part of Congress to limit the remedies to habeas corpus.

Justice White's dissent dwelled longer on this point. He stated that jurisdiction under 28 U.S.C. § 1343(4) was proper because the Indian Civil Rights Act created federally protected rights which implied that they could be enforced through a civil rights action.[181] The existence of these statutory rights implied all necessary and appropriate remedies. Obviously, Justice White found this controlling.[182] One would have difficulty in finding a more appropriate situation for the application of this rule.

The majority's examination of the legislative history lends little support to its eventual finding of no jurisdiction. The majority found shelter in the fact that the provision of the Act that originally called for *de novo* review of criminal convictions obtained in tribal courts was modified to the now existing habeas corpus remedy. This consideration of a provision calling for review of criminal convictions is of little relevance in the determination of whether civil remedies were implied. In any event, only the degree of intrusion is modified.

The majority attempted to find similar significance in removal of a provision authorizing the Attorney General to investigate complaints relating to rights under the Act. The removal of this provision indicates a distrust of administrative involvement and the complications that would follow. In a court action, an individual would be required to press his own claim instead of having a federal agency carrying the burden.

---

179. *See* text accompanying notes 132-37 *supra*.

180. Santa Clara Pueblo v. Martinez, 436 U.S. 49, 60 n.10, 74, citing Court v. Ash, 422 U.S. 66 (1975): (1) whether the plaintiff is one of the class for whose benefit the statute was created (2) whether there is any indication of legislative intent to create or deny a remedy (3) whether the remedy is consistant with the underlying purpose of the Act (4) whether the action is one traditionally regulated by state (tribal) law.

181. Santa Clara Pueblo v. Martinez, 436 U.S. 49, 73 (1978) (White, J., dissenting).

182. *Id.* at 74, citing Sullivan v. Little Hunting Park, Inc., 396 U.S. 229, 239 (1969).

The majority appears to have overlooked the fact that the Act on its face implies additional remedies. The majority opinion states that Congress sought to protect and upgrade tribal self-government by the Act. This purpose is clear, but the goal of protecting individual rights from tribal oppression certainly was the dominant purpose of the Act. Small consolation is found in the majority's statement that tribal courts are available to vindicate rights created by the Act. This ignores both the legislative history of the Act and the political realities of tribal government. Overlooked is the fact that at the hearings on the Act it was discovered that almost half of the tribes operating with constitutions already had provisions protecting individual civil rights. This indicates that Congress felt the tribes were not enforcing the civil rights provisions of the tribal constitutions, otherwise mere amendment of tribal constitutions would have solved the problem. Also ignored were the shocking revelations the committee received about the quality of the tribal courts.[183] The dissent in *Santa Clara* points out that the tribe's legislative and judicial powers were vested in the same body, thus limiting a plaintiff to a hearing before the same body he claims is denying him his rights.[184] Unfortunately, this situation is far from unique. Ignored is the presence of the numerous cases previously mentioned in this article, and numerous others, where federal courts found a violation of protected rights and found that the tribal courts had denied the individual an adequate remedy. The majority couches its argument on the basis of maintaining tribal cultural identity and self-government. This does not recognize the extreme caution the federal courts had exercised in avoiding interference with tribal cultural interests, and the procedures established to promote tribal self-government.

THE AFTERMATH

In light of this decision, the only forum remaining for suits seeking declaratory and injunctive relief under the Act is the tribal courts. With the ongoing upgrading of these courts, one can hope that plaintiffs will now face a better situation than they did prior to the Act's passage. Of course the habeas corpus remedy remains available to persons "detained" by a tribe. Also, a few plaintiffs may be able to bring a suit for damages under 42 U.S.C. § 1985(3), in situations involving deprivations of voting rights.[185] Even though the Supreme Court did not mention 28 U.S.C. § 1331 in its opinion, it would seem that the reasoning applied to 28 U.S.C. § 1343(4) also would be applicable to this section and would deny federal court jurisdiction. In some situations, a tribe may want to waive its sovereign immunity and allow federal court jurisdiction.

---

183. Burnett, *supra* note 31, at 579.
184. Santa Clara Pueblo v. Martinez, 436 U.S. 49, 83 (1978).
185. 42 U.S.C. § 1985(3) (1974). In Means v. Wilson, 522 F.2d 833, 837 (8th Cir. 1975), the court found jurisdiction for a claim under this section.

Of course Congress could provide for an extension of remedies under the Act. The Supreme Court invited such action in the *Santa Clara Pueblo* opinion.[186]

One question that cannot begin to be explored within the limits of this article is the effect of the *Santa Clara* decision on judgments already rendered under the Act. Are these judgments void for lack of jurisdiction, and therefore face the possibility of being vacated?

Conclusion

The *Santa Clara* decision has all but destroyed any possible federal court protection of Indian political rights. It is immaterial now whether the oversight was on the part of the Supreme Court or of Congress. From an examination of the cases heard before the *Santa Clara* decision, it is obvious that some federal protection is necessary to safeguard the political rights enumerated in the Act. Federal legislation is needed to extend the remedies under the Act; otherwise, the Act will be left as "a mere unenforceable declaration of principles."[187]

Dennis R. Holmes

---

186.   As we have repeatedly emphasized, Congress' authority over Indian matters is extraordinarily broad, and the role of courts in adjusting relations between and among tribes and their members correspondingly restrained. . . . Congress retains authority expressly to authorize civil actions for injunctive or other relief to redress violations of § 1302, in the event that the tribes themselves prove deficient in applying and enforcing its substantive provisions. But unless and until Congress makes clear its intention to permit the additional intrusion on tribal sovereignty that adjudication of such actions in a federal forum would represent, we are constrained to find that § 1302 does not impliedly authorize actions for declaratory or injunctive relief against either the tribe or its officers.

Santa Clara Pueblo v. Martinez, 436 U.S. 49, 72 (1978) (citation omitted).
187.   Martinez v. Santa Clara Pueblo, 540 F.2d 1039, 1042 (10th Cir. 1976).

CONSTITUTIONAL LAW: EQUAL PROTECTION:
Martinez v. Santa Clara Pueblo[1]—SEXUAL EQUALITY UNDER THE INDIAN CIVIL RIGHTS ACT

Andra Pearldaughter *

Introduction

An assortment of laws, including constitutional provisions, treaties, statutes, judicial decisions, and administrative regulations, governs the relationship of Native Americans to the federal and state governments.[1] This body of law reflects the vacillation between two conflicting views of the proper role of Native Americans in the dominant culture—separatism or assimilation.[2] One line of cases, statutes, and administrative policies maintains that Native American groups are sovereign entities and as such should be permitted, if not encouraged, to preserve their separate cultural identities and should not be forced to merge with white society.[3] Although repeatedly acknowledged as sovereigns, the powers of Indian tribes have also consistently been limited under the rubric of their status as wards of the federal government.[4]

In contrast, the theory of assimilation espouses the integration of Native Americans, as other minorities, into the mainstream of life in the United States.[5] However, such integration would inevitably lead to the destruction of the cultural identities of Native Americans. Thus, Native Americans are put to a choice between cultural extinction through integration and a special relationship

*J.D., 1977, Golden Gate University School of Law.

The author wishes to acknowledge the assistance of Nancy C. Carter, Librarian, in the preparation of this note.

1. *See generally* F. COHEN, FEDERAL INDIAN LAW (1942), for an overview of the statutes, treaties, federal court cases, Department of the Interior rulings, and Attorney General opinions relevant to the legal status of Native Americans in white society.

2. *See* Burnett, *An Historical Analysis of the 1968 'Indian Civil Rights' Act,* 9 HARV. J. LEG. 557 (1972), for a comprehensive discussion of the history of Indian tribal sovereignty which sets forth in detail the vacillation in national policy between assimilation and separatism. *Id.* at 558-74. *See also* 21 STAN. L. REV. 1236, 1237-40 (1969), for a brief discussion of these themes.

3. *See, e.g.,* United States v. United States Fidelity Co., 309 U.S. 506, 512 (1940); Talton v. Mayes, 162 U.S. 376 (1896); Worcester v. Georgia, 31 U.S. (6 Pet.) 515 (1832); Cherokee Nation v. Georgia, 30 U.S. (5 Pet.) 1 (1831).

4. *See* United States v. Kagama, 118 U.S. 375 (1886); Cherokee Nation v. Georgia, 31 U.S. (6 Pet.) 515 (1831).

5. *See* Indian General Allotment Act of 1887, Act of Feb. 8, 1887, ch. 119, 24 Stat. 388; Indian Citizenship Act, 8 U.S.C. § 3(c) *amended* 8 U.S.C. § 1401(a)(2) (1970); Pub. L. 93-280, Act of Aug. 15, 1953, 67 Stat. 588, *as amended* 18 U.S.C. § 1162 (1970) and 28 U.S.C. § 1360 (1970).

with the federal government which buffers the effects of white society but which also impinges on native self-government.[6]

The most recent major federal legislation concerning Native Americans, the Indian Civil Rights Act,[7] reflects a compromise between the assimilative and separatist approaches.[8] Congress, exercising its plenary authority over Native Americans, imposed on tribal governments specific restraints taken almost verbatim from the Bill of Rights.[9] Thus, Congress attempted to further the assimilation of Native Americans by the extension of many individual rights to tribal members that have long been guaranteed to all other American citizens. Omitted out of deference to cultural differences were the first amendment requirement of nonestablishment of religion and the fifteenth amendment prohibition of racial classification in voting.

The rights accorded Native Americans in their relations with federal and state governments are the same as those of any

6. *See* E. CAHN, OUR BROTHER'S KEEPER: THE INDIAN IN WHITE AMERICA 14 (1969), for a discussion of this dilemma.

7. Act of Apr. 11, 1968, Pub. L. No. 90-284, tit. II, 82 Stat. 77, *codified at* 25 U.S.C. §§ 1301-1303 (1970).

8. *See generally* Burnett, *supra* note 2, at 574-614, 617, for a thorough treatment of the differing philosophies of supporters and opponents of the Indian Civil Rights Act and the legislative compromises resulting from these conflicts. *See also* Note, *The Indian Bill of Rights and the Constitutional Status* of Tribal Governments, 82 HARV. L. REV. 1343 (1969) [hereinafter cited as Note, *Constitutional Status*]. The congressional attitude toward assimilation is specifically discussed. *Id.* at 1359-60.

9. 25 U.S.C. § 1302 (1970), which sets forth the individual rights guaranteed by the Act, provides: "§ 1302 Constitutional rights.

"No Indian tribe in exercising powers of self-government shall—

"(1) make or enforce any law prohibiting the free exercise of religion, or abridging the freedom of speech, or of the press, or the right of the people peaceably to assemble and to petition for a redress of grievances;

" (2) violate the right of the people to be secure in their persons, houses, papers, and effects against unreasonable search and seizures, nor issue warrants, but upon probable cause, supported by oath or affirmation, and particularly describing the place to be searched and the person or thing to be seized;

"(3) subject any person for the same offense to be twice put in jeopardy;

"(4) compel any person in any criminal case to be a witness against himself;

"(5) take any private property for a public use without just compensation;

"(6) deny to any person in a criminal proceeding the right to a speedy and public trial, to be informed of the nature and cause of the accusation, to be confronted with the witnesses against him, to have compulsory process for obtaining witnesses in his favor, and at his own expense to have the assistance of counsel for his defense;

"(7) require excessive bail, impose excessive fines, inflict cruel and unusual punishments, and in no event impose for conviction of any one offense any penalty or punishment greater than imprisonment for a term of six months or a fine of $500, or both;

"(8) deny to any person within its jurisdiction the equal protection of its laws or deprive any person of liberty or property without due process of law;

"(9) pass any bill of attainder or ex post facto law; or

"(10) deny to any person accused of an offense punishable by imprisonment the right, upon request, to a trial by jury of not less than six persons. (Pub. L. 90-284, title II, § 202, Apr. 11, 1968, 82 Stat. 77)"

188

American citizen.[10] However, prior to the enactment of the Indian Civil Rights Act, the federal judicial doctrine of constitutional immunity had exempted tribal governments from constitutional restraints in their exercise of power over tribal members.[11] Consequently, most tribal governments had not extended certain individual rights to tribal members.[12] This was partially due to the lack of the necessary finances and education.[13] Another significant factor, though, was the abiding concept of separate ethnic communities which had as an important goal the retention of cultures developed in a context entirely different from that of Anglo-American constitutional history.[14]

10. *See, e.g.,* Harrison v. Laveen, 67 Ariz. 337, 196 P.2d 456 (1948); Montoya v. Bolack, 70 N.M. 196, 372 P.2d 387 (1962). United States citizenship was granted to Native Americans by an Act of June 2, 1924, ch. 233, 43 Stat. 253.

11. *See* Note, *Constitutional Status, supra* note 8, at 1346-53. The author discusses the history of the constitutional immunity doctrine and the impact of the Indian Civil Rights Act on it.

12. *See, e.g.,* Talton v. Mayes, 163 U.S. 376 (1896) (sixth amendment right to grand jury); Native American Church v. Navajo Tribal Council, 272 F.2d 131 (10th Cir. 1959) (first amendment freedom of religion); Barta v. Oglala Sioux Tribe, 259 F.2d 553 (8th Cir. 1958) (fifth amendment due process); Glover v. United States, 219 F. Supp. 19 (D. Mont. 1963) (sixth amendment right to counsel). This situation was viewed as offensive by many Anglo-Americans. However, some commentators deplore the extent to which the Indian Civil Rights Act will undermine the autonomy of the Indian tribes. They argue the effect will be to usurp yet another area from tha already limited jurisdiction of the tribal courts and make the federal courts the final arbiter. *See, e.g.,* Note, *Equitable and Declaratory Relief Under the Indian Civil Rights Act,* 48 N.D.L. REV. 695 (1972). The authors of this note direct their attention to the availability of equitable and declaratory relief under the Indian Civil Rights Act, and suggest possible ways to minimize its undermining impact on tribal autonomy. *See also* Ziontz, *In Defense of Tribal Sovereignty: An Analysis of Judicial Error in Construction of the Indian Civil Rights Act,* 20 S.D.L. REV. 1 (1975); Note, *An Analysis of the Indian Bill of Rights,* 33 MONT. L. REV. 255 (1972), which also takes the position that the Indian Civil Rights Act is a blatant imposition of white values on Native American culture, destructive of tribal sovereignty and self-government.

But see, de Raismes, *The Indian Civil Rights Act of 1968 and the Pursuit of Responsible Tribal Self-Government,* 20 S.D.L. REV. 59 (1975); Note, *Tribal Injustice: The Red Lake Court of Indian Offenses,* 48 N.D.L. REV. 639 (1972) [hereinafter cited as Note, *Tribal Injustice*]. The author argues forcefully for application of the Indian Civil Rights Act because of the inadequacies of the tribal court system. These inadequacies include the selection of judges as part of a spoils system, the courts' lack of independence from the Bureau of Indian Affairs, and the partiality engendered by tribal politics. The author notes that, ironically, this system is now defended by many as a preserver of tradition although it was originally designed to eradicate the historic way of life of the Native American people. He attacks the tribal sovereignty argument by observing that all tribal legislation must be approved by the Bureau of Indian Affairs and that no tribe could long exist without federal aid. He concludes that the tribal court he is considering could comply with the Indian Civil Rights Act without diminishing the present state of that tribe's sovereignty.

13. *See* Commission on the Rights, Liberties, & Responsibilities of the American Indian, THE INDIAN: AMERICA'S UNFINISHED BUSINESS 37 (W. Brophy & S. Aberle eds. 1966); Burnett, *supra* note 2, at 581; Note, *The Constitutional Rights of the American Indian,* 51 VA. L. REV. 121, 138 (1965).

14. *See* Note, *Constitutional Status, supra* note 8, at 1344.

189

Conflicts have inevitably arisen as the preservation of native cultural integrity and the promotion of Anglo-American constitutional ideals have been considered by the courts. Illustrative of this conflict is the case of *Martinez v. Santa Clara Pueblo*.[15] The *Martinez* Court considered a question of first impression: whether an ordinance differentiating between the rights of tribal members on the basis of sex was violative of the equal protection clause of the Indian Civil Rights Act.[16]

Facts of Martinez

Plaintiffs Julia Martinez and her daughter Audrey Martinez brought suit on behalf of themselves and others similarly situated, to challenge the membership ordinance of the Santa Clara Pueblo in New Mexico. The ordinance granted membership to all children

15. 98 S.Ct. 1670 (1978).

16. This is the first time that discrimination on the basis of sex by an Indian tribe has been considered. However, membership ordinances have previously been attacked for reasons other than sex discrimination.

In Laramie v. Nicholson, 487 F.2d 315 (9th Cir. 1973), the plaintiffs were children whose mothers were members of the Colville Confederated Tribe. The children were refused enrollment in the tribe solely because they had been previously enrolled as members of another tribe. The children met all other requirements for membership. The plaintiffs also alleged that others with the same supposed disqualification were allowed to enroll as members of the tribe. The trial court found no jurisdiction under the Indian Civil Rights Act, but the appellate court reversed and remanded for further proceedings. *Id.* at 316. The United States Supreme Court denied certiorari to Laramie in Tonasket v. Thompson, 419 U.S. 871 (1974). Evidently, *Laramie* was consolidated with *Tonasket*, a case which presented the same issue and was decided by the same Ninth Circuit panel.

The plaintiffs in Slattery v. Arapahoe Tribal Council, 453 F.2d 278 (10th Cir. 1971), alleged the discriminatory application of a membership ordinance requiring one-quarter degree Indian blood. The court found that the plaintiffs could not invoke the Indian Civil Rights Act where the pleadings showed that the tribal council had acted in accord with the ordinance, which was not itself under attack. Thus, no jurisdiction existed under which the court could consider the claim. *Id.* at 282.

The case of Yellow Bird v. Oglala Sioux Tribe, 380 F. Supp. 438 (D.S.D. 1974), also involved an equal protection challenge to a tribal membership provision. In that case, the court granted defendants' motion to dismiss, holding that it lacked subject matter jurisdiction over the case. The plaintiffs sought to run as candidates for tribal office in the Oglala primary election. The Oglala Sioux tribal election board refused to place their names on the ballot, evidently on the grounds that the plaintiffs were barred from tribal membership by a tribal constitutional provision which restricted membership to children born to tribal members who were residents of the reservation at the time of the child's birth.

The court found that absent allegations that membership provisions were not uniformly applied, such provisions were not subject to the equal protection requirements of the Indian Civil Rights Act. Thus, the court dismissed the suit for lack of subject matter jurisdiction under the Act. *Id.* at 440-41.

See also Note, *Equal Protection Under the Indian Civil Rights Act: Martinez v. Santa Clara Pueblo*, 90 HARV. L. REV. 627 (1977). The author of this note considers *Martinez* from the perspective of another membership ordinance case requiring the resolution of cultural autonomy with application of the Indian Civil Rights Act. However, he does not consider seriously the philosophical problems raised by the conflict between invidious discrimination and cultural autonomy.

190

born of marriages between male members of the Pueblo and non-members, while denying membership to all children born of marriages between female members of the Pueblo and nonmembers.[17] The primary motivation for passage of the ordinance in 1939 was the fear of the economic consequences of a marked increase in the Pueblo's population caused by a sharp rise in intermarriage.[18] Prior to its enactment, membership in the Pueblo for children of mixed marriages had been determined on an individual basis.[19]

Plaintiff Julia Martinez, whose parents were Santa Clarans, is a member of the Pueblo. Her husband is a fullblood Navajo and is not a member of the Pueblo.[20] Their eight living children, including plaintiff Audrey Martinez, are, as a result of the ordinance, barred from membership in the Pueblo. The Martinezes have lived at the Pueblo continuously since their marriage in 1941. All of the Martinez children were reared at the Pueblo; all speak Tewa, the traditional and official language of the Pueblo; all are allowed to practice the traditional religion. Culturally, the Martinez children are an integral part of the Pueblo.[21] Since 1946, Mrs. Martinez has attempted to enroll her children in the Pueblo through all procedures available under the Pueblo government.[22] When she exhausted the tribal remedies, she and her daughter filed suit in the federal district court in New Mexico.

Plaintiffs alleged that the ordinance deprived nonmember children of various rights, including residence at the Pueblo as a

17. Martinez v. Santa Clara Pueblo, 540 F.2d 1039, 1040 -41 (10th Cir. 1976), rev'd; 98 S.Ct. 1670 (1978). The ordinance is as follows: "Be it ordained by the Council of the Pueblo of Santa Clara, New Mexico, in regular meeting duly assembled, that hereafter the following rules shall govern the admission to membership to the Santa Clara Pueblo:
1. All children born of marriages between members of the Santa Clara Pueblo shall be members of the Santa Clara Pueblo.
2. All children born of marriages between male members of the Santa Clara Pueblo and non-members shall be members of the Santa Clara Pueblo.
3. Children born of marriages between female members of the Santa Clara Pueblo and non-members shall not be members of the Santa Clara Pueblo.
4. Persons shall not be naturalized as members of the Santa Clara Pueblo under any circumstances." Appellants are attacking sub-paragraphs 2 and 3 of the ordinance.
18. Martinez v. Santa Clara Pueblo, 540 F.2d 1039, 1040 (10th Cir. 1976), rev'd, 98 S.Ct. 1670 (1978).
19. Id.
20. Martinez's marriage to a Native American, although a member of a different tribe, may seem less serious than marriage to a non-Indian. However, this is significant only from an Anglo-American view of pan-Indianism, which is not a pervasive Native American notion. See generally H. HERTZBERG, THE SEARCH FOR AN AMERICAN INDIAN IDENTITY 1-12 (1971), for a discussion of the attempts to organize pan-Indian movements, the need for such a cohesive political response, and the diversity of Native American cultures causing such attempts to fail.
21. Martinez v. Santa Clara Pueblo, 540 F.2d 1039, 1041 (10th Cir.·1976).
22. Id.

191

matter of right; political rights such as voting, holding secular office, and bringing matters before the Pueblo Council; and sharing in the material benefits of Pueblo membership by using the land and hunting and fishing.[23] Plaintiffs also contended the ordinance prevented Mrs. Martinez from passing her possessory interest in Pueblo property to her children.[24]

Decision of the District Court

The trial court found that under the Indian Civil Rights Act it had jurisdiction over the plaintiffs' claims.[25] Moreover, it held that the ordinance did not violate the Indian Civil Rights Act.[26] The court based this conclusion on its holding that the equal protection provision of the Indian Civil Rights Act was not coextensive with the constitutional guarantee of equal protection. "[T]he Act and its equal protection guarantee must be read against the background of tribal sovereignty and interpreted within the context of tribal laws and customs."[27] Accordingly, it reasoned that courts should not invalidate tribal membership ordinances which use classifications based on criteria traditionally employed by the tribe in considering membership questions, even though such classifications might be unacceptable under constitutional standards.[28]

Judge Mechem treated the patrilineal and patrilocal traditions of the Pueblo as indications of a cultural tradition which made acceptable the male-female distinctions in classifying children of mixed marriages as members or nonmembers.[29] He also recognized the Pueblo's economic and cultural interests in membership policies generally and in the 1939 ordinance specifically.[30] If the Pueblo's ability to define Santa Clara membership "is limited or restricted by an external authority, then a new definition of what it is to be a Santa Claran is imposed, and the culture of Santa Clara is inevitably changed."[31] Additionally, he noted the interrelation of the

23. *Id.*
24. *Id.*
25. Martinez v. Santa Clara Pueblo, 402 F. Supp. 5 (D.NM. 1975). The Tenth Circuit had not ruled on the issue of jurisdiction under the Indian Civil Rights Act at that time. The district court discussed the relevant authorities at length in concluding jurisdiction existed. *Id.* at 7-11.
26. *Id.* at 18.
27. *Id.* at 17, *citing* Crowe v. Eastern Band of Cherokee Indians, 506 F.2d 1231 (4th Cir. 1974); Means v. Russell, 383 F. Supp. 378 (D.S.D. 1974).
28. Martinez v. Santa Clara Pueblo, 402 F. Supp. 5, 18 (D.N.M. 1975).
29. *Id.* at 16.
30. *Id.* at 15, 16.
31. *Id.* at 15.

192

economic and cultural interests, pointing out that economic survival is a prerequisite to maintaining cultural autonomy and identity.

Decision of the Appellate Court

Writing for the Tenth Circuit, Judge Doyle reversed the district court's decision.[32] The *Martinez* panel considered three issues in its analysis: (1) sovereign immunity and jurisdiction; (2) the test for violations of equal protection under the Act; and (3) whether the ordinance survived the equal protection challenge.

The court held that federal jurisdiction existed and that to the extent the Indian Civil Rights Act applied, tribal immunity was thereby limited.[33] The Act was designed to provide protection against tribal authority[34] and therefore a congressional intent to allow suits against the tribe was essential to the goal of protection. To hold otherwise would reduce the Act to a mere unenforceable declaration of principles.

The *Martinez* panel held that a balancing test which weighs the

32. Martinez v. Santa Clara Pueblo, 540 F.2d 1039, 1048 (10th Cir. 1976).

33. *Id.* at 1042. The *Martinez* panel upheld jurisdiction and found that sovereign immunity was waived, almost without discussion, on the basis of its decision in Dry Creek Lodge, Inc. v. United States, 515 F.2d 926 (10th Cir. 1975). *Dry Creek Lodge* was decided a few weeks prior to the district court's decision in *Martinez* (June 25, 1975).

In *Dry Creek Lodge*, the court notes that the general issue of jurisdiction under the Indian Civil Rights Act had been before the Tenth Circuit on three occasions. However, those courts never reached the present issue. (515 F.2d 926, 933 (10th Cir. 1975)). In McCurdy v. Steele, 506 F.2d 653, 656 (10th Cir. 1974), the court refrained from ruling on jurisdiction under Section 1302 because the plaintiffs had not exhausted tribal remedies. The complaint in Slattery v. Arapahoe Tribal Council, 453 F.2d 278, 281-82 (10th Cir. 1971), failed to disclose a denial of due process or equal protection. Thus, since the Indian Civil Rights Act was not brought into play, the court found there was no jurisdiction. In Groundhog v. Keeler, 442 F.2d 674 (10th Cir. 1971), plaintiffs challenged the statutory provision for the appointment of a tribal chief by the Secretary of the Interior. The *Groundhog* court found there was no jurisdiction because the complaint was so lacking in substance and so contrary to well-established law enunciating the power of Congress to legislate concerning Native American affairs as to afford no substantial basis for a claim of federal jurisdiction. *Id.* at 678. The *Dry Creek Lodge* panel then turned to the opinions of other circuits from which it concluded jurisdiction existed under the Indian Civil Rights Act, in conjunction with 42 U.S.C. § 1343. 515 F.2d 926, 933 n.6 (10th Cir. 1975).

In considering the issue of sovereign immunity, the *Dry Creek Lodge* court summarily held the Indian Civil Rights Act functioned as a waiver by Congress of any immunity. *Id.* at 934 n.9, *citing* Brown v. United States, 486 F.2d 658 (8th Cir. 1973); Johnson v. Lower Elwha Tribal Community, 484 F.2d 200 (9th Cir. 1973); Daly v. United States, 483 F.2d 700 (8th Cir. 1973); Loncaission v. Leekity, 334 F. Supp. 370 (D.N.M. 1971); Seneca Constitutional Rights Organization v. George, 348 F. Supp. 48 (W.D.N.Y. 1972); McCurdy v. Steele, 353 F. Supp. 629 (D. Utah 1973). The *Martinez* panel adopted this position, relying on *Dry Creek Lodge*. Even though the circuit court considered the issue of sovereign immunity, it was not mentioned in the district court opinion.

34. Martinez v. Santa Clara Pueblo, 540 F.2d 1039, 1042 (10th Cir. 1976).

193

tribal interest against the individual's right to fair treatment under the law is appropriate under the equal protection provision of the Indian Civil Rights Act.[35] Using this test, Judge Doyle applied a compelling interest standard and found the Pueblo's interest in the ordinance not to be compelling.[36]

In determining the appropriate test, the *Martinez* court considered the legislative history of the Indian Civil Rights Act, as well as case law.[37] The Act emerged from a series of congressional bills designed to safeguard Native Americans' constitutional rights. One bill, S. 961,[38] provided that an Indian tribe, in exercising its powers of local self-government, was subject to the same limitations and restraints as those imposed on federal and state governments by the Constitution. Senator Sam Ervin, sponsor of S. 961, stated that the bill was intended to guarantee to individual Indians the same rights that other American citizens had under the Constitution.[39] It was pointed out by other supporters that off-reservation Native Americans enjoyed the same rights as other American citizens, but on the reservation their rights depended upon the benevolence of tribal governments.[40] The comprehensive extension of rights was rejected, however, when further consideration indicated that this approach could undermine tribal structure. For example, giving equality in voting rights might conflict with the recognized power of the tribes to set blood quantum requirements for membership and voting.[41] Also, the first amendment nonestablishment clause would have endangered the continued existence of Pueblo theocracies.[42] While problems were seen in extending some constitutional guarantees, none were suggested with respect to equal protection. In fact, it was frequently characterized as a basic or fundamental right among the guarantees.[43]

35. *Id.* at 1045.

36. *Id.* at 1047.

37. *See generally* Burnett, *supra* note 2, at 574 -614, for extensive commentary on the legislative history of the Indian Civil Rights Act. *See also* Ziontz, *supra* note 12, at 3-20; de Raismes, *supra* note 12, at 72-76; Reiblich, *Indian Rights Under the Civil Rights Act of 1968*, 10 ARIZ. L. REV. 617, 621-23 (1968).

38. *See* S. REP. No. 841, 90th Cong., 1st Sess. 5-6 (1967).

39. 113 CONG. REC. 35473 (1967).

40. *See, e.g., Hearings on Constitutional Rights of American Indians Before the Subcomm. on Constitutional Rights of the Senate Comm. on the Judiciary,* 87th Cong., 1st Sess., pt. 1 (1962), 87th Cong., 1st Sess., pt. 2 (1963), 87th Cong., 2d Sess., pt. 3 (1963), and 88th Cong., 1st Sess., pt. 4 (1964) 3, 8, 286, 447 [hereinafter cited as *1961-63 Hearings*]; *Hearings on S. 961-68 and S.J. Res. 40, Before the Subcomm. on Constitutional Rights of the Senate Comm. on the Judiciary,* 89th Cong., 1st Sess., 165, 221 (1965) [hereinafter cited as *1965 Hearings*].

41. *1965 Hearings, supra* note 40, at 65, 221.

42. *Id.*

43. *E.g., 1965 Hearings, supra* note 40, at 18, 61.

194

In the subcommittee on constitutional rights of the Senate Judiciary Committee, there were conflicting statements regarding the need to refrain from undermining tribal authority. The subcommittee members stated at hearings, in Committee reports, and in floor debates their intent to extend broad constitutional protections to individual Indians.[44] Yet, once cognizant of the negative consequences of a comprehensive extension of constitutional guarantees, the original bill was amended to delete the nonestablishment clause and the fifteenth amendment, as well as to specify the guarantees granted from the first amendment, the fourth through eighth amendments, and the equal protection clause of the fourteenth amendment.[45] In this amended form, S. 961 became the Indian Civil Rights Act of 1968.

From this investigation of the legislative history, the court concluded that congress had individually considered the various protections contained in the Bill of Rights. Those considered essential and workable were retained, while those deemed out of harmony with Native American culture were eliminated.[46] The legislative history contained some evidence that Congress had anticipated that in an evaluation such as *Martinez* the cultural autonomy and integrity of the tribes would be weighed.[47] However, the court perceived nothing in the legislative history that resembled a formula for resolution of these conflicting interests.[48]

The *Martinez* panel concluded that the only way to resolve a conflict between constitutional values and tribal traditions was to consider the scope, extent, and importance of the tribal interest. Against this, the individual's right to fair treatment under the law, in light of the clearness of the guarantee and the magnitude of the interest, both generally and as applied to the particular facts, was to be weighed.[49] Recognition of the specific constitutional guarantee, unless the value of the tribal custom or principle outweighed it, was thereby found to be compatible with congressional intent as manifested in the legislative proceedings.[50]

The court next considered case law concerning equal protection under the Indian Civil Rights Act. Many cases had concluded that

44. Martinez v. Santa Clara Pueblo, 540 F.2d 1039, 1044 (10th Cir. 1976).
45. S. 1843; passed unanimously, 113 CONG. REC. 35471-77 (1967).
46. Martinez v. Santa Clara Pueblo, 540 F.2d 1039, 1044 (10th Cir. 1976.) *See also* Burnett, *supra* note 2, at 574-604 and Note, *Constitutional Status, supra* note 8, at 1359-60.
47. *Id.* at 1045. *See also* Burnett, *supra* note 2, at 574-604 and Note, *Constitutional Status, supra* note 8, at 1360.
48. *Id.*
49. *Id.*
50. *Id.*

195

Congress did not intend the equal protection provision of the Indian Civil Rights Act to be coextensive with the constitutional guarantee. Cases challenging blood quantum requirements for tribal membership or office-holding exemplify this.[51] The court distinguished the blood quantum requirement cases as having "some semblance of basis for the classification," unlike the sex discrimination of the present case.[52] The Tenth Circuit also noted that other courts considering the equal protection provision of the Act invariably looked to the fourteenth amendment for guidance. The line of election requirement cases which dealt with age and residency requirements for voting and holding office, apportionment of tribal legislatures, and irregularities in the conduct of elections are illustrative.[53] The *Martinez* panel "conceded that under the fourteenth amendment the ordinance would clearly be invalid because of its classification scheme based solely on sex."[54] In con-

51. *See* Slattery v. Arapahoe Tribal Council, 453 F.2d 278 (10th Cir. 1971); Daly v. United States, 483 F.2d 700 (8th Cir. 1973).

52. Martinez v. Santa Clara Pueblo, 540 F.2d 1039, 1046 (10th Cir. 1976).

53. *See* Howlett v. Salish & Kootenai Tribes, 529 F.2d 233 (9th Cir. 1976) and Two Hawk v. Rosebud Sioux Tribe, 404 F. Supp. 1327 (D.S.D. 1975) (residency requirements); Means v. Russell, 522 F.2d 833 (8th Cir. 1975) (election irregularities); Wounded Head v. Tribal Council of Oglala Sioux Tribe, 507 F.2d 1079 (9th Cir. 1975) (age requirement); Daly v. United States, 478 F.2d 700 (8th Cir. 1973) and White Eagle v. One Feather, 478 F.2d 1311 (8th Cir. 1973) (reapportionment).

54. Martinez v. Santa Clara Pueblo, 540 F.2d 1039, 1046 (10th Cir. 1976). During the years of the Warren Court, a dual-level equal protection analysis evolved. Usually, the rational relationship standard was applied, which required merely that the classification be rationally related to a legitimate governmental objective. Almost any relationship alleged by the state was sufficient. *See, e.g.*, McGowan v. Maryland, 366 U.S. 420 (1961) (Sunday closing laws upheld). When a suspect classification or fundamental right was involved, however, a compelling state interest was required to sustain the classification. *See, e.g.*, Shapiro v. Thompson, 394 U.S. 618 (1969) (one-year residency requirement for welfare applicants struck down).

With the advent of the Burger Court, there was a shift in analysis. In seven cases during the 1971 Term, the Court found substantial bases for constitutional challenges even though the traditional rational relationship criteria were recited. *See, e.g.*, Reed v. Reed, 404 U.S. 71 (1971), and Eisenstadt v. Baird, 405 U.S. 438 (1972). Since then, the Burger Court has continued to find constitutional violations on old equal protection grounds. *See, e.g.*, Weinberger v. Weisenfeld, 420 U.S. 636 (1975). Gerald Gunther attempts to explicate this trend in *Foreword: In Search of Evolving Doctrine on a Changing Court: A Model for a Newer Equal Protection*, 86 HARV. L. REV. 1 (1972). Justice Marshall's concurrence in Department of Agriculture v. Murry, 413 U.S. 508 (1973), sheds some light on these developments. He sets forth a "sliding scale" theory of equal protection which considers the impact of the rule on the individual, the nature of the right involved, the invidiousness of the classification, the governmental interest at stake, and possible safeguards or less restrictive alternatives. Marshall notes this approach utilizes traditional elements from both due process and equal protection. Perhaps this explains the Court's reliance on Frontiero v. Richardson, 411 U.S. 677 (1973). Although a plurality of the Court in *Frontiero* held sex to be a suspect category, it is inaccurate, based on *Frontiero*, to say, without more, that a classification predicated solely on sex violates equal protection. The Court also refers the reader to Stanton v. Stanton, 421 U.S. 7 (1975), Weinberger v. Weisenfeld, and Reed v.

trast, the district court had not given cognizance to the sex discrimination issue.

Despite its conclusion that equal protection standards did not apply with full force, the Tenth Circuit discussed the facts of *Martinez* in light of whether the tribal interest was compelling. The court noted that the use of the membership classification was of relatively recent origin and, when applied, it caused incongruous and unreasonable results.[55] Rejecting as conclusory the district court's characterization of the Santa Clara culture, the appeals court deemed reliance on the supposed patrilineal and patrilocal nature of the Pueblo an inappropriate justification of the ordinance.[56] Additionally, the ordinance was found not to represent Santa Clara tradition. Prior to its passage, the children of Santa Clara women in mixed marriages were sometimes admitted to Pueblo membership.[57] The ordinance was actually the product of economic concerns which could have been addressed by other, nondiscriminatory solutions.[58]

Through this analysis, the court concluded that the ordinance was repugnant to the equal protection provision of the Indian Civil Rights Act. To have let the ordinance stand, as in disclaiming jurisdiction, would have rendered the Indian Civil Rights Act ineffectual except as an abstract statement of principle.[59]

Decision of the Supreme Court

The Supreme Court, in an opinion by Justice Marshall, reversed the decision of the appellate court, finding that the Indian Civil Rights Act neither expressly nor implicitly authorized civil actions for declaratory or injunctive relief to enforce its substantive provisions.[60] Justice White wrote a dissenting opinion.[61]

The Court first addressed the issue of the sovereign immunity of the tribe. Unlike the appellate court, which found that tribal immunity was limited to the extent that the substantive portions of

---

Reed, 404 U.S. 71 (1971). Each of these cases struck down classifications based solely on sex. The *Martinez* panel did not clearly set forth the level of scrutiny it used to invalidate the classification. Although it alluded to the need for a compelling interest, it also discussed the factors set forth by Marshall in *Murry*. Perhaps this is an example of the "newer" equal protection theorized by Gunther.

55. Martinez v. Santa Clara Pueblo, 540 F.2d 1039, 1047 (10th Cir. 1976).
56. *Id.*
57. *Id.*
58. *Id.*
59. *Id.* at 1048.
60. Martinez v. Santa Clara Pueblo, 98 S.Ct. 1670 (1978).
61. *Id.* at 1684.

197

the Act were applicable, Justice Marshall concluded that the doctrine of tribal sovereign immunity bars suits against the tribe absent an express waiver by Congress. Because the Indian Civil Rights Act contains no such waiver, the Court held that the federal courts had no jurisdiction to hear an action aginst the tribe pursuant to the Act.[62] Despite the lack of jurisdiction, the Court conceded that the Act had modified the substantive law applicable to the tribe.[63]

The Court then examined whether the Act impliedly authorized a private right of action against tribal officers for declaratory and injunctive relief. *Cort v. Ash*[64] stated the test for determining whether a private remedy is implicit in a statute not expressly providing one. The four relevant factors enumerated in *Cort* are the following: (1) whether the plaintiff is one of the class for whose benefit the statute was enacted; (2) whether there is an indication of the legislative intent to create or deny such a remedy; (3) whether it is consistent with the underlying purposes of the legislative scheme to imply a remedy; (4) whether the cause of action is one traditionally relegated to state [or tribal] law, in an area basically the concern of the states [or tribes], so that it would be inappropriate to infer a federal cause of action.[65]

The Court conceded that the plaintiff was a member of the class intended to be benefitted by the Act.[66] The Court next considered whether a private right of action would be consistent with the purposes of the Act. The majority found that Congress had pursued two goals in the Act: the strengthening of the position of individual tribal members *vis-a-vis* the tribal government, and the protecting and furthering of native self-government.[67] The Court believed the creation of a federal cause of action would undermine the latter goal by eroding the authority of the tribal courts and imposing serious financial burdens on the already financially disadvantaged tribes.[68] Thus, the omission of a private right of action was interpreted as Congress' method of balancing these two competing interests and implying a right of action would not be consistent with the goals of Congress.[69]

62. *Id.* at 1677, *relying on* United States v. Testan, 424 U.S. 392, 399 (1976).
63. 98 S.Ct. 1670, 1677 (1978).
64. Cort v. Ash, 422 U.S. 66 (1975).
65. *Id.* at 78.
66. Martinez v. Santa Clara Pueblo, 98 S.Ct. 1670, 1678 (1978).
67. *Id.* at 1679, 1680.
68. *Id.* at 1680, 1681. However, the Court seems to ignore that most individual Native Americans seeking enforcement of Section 1302 would be as financially disadvantaged as the tribe, if not more so.
69. *Id.* at 1681.

198

In contrast, Justice White believed there was no inconsistency. His dissent cites portions of the legislative history which he found to indicate Congress' concern, not only about Native Americans' lack of substantive rights, but also about the lack of remedies to enforce whatever rights she or he might have.[70]

In looking to the third relevant factor established in the *Cort* test, the Court further reviewed the legislative history of the Indian Civil Rights Act. Congress considered and rejected three different proposals for federal review in a civil context. The first proposal was *de novo* review by federal courts of criminal convictions by tribal courts. Instead, the habeas corpus provision of Section 1303 was adopted.[71] The second consisted of an administrative procedure whereby the Department of the Interior would review alleged civil violations of the Act and make referrals to the Attorney General for bringing suit.[72] The last proposal, offered as a substitute for the second, would have authorized adjudication of civil complaints by the Department of the Interior with review by the district courts.[73] The Court found that the rejection of these proposals indicated an intent to deny a private remedy.[74]

Justice White found the rejection of the first proposal to be of limited relevance to the civil context because it involved criminal convictions. Also, the habeas corpus remedy was adopted rather than the original because the *degree* of intrusion was less. He opined that the degree of intrusion permitted by a private cause of action in the civil context would be no greater than that of the habeas corpus remedy.[75]

The rejection of administrative review with initiation of suits by the Attorney General was not a persuasive indication to Justice White of a rejection of federal judicial review.[76] Moreover, testimony indicated that the focus of this suggestion was off-reservation violations by non-Indians, *e.g.*, illegal detention of reservation Indians by state and tribal officials; arbitrary decision making by the Bureau of Indian Affairs; and denial of various state welfare services to Native Americans living off the reservation. Two witnesses did express the fear of disruption of tribal governments by the suggested procedure, but many others ex-

---

70. *Id.* at 1686-90.
71. *Id.* at 1687.
72. *Id.*
73. *Id.*
74. *Id.* at 1683.
75. *Id.* at 1686.
76. *Id.*

199

pressed the view that the Attorney General already possessed the authority to bring suits.[77]

The last proposal had been made in tandem with a provision that allowed the appeal of criminal convictions in the tribal court to the Secretary of the Interior, who could affirm, modify, or reverse the tribal decision. Most of the discussion concerning this joint proposal centered on the review of criminal proceedings and consequently was of limited relevance to congressional views on civil remedies. Further, several witnesses expressed objections to appeals from judicial proceedings to the executive branch.[78] Justice White concluded these rejections were of limited significance because the proposals primarily involved criminal convictions and because . many objections to them, other than tribal autonomy, were raised.

Finally, the Court considered the appropriateness of a federal forum to vindicate the rights in question. The Court reasoned that tribal courts, which were recognized as appropriate forums for adjudicating disputes concerning both Native Americans and non-natives, were available for the enforcement of the substantive provisions of the Act.[79] Thus, contrary to the holding of the Tenth Circuit, a federal cause of action was not plainly required to give effect to the extension of constitutional norms to tribal governments.[80] Furthermore, the Court declared that Congress, in not exposing tribal officials to suit, "may have considered" that civil actions would frequently depend on questions of tribal traditions which tribal forums might be in a better position to evaluate.[81]

Justice White responded that it was both unrealistic and in contravention of Congress' intent to suggest that the tribal body which had allegedly violated an individual's rights was the appropriate forum for the adjudication of that alleged deprivation.[82] In closing, he noted that the majority had acknowledged the Court's frequent recognition of the propriety of inferring a federal cause of action for the enforcement of civil rights.[83]

Thus, after review of the legislative history, the majority found that Congress was committed to the goal of tribal self-determination and that creation of a federal cause of action would

77. *Id.* at 1687.
78. *Id.*
79. *Id.* at 1681.
80. *Id.* at 1680.
81. *Id.* at 1684.
82. *Id.* at 1689.
83. *Id.* at 1690.

200

not comport with this goal. Because tribal courts are available to adjudicate disputes arising under the Act, creation of a cause of action is not plainly required. The rejection of various proposed remedies indicated the belief of Congress that habeas corpus would protect the individual interests at stake while avoiding needless intrusion on tribal governments.

In contrast, the legislative history demonstrated to Justice White that Congress was as concerned with providing remedial relief as with changing the substantive law of the tribes. The relevance of the rejection of various proposals was very limited, particularly since most dealt with criminal convictions. Finally, reliance on tribal courts as forums was unrealistic due to their dual roles as legislative and judicial institutions, and such reliance was inconsistent with Congress' intent to extend constitutional protections.

Criticism of the Court's Decision

The enforcement of the Indian Civil Rights Act and the extension of federal constitutional protections to Native American citizens dictate some intervention of the dominant culture into the affairs of native cultures. As Justice White pointed out, "The extension of constitutional rights to individual citizens is *intended* to intrude upon the authority of government."[84] The majority seems unable to accept that such legislation must have as a basic presumption that the status of Native American tribes is little different from that of the states, or alternatively, Native American groups deserve no greater recognition than that given to other cultural groups such as the Amish.[85]

84. *Id.* at 1689 (emphasis in original).
85. Some commentators have argued that the position of Native Americans is analogous to that of the Amish people in Wisconsin v. Yoder, 406 U.S. 205 (1972). In *Yoder,* the Supreme Court upheld the right of Amish parents to be exempt from the Wisconsin compulsory education law under a first amendment "free exercise of religion" rationale. The Amish community does not enjoy the same long-standing recognition of sovereign status accorded to Native Americans. No treaty or other obligation exists between the United States or the state of Wisconsin and the Amish people, unlike the relationship between the United States and Native Americans. Also, religion and culture are either interdependent or equivalent for Native American tribes. Thus, an even stronger argument than that made by Amish parents could be made by Native Amercans that they have a right to a separate mode of life.

Even if the principle of *Yoder* were found to limit application of the Indian Civil Rights Act, Native Americans would bear a heavy burden in making out a free exercise claim. The showing necessary in *Yoder* to sustain such a claim included (1) the law in question gravely endangered or destroyed the free exercise of the religious beliefs; (2) a long history as an identifiable religious sect; (3) a long history as a successful and self-sufficient segment of American society; (4) a convincing demonstration of the sincerity of the religious beliefs; (5) a demonstration of the interrelationship between the religious belief and the mode of life; (6) a persuasive showing of the vital role the belief plays in the survival of the community; (7) a demonstration of the hazards presented by the enforcement of the statute in

201

Cultural autonomy is a legitimate goal. However, it is a complex and many-faceted problem which raises numerous questions. How does one define the culture that is being respected and preserved?[86] Does the culture to be protected consist only of those values traditionally held from a prior time? If so, from what time? Does cultural autonomy instead mean the right for a culture to evolve? Assuming that a culture is best defined internally, are all internal definitions inherently valid? Is cultural autonomy possible at all in today's world of increased interdependence? Is Native American culture now so adulterated by white influences that it makes no sense to speak of preserving it?[87] Are not the procedures and rules at issue, including those in *Martinez*, frequently those that have been adopted as concessions or adaptations to white society, rather than expressions of a separate culture?

The issue of cultural autonomy is further complicated by the ramifications of sovereignty. *Martinez* is merely another example of the ambivalent sentiments of the white courts, the white legislatures, and ultimately, the white people. Sovereignty may well be a bogus issue, for while the sovereignty of Native American peoples has been repeatedly upheld,[88] that same sovereignty has been curtailed under the euphemism of guardianship when expedient for white objectives.[89] Similarly, it has been manipulated to serve the goals of whites.[90]

Even assuming that native tribes possess more than the trappings of sovereignty, should any group, by virtue of sovereignty,

---

question; (8) a demonstration of the adequacy of the alternative mode of life; (9) a convincing showing that few other groups could qualify for the exemption. *See* Ziontz, *supra* note 12, at 53-56, for criticism of this possible application of *Yoder* as narrow and insensitive to tribal integrity. *But see* de Raismes, *supra* note 12, at 82-90, for a discussion supporting a *Yoder* analysis as an appropriate limit on the Indian Civil Rights Act.

86. Not only are there different cultural philosophies represented among tribes, but also there exist differences in perspective within a given tribe. *See* Burnett, *supra* note 2, at 574-602 for a narration of the variety of reactions by Indians to proposals for the Indian Civil Rights Act. There are specific allusions to Pueblo communities and their reactions. *Id.* at 601, 614-15.

87. *See* Bysiewicz & Van de Mark, *The Legal Status of the Dakota Indian Woman,* 3 AM. INDIAN L. REV. 255 (1975) for an example of such adulteration. The authors discuss in detail the negative impact of white culture upon the traditional status of Dakota women. *See also* the discussion in Burnett, *supra* note 2. at 657-59, concerning the white origins of the present tribal court system.

88. See note 3, *supra*, and accompanying text.

89. See note 4, *supra*, and accompanying text. *See also* Tee-Hit-Ton Indians v. United States, 348 U.S. 272, 290-91 (1955).

90. *See* Burnett, *supra* note 2, at 559-60, for a discussion of white creation and retention of native police forces and courts to set examples of acculturation and to undermine recalcitrant chieftains and councils.

be able to utilize cultural structures that destroy or limit the growth and potential of whole classes of human beings?

Examination of this question in the abstract presents an insoluble dilemma. The entities identified as destructive will vary depending upon who is doing the identifying. Realistically, all one can do in addressing these complex issues is to remain constantly aware of the tension between cultural values and the inherent biases each person possesses. In *Martinez*, such awareness is particularly difficult. No separate, recognized "women's culture" exists. Yet, the conflict must be viewed as involving differences in sexual values *as well as* differences in racial/ethnic values. Sexual values are not merely a function of racial/ethnic culture.

Conclusion

The federal court system has been less than totally successful in exercising a self-awareness of bias and a sensitivity to differences in sexual values.[91] The district court in its decision on the merits in *Martinez* seemed oblivious to this aspect of concern. One wonders whether the Supreme Court would have reached a different result in resolving the tension between racial/ethnic cultures had some interest more central to white *male* institutions been in conflict with the sovereignty and cultural autonomy of Native Americans.

On the other hand, the Tenth Circuit's decision illustrates a sensitive consideration of all the relevant values. The *Martinez* panel made a detailed analysis, identifying each party's interest.[92] The

---

91. *See, e.g.*, Geduldig v. Aiello, 417 U.S. 484 (1973) and Gilbert v. General Electric, 429 U.S. 125 (1976) (the Court found that discrimination in employment benefits based on pregnancy was not sex discrimination); Kahn v. Shevin, 416 U.S. 351 (1974) (Florida tax law giving exemption to widows but not widowers was not impermissible sex discrimination).

The Canadian government and Canadian Indians have faced the same problem of resolving the idea of cultural autonomy with individual rights. In *In re* Lavell, 38 D.L.R. 3d 481 (Sup. Ct. 1973), § 12(1)(b) of the Indian Act, CAN. REV. STAT. c. I-6 (1970) was challenged. This section provides that an Indian woman loses her status as an Indian if she marries a non-Indian. Plaintiffs contended this section violated the equal protection provision of the Canadian Bill of Rights. However, the Supreme Court rejected this argument, reasoning that equal protection referred only to nondiscriminatory application of the laws. This case is even more disturbing in its implications than many United States cases because the rule being upheld is not one promulgated by a tribal authority, but rather one legislated by the dominant culture. This indicates that sexism is recognized as the destructive force it is even to a lesser degree outside the United States. *See* Sanders, *Status of Indian Women on Marriage to Person Without Indian Status*, 38 SASKATCHEWAN L. REV. 243 (1974), and Note, *Civil Rights: Loss of Indian Status by Indian Woman Marrying Non-Indian under Indian Act (Can.)*, § 12(1)(b), 6 OTT. L. REV. 635 (1974), for differing views on the *Lavell* case.

92. Martinez v. Santa Clara Pueblo, 540 F.2d 1039, 1041-48 (10th Cir. 1976).

203

court then balanced these interests acknowledging the differences in sexual values as well as racial/ethnic values.[93]

Beyond intervention, the tribe itself must again critically examine the issues raised in *Martinez*. The district court found that, "To abrogate tribal decisions, particularly in the delicate area of membership, for whatever 'good' reasons, is to destroy cultural identity under the guise of saving it."[94] Likewise, the effect of the tribe's use of a sex-based criterion to exclude from membership those who would be culturally and racially identified as Santa Clarans, but for the sex of the Santa Claran parent, is to diminish its human resources under the guise of preserving them.

93. *Id.* at 1047. The *Martinez* panel did not clearly set forth the standard it used to balance these interests. It merely stated that under the fourteenth amendment the ordinance would clearly be invalid because of its classification scheme based solely on sex." *Id.* at 1046. Some insight into the *Martinez* panel's conclusion may be gained from a review of the development of the law by the Supreme Court concerning equal protection. See note 54, *supra*.

94. Martinez v. Santa Clara Pueblo, 402 F. Supp. 5, 18-19 (D.N.M. 1975).

204

After *Martinez*: Civil Rights Under Tribal Government

BY ALVIN J. ZIONTZ*

Santa Clara Pueblo v. Martinez,[1] decided last year, was the first Supreme Court review of the Indian Civil Rights Act of 1968 (ICRA).[2] The ICRA reflected a majoritarian view[3] that all Indian tribal governments must be required to respect the rights and liberties of persons coming under their authority.[4] While Indian tribes are not bound by the United States Constitution,[5] they are bound by acts of Congress, which have been held to have plenary authority over them.[6] Consequently, the ICRA which makes the constitutional guarantees of liberty and property binding on Indian tribes, has the effect of creating new rights against tribal governments. Strictly speaking, it is inaccurate to call them constitutional rights, since they derive from statute. The statute repeats the language of the Constitution, however, and covers most of the rights and liberties found there,[7] with some notable excep-

---

* Partner, Ziontz, Pirtle, Morisset, Ernstoff and Chestnut, Seattle, Washington. LIB., University of Chicago.

[1] 436 U.S. 49 (1978).

[2] 25 U.S.C. §§ 1301-1341 (1976). The discussion in this article concerning the ICRA is directed to § 1302 which codifies the protection of individual rights.

[3] *See,* Bishin, *Judicial Review in Democratic Theory,* 50 S. CAL. L. REV. 1099, 1102 (1977); Ratner, *Constitutions, Majoritarianism and Judicial Review: The Function of a Bill of Rights in Israel and the United States,* 26 AM. J. COMP. L. 373 (1978).

[4] Prior to the passage of the Indian Civil Rights Act, 117 tribes had provisions protecting civil rights in their tribal constitutions, while 130 tribes had no such provision. In addition, 188 tribes or bands were not organized under any form of tribal constitution. *See* Burnett, *An Historical Analysis of the 1968 Indian "Civil Rights"Act,* 9 HARV. J. LEGIS. 557, 579 (1972).

[5] Talton v. Mayes, 163 U.S. 376 (1896); Native American Church v. Navajo Tribal Council, 272 F.2d 131 (10th Cir. 1959).

[6] Cherokee Nation v. Hitchcock, 187 U.S. 294 (1902); Lone Wolf v. Hitchcock, 187 U.S. 294 (1902); Talton v. Mayes, 163 U.S. 376 (1896); United States v. Kagama, 118 U.S. 375 (1886); United States v. Holliday, 70 U.S. (3 Wall.) 407 (1866); Buster v. Wright, 135 F. 947 (8th Cir. 1905), *appeal dismissed,* 203 U.S. 599 (1906); *See also* Santa Clara Pueblo v. Martinez, 436 U.S. 49 (1978).

[7] 25 U.S.C. § 1302 (1976). Constitutional rights

tions. These exceptions were intended to avoid infringing upon the right of tribes to preserve their identity and cultural autonomy.[8]

With the exception of a narrow provision for habeas corpus review of detention,[9] the Act contains no reference to enforcement

---

No Indian tribe in exercising powers of self government shall—

(1) make or enforce any law prohibiting the free exercise of religion, or abridging the freedom of speech, or of the press, or the right of the people peaceably to assemble and to petition for a redress of grievances;

(2) violate the right of the people to be secure in their persons, houses, papers, and effects against unreasonable search and seizures, nor issue warrants, but upon probable cause, supported by oath or affirmation, and particularly describing the place to be searched and the person or thing to be seized;

(3) subject any person for the same offense to be twice put in jeopardy;

(4) compel any person in any criminal case to be a witness against himself;

(5) take any private property for a public use without just compensation;

(6) deny to any person in a criminal proceeding the right to a speedy and public trial, to be informed of the nature and cause of the accusation, to be confronted with the witnesses against him, to have compulsory process for obtaining witnesses in his favor, and at his own expense to have the assistance of counsel for his defense;

(7) require excessive bail, impose excessive fines, inflict cruel and unusual punishments, and in no event impose for conviction of any one offense any penalty or punishment greater than imprisonment for a term of six months or a fine of $500, or both;

(8) deny to any person within its jurisdiction the equal protection of its laws or deprive any person of liberty or property without due process of law;

(9) pass any bill of attainder or ex post facto law; or

(10) deny to any person accused of an offense punishable by imprisonment the right, upon request, to a trial by jury of not less than six persons.

[8] Section 1302 omits the establishment clause language of the first amendment in order to permit Indian theocratic governments; the 2nd and 3rd amendment provisions dealing with the right to bear arms and protection against quartering of soldiers; and the 5th amendment grand jury indictment provisions. In the statute, the 6th Amendment right-to-counsel clause provides that counsel is at the expense of defendant. Section 1302 further deletes the 7th amendment guaranty of jury trial in civil cases and authorizes a jury of only six members in criminal cases. Finally, the ICRA omits the 13th amendment proscription against involuntary servitude and the 15 amendment prohibition against abridgement of voting rights on account of race or color. The latter omission presumably enables tribes to restrict voting rights to their members.

[9] 25 U.S.C. § 1303 (1976).

procedures. Lower courts, however, had ruled that both federal question[10] and civil rights[11] jurisdiction existed. Furthermore, these courts implied a federal cause of action as necessary to enforce the ICRA[12] and deemed Indian tribes' sovereign immunity[13] waived by implication.[14] The consequence of the lower court interpretations was a decade of litigation against Indian tribal governments and their officers.[15] The Supreme Court, however, had declined review of ICRA cases[16] until its May 1978 decision in *Santa Clara Pueblo v. Martinez*.[17]

In its landmark *Martinez* decision, the Court held that, except for habeas corpus petitions, federal courts have no jurisdiction to hear ICRA cases.[18] The Court considered the absence of any provision in the Act granting a remedy against tribes or their officers fatal to claims brought under the Act.[19] Thus, the Court concluded that tribal governments themselves are the proper forums for deciding questions arising under the ICRA.[20] Seemingly,

---

[10] 28 U.S.C. § 1331(a) (1976).

[11] 28 U.S.C. § 1343(4) (1976).

[12] Bivens v. Six Unknown Named Agents of the Federal Bureau of Narcotics, 403 U.S. 388 (1971); Jones v. Mayer, 392 U.S. 409 (1968); Bell v. Hood, 71 F.Supp. 813 (S.D. Cal. 1947), *on remand from* 327 U.S. 678 (1946).

[13] Puayallup Tribe, Inc. v. Washington Department of Game, 433 U.S. 165 (1977); United States v. United States Fidelity & Guaranty Company, 309 U.S. 506 (1940); Turner v. United States, 248 U.S. 354 (1919).

[14] Dry Creek Lodge, Inc. v. United States, 515 F.2d 926 (10th Cir. 1975); Dailey v. U.S., 483 F.2d 700 (8th Cir. 1973); Johnson v. Lower Elwha Tribal Community of Lower Elwha Indian Reservation, 484 F.2d 200 (9th Cir. 1973); Slattery v. Arapahoe Tribal Council, 453 P.2d 278 (10th Cir. 1971); Loncassion v. Leekity, 334 F.Supp. 370 (D.N.M. 1971).

[15] Fifty-eight published decisions are annotated as of 1978. *See* cases collected in 25 U.S.C.A. § 1302 (West Cum. Supp. 1978).

[16] Means v. Wilson, 522 F.2d 833 (8th Cir. 1974), *cert. denied* 424 U.S. 958 (1975); United States ex rel. Cobell v. Cobell, 503 F.2d 790 (9th Cir. 1975), *cert. denied*, 421 U.S. 999 (1975); Thompson v. Tonasket, 487 F.2d 316 (9th Cir. 1973), *cert. denied*, 414 U.S. 871, 95 S.Ct. 132 (1974).

[17] 436 U.S. 49 (1978).

[18] *Id.* at 59. "Nothing on the face . . . of the ICRA purports to subject tribes to the jurisdiction of the federal courts in civil actions for injunctive or declaratory relief."

[19] As to the tribe, the court said, "In the absence here of any unequivocal expression of contrary legislative intent, we conclude that suits against the tribe under the ICRA are barred by its sovereign immunity from suit." *Id.* at 59. As to tribal officers, *see* the discussion *Id.* at 59-70.

[20] *Id.* at 65-66, 71-72. Williams v. Lee, 358 U.S. 217 (1958). United States v. Quiver, 241 U.S. 601 (1916); Jones v. Meehan, 175 U.S. 1 (1899); Roff v. Burney, 168 U.S. 218 (1897); United States v. Kagama, 118 U.S. 375 (1886). The opinion restates the familiar language of Worcester v. Georgia, 31 U.S. (6 Pet.) 515

Martinez was not only the first ICRA case decided by the high court, but with the exception of habeas corpus cases, it well may be the last.

This article first examines the *Martinez* decision and some of the consequnces of the absence of federal jurisdiction to enforce the substantive provisions of the ICRA. The article then addresses the ability of tribal courts to undertake responsibility as the primary enforcement mechanism for the ICRA. It particularly discusses the authority and practical ability of tribal courts to exercise judicial review over the actions of tribal councils.

Since much of the earlier litigation under the ICRA involved challenges to the actions of tribal councils, *Martinez* is likely to result in increased pressure on the tribal court system to adjuciate ICRA complaints against the councils. Judicial review of legislative actions, however, is outside the experience of most tribal courts. The article focuses, therefore, on the resultant political and practical consequences of the absence of the peculiarly American institution of judical review of legislative decisions within the Indian tradition. It considers the institution of judicial review from a non-American perspective and then takes a case study of an attempt by the Navajo courts to exercise judicial review in the face of opposition from the tribal council.

The last section of the article considers the potential threat to tribal autonomy arising from the possibility of congressional amendment to the ICRA to authorize federal judicial remedies. This may act as a spur to improving tribal response to the ICRA and several methods are suggested by which the tribes could deal more effectively with ICRA violations within the traditions and present structure of tribal government. Finally, the article examines the existing threat to tribal autonomy arising from the view of the Interior Department that *Martinez* mandates

---

(1832), that Indian tribes are 'distinct independent political communities retaining their original natural rights,' and goes on to recite the cases holding that Indian tribes retain the power of regulating their internal and social relations, making their own substantive laws in internal matters and enforcing that law in their own forums. United States v. Kagama, 118 U.S. 375 (1886); United States v. Wheeler, ____ U.S. ____, 98 S.Ct. 1079 (1978); Roff v. Burney, 168 U.S. 218 (1897); Jones v. Meehan, 175 U.S. 1 (1899); United States v. Quiver, 241 U.S. 602 (1916); Williams v. Lee, 358 U.S. 217 (1958). For some current views on the status of tribal sovereignty theory, *see* Mettler, *A Unified Theory of Indian Tribal Sovereignty*, 30 Hastings L. J. 89; Werhan, *The Sovereignty of Indian Tribes: A Reaffirmation and Strengthening in the 1970's*, 54 NOTRE DAME LAW. 5.

that it intervene in tribal government in order to fill what it perceives to be the jurisdictional void left by the decision. That claim is critically examined. The article concludes that the objectives of the ICRA can be attained without compromising tribal autonomy by federal intervention.

I. THE MARTINEZ DECISION

The holding of the Supreme Court in *Santa Clara Pueblo v. Martinez*[21] came as a surprise to many observers. Few expected the Court to invalidate ten years of decisionmaking by the lower federal courts.[22] The decision turned on the Court's reading of congressional intent underlying the ICRA: preservation of individual rights within tribal government.[23] The case is, therefore, a major restatement of the vitality of tribal sovereignty.

In *Martinez* the Santa Clara Pueblo petitioned from a Tenth Circuit decision holding the Pueblo's membership ordinance violated the ICRA's equal protection guaranty. The Pueblo raised fundamental jurisdictional questions by motion to dismiss, which were denied by the district court[24] and the Tenth Circuit.[25] The lower courts then decided the case on the merits.[26]

When the Supreme Court granted certiorari in *Martinez*,[27] most observers focused their attention on the equal protection issue. The question was whether a tribal ordinance which admitted into membership the offspring of male members who married outside the Pueblo, while denying membership to offspring of female members who married outside the Pueblo could stand under the ICRA.[28] The question was intriguing because the validity of tribal classifications which discriminate between the sexes on the basis of traditional values and beliefs was at issue.

In the Supreme Court, however, the Pueblo not only defended the legality of its ordinance, but also renewed its jurisdictional challenge. The ICRA, it asserted, vested no jurisdiction in federal courts except for writs of habeas corpus. The Pueblo argued further that the Act created no federal cause of action and did not

---

[21] 436 U.S. 49 (1978).

[22] *See generally,* cases collected in 25 U.S.C.A. § 1302 (West Cum. Supp. 1978).

[23] Santa Clara Pueblo v. Martinez, 436 U.S. 49, 58-72 (1978).

[24] Martinez v. Santa Clara Pueblo, 402 F.Supp. 5 (D. N.M. 1975).

[25] Martinez v. Santa Clara Pueblo, 540 F.2d 1039 (10th Cir. 1976).

[26] Martinez v. Santa Clara Pueblo, 402 F.Supp. 5 (D. N.M. 1975); Martinez v. Santa Clara Pueblo, 540 F.2d 1039 (10th Cir. 1976).

[27] Santa Clara Pueblo v. Martinez, 431 U.S. 913 (1977).

[28] Santa Clara Pueblo v. Martinez, 436 U.S. 49, 51-52 (1978).

waive tribal immunity from suit.[29] While these claims had been made in earlier cases under the ICRA, they had been uniformly denied.[30] These holdings had provoked some critical comment,[31] but most observers felt that these issues were clearly settled. Given the unanimity of four circuits on this issue,[32] most felt the Supreme Court was not likely to upset the jurisdictional apple cart. In a 7 to 1 decision, however, the Court ruled that the ICRA did not give federal courts jurisdiction over Indian tribes or their officers, except for the narrow remedy of habeas corpus to test the legality of detention.[33]

Justice Marshall, speaking for the Court, first considered the question of whether the ICRA waived tribal immunity from suit.[34] Despite the fact that four circuits had found waiver by implication, Justice Marshall disagreed and ruled that waiver of sovereign immunity cannot be implied. Intent to waive immunity must be "unequivocally expressed."[35] Since there is nothing in the Act expressing waiver, the tribe remained immune from suit.[36]

Justice Marshall analyzed the issue of tribal officers' liability under the ICRA differently, however, since tribal officers do not enjoy absolute immunity from suit.[37] The analysis dealt not with

---

[29] *Id.*

[30] Luxon v. Rosebud Sioux Tribe, 337 F.Supp. 243 (D. S.D. 1971), 455 F.2d 698 (8th Cir. 1974); Loncassion v. Leekity, 334 F. Supp. 370 (D.N.M. 1971); Solomon v. La Rosa, 335 F. Supp. 715 (D. Neb. 1971); Spotted Eagle v. Blackfeet Tribe, 301 F.Supp. 85 (D. Mont. 1969); Dodge v. Nakai, 298 F.Supp. 17, 26 (D. Ariz. 1968).

[31] Ziontz, *In Defense of Tribal Sovereignty: An Analysis of Judicial Error in Constructon of the Indian Civil Rights Act,* 20 S.D.L.Rev. 1 (1975); Note, *Implication of Civil Remedies Under The Indian Civil Rights Act,* 75 Mich. L. Rev. 210 (1976).

[32] Dry Creek Lodge, Inc. v. United States, 515 F.2d 926 (10th Cir. 1975); Crowe v. Eastern Band of Cherokee Indians, Inc., 506 F.2d 1231 (4th Cir. 1974); Johnson v. Lower Elwha Tribal Community, 484 F.2d 200 (9th Cir. 1973); Luxon v. Rosebud Sioux Tribe, 337 F.Supp. 243 (D. S.D. 1971) *aff'd,* 455 F.2d 698 (8th Cir. 1972) *supra,* n.4.

[33] Santa Clara Pueblo v. Martinez, 436 U.S. 49, 72 (1978).

[34] *Id.* at 58-59.

[35] *Id.,* citing United States v. Testan, 424 U.S. 392 (1976).

[36] Santa Clara Pueblo v. Martinez, 436 U.S. 49, 59 (1978).

[37] *Id.* The Court's flat statement that one of the officers of the Pueblo was "not protected by the Tribe's immunity from suit" must be understood to mean that the officer does not have the absolute immunity of the Tribe. His immunity may be lost, for purposes of constitutional challenge, under the doctrine that an official who acts unconstitutionally is "stripped of his official character." *Id.* at 59, *citing* Ex Parte Young, 209 U.S. 123 (1908). However, Justice Marshall's citation of *Puyallup Tribe, Inc. v. Washington Department of Game,* 433 U.S.

whether the Act waived immunity, but rather with whether it implied a cause of action against tribal officials. The lower courts had overcome that obstacle by implying a cause of action.[38] But the Supreme Court, concerned over the interference with tribal autonomy which such an implication would create, turned to the legislative history of the ICRA to determine whether there was congressional intent to either create or deny a remedy.[39]

The Court, in analyzing the ICRA's legislative history found two separate but competing purposes for the ICRA: to impose protections for individual members of the tribes and to further Indian tribal self-government.[40] While implying a cause of action might further the former purpose, it would disserve the latter. The Court observed, for example, that implication of a remedy would impose serious financial burdens on already financially disadvantaged tribes.[41] Furthermore, citing, *Fisher v. District Court,*[42] the Court pointed out that resolution of a dispute arising on the reservation, affecting reservation Indians in a non-tribal forum might undermine the authority of the tribal court and thereby infringe on the right of Indians to govern themselves.[43] Such an infringement would constitute a greater interference with tribal autonomy and self government than the change effected by the ICRA in the substantive law. The Court concluded that the legislative history of the Act did not support the creation of a federal cause of action and indeed, would actually conflict with the congressional goal of protecting tribal self government.[44]

The Court rejected the argument that without federal court review, the substantive provisions of the ICRA would be mean-

---

165 (1977) for the same proposition is puzzling since that case does not deal with the immunity of tribal officers and merely holds that tribal members have no immunity from suit. *Id.* Tribal officers have been held to enjoy the same immunity as other public officers when acting within the scope of their authority. Graves v. White Mountain Apache Tribe, 570 P.2d 804 (Az. 1977); White Mountain Apache Tribe v. Shelley, 480 P.2d 654 (Az. 1971); Davis v. Littell, 398 F.2d 83 (9th Cir. 1968).

[38] *See* note 13 *supra.*

[39] The Court thus followed the test enunciated in Cort v. Ash, 422 U.S. 66 (1975).

[40] Santa Clara Pueblo v. Martinez, 436 U.S. 49, 62 (1978). The Court stated, "In addition to its objective of strengthening the position of individual members vis-a-vis the tribe, Congress also intended to promote the well-established federal policy of furthering Indian self-government." *Id.* at 62.

[41] *Id.* at 60.

[42] 424 U.S. 382 (1976).

[43] Santa Clara Pueblo v. Martinez, 436 U.S. 49, 72 (1978).

[44] *Id.* at 72.

ingless, as lower courts had reasoned in ICRA cases. In a key passage,[45] the Court pointed out that the tribes' own forum might include both tribal courts and other, nonjudicial tribal institutions.[46]

In support, the Court noted that in 1973 there were 117 operating tribal courts which handled approximately 70,000 cases.[47] In some circumstances these tribal court decisions were found to be entitled to full faith and credit.[48] The Court emphasized that tribal courts were not the only appropriate forums, pointing out that the Santa Clara Pueblo had vested judicial authority in its tribal council by the terms of its constitution,[49] which had been approved by the Secretary of the Interior under the Indian Reorganization Act of 1934.[50]

Thus, the Supreme Court concluded that a federal judicial remedy was not essential to the effectiveness of the ICRA.[51] Rather the effectiveness of the ICRA would be realized within the framework of tribal government. The ICRA would not only guide the tribal government's actions and decisions, but would also challenge tribal governments to provide forums within which individual members could vindicate grievances under the Act.[52]

---

[45] The Court states:

> Moreover, contrary to the reasoning of the court below, implication of a federal remedy in addition to habeas corpus is not plainly required to give effect to Congress' objective of extending constitutional norms to tribal self-government. Tribal forums are available to vindicate rights created by the ICRA, and § 1302 has the substantial and intended effect of changing the law which these forums are obliged to apply. Tribal courts have repeatedly been recognized as appropriate forums for the exclusive adjudication of disputes affecting important personal and property interests of both Indians and non-Indians. [citations omitted] Nonjudicial tribal institutions have also been recognized as competent law applying bodies. [citations omitted] Under these circumstances, we are reluctant to disturb the balance between the dual statutory objectives which Congress apparently struck in providing only for habeas corpus relief.

Id. at 65-66.

[46] *Id.*
[47] *Id.* n.21.
[48] *Id.*
[49] *Id.* at 66 n.22.
[50] 25 U.S.C. § 476 (1970).
[51] *See* note 45 *supra.*
[52] As the Court noted, Congress retains control to change the situation. Santa Clara Pueblo v. Martinez, 436 U.S. 49, 72 (1976). Thus, the tribes have an incentive to provide effective redress. *See* discussion in text accompanying notes 126-128, *infra.*

Henceforth tribal councils and tribal courts would play the major roles in protecting and adjudicating individual rights in tribal life.[53]

The *Martinez* decision, however, emphasizes the need to understand the political structure of tribal governments. It would be a mistake to assume that tribal government's institutions will function like their counterparts in American government. There are crucial differences which require consideration. Furthermore, the elimination of federal court review appears to have made administrative intervention in tribal government by the Department of the Interior more likely. Both of these matters raise serious and difficult questions which the remaining sections discuss.

---

[53] Since the decision holds there is no federal jurisdiction, all pending cases are subject to dismissal and a number have been dismissed. *See, e.g.,* Mousseaux v. Rosebud Sioux Tribe, 582 F.2d 1287 (8th Cir. 1978), reported in 5 I.L.R. C-34; Crowe v. Eastern Band of Cherokee Indians, Inc., No. 77-2631 (4th Cir. Sept. 28, 1978) reported in 5 Indian L. Rep. (hereinafter I.L.R.) § B at 26; Sturdevant v. Wilbur, No. 75-C-381 (E.D. Wisc. 1978), reported in 5 I.L.R. at 176; Salt River Project Agricultural Improvement & Power Dist. v. Navajo, Civ. No. 78-352 Phx. WPC (D. Ariz. 1978), reported in 5 I.L.R. § F at 116, (appeal pending); Boe v. Fort Belknap Indian Community of Fort Belknap Reservation, No. CV 78-10-GF (D. Mont. 1978); Olympic Pipeline Co. v. Swinomish Tribal Community, No. C 76-550V (D. Wash. 1978) (the ICRA claim was dismissed, but the plaintiff's counterclaim to the Tribe's complaint was allowed to stand); Wardle v. Ute Indian Tribe, No. C 74-330 (D. Utah 1978), reported in 5 I.L.R. § L at 20 (appeal pending). Since the decision in Martinez did not limit its retroactivity, presumably it will be retroactive in effect. *See* England v. Louisiana State Bd. of Medical Examiners, 375 U.S. 411 (1964); Great Northern R. R. Co. v. Sunburst Oil & Ref. Co., 287 U.S. 358 (1932). At least three federal district courts have so ruled. Sturdevant v. Wilbur, No. 75-C-381 (E.D. Wisc. 1978); Mousseaux v. Rosebud Sioux Tribe, 582 F.2d 1287 (8th Cir. 1978); reported in 5 I.L.R. § C at 34; Dry Creek Lodge, 415 F.2d 926 (10th Cir. 1975); *on remand sub. nom.* Dry Creek Lodge, Inc. v. Canan, No. C-74-74A (D. Wyo. 1978), (appeal pending). In Dry Creek Lodge, the Martinez decision resulted in the trial court vacating a $525,000 verdict which had been awarded against the Shoshone-Arapahoe Tribes of the Wind River Reservation. *Id.*

Absent any jurisdiction, and given the retroactivity of Martinez, prior federal decisions would appear to be a nullity. *See* United States v. United States Fidelity & Guaranty Co., 309 U.S. 506, 513-514 (1939), holding that where an Indian tribe has been subjected to an adjudication in the absence of congressional waiver of sovereign immunity, the attempted exercise of judicial power is void.

One question of importance to tribal government is the weight to be given prior substantive rulings under the ICRA. While those decisions may no longer stand as conclusive and binding interpretations of the ICRA, they cannot safely be ignored. *See* Note, *Indian Law: The Application of the One-Man-One-Vote Standard of Baker v. Carr to Tribal Elections,* 58 MINN.L.REV. 668 (1974).

II. ICRA ENFORCEMENT UNDER TRIBAL GOVERNMENT

After *Martinez,* a fundamental problem with tribal enforcement of the ICRA still remains: which governmental entity will
decide the legality of the acts of the tribal council? Because of the
political and constitutional position of the tribal courts and council in tribal government, it may not be feasible for tribal courts
to exercise the traditional American power of judicial review over
council action. A functional analysis of tribal courts and tribal
councils strongly suggests that in most cases judicial review is
inappropriate—at least for the present. The attempt of the Navajo courts to exercise that power and the internal governmental
strife which ensued is examined as a case study illustrating the
general problem.

A. *Judicial Review in the American and Tribal Contexts.*

The United States Supreme Court exercises a power of judicial
review of legislative actions unique in its scope compared to the
judiciary of other nations.[54] Unlike most foreign judicial bodies,
the American judiciary has the power to void legislative acts
which conflict with the Constitution.[55] Although the United
States Constitution nowhere expressly delegates this review
power to the judiciary, nevertheless, since Chief Justice Marshall's opinion in *Marbury v. Madison,*[56] it has become well established in American jurisprudence.[57]

The American system of judicial review of legislative action is
perhaps most attributable to the system of checks and balances
created by the United States Constitution. Since the Constitution created the Supreme Court,[58] the Court does not owe its
existence to the legislative body. Moreover, the Constitution
mandates a separate federal judiciary.[59] The Constitution thus
lays the foundation for the judicial independence vital to the
effective exercise of judicial review of legislative actions.

In addition to the constitutional establishment of an independent judiciary as a coordinate branch of government,[60] there also
existed a fundamental notion in American jurisprudence that the

---

[54] *See* R. MCCLOSKEY, THE AMERICAN SUPREME COURT, 225 (1960).

[55] *See generally,* J. NOWAK, R. ROTUNDA & J. YOUNG, CONSTITUTIONAL LAW, 1-
22 (1978); L. TRIBE, AMERICAN CONSTITUTIONAL LAW, 20-156 (1978).

[56] 5 U.S. (1 Cranch) 137 (1803).

[57] *See* R. MCCLOSKEY, *supra* note 54, at 77-80; J. NOWAK, *supra* note 55, at 1.

[58] U.S. CONST., art. III, § 1.

[59] *Id.*

[60] *See* text accompanying notes 54-60, *supra.*

legislature is bound by a "higher law"[61] at the time the judiciary adopted the notion of judicial review.[62] Moreover, this fundamental concept was considered to underlay the Constitution. Thus, it was the source of what Professor McCloskey described as the dualism between popular sovereignty and the doctrine of fundamental law.[63] In essence, the Court is the "guardian" of the fundamental law, yet, it is ultimately dependent on public acceptance for the legitimacy of its power. Thus, the successful development of judicial review has required thoughtful restraint by the Supreme Court and care not to overestimate its power.[64]

When we turn to tribal court systems, sharp contrasts are immediately apparent. Most tribal courts owe their existence to the tribe's legislative bodies.[65] Rather than providing for co-equal branches, tribal constitutions generally assign the central role in tribal government to the tribal council. Tribal courts are, for the most part, the creatures of ordinances enacted by the tribal council.[66] Consequently, a different relationship exists between the legislature and judiciary in Indian and American governments. Historically, the role of tribal courts in tribal government has been quite limited. Furthermore, few tribal judges have had any formal training in law. This seriously undermines the respect of tribal members and other agencies of tribal government for the tribal courts.[66.1] Tribal courts, therefore, do not enjoy the general presumption accorded American judges that their decisions are the product of a learned and impartial application of systematic principles to the case before them.

Tribal councils are generally the central repositories of power on the reservation. Most tribal constitutions delegate to the tribal council the power to manage the economic affairs of the tribe,

---

[61] McCloskey, *supra* note 54 at 11-16; *See also* Nowak, *supra* note 55, at 11-14.

[61.1] *See*, American Indian Lawyer Training Program, Indian Self-Determination and the Role of Tribal Courts, 68 (1977). (Hereinafter cited as Indian Self-Determination.) This study showed that 11 of 76 chief judges of tribal courts surveyed had less than a high school education and only 12 had any legal training.

[62] *See, e.g.*, Marbury v. Madison, 5 U.S. (1 Cranch) 137 (1803).

[63] McCloskey, *supra* note 54, at 11-13.

[64] *Id.* at 225.

[65] *See*, National American Indian Court Judges Association, Indian Courts and the Future—Report of the NAICJA Long Range Planning Project, 37-40 (1978) (hereinafter cited as Indian Courts).

[66] *Id.*

[66.1] Indeed, the Navajo Court of Appeals expressly rested its claim of the power of judicial review on this ground among others in *Halona v. MacDonald* (Navajo Nation Ct. App. filed Jan. 24, 1978) reported in 5 Indian L. Rep. § m at 119 (1978).

provide for law and order and the general welfare of the tribe. Councils function as legislative bodies and frequently as executive and quasi-judicial bodies dealing with individual requests and complaints of members as well as public issues. In addition to their political function, councils function in the business and economic sphere in the same manner as a corporate board of directors: planning, authorizing contracts and expenditures and setting policies. The council usually has power to hire and fire key tribal employees, such as the executive director or business manager, department heads and tribal judges. The council frequently establishes committees, usually headed by a council member, to oversee specific programs and projects in such areas of land and forestry management, finance, leasing, adoption, election procedures, law and order, hunting and fishing, and the like. The council thus has control over a great deal of employment and appointment to tribal governmental positions.

As a practical political matter, moreover, tribal councils tend to be intolerant of any action of other organs of tribal government which appears to challenge their authority. They usually regard themselves as representing the tribe and being the voice of the tribe. For most purposes, the council is the government.

Challenges to council actions, however, occur frequently. Indeed, a review of the pre-*Martinez* cases brought under the ICRA discloses that most involved precisely such challenges in the areas of election procedures, legislative apportionment, qualification and standards for office, tribal membership, and voting.[67] Since *Martinez* has now relegated resolution of ICRA disputes to tribal government,[68] those who challenge the actions of tribal councils in the future will no doubt argue that it is inappropriate for the council to sit as judge of the legality of its own actions. Many will seek to have tribal courts assume the power of judicial review of council action. An examination of the modern history of tribal government suggests that such judicial review is inconsistent with the traditions and the structure of tribal government and is likely to lead to disruptive conflict. In order to understand the difficulties associated with judicial review in tribal government, it is important to examine the origins of the modern tribal courts.

While Indian societies had their own laws and institutions for dealing with anti-social conduct before contact with Anglo-American culture, these institutions and codes gradually disappeared under federal "civilizing" policies.[69] The tribal court system was an outgrowth of the concept of Indian police. An Indian

---

[67] *See* cases collected in 25 U.S.C.A. §§ 1302-03 (West Cum. Supp. 1978).

[68] Santa Clara Pueblo v. Martinez, 436 U.S. 49, 65-66 (1978).

[69] *Supra* note 61.1, at 13-17.

agent established the first regular police force in 1874 on the San Carlos Apache Reservation.[70] Its effectiveness encouraged the establishment of similar Indian police forces on other reservations. The practice took on congressional approval under an 1878 Appropriations Act.[71]

While the official establishment of Indian police in 1878 made no provision for the trial and punishment of offenders, it was the common practice for the Indian agent to act as judge, or to delegate this duty to another subordinate or to a trusted Indian. In 1884, the Secretary of the Interior authorized the establishment of Courts of Indian Offenses, which were soon placed in operation on about two-thirds of the reservations.[72] Indian judges were appointed by agents, who thereafter exercised considerable control over them. These courts operated under Interior Department regulations.[73]

In 1934 Congress passed the Indian Reorganization Act (IRA)[74] to provide a framework for tribes to reestablish their governmental status. Many tribes adopted tribal constitutions under the Act. For the most part, the Interior Department drafted these constitutions. They generally provided for a council elected by tribal membership, which would exercise primary governing authority. They also provided for establishment of a tribal court system and judicial codes *if* the *council* so provided by ordinance. By 1935, most tribes had functioning tribal courts or Courts of Indian Offenses.[75]

Thus, at their inception, the tribal courts were subordinate to the tribal councils which created them. More recently, tribal courts on some reservations have established a degree of judicial independence. Nonetheless, while support for tribal courts is increasing they are still considered a subordinate arm of tribal government on a substantial proportion of the reservations.[76] For example in a 1977 survey, it was found that tribal judges were appointed by the tribal council on 64 reservations and elected by the membership at large only on 19 reservations.[77] Moreover,

---

[70] *See* W. HAGAN, INDIAN POLICE AND JUDGES, 27-39 (1966) (hereinafter cited as HAGAN); Burnett, *An Historical Analysis of the 1968 'Indian Civil Rights' Act,* 9 HARV. J. LEGIS. 557, 558-570 (1972).

[71] *See* Hagan, note 70 *supra,* at 42.

[72] INDIAN SELF-DETERMINATION, *supra* note 61.1, at 17-18.

[73] *Id.* at 11-21.

[74] Act of June 18, 1934, Pub. L. 383, 48 Stat. 984 (current version at 25 U.S.C. §§ 461-492 (1976)).

[75] INDIAN SELF-DETERMINATION, *supra* note 61.1, at 27.

[76] INDIAN COURTS, *supra* note 60, at 40.

[77] *Id.* at 86.

many tribal courts report that it is not uncommon for political influence to be brought to bear upon them.[78]

In 1977 there were federally-recognized tribal court systems on 127 reservations.[79] In 1970 Indian judges formed the National American Indian Court Judges Association, whose function has been to organize judicial education programs for Indian court judges throughout the country and attempt to achieve greater separation of powers between the judicial and executive branches of Indian governments. About 200 tribal judges participated in regional seminars, taught by lawyers, judges and law professors, using case books and other publications specially prepared for Indian courts.[80]

Tribal courts, however, continue to function primarily to mete out punishment to misdemeanants. In a 1977 survey, most tribal courts reported that civil matters comprised less than ten percent of their caseload. The vast majority of these cases involved domestic relations and juvenile cases, with the balance comprised of contract, property and personal injury cases.[81] Unfortunately, most tribal judges have had little training in substantive and procedural civil law and feel ill-equipped to handle these cases.[82]

While tribal courts have acquired substantial familiarity with criminal due process concepts, they have had little experience with the body of constitutinal law applicable to individual liberties in the civil context of the first,[83] fifth[84] and fourteenth amendments.[85] This is not to say that tribal judges have no understanding of these matters, for no doubt many do. But most tribal judges will have great difficulty applying American constitutional analysis to the actions of the tribal councils. They will need substantial training, at least equivalent to what they have received in the area of criminal law.[86]

---

[78] *Id.* at 70, 94. *See also*, BRAKEL, AMERICAN INDIAN TRIBAL COURTS, THE COSTS OF SEPARATE JUSTICE (1978). (The author is a severe critic of tribal courts and the continued existence of Indian reservations and tribal government.)

[79] Indian Courts *supra* note 65, at 36.

[80] Collins, Johnson, and Perkins, *American Indian Courts and Tribal Self-Government,* 63 A.B.A.J. 808 (1970).

[81] INDIAN COURTS, *supra* note 60, at 47; INDIAN SELF-DETERMINATION, *supra* note 61.1, at 46-47.

[82] INDIAN COURTS, *supra* note 60, at 47.

[83] U.S. CONST., amend. I.

[84] *Id.,* amend. V.

[85] *Id.,* amend. XIV.

[86] The National American Indian Court Judges Association, in their 1978 long-range planning project call for training programs in judicial review of tribal legislation. INDIAN COURTS, *supra* note 60, at 188. This is one of fifteen subjects

In addition to acquiring familiarity with American constitutional concepts, given the political organization of tribal government, tribal judges must familiarize themselves with the methods of judicial restraint developed in the American legal system. Otherwise, tribal judges will risk destructive clashes with their tribal councils. The development of judicial restraint by the federal courts exemplifies the need of tribal courts, also, to understand the need for judicial restraint if they are to review legislative action.

Indeed, in tribal government, since the judiciary is dependent upon election by the tribal members or council, development of judicial restraint is even more necessary to avoid conflicts with the legislative body which presumably reflects the popular will. Relevant judicial doctrines developed by the United States Supreme Court include avoiding constitutional issues wherever possible,[87] resting decisions on non-constitutional grounds when possible,[88] showing deference to the legislative judgment in policy matters,[89] and avoiding hypothetical or moot constitutional questions.[90] The political question doctrine would be a particularly useful one for tribal courts, since it is designed to avoid judicial invasion of the legitimate province of the legislative body.

Judicial review is ultimately a delicate institution. Courts must exercise restraint and remain sensitive to the popular will, particularly until the doctrine becomes well established. The tribal judicial system must continue to recognize that it is not yet a coequal branch of government. Because Indian tribes lack a tradition of judicial review, their courts may encounter serious difficulties in identifying the requisite boundaries of the doctrine while simultaneously discharging their responsibilities under the ICRA.

---

proposed for future training curricula. The National Judicial College at Reno, Nevada, has been participating jointly with the National American Indian Court Judges Association in training seminars for Indian tribal judges in such areas as evidence, contracts and trial court procedures.

[87] *See, e.g.,* TRIBE, *supra* note 55, at 120-29.

[88] TRIBE, *supra* note 55, at 56. For a discussion on the extent to which this restraint may vary given the Court's makeup, *see* E. BARRETT, CONSTITUTIONAL LAW 63 (1977).

[89] *See, e.g.,* Laird v. Tatum, 408 U.S. 1 (1972).

[90] *See, e.g.,* DeFunis v. Odegaard, 416 U.S. 312 (1974). *See generally* L. TRIBE, *supra* note 55, at 54, 56-57, 62-68.

[91] *See generally* J. NOWAK, *supra* note 55, at 100-111; and TRIBE, *supra* note 55, at 71-79. Historically, the "political question" doctrine has been one of the Supreme Court's major tools of judicial restraint. The Court will refrain from deciding issues which would require the invasion of the legitimate province of a coordinate branch of government. Although the future of the political question

Moreover, most tribal judges at present are likely to feel that they are without power to effectively overrule any action of the tribal council. This may be changing, however, as more lawyers, or people with some legal training, come to preside over tribal courts. But such people may also rashly assume that the American model of judicial review is the sole means for resolution of intragovernmental disagreement. Failure to appreciate the unique milieu in which tribal courts function could lead tribal courts to exacerbate tribal strife rather than alleviate it.[92] Furthermore, a glance at the legal systems of other countries suggests that judicial review of legislative action is not a necessary component of an effective and equitable legal system.

Judicial review of legislation has not been characteristic of most legal systems outside of the United States.[93] In Europe and Japan, there is, however, a centralized system which divorces judicial review from ordinary litigation and confines it to special proceedings brought directly before a constitutional court.[94] In England, Parliament is supreme and the courts do not question the constitutionality of its action. Accordingly, in the Commonwealth countries, judicial review has been exercised very sparingly.[95]

Although most of the Latin American republics provide for some sort of judicial review, in practice it is rarely exercised. Those countries have developed highly refined versions of the political question doctrine.[96] In Africa, where strong central gov-

---

doctrine is in doubt, in light of the Court's decision in Baker v. Carr, 369 U.S. 186, 1962, the principles underlying the doctrine are nevertheless useful for avoiding disruptive conflict between the judicial and legislative branches of government. *Id.* at 217. Thus, tribal courts should heed the teachings of American judicial review. *See* Sharp, *Judicial Review & A Functional Analysis,* 75 YALE L.J. 517 (1966); *cf.* Hankin, *Is There a "Political Question" Doctrine?,* 85 YALE L.J. 597 (1976).

[92] *See* discussion accompanying notes 102-125, *infra.*

[93] Judicial review of administrative action is, of course, a wholly different matter.

[94] *See* Bishin, *Judicial Review in Democratic Theory,* 50 So.CAL. L.REV. 1099 (1977). Civil law countries have resorted to this system because they conceive of the process of determining constitutionality as a political function, and therefore unsuitable for the ordinary judiciary. This approach has been adopted in the Federal Republic of Germany, Japan, Norway, Denmark, Sweden, Austria and Switzerland. *See* Cappelleti, *Fundamental Guarantees of the Parties In Civil Litigation; Comparative Constitutional and Social Trends,* 25 STAN. L.R. 651 (1973).

[95] McWhinney, *Constitutional Review in Canada and the Commonwealth Countries,* 35 OHIO ST. L.J. 900, n.30 (1974).

[96] "Constitutions, like virgins, are born to be violated," goes a Latin American

ernments characterize the political systems, court decisions have rarely opposed governmental action.[97]

While some students admire the American institution of judicial review, others are critical. Professor Schmeiser of Canada argues that fundamental rights always involve the question of where to draw the line and this, he says, is basically a policy question, not a legal one.[98] He points to the United States Supreme Court's dramatic reversals of position over time in such areas as regulation of the conditions of employment of wage earners[99] and racial segregation.[100] Professor Schmeiser further argues that judicial review fosters litigation, since an attack on the constitutional validity of legislation is always possible. This, he says, has given rise to literally thousands of cases containing frivolous allegations of unconstitutionality.[101]

The total absence or restricted versions of the doctrine of judicial review in other countries suggests that it may not be absolutely necessary for the protection of fundamental human rights. It is a complex and difficult undertaking for courts in even the most advanced countries to overrule acts of the lawmaking body in the absence of an established tradition of judical supremacy. For Indian tribes which have no such tradition, the exercise of judicial review by a tribal court, may well lead to a confrontation. Such an event occurred on the Navajo Reservation in 1978. The entire episode is worthy of careful study.

---

quip. While some Latin American courts have struck down legislation they deem unconstitutional, it is recognized that this power is fragile. Judicial independence is rare in Latin America. *See* Rosenn, *Judicial Review In Latin America,* 35 OHIO ST. L.J. 785 (1974).

[97] While all of the Anglophonic constitutions were designed to protect democratic liberties, the whole system has been described as basically a failure in Africa. The protection of fundamental freedoms has depended on the independence of the judges and institutions, and properly trained civil service employees. Seidman, *Judicial Review and Fundamental Freedoms in Anglophonic America,* 35 OHIO ST. L.J. 820 (1974); Paul, *Some Observations on Constitutionalism, Judicial Review and Rule of Law in Africa,* 35 OHIO ST. L.J. 851 (1974).

[98] D. SCHMEISER, CIVIL LIBERTIES IN CANADA, at 26 (1964) (hereinafter SCHMEISER).

[99] *Cf.,* Lochner v. New York, 198 U.S. 45 (1905), holding wage and hour laws unconstitutional and West Coast Hotel Co. v. Parrish, 300 U.S. 370 (1937), *reversing* Lochner.

[100] *Cf.,* Plessy v. Ferguson, 163 U.S. 537 (1895), upholding the constitutionality of segregation statutes, and Brown v. Board of Education, 347 U.S. 483 (1954), *reversing* Plessy.

[101] SCHMEISER, *supra* note 97 at 22-36.

B. *Judicial Review in the Navajo Courts: A Case Study*

The Navajos have what is probably the most highly developed and sophisticated tribal judicial system among the tribal governments in the United States. While it is not characteristic, it serves as a model for other tribal judicial systems.

The Navajo Tribe operates without a tribal constitution, instead having an extensive and highly-formal tribal code, promulgated by the Navajo Tribal Council. An entire title of the Code is devoted to courts and procedure.[102] The judicial branch is treated as a separate branch of the Navajo tribal government, and consists of the Trial Court and the Court of Appeals.[103] The Code provides that all of the Trial judges, and the Chief Justice of the Navajo Court of Appeals are appointed by the Chairman of the Tribal Council with the approval of the Tribal Council.[104] The initial appointment of these judges is for a two-year probationary term. Thereafter, they are eligible for permanent appointment. This is done by action of the Tribal chairman with approval of the council. From then on, they have tenure "during good behavior" or until age 70. Removal is by action of the tribal council.[105]

The Code does not expressly give the tribal courts jurisdiction over claims brought against the Tribe, the Council or tribal officers. Jurisdiction is merely described as reaching, "All civil actions in which the defendant is an Indian and is found within its territorial jurisdiction."[106] On the other hand, there is no limitation of tribal court jurisdiction in the code with respect to such claims.

The confrontation between the Navajo Tribal Court and the Navajo Council may be said to have begun in 1973 when the Navajo Court considered the case of *Dennison v. Tucson Gas and Electric Co.*[107] A claim was brought by the members of a Navajo family against the tribal chairman, tribal employees, the Council, the Tribe, a public utility company and its contractor. The family claimed illegalities and improprieties in connection with a power

---

[102] Title 7, N.T.C. (1977).

[103] 7 N.T.C. § 201 (1977).

[104] *Id.* §§ 251, 301. The code's statement of background explains that the decision to change from elected to appointed judges was based on the desire to remove the judges from the pressure of politics in making decisions and enforcing the law. History, at 278.

[105] 7 N.T.C. § 352 (1977).

[106] *Id.* § 253.

[107] No. A-CV-12-74 (Navajo Ct. App., filed Dec. 23, 1974) reported in 2 Indian L. Rep. No. 4, at 52 (1975).

line right-of-way. The case was ultimately decided by the Navajo Court of Appeals in 1974.

Employees of the Navajo Office of Land Administration and employees of the Bureau of Indian Affairs and Tucson Gas and Electric Company had negotiated with the plaintiffs and secured their written consent to construct a power line over their traditional use area. The plaintiffs had accepted the public utility company's check in the amount of $5,000 but had never cashed it. They brought their action to cancel their consent on the ground of fraud, deceit and duress, and sought to enjoin all the defendants from trespass to their property. They also asked for punitive damages and offered to return the uncashed check.

Pointing out that the case involved the exercise of the power of eminent domain, the court found that all of the defendants had acted in disregard of Navajo statutory procedures in undertaking to negotiate a private consent with the plaintiffs. The court made no finding on the claim that the plaintiffs' consent was procured by "fraud, deceit and duress". Instead, the Court of Appeals found the written consent a nullity. The opinion chastised all those who had part in the transaction for ignoring the strict provision of Navajo law concerning the exercise of the power of eminent domain.

The court rejected the tribal officials' claim that they were shielded by the Tribe's sovereign immunity. In holding that tribal officials acted beyond their authority in attempting to negotiate a private consent to a right-of-way, the Court had, in effect, held that their acts were *ultra vires*. The court not only rejected the sovereign immunity defense, it expressed indignation and contempt that the defense would even be raised, saying:

> This court has always upheld and presently does uphold the sovereign immunity doctrine of the Navajo Nation, but for anyone to seriously impose that defense under the facts of this case causes concern among the court, regarding the competency of the legal advisors to the prosecutor and the competency of the legal advisers (sic) to the office of the Navajo land administration. *All that the plaintiffs would be entitled to from the Navajo Nation under the statute, in any event, would be, just compensation.* How could they be deprived of this simpy because some officials and employees in the executiv branch, to put it mildly, neglected to follow the law?[108]

The court's view of sovereign immunity seemed to be that since the plaintiffs were absolutely entitled to just compensation, they were not asking for anything from the Navajo Nation beyond what the Nation has already conceded to be their right—in effect,

---

[108] *Id.* at 55.

a waiver of immunity. In this respect, the court's opinion is in agreement with that of numerous state courts which have considered similar questions.[109]

The *Dennison* decision, however, seems to have been poorly thought out. It implied that a negotiated consent could never be lawful. Surely this was not the intention of the Navajo condemnation law. Indeed, it is doubtful that the court even intended such a sweeping rule. Furthermore, the court may have been remiss in not exercising restraint. Remanding for findings on the manner in which the consent was obtained might have led to a better result. The court seemed over-eager to chastise tribal officials, and this resulted in a decision which confused Navajo eminent domain law.

In *Dennison* the Navajo court was adjudicating the legality of executive rather than legislative action. However, its boldness in striking down the action of the Chairman of the Council as well as brushing aside the Chairman's claim of sovereign immunity no doubt had much to do with its confidence in approaching the problem of judicial review of Council action which was to come before it in 1978. *Dennison* may be seen as an important stepping-stone to the exercise of judicial review in the 1978 decision of *Halona v. MacDonald.*[110]

Halona v. MacDonald was an action brought by several tribal members, including some members of the Tribal Council, to enjoin an appropriation voted by the Tribal Council to pay the legal expenses of the Chairman, Peter MacDonald. Mr. MacDonald had been indicted for misapplication of tribal funds. He had retained a noted criminal attorney, to represent him, and the Council passed a resolution appropriating $70,000 in tribal funds to pay the attorney. The suit sought to enjoin the expenditure of any portion of the appropriation.

The plaintiffs contended that the Council's appropriation of funds was invalid because the measure had not first been submitted to the Budget and Finance Committee on the Council. A general ordinance of the Council requiring all appropriations to be so referred had been adopted only two months earlier. But the defendants claimed that the tribal court had no authority to review the legality of actions of the Council.

---

[109] Boxberger v. State Highway Dept., 126 Colo. 438, 250 P.2d 1007 (1952); Anselmo v. Cox, 135 Conn. 78, 60 A.2d 767 (1948), *cert. denied* 335 U.S. 859; Grant Const. Co. v. Burns, 92 Idaho 408, 443 P.2d 1005 (1968); Ancelle v. State, 212 La. 1069, 34 So.2d 321 (1948).

[110] Navajo Ct. App. (filed Jan. 24, 1978) reported in 5 INDIAN L. REP. § M at 12 (1978).

The court squarely faced this challenge and ruled that it had such power. First, the court held that the Navajo Tribal Code did not exclude judicial review of council action. The court relied most heavily on the Indian Civil Rights Act, however, viewing it as a mandate for judicial review of any allegedly illegal activities by tribal government. The Navajo Court said, "We cannot imagine how any legislative body accused of violating these primary rights could be the judge of its own actions and at the same time comply with the federal law."[111]

The Navajo Court also attempted to claim that the doctrine of judicial supremacy had the hallowed status of Navajo traditon, stating:

> When all have been heard and the decision is made, it is respected. This has been the Navajo way since before the time of the present judicial system. The Navajo people did not learn this principle from the white man. They have carried it with them through history.[112]

Further, the court pointed out, if the Tribal Court cannot exercise this power, the only alternative is federal court review. In what seemed to be a message to the Council, the court said it was inconceivable that the Council would prefer review of its actions by "far-away federal courts unfamiliar with Navajo customs and laws" to review by the Navajo court. Finally, the court drew on the absence of legislative interference with the court jurisdiction following its decision in *Dennison,* concluding that acquiescence meant Council approval.

Having disposed of challenges to its right to decide the issue, the court ruled on the merits that the failure to submit the appropriation to the Budget and Finance Committee was fatal to the legislation. The court viewed its *ad hoc* character, making no reference to prior legislative procedure either repudiating or suspending the prior procedural ordinance, as raising a due process issue. To the court, due process apparently meant deliberate legislative action with full acknowledgment of and harmony with existing law.

The court suggested it was really avoiding disrespect to the Council by upholding its procedural ordinance while striking down its conflicting *ad hoc* ordinance. It rejected the argument that, in the absence of a constitution, prior legislation stood on no higher plane than the subsequent legislation and was thus impliedly amended or repealed. The court found that the "higher law" here was the due process clause in the Indian Civil Rights

---

[111] *Id.* at 16.
[112] *Id.*

Act and that failure to give heed to this law could result in federal intervention to correct violations of federal law.

One may question whether the Navajo court in *Halona* decided the case wisely. The defendants had strongly argued that the issue was nonjusticiable—that it presented a political question which was not subject to judicial review. In the American legal system, the political question argument would carry great weight where the issue was whether a legislative appropriation of funds, otherwise validly enacted, could be struck down because of failure to submit it to a legislative committee, as required by a prior law.[113]

Regardless of how one views the wisdom or correctness of the decision, it is clear that the court was determined to establish its judicial supremacy. Its opinion pulled out all the stops; invoking the "higher law" of Navajo tradition,[114] the federal Indian Civil Rights Act,[115] the duty of the judiciary, the sanctity of the Council's own general laws and finally, suggesting that the Council could validly enact such an appropriations ordinance if it expressly recited that it suspended prior review procedures required by prior law. *Halona v. MacDonald* is the *Marbury v. Madison*[116] of Navajo jurisprudence. But the power which the Navajo court claimed for itself was soon to be taken from it by the Council.

The *Halona* decision made it clear that the tribal courts claimed judicial supremacy. Pending before the Tribal Court was a voting reapportionment plan which had been adopted by the Council. The *Halona* decision and the possibility that the Tribal Court would strike down the council's reapportionment plan triggered Council action. On January 27, 1978, the Tribal Council enacted a resolution stripping the tribal courts of jurisdiction over reapportionment plans and authority to determine the validity of any resolution of the Council in the absence of a specific grant of jurisdiction.[117]

Undaunted, the Navajo tribal courts ignored the resolution and proceeded in two cases to override the Council and the executive branch of the Navajo government. In *Yazzie v. Navajo Tribal*

---

[113] *Cf.* dictum in Baker v. Carr, 369 U.S. 186, 214 (1962), to the effect that the judiciary should be reluctant to inquire into compliance with the formalities of legislative procedure.

[114] Halona v. MacDonald, (Navajo Nation Ct. App. filed Jan. 24, 1978) reported in 5 INDIAN L. REP. § M at 119 (1978).

[115] 25 U.S.C. §§ 1301-1341 (1976).

[116] 5 U.S. (1 Cranch) 137 (1803).

[117] Navajo Tribal Council Resolution CJA-14-78 (Jan. 27, 1978) (on file U.C. Davis Law Review Office).

Board of Election Supervisors,[118] the tribal court struck down the Tribal Council's reapportionment plan and ordered the Board of Elections Supervisors to implement a court-designed reapportionment plan. Shortly thereafter, the Court of Appeals of the Navajo Nation in *Gudac v. Marianito, et al.*[119] enjoined executive branch officers from terminating the employment of the plaintiff, the Judicial Branch Fiscal Officer. The court ruled that the ICRA precluded the executive branch from applying its personnel policies to judiciary employees since this would threaten judicial independence.

The defiance of the Council's restriction of tribal court jurisdiction led to a grave crisis in Navajo government. The Judicial Committee of the Navajo Trial Council requested the assistance of Edgar S. and Jean Camper Cahn, co-deans of the Antioch School of Law, to help find a solution. After studying the legal, plitical and cultural issues, the Cahns submitted a report to the Committee.[120] They concluded that the Council had the power to limit the Tribal Court's jurisdiction but pointed out that this would not resolve the problem. The Court would still have to decide whether to apply the resolutions and ordinances of the Council, and if they found them invalid, they could frustrate Council action. They also pointed out that some of these tribal disputes would end up in the federal courts under the Indian Civil Rights Act.

The Cahns report proposed five alternatives: (1) do nothing further and operate under the existing ordinance restricting the power of judicial review, (2) accept judicial review by the tribal court, (3) terminate the entire tribal court system and return to traditional Navajo methods of settling disputes, (4) discharge four of the five judges who were in probationary status and provide for elected judges, and (5) create a special court inside the Tribal Council and take political cases out of the tribal courts.[121]

The Cahns discussed the advantages and disadvantages of each of the proposed alternatives. In the end, however, they recommended establishment of a special tribunal composed of both tribal judges and Council members to consider cases involving

---

[118] No. WR-C-216-77 (Navajo Ct. App., filed Feb. 15 and Feb. 24, 1978) reported in 5 Indian L. Rep. § L at 6.

[119] (Navajo Ct. App., filed Feb. 28, 1978) reported in 5 Indian L. Rep. § L at 6.

[120] E. Cahn & J. Cahn, *Preliminary Report to the Judicial Committee of the Navajo Tribal Council* (on file in U.C. Davis Law Review Office) (hereinafter cited as Cahn.)

[121] *Id.* at 4-12.

the propriety of the actions of the Council or officials of the Tribe.[122] With some changes the Council adopted this recommendation. On May 4, 1978, the Council established a new Navajo judicial institution: the Supreme Judicial Council of the Navajo Tribal Council.[122.1]

The Navajos' solution preserved the principle of judicial review but overturned the principle of judicial supremacy. It did this in a curious way. The Navajo Supreme Judicial Council functions as a review body to hear challenges of Navajo Court of Appeals rulings regarding the validity of any action of the Tribal Council or its advisory committee. The Supreme Judicial Council has power to stay any challenged acti n of the Navajo trial court or Court of Appeals.

The Judicial Council consists of eight members: three judges and five Tribal Council members.[123] In addition, there are two panels of advisors, one composed of licensed attorneys and the other of persons learned in "Navajo law, custom, tradition and culture, including medicine men, retired judges, chapter officers, anthropologists, advocates, professors, and other professionals."[124] The Supreme Judicial Council is to designate one qualified member of each panel to sit on each case that comes before it and provide advice and assistance.

The Supreme Judicial Council has authority to function as a court: to issue writs, to stay actions and to issue decisions reversing or sustaining lower court decisions involving the validity of Council action. The ordinance creating the new institution contains an elaborate mechanism to insure that the Tribal Council is given a substantial opportunity to adopt any of the Supreme Judicial Council's recommendations. But most important, the Tribal Council retains ultimate sovereignty. This is accomplished by providing

> that the Navajo Tribal Council shall retain the ultimate authority to overturn a decision of the Supreme Judicial Council by a vote of a majority of its total membership and that vote shall be final and conclusive, subject only to review in federal court or by federal officials in accordance with federal law.[125]

Thus the Navajo Tribal Council repudiated the confident assertions of the Navajo Trial Court in *Halona* that it alone could properly pass on the legality of Council action.

---

[122] *Id.* at 15-17.
[122.1] Navajo Tribal Council Resolution, CMY-39-78 (May 4, 1978).
[123] Cahn at i-ii.
[124] *Id.* at iv.
[125] Navajo Tribal Council Resolution CMY-39-78 (May 4, 1978).

The method adopted by the Navajo Nation to deal with ICRA issues bears some resemblance to the special constitutional courts of Western Europe established to deal with questions of the constitutionality of legislative action. This is only a resemblance, however, and not an identity. The Council was careful to insure that it retained ultimate sovereignty.

The future of the Navajo judiciary might have been made more secure if the court had seen fit to apply a measure of judicial restraint in dealing with the challenge before it in *Halona*. The lesson is clear: lacking their own constituency and a tradition of judicial supremacy, the Tribal Court acted at its own risk in overruling Council action.

The conflict which embroiled the Navajo Tribal Court is by no means certain to arise elsewhere. But when a highly-sophisticated and well-established judiciary, such as that of the Navajo, found its authority challenged by the Tribal Council, the risk is certain to be greater on reservations where the tribal court is less solidly established.

It is a mistake to assume that institutions of tribal government will function like their counterparts in American government. There are crucial differences. Furthermore, the elimination of federal court review appears to have made administrative intervention in tribal government by the Department of Interior more likely. Both these matters raise serious and difficult questions which are discussed in the remaining sections.

III. PRESERVATION OF TRIBAL AUTONOMY

Any analysis of problems connected with tribal resolution of ICRA complaints must take into account Congress' ultimate power over tribal governments. Since Congress may always revise the ICRA to provide nontribal remedies, tribes are under some constraint to insure compliance with the Act. This is a federal power which only Congress can exercise, however, and should be used only if there is compelling evidence of need for federal intervention in tribal government. Any intervention by other branches of government, such as the Department of Interior, are inappropriate and of questionable legality after *Martinez*. This section discusses the implication of Congressional overview and problems with Interior Department interference.

A. *Congressional Power and Improving Tribal Response to the ICRA*

Martinez brought to an end federal court review of tribal governmental action. If tribal governments fail, however, to deal responsibly with ICRA problems,[126] *Martinez* will only have resulted in a reprieve, and there will be calls for Congress to amend the Indian Civil Rights Act so as to empower federal courts to review tribal action.

Tribal councils can take steps to improve the handling of ICRA complaints, so as to avoid internal strife and external pressure. Given the lack of federal court review, it seems likely tribal courts will be placed under increasing pressure to decide whether council action violated the ICRA. While some tribal courts may disclaim any power to make such decisions,[127] others, like the Navajo Tribal Courts, will not be so reticent. Thus, in order to provide effective redress of ICRA complaints and retain ICRA jurisdiction, tribes should determine in advance the tribal court's authority rather than place burdens and risks on tribal judges. The alternatives available to tribal councils range from affirming broad tribal court authority to decide all questions of propriety of tribal action, to prohibiting courts from deciding any such questions.[128]

For instance, tribal councils could enact express limited waivers of immunity and grants of jurisdiction to tribal courts. Tribes might be well advised to draft ordinances waiving sovereign immunity from tort liability to the extent of insurance coverage in force and authorizing tribal courts to adjudicate any claims against the tribe, its agents or employees in tribal courts. Similarly, tribal councils can enact resolutions authorizing tribal courts to hear and determine claims against the tribe based on contract where the contract contains an express waiver of immunity.

Obviously, tribal courts must be able to deal with these new civil and constitutional issues. This will require vastly expanded training of tribal judges, and perhaps providing them with legal

---

[126] *See, e.g.*, De Raismes, *The Indian Civil Rights Act of 1968 and the Pursuit of Responsible Tribal Self-Government*, 20 S.D. L. Rev. 59 (1975).

[127] *See, e.g.*, Howlett v. Salish & Kootenai Tribes, 529 F.2d 233 (1976).

[128] For instance, the constitution for the Pueblo of Isleta, art. IX, § 5, declares that the Isleta Pueblo Tribal Court "shall determine the constitutionality of enactments of the [Isleta Pueblo] Council submitted to the court for review. *Id. cited in* INDIAN SELF-DETERMINATION, *supra* note 61.1, at 37 nn.5, 6. The Oglala Sioux Tribal Council, on the other hand, enacted a resolution which prohibits the tribal court from entertaining any action or suit against the Tribe, its agencies or officials unless the plaintiff has first exhausted his administrative remedies by filing his complaint with the Tribal Executive Committee. Oglala Sioux Resolution No. 76-03 (Sept. 16, 1977) (cited in Pine Ridge Village Council v. Trimble, 5 Indian Law Rep. § M, 6, 7).

advisors. Tribal courts are not likely to engender respect among tribal members if their handling of civil and constitutional issues reveals a lack of competency. Attainment of competency over the substance of civil and constitutional law is not enough. Tribal courts will have to learn the techniques of judicial restraint in order to cope with challenges to council action. Perhaps most importantly of all, tribal courts will have to achieve judicial independence.

Finally, tribal councils may desire to entrust the process of judicial review to courts in whose special competency they and their members may have some confidence. They can consider the establishment of a special constitutional court, such as the Navajo Judicial Supreme Council, or they may wish to improve the structure of their appellate court system. There is no reason why tribes cannot design an appellate court system utilizing intertribal judicial arrangements so as to insure maximum impartiality.

Regardless of the possible expansion of the role of the tribal court system in deciding ICRA issues, it is likely that the tribal councils will continue to dominate tribal government. Councils may deliberately reject the legitimacy of judicial review, either explicitly or by simply ignoring the rulings of tribal courts. In some cases there are good arguments for such a course of conduct. There is no denying that some tribal courts are not presently capable of dealing responsibly with constitutional issues. Some of the tribal courts are often as political as councils, thus accordingly impairing the acceptability of their decisions.

The Indian Civil Rights Act does not necessarily mandate judicial review. In *Howlett v. Salish and Kootenai Tribes,*[128.1] the Ninth Circuit ruled that the ICRA does not preclude the Indians from vesting the power to interpret the tribal constitution in the tribal council rather than in a tribal court. Moreover, *Martinez* makes it clear that the tribal council may well be an appropriate forum in which to decide ICRA issues.

There is still another reason why tribal councils may not see the wisdom of deferring to the judgment of tribal courts. At the present stage of development, the expertise of tribal judges in noncriminal constitutional law is not demonstrably superior to council members. In fact, the reverse may be the case. Furthermore, the tribal council usually has better access to legal advice than the tribal judge. Tribal councils are accustomed to dealing directly with tribal attorneys and requesting their assistance and

---

[128.1] 529 F.2d 233 (1976).

advice in the drafting of ordinances, or in the undertaking of official action. Tribal judges often seek advice from the very same sources. There is no reason then, why the tribal council cannot make decisions as responsibly as tribal courts. Moreover, it is necessary to remember that there is nothing sacrosanct about judicial review as the sole means of determining legality of legislative action, particularly under the circumstances of Indian tribal societies in America today.

B. *Department of the Interior Review of ICRA Complaints*

Martinez seems to have raised the possibility that there will be increased interference with tribal autonomy by the Interior Department. It would be ironic if the effect of *Martinez* was to end federal court intervention in tribal government, only to have it replaced by Interior Department intervention. Yet, recent actions of the Interior Department indicate this result.

Shortly after the *Martinez* decision, an Interior Department official stated that the lack of a federal court remedy would impel the Secretary of the Interior to assume greater responsibility over tribal members' complaints against the action of tribal government. Specifically, the official asserted that if an action of the tribe or its officers is found violative of the tribal constitution, the Department may take what it deems to be appropriate action. This may include withholding approval of tribal budgets, restricting the flow of Bureau of Indian Affairs (BIA) funds to tribal programs, and withdrawing recognition of tribal governments or officials.[129]

Interior Department intervention in tribal affairs is not new.[130] Indeed, prior to the Indian Reorganization Act,[131] the BIA completely dominated tribal affairs. Since then, however, particularly under the policy of Indian Self-determination,[132] and the

---

[129] Letter from R. Lavis, Deputy Assistant Secretary, Indian Affairs, to Charles Moon (July 28, 1978).

[130] *See* Potts v. Bruce, 533 F.2d 527 (10th Cir. 1976); U.S. v. Pawnee Business Council, 382 F.Supp. 54 (1974). *See also* Note, *Administrative Law: Self-Determination and the Consent Power: The Role of the Government in Indian Decisions*, 5 AM. IND. L. REV. 195 (1977).

[131] 25 U.S.C. §§ 461-492 (1970) (Act of June 18, 1934, 48 Stat. 984, *as amended by*, Pub. L. 91-229, 84 Stat. 20).

[132] The self-determination policy is generally regarded as having first been propounded by President Nixon in his Special Message to Congress, July 8, 1970. It became the official policy of the Bureau of Indian Affairs thereafter. *See* TYLER, A HISTORY OF INDIAN POLICY (1973). It was expressed by law in the Indian

growing assertion of sovereign authority by the tribes, the Bureau has been considerably more restrained in interfering with tribal government.[133]

Two examples of post-*Martinez* Interior Department interventions in the affairs of tribal government suggest, however, that the Interior Department has no intention of allowing the tribal governments full autonomy after *Martinez*. In July of 1978, the BIA became involved in an intra-tribal dispute involving the Wichita and Affiliated Tribes of Oklahoma. A group of members had petitioned for removal of the President of the Tribe. The governing resolution appeared to require calling a special meeting. When this was not done, the Superintendent gave notice to the President that unless the meeting was called, the Bureau would withdraw its recognition of him. The President refused, apparently contending that the regular meeting of the Council sufficed. The Superintendent notified him that the BIA no longer recognized him as President and instead recognized the Vice President as the acting chief executive officer. The Superintendent then urged the Vice President to proceed to call the special meeting.[134]

The Office of the Assistant Secretary for Indian Affairs attempted to justify this action on two grounds. It asserted that whenever the Superintendent takes actions affecting trust property, or appropriated funds, he is required to deal with the individuals who hold elected office pursuant to the provisions of the Secretarially-approved governing document. In addition, the Assistant Secretary's Office contended that whenever the BIA approves a tribe's governing document, the BIA becomes a party to the document and is bound by its terms.[135]

The assertion that disposition of trust property or appropriated funds places the Secretary under a duty to deal only with properly elected officials stems from the Supreme Court ruling in *Seminole Nation v. United States*.[136] In that case the Court held that the United States could be liable for payment of funds appropriated for the benefit of tribal members to tribal officials known to be corrupt and faithless. The Court applied the equita-

---

Self-Determination & Assistance Act of 1975, 25 U.S.C. §§ 450-450n. (Pub. L. 93-638, 88 Stat. 2203).

[133] M. Price, Law and the American Indian 724 (1973).

[134] Letter from Superintendent, Anadarko Agency, to Newton Lamar (Aug. 9, 1978).

[135] Letter from Superintendent, Anadarko Agency, to Newton Lamar (July 18, 1978); letter from R. C. Lavis, Acting Assistant Secretary, Indian Affairs, to Sen. Dewey F. Bartlett (Sept. 25, 1978).

[136] 316 U.S. 286 (1941).

ble principle of trust-law that a third party paying a fiduciary for the beneficiary's benefit with knowledge that the fiduciary intends to misappropriate the money or to be otherwise false to his trust is a participant in the breach of trust and liable to the beneficiary.[137] The holding in *Seminole,* however, does not support intervention into the affairs of tribal government. Claims of election irregularities do not in themselves impair the ability of the United States to deal with *de facto* tribal officers.[138]

The other justification offered by the Assistant Secretary for Indian Affairs is based on the notion that Secretarial approval of tribal constitutions and law and order codes renders them tantamount to contracts or compacts with the United States. The theory was subsequently more fully articulated by the Assistant Secretary in the *Plumage v. Fort Belknap Election Board*[139] case.

In March, 1978, the Fort Belknap Community Court invalidated the results of a tribal election on the ground that one of the candidates did not meet the Tribe's constitutional qualifications.[140] The Billings Area Director recognized the tribal court's ruling as valid and binding. The aggrieved parties appealed the Area Director's action to the Secretary.[141]

On August 23, 1978, the Assistant Secretary issued a written decision upholding the tribal court.[142] He took pains to point out that the Department had no alternative but to scrutinize the decision of the Fort Belknap court once an appeal had been taken from the Area Director's determination to recognize that court's ruling. His decision emphasized that "the Department of the Interior *is not* a judicial appeal level above tribal judicial forums empowered to sustain or reverse decisions of those forums." But, he declared that the Department views tribal constitutions and law and order codes as contracts with the Interior Department and concluded: "We cannot be bound or compelled to recognize any tribal action which may be in violation of those agreements."

---

[137] *Id.* at 296.

[138] *See* United States v. Royer, 268 U.S. 394 (1925); Lyons v. Woods, 153 U.S. 649 (1894); Re Manning, 139 U.S. 504 (1891); Ralls County v. Douglas, 105 U.S. 729 (1881).

[139] 5 Indian L. Rep. § L at 7 (Mar. 15, 1978).

[140] *Id.*

[141] 25 C.F.R. Pt. 2 authorizes appeals from administrative actions to the Commissioner of the BIA, and to the Board of Indian Appeals. This Board is also authorized to conduct appeals and make decisions for the Secretary. 43 C.F.R. Pt. 4.

[142] Assistant Secretary's opinion, reported in 5 Indian L. Rep. § H at 17 (Aug. 23, 1978).

In making this claim, however, the Assistant Secretary may have placed the Interior Department in precisely the position he earlier disclaimed. While the opinion went to great lengths to affirm the tribal court's authority to exercise judicial review,[143] it also reserved for the Department the right to decide whether the tribal court's interpretation was arbitrary or unreasonable. Thus, although the Department would give great weight to the decision of the tribal court, it would not accept any interpretation "so arbitrary or unreasonable that its application would constitute a violation of the right to due process or equal protection".[144]

Applying this standard, the Assistant Secretary upheld the tribal court's ruling in the *Plumage* case.[145] Thus, the Assistant Secretary now claims administrative authority to review and ultimately determine the constitutionality of the action of tribal governments. This promises to open up an entirely new field of ICRA administrative review, for it is certain that determined litigants will resort to the Interior Department and its appellate process. In light of the importance of this potential for interference with tribal self government, the Department of the Interior's rationale for intervention in tribal government deserves closer examination.

In the past, the Department of Interior has relied on the broad statutory authority contained in 25 U.S.C. § 2[146] to justify intervention in tribal affairs. This statute provides that the Commissioner of Indian Affairs shall "have the management of all Indian affairs and of all matters arising out of Indian relations"[147] under Secretarial regulations. The Secretary has construed this section to give a broad charter to do almost anything deemed advisable in the management of Indian Affairs.[148] That section, originally enacted in 1832,[149] was followed by a major policy change in 1934 with the enactment of the Indian Reorganization Act.[150] One of the principal features of the IRA provided for establishment of

---

[143] The Assistant Secretary upheld the court's exercise of judicial review on the authority of Marbury v. Madison 5 U.S. (1 Cranch) 137 (1803), in support of the proposition that the tribal court may interpret the tribe's organic documents, even where they do not explicitly give such authority to the court. Assistant Secretary's opinion, reported in 5 I.L.R. § H at 17, 18 (Aug. 23, 1978).

[144] *Id.* at 18.

[145] *Id.* at 17.

[146] 25 U.S.C. § 2 (1976).

[147] *Id.*

[148] *See* Cohen, *The Erosion of Indian Rights, 1950-1953: A Case Study in Bureaucracy,* 62 YALE L.J. 348 (1953).

[149] Acts of July 9, 1832, ch. 174, § 1, 4 Stat. 564 (1832).

[150] Act of June 18, 1934, ch. 576, 48 Stat. 984 (1934).

tribal organizations and was expressly intended to eliminate the broad authority which the Interior Department had exercised over tribes.[151] The original bill retained broad governmental powers to review and even veto tribal actions,[152] but these provisions were ultimately discarded.[153]

The Indian Reorganization Act provides that Indian tribes shall have the right to organize and adopt appropriate constitutions and by-laws.[154] The Secretary of the Interior is to prescribe by regulation the manner of conducting a special election to adopt the tribal constitution and must thereafter approve the constitution adopted by the tribe. The only other reference to secretarial authority is the requirement that any amendment of the constitution and by-laws be ratified and approved in the same manner as the original constitution and by-laws. There is no mention in the IRA of any further authority in the Secretary once the tribe's constitution has been adopted and approved.

Moreover, Congress considered and rejected secretarial intervention in tribal affairs again while considering the enactment of the ICRA. The Interior Department proposed a substitute bill providing that the Secretary review any tribal action which infringed upon a right or freedom protected by the ICRA. The Interior Department's bill empowered the Secretary to require tribal government to take such corrective action deemed necessary. Review would have been available in the federal courts.[155] Congress rejected the Department's bill, however, and the ICRA as enacted contains no provision authorizing Secretarial review of ICRA complaints. The Supreme Court expressly noted Congres-

---

[151] President Franklin D. Roosevelt wrote the Senate Indian Affairs Committee concerning the proposed bill and said, in part:

> . . . We can and should, without further delay, extend to the Indian the fundamental rights of political liberty and local self-government. . . . Certainly the continuance of autocratic rule, by a federal department, over the lives of more than 200,000 citizens of this Nation, is incompatible with American ideals of liberty. . . .

SENATE COMM. ON INDIAN AFFAIRS, REPORT NO. 1080, 73D CONG., 2ND SESS. 3-4 (1934); *see also* Note, *Tribal Self-Government and the Indian Reorganization Act of 1934,* 70 MICH. L. REV. 955 (1972).

[152] S. 2755, 73rd Cong., 2d Sess., Tit. I, §§ 3-5, 9, (1934).

[153] Comment, *Tribal Self-Government and The Indian Reorganization Act of 1934,* 70 MICH. L. REV. 955, 962-63, 967 (1972).

[154] 25 U.S.C. § 476 (1976).

[155] *Hearings on S. 961-968 & S.J.Res. 40 Before the Subcomm. on Constitutional Rights of the Senate Judiciary Comm.,* 89th Cong., 1st Sess. 318-319 (1965) (hereinafter cited as *1965 Hearings).*

sional rejection of Interior Department review in the *Martinez* opinion.[156]

The Interior Department now appears to claim precisely that authority which it sought and Congress denied in 1934 and 1968. Regardless of the Department's rationale, there is no statutory support for the authority claimed by the Department. Moreover, such a claim directly contravenes congressional policy. In similar circumstances, the Supreme Court has struck down claims of executive authority.[157]

Admittedly, the Secretary is faced with a dilemma. On the one hand, direct review of complaints of violations of the ICRA and tribal constitutions should be precluded by virtue of congressional rejection of such authority. Conversely, the Secretary legitimately may be concerned about placing the federal government in complicity with illegal conduct. The fact remains, however, that Congress explicitly chose not to vest the Department with the power of administrative review.[158] Instead, the Congress deferred to the sovereignty of tribal governments and the Interior Department should respect that decision.

The Department now claims authority to withdraw tribal funding or recognition. Such a determination is a matter of utmost gravity. Prior to *Martinez,* a federal court would not issue a temporary restraining order or injunction without the necessary showing of irreparable harm, lack of alternate remedies and probability of success. The Interior Department should have no lighter burden. The Office of the Secretary should afford the tribal institutions and officers the same measure of due process heretofore afforded tribal governments by federal courts. At the very least, the Secretary should promulgate clear standards for administrative intervention and insure that all parties be afforded notice and the opportunity to be heard. The Secretary must bear in mind that *Martinez* was a mandate for tribal self government, not for the substitution of administrative review for judicial review.

---

[156] Santa Clara Pueblo v. Martinez, 436 U.S. 49, 68 (1978). The Court also noted, however, that many tribal constitutions require that tribal ordinances not be given effect until the Department of Interior gives its approval. The Court suggested that persons aggrieved by such laws might be able to seek relief from the Department of Interior. *Id.* at 66, n.22.

[157] *See* Youngstown Sheet & Tube Co. v. Sawyer, 343 U.S. 579 (1952); New York Times Co. v. U.S., 403 U.S. 713, 746-747 (1971), (Marshall, J., concurring).

[158] *1965 Hearings, supra* note 154.

IV. CONCLUSION

The climate of opinion in the United States now is probably less sympathetic to Indian rights than at any time since the termination era of the early 1950's. The condition is sometimes referred to as the "backlash," a reaction to Indian claims and victories in the courts. The recent decision of the Supreme Court in *Oliphant v. Suquamish Tribe,*[159] holding that tribal courts have no inherent authority to try and punish non-Indians has relieved some political pressure to subject tribal government to judicial review in state or federal courts.[160] Nevertheless, if substantial numbers of Indians or non-Indians feel their rights have been denied by Indian tribes or their officials, there may be renewed pressures for legislative change. Although *Martinez* ends the potential for much litigation over tribal action, it certainly does not lessen tribal responsibility for observance of ICRA proscriptions. As the Supreme Court noted, the ICRA is binding on all organs of tribal government in all areas of tribal governmental activity. All that has changed is that tribal actions will no longer be subject to the scrutiny of federal judges.

Respect for the individual rights guaranteed by ICRA, and awareness of the restrictions placed on tribal government will require sensitivity and training on the part of all of the organs of tribal government. This includes not only the tribal council and tribal courts, but also such bodies as election committees, membership committees, and tribal police.

Frequently, tribal councils have the benefit of legal advice from tribal attorneys concerning the constitutionality of proposed action. Tribal courts and police have frequently been exposed to training programs which include criminal due process material. However, all branches of tribal government should have some education in the concepts of personal and property rights incorporated in the ICRA. Tribes and inter-tribal organizations should be able to organize seminars and workshops for council members and other officials of tribal government to familiarize themselves with the nature of the restraints imposed by the ICRA.

There will be many who will urge that tribal resolution of ICRA complaints requires that tribal courts rapidly expand their function to encompass judicial review. However, such a view may in part be attributed to a conscious or unconscious ethnocentricism

---

[159] 435 U.S. 191 (1978).

[160] H.R. 9950, 95th Cong., 1st Sess. (1979), would have expressly abrogated tribal sovereign immunity and made tribes and their members subject to suit in state courts. The bill did not progress even to hearings.

regarding the role of courts. Moreover, given the diversity of tribal governments, each tribe should determine for itself the appropriateness of judicial review. Tribal courts and tribal councils must proceed thoughtfully if they are to continue to strengthen the institutions of tribal government.

The principle of judicial review may well take root in Indian government. However, it may require revision of tribal constitutions in order to establish the independence and coordinate status of the tribal judiciary. But even this is no guarantee that deadlock will not occur on important issues. In the meantime, greater attention must be given to helping tribal councils deal with their responsibilities under the ICRA to focus on protection of constitutional rights.

The Secretary of the Interior bears a heavy responsibility to avoid interfering with tribal self-government. Such interference is repugnant to the letter and spirit of the Indian Reorganization Act and is unwarranted by statute or congressional intent. The Secretary must proceed with great deference to the autonomy of tribal government. This is clearly required by the central principle of *Martinez:* in the absence of contrary congressional direction, ICRA complaints are to be resolved by the institutions of tribal government.

Admittedly, tribal sovereignty, like state sovereignty, has always been subject to the supreme authority of the United States. Where Secretarial action is deemed absolutely necessary, however, it must be exercised with full awareness of the position of the Indian tribes in the United States: a separate and autonomous system of government.

Martinez has provided tribes with the opportunity to demonstrate their capability of dealing fairly with their members and others while developing sensitivity to Anglo-American notions of individual rights and equality. The ICRA remains, of course, an imposition of values of the dominant American culture which sharply conflicts with the tradition of many tribes. But *Martinez* allows the tribes to implement the ICRA in a manner which preserves their ability to decide difficult questions in accordance with tribal values, and more importantly, in a manner consistent with tribal sovereignty.

---

[161] U.S. v. Wheeler, 435 U.S. 313 (1978).

Acknowledgments

Wunder, John R. "The Indian Bill of Rights." In *"Retained by The People": A History of American Indians and the Bill of Rights* (New York: Oxford University Press, 1994): 124–46. Reprinted with the permission of Oxford University Press.

Burnett, Donald L., Jr. "An Historical Analysis of the 1968 'Indian Civil Rights' Act." *Harvard Journal on Legislation* 9 (1972): 557–626. Reprinted with the permission of the Harvard University Law School.

Lazarus, Arthur, Jr. "Title II of the 1968 Civil Rights Act: An Indian Bill of Rights." *North Dakota Law Review* 45 (1969): 337–52. Reprinted with the permission of the *North Dakota Law Review*.

Reiblich, G. Kenneth. "Indian Rights Under the Civil Rights Act of 1968." *Arizona Law Review* 10 (1968): 617–48. Copyright (1968) by the Arizona Board of Regents. Reprinted by permission.

Ziontz, Alvin J. "In Defense of Tribal Sovereignty: An Analysis of Judicial Error in Construction of the Indian Civil Rights Act." *South Dakota Law Review* 20 (1975): 1–58. Reprinted with the permission of the *South Dakota Law Review*.

Johnson, Ralph W. and E. Susan Crystal. "Indians and Equal Protection." *Washington Law Review* 54 (1979): 587–631. Reprinted with the permission of the Washington Law Review Association.

Holmes, Dennis R. "Political Rights Under the Indian Civil Rights Act." *South Dakota Law Review* 24 (1979): 419–46. Reprinted with the permission of the *South Dakota Law Review*.

Pearldaughter, Andra. "Constitutional Law: Equal Protection: *Martinez* v. *Santa Clara Pueblo*—Sexual Equality Under the Indian Civil Rights Act." *American Indian Law Review* 6 (1978): 187–204. Reprinted with the permission of the *American Indian Law Review*.

Ziontz, Alvin J. "After *Martinez*: Civil Rights Under Tribal Government." *University of California, Davis, Law Review* 12 (1979): 1–35. Reprinted with the permission of the *University of California, Davis, Law Review*.